The R   ᴸ ʳadition

*Revolutionaries, Resistance
Fighters and Firebrands*

Donny Gluckstein
and Janey Stone

About the authors

Donny Gluckstein is the son of an anti-Zionist Jewish Palestinian refugee father and Jewish South African mother. He is the author of several works that touch on the subject matter of this book, including *The Nazis, Capitalism and the Working Class*, *A People's History of the Second World War*, *The Western Soviets* and *The Tragedy of Bukharin*. He edited *Fighting on all Fronts: Popular Resistance in the Second World War*.

Janey Stone is a lifelong socialist and political activist. She has been a union delegate and participated in the student, anti-Vietnam war and women's liberation movements. As an anti-Zionist Jew, she has written and presented about resistance to the Nazis in Germany and Poland, and by Jews, and many other topics including women workers, sexual politics, the Middle East and the radical Jewish tradition.

Dedication

This book is dedicated to Chanie Rosenberg (1922–2021), someone who embodied in practice the finest elements of the Jewish radical tradition. Teacher, artist, union branch secretary, socialist activist in South Africa, Palestine and the UK, she remained a committed revolutionary throughout her long life and was a role model for many.

The Radical Jewish Tradition

Revolutionaries, Resistance Fighters and Firebrands

*Donny Gluckstein
and Janey Stone*

Bookmarks Publications

The Radical Jewish Tradition: Revolutionaries, Resistance Fighters and Firebrands
by Donny Gluckstein and Janey Stone

Published 2023 by Bookmarks Publications
c/o 1 Bloomsbury Street, London WC1B 3QE
© Bookmarks Publications

Cover design by Roger Huddle
Typeset by Peter Robinson
Printed by Halstan Ltd

ISBN paperback 978-1-914143-97-7
Kindle 978 1 917020 00 8
ePub 978 1 917020 01 5
PDF 978 1 917020 02 2

Cover images: *Left*: mass parade of Jewish and non-Jewish socialists and Bundists to commemorate the victims of pogroms in Vilna (Tsarist Russia) 1905, © Getty Images. *Centre*: police arrest a protester during the Battle of Cable St, London East End, 4 October 1936, when Jews and non-Jews massed to prevent Mosley's British Union of Fascists from marching. *Right*: the Uprising of the 20,000: garment workers' strike, New York, 1909. Note the placard in English and Yiddish. The sign reads "We will aid the strikers until victory is theirs".

Contents

Introduction¹

[S]tories survived, countless tales of partisans and revolutionaries, resistance fighters and firebrands engaged in a fiery struggle for redemption and deliverance.[2]

These words from Arnold Zable, Australian writer and social activist, are of his Jewish forebears and the communities in Eastern Europe of which they were part. They belie the contemporary narrative of Jewish history that starts with ghettos, pogroms, suffering, oppression—Jews as the eternal victims. The climax of such a view, what Maxime Rodinson calls the "lachrymose conception of Jewish history",[3] is the Holocaust, when Jews supposedly went to the gas chambers like lambs to the slaughter. It is a narrative that has been adopted by Western governments and Zionists and is used to justify the existence of, and ongoing support for, the state of Israel; only an armed entity in the Middle East, it is argued, can defend world Jewry against antisemitism and ensure their safety.

This central argument is used to justify all the horrors of the apartheid Israeli state. The persecution and expulsion of the existing local Palestinian population, the suppression of democracy in the interest of maintaining the state, the militarisation of society and the decline of civil society because of the increasing domination of religious zealots—all these issues are subordinated to the idea that in no other way can Jews escape the historical existence of antisemitism and cease to be victims.

The title of this book, taken from Zable's words, encapsulates our approach to the radical Jewish tradition. This is an alternative view of modern Jewish history and an alternative solution to perpetual victimhood. We depict Jews not as victims, or a group apart, but as people who have repeatedly fought their oppression, and often in solidarity with other social groups. The lachrymose conception of Jewish history requires suppression of the stories of those partisans and revolutionaries, resistance fighters and firebrands because such stories suggest that Jews have it within their own power to respond to oppression and that others will in fact support them.

This is why so much of the radical story has disappeared from public consciousness. US Jewish commentator Rachel Cohen noted in 2014 how the "American-Jewish diaspora fears, and consequently, avoids reckoning with its radical history; such an interrogation would demand revisiting the basic lens through which we've conceptualised the past 120 years".[4]

> It's not a coincidence that the erasure of radical history has coincided with the creation of an American-Jewish consensus that was built and maintained in large part to drive specific politics around Israel. For a time, there were many different but legitimate answers to the question of Jewish self determination…[the] tantalising idea of Jewish unity was always a myth—one that grew and flourished through the exclusion and expulsion of select groups of Jewish voices, groups, and movements.[5]

This book, then, is the story of the radical Jewish working class. The core concept is an understanding of how Jewish workers and their supporters responded with extraordinary vigour to twin experiences—those of exploitation and oppression. The development of their class consciousness, workers' organisations, and socialist ideas was inseparable from their experience of antisemitic discrimination and violence. Furthermore, the radical Jewish current developed alongside and was part of the broader movement; radical Jews acted together with others who were fighting to change the world, as socialists and revolutionaries.

The book is divided into four sections. The first section, Firebrands, reviews what might be called "the Jewish question". A core topic is the nature of antisemitism. The lachrymose conception is founded on an assumption that all Jews, everywhere and at all times, have been the victims of an anti-Jewish hostility that is inherent in all non-Jews. We show instead that modern antisemitism is a product of the capitalist system. As a social construct, it can be defeated. The other chapters in this section provide a summary of the sociology and development of Jewry over time, and briefly outline important Jewish political currents.

Section two, Revolutionaries, presents the history of the radical Jewish tradition in four localities, Russia, London's East End, New York and Poland. The section is structured geographically, with two chapters on each, pre-First World War and the interwar years, except for Poland whose pre-First World War experience as part of the Tsarist Empire is covered in Chapter 4. The section starts with Jewish concentrations in the pre-First World War Tsarist Empire and post-First World War USSR,[6] and then follows emigration from there to London and New York. The section ends with an account of pre-Second World War Poland and sets the scene for the next section.

We do not attempt to provide encyclopaedic coverage of the history of Jews. We aim rather to provide the highlights of the radical Jewish experience in each region. In particular, we have restricted the story in the UK to the East End of London and the story in the US to New York City. Much more could be written about other parts of both countries. We could also have extended the geographical range to include, for example, the Galician province of the Austro-Hungarian Empire.[7] However, the places dealt with are the crucial core arenas which we believe adequately demonstrate our argument within the limits of a book of readable length.

Section 3, Resistance Fighters, looks first at how the Jewish radical tradition was destroyed in Germany. We then take up the vexed matter of the Holocaust and the question: Is it true that the Jews went like lambs to the slaughter? The lachrymose conception of Jewish history is nowhere stronger than on this question.

The last section focuses on the impact of Palestine, ending the historical accounts in this book with the establishment of the State of Israel in 1948. As long as such a state remained an aspiration, some Zionists were able to partition their consciousness and engage in local radical struggles while still believing in the need for such a state. Once the state came into existence, and in doing so became a centrepiece of world imperialism and centre of the persecution of Palestinians, such partitioning was no longer possible. All serious radicals from that point on had to take sides.

We have brought together a story that is known only in a fragmentary way due to most works dealing with partial aspects of the Jewish radical tradition. An example is the mass demonstration against the fascists in London's Cable Street in 1936. For the left, this is familiar ground and is a standard component of any work on how to fight fascism. But this inspiring event did not appear out of nowhere. It was the culmination of decades of anti-fascist activity by Jews and non-Jews in London and other British cities. It was also inextricably linked with earlier strikes and struggles of Jewish immigrants to the UK, and with concurrent campaigns over issues such as housing, most of them led by socialists and other radicals.

We did not commence on this collaboration as an academic exercise, although we hope the material and arguments are well substantiated. We are both passionately committed to the use of history as a weapon in the on-going struggle for justice and a future for all.

As far as we are aware, no other book brings together the material in this way. Most books on specifically Jewish topics have in mind a Jewish audience. Ours is aimed as much at non-Jews as at Jews. Furthermore, most existing books treat Jews as homogeneous and in isolation from society. We focus on a specific layer of the Jewish population—the Jewish working class and radical activists who were a component of the wider left. And, finally, most existing books by Jews on the topic are by authors with some sympathy towards the Israeli state or Zionists. We publicly stand as Jewish anti-Zionists.

A genuine account of Jewish radical history can counter the amnesia that Cohen referred to, an amnesia that is so widespread that it sometimes even influences the left. Cohen was referring to a trend among Jews, but many non-Jewish supporters of Palestinian rights who want to oppose and reject Zionism can also find themselves overlooking much of Jewish experience. This may be because it appears to be only available refracted through the lens of support for Israel or because most are not aware of the scale of pre-Second World War Jewish history. We set out to re-establish awareness of a working-class tradition founded in struggles against the ruling class and imbued with a conviction that fundamental social change was possible. This tradition was not firmly rooted in the entire Jewish population (however this is defined); it involved workers' solidarity on a class basis. For this reason, Jewish radical history is not a niche subject. Rather, it is central to the socialist movement as a whole and contains lessons for all struggles against oppression.

A note on language and the Pale of Settlement

Yiddish is the language historically spoken by the Ashkenazi Jews of Eastern Europe. It is Germanic but contains many elements from Hebrew and Slavic languages, and there is significant regional variation in vocabulary and pronunciation. It is written using Hebrew script. There is no one standard spelling in English, and, furthermore, the sources used for this study were written over an extensive period, during which conventions changed. This presented the authors with a number of problems, particularly with the names of people and organisations. For example, the Yiddish writer David Edelshtat sometimes appears in English-language sources as Dovid Edelstadt and many other variations. For the purposes of this study, the primary aim has been internal consistency not scholarly exactitude so we have chosen common variants. The result is somewhat arbitrary but we hope it is accessible for the non-expert reader. In a couple of places, there are transliterations of Hebrew words. Here we have used spellings common for English-speaking readers.

A similar problem occurs with the names of towns in Eastern Europe which have undergone significant changes over the time period. Lviv in Ukraine has previously been known as "Lwów", "Lvov", and "Lemberg". Vilna (or Vilno) is now known as Vilnius. Again, we have rather arbitrarily chosen a commonly used variant from the period written about and then kept it consistent through the book.

The establishment of the Pale of Settlement in the Tsarist Empire underpinned all the persecution and oppression that followed. From the time of the first partition of Poland in 1772 onward, the tsars sought to control the Jewish population now within their territory for economic and political purposes. The prime mechanism was a declaration that Jews were only allowed to reside in very restricted regions. Tsar Nicholas III coined the term "Pale" and drew new boundaries resulting in the concentration of Jews in the region of the empire near the western border, the annexed parts of Poland and most of modern-day Ukraine, Lithuania and Belarus. Poland itself now existed within the Tsarist Empire in two parts—so-called Congress Poland, theoretically with some autonomy but in actuality a puppet state, and the eastern part which was annexed outright by the tsar.

Acknowledgements

During the journey to create this work, we have received input, constructive criticism, suggestions and support from many people. We would like to acknowledge and thank Leo Bild, Alex Callinicos, Joel Geier, Anna Gluckstein, Eris Harrison, Omar Hassan, Christian Hogsbjerg, Roger Huddle, Rick Kuhn, Tess Lee Ack, Tom O'Lincoln, Louise O'Shea, Peter Robinson, John Rose, Camilla Royle, Sandra Shepherd, Mike Simons and Carol Williams. And, above all, we wish to express our great appreciation to Rob Ferguson, who provided detailed and very constructive feedback and criticism. Of course, the content of the book as it stands is entirely our responsibility.

Section 1

Firebrands:
Understanding the
Jewish Question

Antisemitism and its adversaries

In 1881 there was a wave of pogroms against Jews in Russia. In the period following that, Jews became a crucial part of opposition to capitalism across the world. Many were promoted to the highest ranks of radical parties and movements, often by people who were not Jewish. Alongside these mixed formations there were also specifically Jewish organisations of the left such as the Jewish Labour Bund. Ezra Mendelsohn explains why involvement was so intense:

> On the face of it the answer seems fairly obvious. Would not a people confronting discrimination, hatred, and humiliation (in Eastern Europe in particular but in the West as well), a people blessed or cursed, with a large, poverty-stricken working class and lower middle class—would not many members of such a group inevitably gravitate toward the only political force dedicated to revolutionary change? This in many countries was the left, the only group that firmly and bravely opposed Nazism, fascism, and other antisemitic movements.[1]

This phenomenon was not incidental or superficial. The Jewish radical tradition *was* the radical tradition.

The roots of antisemitism: the conventional account

These days we are told something different. For example, the Jewish historian Lars Fischer says "That mainstream Marxism has a staggering track record of tolerating, excusing, and all too often itself propagating problematic attitudes toward Jews that gravitate toward, and in some cases themselves constitute, antisemitism is well known".[2] Rabbi Julius Carlebach writes "Marx is a logical and indispensable link between Luther and Hitler".[3] David Cesarini adds that Marx "saw no intrinsic value in Judaism or the continuation of Jewish life [and] predicted that the Jews would eventually liquify. So, for Orthodox Marxists the defence of Jews would always be quixotic".[4] We are informed that the Polish revolutionary Rosa Luxemburg's "attitude towards antisemitism was notorious".[5] Another writer says that in the 1917 Russian Revolution (which secured Jewish emancipation with Leon Trotsky playing a commanding role) there was an "explosive overlap between antisemitism and revolutionary politics".[6]

If these statements were true, then it is difficult to comprehend how the tradition which these writers are so eager to criticise could ever have existed in the first place. Why would so many Jews join with leftists who detested them?[7] And if the non-Jewish left were antisemitic, why would it put Jews into leadership positions and fight together with them against antisemitic regimes in Russia and Germany?

Full of sound and fury, the recently conceived "antisemitism of the left" theory builds on a particular view of oppression developed in Theodor Herzl's 1896 *The Jewish State*, the founding document of Zionism. He believed that whenever Jews were in contact with others, hatred was inevitable:

> The Jewish question exists wherever Jews live in perceptible numbers. Where it does not exist, it is carried by Jews in the course of their migrations. We naturally move to those places where we are not persecuted, and there our presence produces persecution. This is the case in every country.[8]

Wherever they went, and whoever they were, they would be treated as an alien race by non-Jews (and today this is taken to include anti-racists): "Anti-Semitism increases day by day and hour by hour among the nations; indeed, it is bound to increase".[9] Struggling for equality only made the situation worse: "In the principal countries where Anti-Semitism prevails, it does so as a result of the emancipation of the Jews".[10] Little matter that at the time Herzl was writing, the most notorious place for anti-Jewish terror was the last major European country without emancipation (formal Jewish equality before the law)—Russia. Herzl was springing to the defence of his community, but his counter-strategy relied on the same belief in racial incompatibility that was standard fare for the colonial imperialists and antisemites of late 19th century Europe.

There are recent variations on his theme. In their book *Why the Jews?*, Dennis Prager and Joseph Telushkin exclude every possible alternative explanation: "economic factors, the need for scapegoats, …do not explain antisemitism; they only explain what factors have exacerbated it and caused it to erupt in a given circumstance. None accounts for the universality, depth, and persistence of antisemitism".[11] They say "Jews were never asked, 'Why the Jews?'. They knew why. Throughout their history, Jews have regarded Jew-hatred as an inevitable consequence of their Jewishness",[12] which for them consists of "God, Torah, Israel, and Chosenness".[13]

Attributing antisemitism to Jewish migration or Jewishness indicts the victims for their own victimisation—a lachrymose conception if ever there was one.

Götz Aly, author of valuable books on the Holocaust, thankfully absolves them but suggests human nature is the cause. In doing so he too rejects any social explanation for antisemitism and approvingly quotes this statement: "The legend of the evil capitalists who raped the masses with the help of National Socialism cannot be dispelled vigorously enough".[14] *In Why the Germans? Why the Jews?* Aly argues that "envy, fear of failure, resentment, and greed fuelled German antisemitism. These were forces of evil that mankind has feared and has tried to rein in with civilisation since the dawn of time".[15]

Blaming any oppressed group or human nature for oppression itself exonerates the social system from any responsibility. Its opponents become irrelevant or part of the problem, and the oppressed who associate with them must be "self-hating". Playing on August Bebel's famous quip that "antisemitism is the socialism of fools", the Canadian writer Moishe Postone says today's left suffers from "the anti-imperialism of fools", presumably due to its supporting Palestinian rights. He accuses the left of believing antisemitism is "emancipatory" and a "fetishised form of anticapitalism" that differs little from the far right.[16]

The social origins of oppression

The left believes antisemitism is not natural but is founded upon a lie, an ideological construct. The culprit for this deception is not Jews or human nature, but the deceiver. The historical record shows who that was. Persecution of Jews was driven from the top downwards. French kings expelled them in 1182, 1254, 1306, 1322, 1359 and 1394. In 1290 it was King Edward I of England, followed by King Louis I of Hungary in 1360. The largest expulsion took place by order of King Ferdinand and Queen Isabella of Spain in 1492. After 1881 Tsar Alexander III imposed draconian laws and waves of pogroms on the world's greatest concentration of Jews. The German Führer, Hitler, exterminated two out of three European Jews.

Of course, antisemitic beliefs penetrated down to all levels of society. That was their entire purpose. Many people were duped into believing conspiracy theories, shameless fabrications such as the medieval libel (that Jews murdered Christian children for blood in religious rituals), *The Protocols of the Elders of Zion* (concocted in Russia by tsarist police in 1903), or the idea that Jewish financiers were responsible for the economic woes of the 1930s. But if there was no substance to them, why did these lies exist and influence people?

Oppressive attitudes are not a human trait but arise from society. Karl Marx and Engels argue that "The phantoms formed in the human brain are…sublimates of their material life-process".[17] The production process gives rise to different classes: exploiters at the top, and beneath them the exploited and intermediate groupings.

Ruling classes surmount the discontent that privilege and exploitation generates among subordinates through physical coercion and ideology.[18] The latter directs the frustrations people feel with existing social arrangements towards false and innocent targets. The technique is an old one. It is, as the Romans put it, *divide et impera*—divide and rule. Those at the receiving end experience this as oppression. Thus, oppression and exploitation are inter-related though distinct. Exploitation is associated with labour and the production process and is fundamental to the economics of capitalism. Any business that dispenses with exploitation for profit making would disappear. Oppression, on the other hand, is ideological and stimulated by attitudes fed down from the top.

The choice of target can be arbitrary and it can change over time,[19] but each oppression has specific characteristics. For example, women's oppression through the institution of the family serves both the capitalist division of labour and reproduction of the next generation. Racist attitudes towards Black people justified enslaving Africans to meet labour demands in the American colonies and continues to be used to divide and rule. The stoking up of Islamophobia in recent years assisted the latest imperialist adventures for the control of oil in the Middle East.

To drive divisions through the population, certain features such as appearance, religion, birthplace, ethnicity, sexual orientation, or gender role are suggested to have negative significance. By reducing the humanity of an individual from their entirety to this single stigma, they are made to seem "other", inferior and deserving of ill-treatment.

Whether dealt out by the deceivers at the top or by the duped below venting their ire, one cruel outcome of oppression is suffering. Prejudice and hostility take many forms: discrimination, micro-aggressions, hate-crimes including physical attacks, and much more. Because the source of oppression is the class system, the most obnoxious attitudes and actions commonly reside in the ruling-class institutions. These reinforce the dehumanising of scapegoats by deliberately humiliating them in order to confirm the sense of "otherness".

Prejudice affects everyone in the scapegoated group to some degree irrespective of class. Though scapegoats suffer, when myths are used to mask the real cause of social misery, it is a misfortune for both the oppressed and the exploited. Marx gave one example:

> The ordinary English worker hates the Irish worker as a competitor who lowers his standard of life. In relation to the Irish worker he regards himself as a member of the *ruling* nation and consequently he becomes a tool of the English aristocrats and capitalists against Ireland, thus strengthening their domination *over himself*... His attitude towards him is much the same as that of the "poor whites" to the Negroes in the former slave states of the USA... This antagonism is artificially kept alive and intensified by the press, the pulpit, the comic papers, in short, by all the means at the disposal of the ruling classes... It is the secret by which the capitalist class maintains its power. And the latter is quite aware of this.[20]

Oppression will only end if the class system behind it is abolished. The working class has the numbers and economic strength to do this. For the working class to be liberated, an awareness that its exploitation is secured by divide and rule is necessary. Equally, the oppressed, who are often a minority and therefore lack sufficient social strength to achieve ultimate liberation unaided, need to understand the importance of struggle in cooperation with others.

Unique yet emblematic: the case of antisemitism

The deadly nature of antisemitism, one of the many forms of oppression, was underlined by the Holocaust. There has been nothing comparable to this deliberate, industrialised mass murder aimed at completely exterminating an entire population. However, European Jews had long been "the archetypal minority" whose condition was a bellwether for "the way states would treat not only other minorities but indeed all of their citizens and subjects".[21]

Russia's tsarist autocracy blamed Jews for the miserable, short lives of its population, and Hitler's totalitarian regime vilified them in every way possible. It is true a "bare-footed brigade" took part in Russia's pogroms and Brownshirt violence erupted on German streets. The authorities alleged this was the instinctive expression of the masses justifiably bent on revenge against those causing their woes. But Jews were not the instigators, just as a lightning rod does not create lightning. The gullible paid a high price for their delusions. The bare-footed remained hungry and unshod, while 3 million Germans were incarcerated in Nazi concentration camps and over 4 million died in Hitler's war.

Ber Borochov, a socialist Zionist in tsarist Russia, accepted antisemitism had social causes, rather than being the result of racial incompatibility, but denied the ruling class was culpable. He wrote that antisemitism "flourishes because of the national competition between the Jewish and non-Jewish petty bourgeois and between the Jewish and non-Jewish proletarianised and unemployed masses".[22] But "national competition" is a function of capitalist rivalry, even if ordinary people are taken in by it.

Abram Leon, the Trotskyist theoretician who wrote *The Jewish Question* just before his death at the hands of the Nazis, had a different approach. He emphasised that hatred of Jews was a product of society which appealed to a particular group. Leon recognised "the savage anti-Semitism of the middle classes, who are being choked to death under the weight of capitalist contradictions", but it was "big capital [which] exploits this elemental anti-Semitism of the petty bourgeoisie in order to mobilise the masses around the banner of racism".[23]

Critics of the Marxist social analysis of antisemitism allege it cannot assist Jews because Marxism is itself antisemitic, despite its record of opposing racism and championing equal rights for all, including Jews. That is ignored because Zionist theory denies racism against Jews can end or that equal treatment is even possible. The allegation therefore depends on presenting texts in a certain way. Reference is often made to Marx's early article *On the Jewish Question*, from which passages are selected, deprived of context, and a smoking gun is discovered.

In 1843 Marx's focus was on how both religion and society negatively impact on human freedom.[24] Enzo Traverso shows that *On the Jewish Question* was written to argue for "the emancipation of the Jews in opposition to Bruno Bauer, who denied them this right considering them as inferior to Christians" because of their Jewishness.[25] Nonetheless it is a difficult text.[26] Confirming Marx's own premise about how ideas develop, his thinking was not divorced from the outside world. The debate was about where emancipation should lead, but that was recent and Jews were only beginning to escape the restricted functions imposed by ghetto conditions (see Chapter 2). As yet, wider roles, including radicalism, were embryonic, though Marx himself was a pioneering exemplar.[27] The full liberation from oppression he posited for Jews could only be sketched in abstract terms and it would take until the 20th century for the mature Marxist strategy to be fleshed out.

As the following passage shows, *On the Jewish Question* is couched in opaque Hegelian phraseology using metaphor:

> Christianity sprang from Judaism. It has merged again in Judaism. From the outset, the Christian was the theorising Jew, the Jew is, therefore, the practical Christian, and the practical Christian has become a Jew again.[28]

Though this does not discriminate between communities, its language can obscure the distinction Marx makes, and which Bauer refused to make, between the person and the *structural constraints shaping them*.

Sentences in *On the Jewish Question* that today would be classed as antisemitic such as "What is the worldly religion of the Jew?

Huckstering. What is his worldly God? Money"[29] refer only to the structural aspects. Herzl does the same, writing of Jews' "terrible power of the purse", "the Jewish spirit of enterprise"[30] and suchlike, but no one accuses Zionism of being antisemitic because his phrases are seen as part of a larger picture—his overall programme.

So, while there is no point glossing over problematic language, Marx's larger picture—what he intended—is more important. The crux of it was that while "the Jews (like the Christians) are fully politically emancipated in various states both Jews and Christians are far from being humanly emancipated";[31] and yet both should be. The Jewish person who, for the Zionist, was a fixed and impotent victim of unchallengeable antisemitism, was for Marx a person with vast potential if liberated.

To achieve this aim, the external and internal bonds of the Jewish straitjacket must be broken. Marx was thus treating Jews as humans, not powerless representations of a race or stereotype. Regarding the external bond, he wanted to go beyond legal equality so that Jews could participate in humankind's quest for progress. Internally, Marx grasped how circumstances encouraged submission to the dictates of religious belief but wished a free choice in this matter. So, Jews were entitled to, and capable of, self-determination unrestrained by either outside prejudice or their own communal institutions. Once humanly emancipated, Jews (and Christians) would be free to choose how to live their lives, and whether or not this conformed to expected stereotypes would be up to them.

Far from being "quixotic" or dismissive, Marx wrote copiously about Jews, doing so again in a substantial book published one year after *On the Jewish Question*, *The Holy Family*, his first collaboration with Friedrich Engels.[32] As an emblematic group chained down for centuries, Jews were not peripheral but central to their vision of human liberation. That is why Marx spotlighted the community so early in a lifetime project about which he wrote, aged 17, the "chief guide…is the welfare of mankind".[33] Later research led him to focus on agency, with emphasis on class and the economic system, but this was not a break from but an advance along the path trodden in 1843.[34]

Actions speak louder than words, and the real test of Marxist theory was not this or that early formulation, but developments over the next hundred years. Jews themselves would vindicate Marx's position through their deeds. We shall see in the chapters that follow that far from relishing their straitjacket, or human emancipation being antithetical to them, millions aspired to freedom (even if they did not all become left-wing activists to bring it about). Zionist critics see this yearning as giving up on being Jewish. Another view is that Jews wanted to be themselves, free from oppression.

It would take a series of calamities—the rise of fascism, Stalinist counter-revolution in Russia, the Holocaust, and worldwide refusal to accept Jewish refugees—to replace the radical hope of universal liberation with a very inadequate substitute: the establishment of a small militarised Middle Eastern state oppressing others.

Luther, Voltaire and Wagner

That prejudice against Jews was not a fixed human reaction is confirmed by the way individual attitudes changed depending on circumstances. The biographies of the three people held to be the most influential promoters of Jew-hatred between the Middle Ages and the 20th century cast light on this.

The Reformation movement led by Martin Luther began in the German speaking lands in 1517. A rising middle class was beginning to challenge feudalism. Luther condemned the Catholic underpinning of society, posing this challenge in theological terms. Prior to 1517 Luther reflected standard anti-Jewish views,[35] but afterwards he underlined "the commonality of all men as the good creations of God".[36] *That Christ was Born a Jew*, written in 1523, says:

> The papists have so demeaned themselves that a good Christian would rather be a Jew than one of them... What good can we do the Jews when we constrain them, malign them, and hate them as dogs? When we deny them work and force them to usury, how can that help? We should use toward the Jews not the pope's but Christ's law of love.[37]

His tone changed drastically after 1525 when German peasants revolted against feudal landowners. Proto-communist teachings by the Anabaptists threatened both bourgeois and aristocratic property.[38] To defend wealth in general Luther turned on the insurgents:

If the peasant is in open rebellion, then he is outside the law of God…
Therefore, let everyone who can, smite, slay, and stab, secretly or openly,
remembering that nothing can be more poisonous, hurtful, or devilish
than a rebel.[39]

The very next year he began vilifying Jews, and this reached a cre-
scendo when he called on people to "set fire to their synagogues or
schools and to bury and cover with dirt whatever will not burn…that
their houses also be razed and destroyed".[40] Luther's change of heart
was prompted, as one writer puts it, by "concern over the effectiveness
of his mission from the viewpoint of the peasant revolt".[41]

Voltaire was a leader of the 18th century Enlightenment, which
furthered the ideological confrontation begun by the Reformation. He
went beyond Luther to champion a society based on reason as against
religious superstition. Consequently, Voltaire lived a life of exile, having
had several brushes with the authorities including two spells in the
Bastille. Henceforth he tried to avoid open confrontation. Whether or
not he used Judaism as a covert means of criticising religion in general,[42]
he wanted to be on good terms with the cream of Europe's "enlightened
despots"[43] and felt no need to confront their prejudice.[44] He wrote "the
Hebrews have ever been vagrants, or robbers, or slaves, or seditious".[45]

Unlike Voltaire, who appealed to the establishment to run society
based on reason, there was a wing of the Enlightenment that opposed
aristocratic rule on principle. Civil rights for Jews was one of its battering
rams. This trend was represented by the playwright Gotthold Lessing,
author of the pro-Jewish play *Nathan the Wise*, Jean-Jacques Rousseau,
and Charles Montesquieu. In Lessing's play, the Christian character
tells Nathan "you give me more, much more than you have taken".[46]
Rousseau requested the translation of the writings of Enlightenment
writer Moses Mendelssohn because "they came from a Jew; for otherwise, there was not a book in the world he would read".[47] He wanted
Jews to enjoy "a free state, schools and universities".[48] Montesquieu
wanted "to get rid of this spirit of intolerance…which differs little
from that of the prince".[49] For radical critics of existing society, Jewish
emancipation was an important component of progressive change.

By the 19th century the bourgeoisie had moved from ideas to
the barricades. The composer Richard Wagner was caught up in the

whirlwind. In 1848 a wave of revolutions against vestiges of feudal government swept Europe. A supporter of liberal German unification, Wagner had to flee Dresden after his involvement in an 1849 uprising and that year wrote *Art and Revolution*. Jews were not mentioned anywhere. Instead, he advocated "the new beauty of a nobler Universalism"[50] to counter "Industry", which aimed "to fleece the poor... enervating, demoralising and dehumanising everything on which it sheds its venom".[51] And according to Jacob Katz, "Nothing in his letters and other statements during the previous decades presaged anti-Jewish sentiments".[52] However, a year later, disillusioned by the defeat of the revolution, in search of funds for his opera projects, and now a firm supporter of the status quo, he wrote *Jewishness in Music*. In it he declared "we have been bound to lose even our earlier sympathy for the tragic history" of Jews. He now categorised them as "the most heartless of all human beings",[53] rebuking them for "the attempt to appropriate our hard-earned heritage [using] the power of money".[54] Like Luther and Voltaire, he had formed connections with the establishment, becoming political adviser to King Ludwig II of Bavaria.

It does not follow that the attitude of every bourgeois towards Jews was instrumental or immediately determined by personal relations with the elite. However, these prominent figures in anti-Jewish thinking are indicative.

Jews on the left

Unlike those parts of society that shunned Jews, the left welcomed them; and far from their presence leading to an increase in antisemitism, the integration of Jews and non-Jews worked well in common struggle. By the early 20th century, according to Traverso, Jews were visible in all major revolutionary currents in Europe:

> in all of the currents, from Mensheviks (Julius Martov, Fyodor Dan) to Bolsheviks (Lev Kamenev, Gregory Zinoviev). After the Russian Revolution they were among the leading lights in the Communist International, of which Zinoviev was the first secretary. Jewish intellectuals were at the head of the revolutions that overthrew the central empires and led, as in Bavaria and Hungary, to ephemeral soviet-type

republics of 1919. We need only mention Rosa Luxemburg, Leo Jogiches and Paul Levi in Berlin; Kurt Eisner, Gustav Landauer, Ernst Toller and Eugen Leviné in Munich; Bela Kun and Georg Lukacs in Budapest; Otto Bauer, Max and Friedrich Adler in Vienna.[55]

Jews were one third of delegates at the 1907 Russian Social Democratic Labour Party (RSDLP) Congress.[56] Soviets were a form of direct democracy with all delegates subject to scrutiny and instant recall. It is therefore significant that Trotsky, a Jew, was president of the Petrograd Soviet in 1917 and 11 of the 35 members of its executive were Jewish in a city where Jews were a tiny fraction of the workforce. After the October insurrection, Trotsky, in his role as Red Army commander, was at a level of authority in the country second only to Vladimir Lenin. Jacob Sverdlov, who was Jewish, was president of the Party Central Committee.[57]

There was also a high proportion of Jews lower down the ranks, giving the lie to the claim that Jewish leaders manipulated others. Though just 4 percent of the population, they were 7 percent of members in the Russian Populist movement (the revolutionary movement that preceded Marxist activity) and 5 percent of the Marxist RSDLP.[58] And Jews ran greater risks. In St Petersburg (later Petrograd) they were 30 percent of those indicted for Populism,[59] and the Jewish share of prosecutions in the 1905 Revolution was 34 percent.[60]

Gender oppression was an additional factor. A quarter of the Jews in the early Russian Populist movement were women.[61] They were also a third of activists in the early Jewish socialist organisation under Russian tsarism, the *Algemeyner Yidisher Arbeter-bund in Lite, Poyln un Rusland* (General Jewish Workers' League of Lithuania, Poland and Russia), generally known as the Jewish Labour Bund or simply "the Bund".[62] These were higher statistics than for women in the movement generally. Marx's daughter Eleanor, Angelica Balabanoff (secretary of the Communist International) and Luxemburg were prominent individual examples.[63]

The scale of Jewish involvement was not precisely calibrated to the degree of antisemitism encountered in any one place, or particular events such as pogroms. This is confirmed by the radicalism seen in Britain and the US. Commitment arose out of empathy with others also suffering under capitalism. Oppression furnished a special outsider perspective sometimes described as "marginality".[64] Ludwig Börne (1786–1837), a German-Jewish political writer, exemplified this when he wrote "Yes, because I was born a slave I love freedom more than you do. Yes, because I have learnt all the more about servitude, I understand about freedom more than you do".[65]

The South African example

South Africa demonstrates how marginality and empathy could work. The number of Jews fleeing antisemitism (mainly from Lithuania)[66] climbed from 40,000 in 1914 to 105,000 in 1945. Would oppression make them look inwards, creating a barrier to identifying with others, or would it stimulate solidarity against all suffering?

They entered a society partitioned along racist lines, with the Black majority at the bottom of the heap. Yet anti-Jewish prejudice was also rife, particularly among the Afrikaner element. That became even more pronounced after Hitler's accession to power in Germany. The Afrikaners' ethnically-based Nationalist Party believed Jews were "not far behind 'kaffirs' [a racist term for Black people] in terms of its defined prejudices".[67] Winning all-white elections in 1948, the Party inaugurated an apartheid system that codified earlier political practices.

South African Jews suffered antisemitism but being deemed white themselves were segregated from Black people. This made them acutely aware of their ethnic position. That is why South Africa had the first nationally organised Zionist federation (1898)[68] and why support for Zionism in South Africa was second only to Palestine, Zionism's chosen destination. In 1948, 99 percent of South African Jews were affiliated.[69]

At the same time, South Africa's Jewish radicals repudiated ethnic separatism and embraced social justice for all. Socialist politics was brought to the country from outside, and, as Baruch Hirson puts it, until the end of the First World War, "only the Jewish groups, fed by continued immigration from Eastern Europe survived for any length of time".[70] The International Socialist League (ISL), which would become the Communist Party after the war, had Yiddish speaking branches. An important ISL leaflet of 1918 called on Black workers to realise that "You are the mainstay of the country. You do all the work

[but] are robbed of the fruits of your labour and robbed of your liberty as well".[71] One writer claims that at this time, aside from Durban, "the South African left-wing socialist spectrum was not geographically based but was located within segments of the small Jewish population centred in the major cities".[72] Later on, South Africa's Poale Zion (Workers of Zion), the Yiddisher Arbeter (Workers) Club, and the Zionist Socialist Party also took a stand against racial discrimination.[73]

One hundred and fifty-six people were charged in the "great Treason Trial" against the African National Congress in the 1950s. Of the 23 white people present, Jews constituted more than half. When mass struggle against apartheid took off with the 1960 Sharpeville massacre, the police believed "the contribution of the whites to the underground movement was decisive... One third were Jews".[74] In the Rivonia Arrests of 1963, which led to the incarceration of Nelson Mandela, *all* the whites prosecuted were Jews.[75] A roll call of leading white opponents of apartheid in *The Jewish Chronicle* (who suffered repression, imprisonment or even assassination) tells the tale. Joe Slovo, Ruth First, Ronnie Kasrils, and Sam Kahn were just some of the many Jews involved in the African National Congress at the highest level.[76] Yet at this time Jews formed just 2.5 percent of whites and 0.3 percent of the total population.[77]

However, not all Jews took the road of solidarity. They benefitted materially from the apartheid system and enjoyed incomes many times that of Black workers. Shimoni notes:

> Only when the apartheid system was utterly discredited at home and internationally did South Africa's Jewish Board of Deputies, the umbrella organisation of mainstream Jewry, go beyond vague murmurings to explicitly criticising it.[78]

And leading rabbis still condemned the anti-apartheid campaign.[79] Such attitudes led a frustrated Rabbi Louis Rabinowitz to declare:

> What do we do to loosen the bonds of wickedness, to undo the bonds of oppression?... There are some Jews in the community who do attempt to do something...and when, as a result, they fall foul of the powers that be, the defence put up by the Jewish community is to prove that these are Jews only by name.[80]

Jews as radical leaders

The high proportion of Jewish leaders in the broader left was evidence of personal abilities and the absence of antisemitism among the membership.[81] Swimming against the stream is never easy and most workers, of whatever ethnicity, are burdened with exploitation, long hours, poverty, lack of educational opportunity, and the daily effort required simply to survive. Heavy commitment to running left-wing parties was difficult. Therefore, the skills, education, time and generalised social viewpoint needed for leadership was often found in the socialist "intelligentsia" (a term of Polish/Russian origin).

Marx, Luxemburg and Trotsky on the revolutionary side, and Rudolf Hilferding, Julius Martov and Victor Adler on the reformist wing are characteristic cases. Their background had a common pattern. Their fathers were well-to-do lawyers, merchants and farmers. Where did they get their motivation?

The Jewish community, "the people of the Book", traditionally had a high level of literacy.[82] In Russia in 1897 it was twice that of the general population.[83] Partial liberalisation gave access to broader educational opportunities, and the children of better-off Jews availed themselves. All six people listed above attended university, something rare even for non-Jewish youth at the time, and through study became armed with a broad perspective on sociology, history, politics, economics and so on. However, unlike today, higher education was relatively exclusive and a stepping-stone into the privileged elite. Jewish students found this route barred and remained outsiders.[84] The advantage gained by literacy was snatched away by antisemitism. That was a recipe for opposing the established order at a high theoretical level.

Jews were not the only marginal group to take a disproportionate role on the left. The main theoretician of British Chartism, a working-class struggle for the vote in the 19th century, was Bronterre O'Brien and its chief leader was Feargus O'Connor. Both were from Ireland, Britain's oldest colony which, due to British misrule, suffered a famine that starved 1 million to death and forced 1 million to emigrate—together a quarter of the entire population. William Cuffay was a leading Black Chartist in London. The connection between the fight against oppression, working-class organisation and progressive democratic demands explains the strong involvement of oppressed communities in left-wing movements.

Anita Shapira, an Israeli historian, is therefore wrong to deem Herzl "extremely astute"[85] for suggesting "that antisemitism derived from a new phenomenon in the distribution of power in Europe: the politics of the masses. As the masses' power increased…the risk to Jews rose concomitantly".[86] The complete opposite was true. The risk to Jews came from ruling-class ideology, while possession of working-class democratic rights could curb that influence. Where these rights were absent, such as under the kings and princes of the Middle Ages, Tsarist Russia or Nazi Germany, Jews experienced expulsions, pogroms and genocide.

Antisemites focussed on the presence of Jewish leaders, exaggerated their numbers and traduced their motivations, suggesting non-Jews were being manipulated. The tsar's minister of the interior, Vyacheslav von Plehve, declared Jews were "40 percent of all revolutionaries".[87] A century later Vladimir Putin said the first Soviet government "was 80-85 percent Jewish".[88] A factual correction had to be published in the *Vedemosti* newspaper:

> [I]n the composition of the first Council of People's Commissars Jews were 8%… In the government of the Russian Socialist Federative Soviet Republic of 1917–1922 Jews were 12% (six out of 50 people). Apart from the government, in the Central Committee of the Russian Social Democratic Labour Party (Bolsheviks) on the eve of October 1917 there were 6 out of 30 who were Jewish (20 percent), and in the composition of the first political bureau of the Bolshevik Central Committee it was 40 percent (3 out of 7).[89]

Others who distorted the truth included Winston Churchill, who weighed in with this diatribe in 1920:

> There is no need to exaggerate the part played in the creation of Bolshevism and in the actual bringing about of the Russian Revolution by these international and for the most part atheistical Jews. It is certainly a very great one; it probably outweighs all others… The same evil prominence was obtained by Jews in the brief period of terror during which Bela Kun ruled in Hungary…this madness has been allowed to prey upon the temporary prostration of the German people.[90]

Churchill distinguished between "Good Jews and Bad Jews". The former included the Zionists while the latter was made up of "International Jews...in a sinister confederacy", thus making them "Terrorist Jews".[91]

Hitler made no differentiation, and his approach was the most far-reaching. He said there was an international "Jewish-Bolshevik conspiracy", to which he added three additional false claims. First, that Jews plotted to control the world and lay behind every misfortune. Second, that Jews alone were responsible for all revolutions: "Time and again the Jews have stirred up the various systems of government by means of wars and revolutions, not only political but economic and intellectual revolutions". The third lie insulted the working class: "As the proletariat cannot lead a state, leadership comes into the hands of the Jews".[92]

Far from being manipulators, Jews joined the common struggle and were valued for their contribution. The left has taken numerous forms but Jews played a disproportionate role in all of them because discrimination fuelled sensitivity to human suffering. This was summed up well by Stanislaw Wygodzki, a Polish poet interviewed two decades after emigrating to Israel.

> You want to know whether I still believe in something that was once called Communism. I believe that one should not live from exploitation, that one should not oppress anyone, that one should not subjugate a foreign land and that one should not do anything that takes away from people their humanity. This is what communism means to me and in such a communism I still believe today.[93]

The shaping of modern Jewry

The feudal heritage

These days it is fashionable to get around the existence of radical Jews by suggesting they were not really Jews at all. How can the truth of this be decided? In a world of nation states conventional badges of identity are frequently determined by place, but that does not work for Jews because they have been dispersed across the diaspora for millennia. To determine who is a "real Jew", rather than looking for an arbitrary definition, we must consider the character of the community over time.

What emerges is that far from the radical tradition being extraneous, fake or proof of self-hatred, it was one of a multiplicity of different Jewish identities that emerged in the late 19th century. These were moulded by the interaction of the community's self-image and external oppression. As Leon wrote, "We must not start with religion in order to explain Jewish history; on the contrary [it] can be explained only by the 'real Jew', that is to say, by the Jew in his economic and social role".[1]

Ancient Palestine was located on key trade routes and between warring powers—Egypt, Assyria/Babylon.[2] This situation led to the dispersal of followers of Judaism even before the Babylonian exile (590 BC) and the Roman conquest of Judea (70 AD).[3] They circulated commodities across many different countries helped by communal connections. Schlomo Goitein gives an example from around 870 AD:

> These merchants speak Arabic, Persian, Roman (ie, Greek, which was spoken in the Eastern Roman Empire), the language of the Franks (the inhabitants of present-day France), of the Andalusians (the Christian inhabitants of Spain), and of the Slavs. They journey from west to east and from east to west, partly on land, partly by sea. They take ship in

the land of the Franks, on the Western Sea and steer for Farama (an ancient port in Egypt, which was situated not far from the northern end of the present Suez Canal). There they load their goods on the backs of camels and travel by land to Kolzum (a port on the southern end of the Suez Canal). There they embark into the Eastern Sea and go to India and China.[4]

During the 10th century, the stagnation of the Muslim world shifted the fulcrum of Jewish life to Europe. The medieval European economy was centred on agricultural production and its two major classes—landowners and peasants. Feudal rulers' political dominance was assisted by the Catholic Church in two ways. Firstly, Biblical authority was invoked: "Obey your earthly masters with fear and trembling… not only while being watched, and in order to please them".[5] Secondly, peasant identification with their rulers was cemented by presenting non-Christians as a threat—Muslims in the Crusades, and Jews.

Jews were excluded from the agricultural nexus and were forced to congregate in urban centres[6] where they performed the essential lower status functions the countryside lacked.[7] Using skills acquired in the more advanced culture of the Middle East but absent in Europe,[8] Jewish occupations developed in two directions—artisan manufacture and commerce. A sense of what the former meant in practice is provided by Jewish occupations in a small Spanish town just before the 1492 expulsion. Jews there were listed as basket makers, goldsmiths, cobblers, tailors, blacksmiths and harness makers.[9] Half a millennium later tsarist officials emphasised that in Russia Jews "by their petty and frequently maligned pursuits promote not only rural but commercial life" so that there was "no possibility, and for a long time there will be none, of replacing them".[10]

In terms of commerce Christian involvement in moneylending was restricted on pain of excommunication by decisions such as those of the Third Lateran Council of 1179.[11] Jews were driven to this[12] because, as Luther said, "we deny them work and force them to usury". Feudal lords found Jews essential for financing lavish lifestyles and wars, even if they despised them and repayments were irksome. This gave rise to the phenomenon of the wealthy "Court Jew" enjoying (temporary) princely protection.

Despite economic differentiation within the community itself, the close association of ethnicity with a special economic position, what Leon called a "people-class", made Jews a perfect safety valve for discontent. There were other scapegoats available, such as deviants from the Christian faith (heretics) and objects of misogyny (witches), but targeting followers of an entirely different religion was convenient. Jews were used and then abused: tolerated at one moment and vilified the next. The ruling class periodically cancelled debts by expulsion or massacre and simultaneously kept the masses quiescent.

The episodic expulsions seen in France were therefore reproduced elsewhere, such as in the Bishopric of Speyer in Germany. Jews were driven out in 1405, readmitted in 1421, expelled in 1430, brought back in 1434, banished in 1435, and so on.[13] This fluctuating pattern was also a sign of economic transition in European society:

> The rise of a native Christian class of merchants and usurers [meant] Jews were no longer indispensable and the feudal aristocracy was glad to wriggle out of paying its debts. This period was marked by mass expropriation and wholesale expulsion of Jewish communities. In England, when the Lombards could advance money to the king, the Jews were expelled in 1290... In Western Europe the rise of the native merchant class had broken the monopoly of the Jews, who could be dispensed with. In Eastern Europe, however, feudal economy was at a lower level. No native middle class had yet arisen... The Jews could once again fulfil this function.[14]

Many headed for the Polish-Lithuanian Commonwealth under Casimir III (1333–1370) and later rulers. These were the Ashkenazi Jews. As Borochov puts it, the state "opened wide the gates of commerce and finance and ensured [Jews] freedom of religion and safety of life and property, but at the same time isolated them completely from any external influence and removed them from Poland's political life".[15] After Jews became expendable in Spain, there was the mass expulsion of 1492. These became the Sephardic Jews who fled to the Ottoman Empire and the Middle East. Clearly, although the overall pace of change under feudalism was slow, the situation of Jews was evolving with it.

Where the rising bourgeoisie actively confronted feudalism, Jewish status improved. When the Dutch revolted against Spain and founded a republic (1566–1648),[16] Rembrandt painted rabbis in dignified poses on a par with Christian subjects,[17] while the Jewish philosopher Baruch Spinoza became a key figure of the Dutch Golden Age.[18] Prefiguring Marx he identified the way that religion was used by feudalism: "The greatest secret of monarchic rule…is to keep men deceived and to cloak in the specious name of religion the fear by which they must be checked, so they will fight for slavery as they would for salvation".[19]

Progress towards equality through revolution did not mean denial of identity (religious or otherwise) but toleration, an increased freedom to choose what identity should be. In contrast to reactionary Spain, where the Jews who evaded expulsion in 1492 were forcibly converted to Christianity (the Marranos), during the English Revolution (1642–1660) Oliver Cromwell invited the celebrated Dutch rabbi Menasseh ben Israel to London. Thereafter, for the first time in 300 years, Jews were allowed to re-settle and practise their religion if they chose.[20]

Where the ruling class (and its ideas) were unchallenged no such openings were present. In the absence of revolution Jews remained walled inside literal or figurative ghettos by discriminatory laws. But those inside were not a passive flock simply herded about. To perform its economic function the community was allowed to operate as a semi-independent island supervised by an institution called the *Kehillah* (community). Though tasked with collecting heavy special taxes and keeping Jews orderly and segregated, it provided a degree of security and autonomy, education and community services, and maintained social cohesion.

This was a collaborationist state within a state, a prison, and a free Jewish space which mirrored the class divisions outside. The Kehillah governing council was controlled by a patrician and religious elite that used its power to both defend and represent the community to outsiders and simultaneously pursue its own interests within.[21] Below them were a middle layer of small producers and merchants, while wage-earners and paupers occupied the lowest rank.[22]

In this environment self-image became focussed on Judaism, which also served as a palliative. As Marx wrote at the time *On the Jewish Question* was published, "*Religious* suffering is, at one and the same time, the *expression* of real suffering and a *protest* against real suffering.

Religion is the sigh of the oppressed creature, the heart of a heartless world, and the soul of soulless conditions".[23] Constructing their identity using the social materials available in their confinement, Jewish suffering was expressed and made into a protest by proudly affirming religious difference, seeing what outsiders saw as negative stereotypical traits as positive.

Raphael Mahler notes that with "every increase in economic distress or national oppression, repressive legislation or persecution—the longing of the masses for deliverance became more acute".[24] Widespread expulsions in the 15th century gave rise to the *Kabbalah* religious movement. Mid sixteenth century pogroms stimulated the Sabbatai Zvi sect led by a self-proclaimed messiah, and from around 1760 came the most important of all, a mystical religious revival called Hasidism.[25] The inextricable link between religious and personal identity in the ghetto setting had its positive self-actualising side, but it gave the Kehillah authorities control over daily life—a situation that was tyrannical at the same time.

The double-edged nature of the situation was described by Vladimir Medem, the Bundist leader: "The Jewish world was closed unto itself; closed with two locks: one with which it locked itself off from the outside, strange world and another with which this strange world in turn locked it into a ghetto".[26] This situation bore no hint of radicalism, rather the opposite. Sealed within and cleaving to their religious sanctuary, Jews' minority status meant they had little choice but to act with subservience even if in their minds they were religiously defiant. They showed what Baron calls "loyalty to their respective governments. Only under extreme provocation or a severe persecution did they occasionally waver".[27]

"Men are born and remain free and equal": the strength and limits of bourgeois revolution

The changes initiated in Holland and England began to overcome the impasse. In the following century the Enlightenment's progressive challenge to feudal ideology found an echo inside the Jewish community. Moses Mendelssohn founded the *Haskalah* movement in Germany, taking tentative steps towards the human emancipation

Marx would later talk of. Writing in 1783, Mendelssohn broke with rabbinical dictation: "I recognise no eternal truths except those that can be grasped by human reason". He called for "universal tolerance" and demanded the right for the individual to "speak as he thinks, [and] call on God in his own way".[28]

But the ghetto gates remained locked from the outside in most places until the 1789 French Revolution. When the *sans culottes*, the Parisian masses, stormed the Bastille prison in July, they not only defied Louis XVI, they shattered feudal ideology. A month later the *Declaration of the Rights of Man* announced, "Men are born and remain free and equal in rights".[29]

Turning this into a reality was a challenge. Opponents of the Revolution regarded Catholic hegemony as essential and saw Jewish equality as a tremendous threat to that. While bodies representing the popular masses pressed for an emancipation decree,[30] the aristocracy and clergy played for time.[31] The reactionaries' grip wavered when, in June 1791, women seized the King at Versailles and his escape attempt (the "flight to Varennes") failed. Soon after, inspired by the *Rights of Man*, the largest slave revolt in the history of the Americas broke out in France's Caribbean colony of Saint-Domingue, which became the independent Black republic of Haiti.[32]

In September 1791 three remarkable things happened. On the 28th the Constituent Assembly banned slavery in France and decreed Jewish emancipation. The two were directly connected through Abbé Grégoire. He led the debates on Jewish civil rights[33] and was a founder of Friends of the Negro.[34] Simultaneously, Olympe de Gouges, another leading slavery abolitionist, published her historic *Declaration of the Rights of Women*. Jews were only 0.15 percent of the French population but revolutionary action by the oppressed and exploited—women, Black slaves and *sans culottes*—had created a breakthrough for them.

Formal legal equality meant real progress but it also had limitations. These were famously summed up by the Count of Clermont-Tonnerre: "Everything must be refused to the Jews as a nation; everything must be granted to them as individuals. They must be citizens".[35] It was an historic step but revealed the ambiguity of the Revolution's motto "liberty, equality, fraternity". "Fraternity" extended no further than those living within the territory of the French capitalist state. "The existence of a nation within a nation is unacceptable", said Clermont-Tonnerre.[36] This ill-fitted an international community. One barrier had come down but a new one was erected at the border.

Zionist writers claiming to speak for Jews doubt that ending legal inequality was a step forward in any way whatsoever. Citing the fact that four of Mendelssohn's six children changed their religion, David Vital sees in it little more than Jews "abandoning their own social structures and accepting the culture and values of the host nation".[37] The implication is that they should have put up with subjugation and that emancipation made their lives worse.

They clearly did not think so. Wherever change was on offer, despite the limitations, it was embraced with alacrity. The majority of Jews wanted liberation and what the poet Heinrich Heine called "the entrance ticket to European culture".[38] What it was to be Jewish—the way of life imposed over centuries—had been internalised and moulded into an identity that was both a reflection of and a response to the oppression they encountered. But when the alternative prospect of free self-expression beckoned, the majority ran towards it.

Yet emancipation would fall short of expectations. Even for those from privileged backgrounds, the promised end to discrimination was not fulfilled because bourgeois society still required scapegoats. But at least the road to fighting for more did exist. With the gates open Jews could now take action together with their non-Jewish sisters and brothers. Spasmodic rebellions had occurred during feudalism, such as the French Jacquerie, the English Peasants' Revolt of 1381 or the German Peasant War of 1525. However, long-term movements were not sustainable because insurgents eventually had to return to their farms. Now capitalist urbanisation was concentrating the masses in centres of power, places where most Jews already resided. And after 1789, politics was no longer the exclusive remit of the privileged. Permanent parties and movements that could campaign for those who suffered in society would now be organised.

Forerunners of a tradition

An early sign of what was to come was when the French advanced on Russia in 1812. A leader of the peasants in the town of Vilki (Vilna region), Abraham Marcus, called on the serfs "not to obey the Court, and not to labour for the lord, and whatever might be done by the lord, not to yield but to fight".[39] He and his family were exiled to Siberia.

Then in 1848 Jews were at the forefront of the wave of revolts that spread out from Paris. The ministers of justice and finance in the new French cabinet were Jewish. Jews joined the barricades in Vienna and Adolf Fischhof headed the Committee on Security to become "practically the uncrowned emperor of Austria".[40] Simultaneously Jews were fighting on the barricades in Berlin, capital of Prussia. They suffered almost 10 percent of the casualties while only constituting 2.5 percent of the population.

To unify Germany a national parliament was established in Frankfurt. Gabriel Riesser, a Jew, was elected vice-president. Its most famous decision—the offer of the crown of a united Germany to the Prussian King—was conveyed by its then president Martin Simson, a converted Jew.[41] Italy saw many regional uprisings. In Rome the walls of the ghetto were torn down after 300 years. In Venetia the revolution was led by Daniele Manin, a Jew. His government included Jewish ministers.[42]

Fischhof, Riesser, Simson and Manin were members of a bourgeois class seeking political hegemony. On that score the 1848 revolutions appeared to fail because the traditional regimes recovered. So, when the Frankfurt Parliament was dispersed by counter-revolution, its decree of emancipation throughout Germany was annulled.[43] Despite these setbacks the bourgeoisie gained the upper hand economically and eventually joined the establishment in those places where they had not achieved that status through revolution. At that point their incentive to unite the base of society against divide and rule thinking evaporated.

That heralded a parting of the ways between proletarians and bourgeoisie. Soon the latter would itself need to deflect unrest, so it fell to the new working class in the dark satanic mills to take the lead in challenging oppression. And there were new sorts of radical intellectuals, socialists like Marx and Moses Hess, eager to promote the cause.

The Paris Commune of 1871 was an example. Right-wing conspiracy theorists accused "Red Doctor" Marx in London of being its mastermind. Though an enthusiastic supporter, the charge was inaccurate. The Commune developed independently and represented the first workers' democracy. Its beliefs were embodied in its anthem "The Internationale" with its words about the unity of the human race. Leo Frankel, a Hungarian Jew, was elected as Delegate for Labour, a post only surpassed in importance by the Delegate for War. Another Jew, Gaston Crémieux, led the brief Marseilles Commune.

Paris was violently suppressed, and triumphant reaction led to the Dreyfus Affair, which exposed the limits of emancipation under capitalist rule. In 1894 Alfred Dreyfus, a French Jewish army officer, was falsely accused of spying. That such victimisation could happen in a country supposed to exemplify equality shocked non-Jews and Jews alike. In Paris Herzl was dismayed to discover Jews backed the socialist leader Jean Jaurès, who championed Dreyfus's cause. Herzl's diary noted: "Obviously, there is no helping the French Jews... They seek protection from the Socialists and the destroyers of the present civil order... Truly, they are not Jews any more".[44]

Identity in transition

Herzl's comment raises the important question of what the definition of a Jew might be after emancipation. Simon Dubnov, Russian-born and acknowledged doyen of Jewish historians, shared Herzl's doubts about who qualified. Russian revolutionaries had to use clandestine names (Lenin—Ulyanov, and Stalin—Jughashvili, being examples). According to Dubnov, however, left-wing Jews employed "Russian pseudonyms because they are ashamed of their Jewish origin (Trotsky, Zinoviev etc), but maybe it is their Jewish name which is not genuine, because they have no roots to bind themselves to our people".[45] Though Herzl and Dubnov disagreed on many issues of policy, both were convinced as nationalists that to be Jewish was above all to be a member of a separate nation. This is the latter's definition of that concept:

> Members of a nation are not made, but born (nascuntur, originating from the words natio, nativus)...it is only possible to make oneself a member of an organic group, tribe, or nation...by physically blending with that group... In order to be a member of the French nation, one must be descended from the Gauls or a kindred race; or else, over the course of several generations.[46]

But neither the nation nor race are biological entities. What appears natural is nothing of the sort. Where borders were placed, or who identifies as a member of a nation (and which one), are political and individual decisions. The nation is an interactive social construct and the very word "Jew" must be seen as having a dual content—a label affixed to someone from the outside *and* a label generated by that person from the inside.

Once generations of fixed separation were ended by emancipation, the Jewish persona was in flux, and what that was was up for grabs. A good starting point for judging this is the survey Arthur Ruppin made at the start of the 1930s. Ruppin was an important figure in his own right—founder of Tel Aviv, head of the Jewish Agency in Palestine, sociologist and leading Zionist. He cannot be suspected of deliberately overplaying intercommunal integration or social change because that would undermine the claim that Jews were a single immutable people.

Ruppin describes a community which, though dispersed across 33 European, 12 American, 13 Asian, seven African and two Australasian countries,[47] had been among the least diverse due to segregation behind a "fivefold wall of isolation—consisting of a separate economy, legal status, language, education and religion".[48] Emancipation, however, produced a "weakening of their ethnic homogeneity and of their sense of unity [accompanied by] assimilation to the economic and cultural life of their non-Jewish surroundings".[49] In Ruppin's view, "What it meant to be a people" was now at stake.[50]

Leaving aside that this could be seen differently—as Jews enjoying greater personal freedom and more equality—let us consider "separate economy", the first component of Ruppin's wall. Emigration to places like the US removed Jews from the economic isolation seen in places like Russia. A first-generation immigrant might arrive as a seamstress or tailor at Ellis Island, New York, working with and for Jews. Their children had a much wider range of occupations to move into. Even in the unemancipated heartlands, traditional structures were decaying. For example, the exclusive Jewish artisan guilds and the Kehillah system in Russian Poland ended in 1822.[51] Industrialisation also diluted Jewish concentrations in towns as ever larger numbers of non-Jews congregated there.[52]

Separate legal status vanished in a broad arc stretching out from the more economically advanced countries of the West towards the East. Emancipation began in the US (1790) and France (1791), reaching several German states between 1808 and 1813. Significant European additions were Greece and Belgium (1830), Holland (1834), Denmark (1849), Switzerland (1856), Britain (1858), Italy (1861), the Austrian Empire (1867), Germany (1871), and so on.

Ruppin's third category was language. Yiddish and Hebrew were the main Jewish languages, though the latter was largely used for prayer alone (in the same way as Latin).[53] Reduced isolation transformed communication:

> In Western and Central Europe this linguistic change occurred during the first half of the nineteenth century, in Eastern Germany several decades later, and Yiddish entirely disappeared... Similar changes supervened in France, Holland, England, Italy and the Magyar parts of Hungary.[54]

Russia saw dramatic shifts when emancipation arrived in 1917. Twenty years before, 97 percent of Russian Jews gave Yiddish as their mother tongue.[55] By 1939, 54 percent of Soviet Jews put down Russian.[56] In the US first generation immigrants largely spoke Yiddish, second generation Yiddish and English, and the third English only.[57] Even in countries with the highest concentrations of Yiddish speakers the process of dissolution was rapid. A visitor to Poland in 1932 commented:

> Linguistic assimilation is increasing...in front of our very eyes, the language which they spoke for hundreds of years is being forgotten... The children virtually don't know Yiddish at all and speak Polish.[58]

Attrition was clear even if use of Yiddish remained widespread.[59]

Traditional Jewish schooling was at the *chayder* or *yeshiva*. Education, wrote Ruppin, meant "memorising [religious] texts...the pupil learns nothing in it of the intellectual developments of the last thousand years".[60] With the rapid spread of free state education using the local vernacular, the decline of specifically Jewish schools was predictable. This evolution was taking place in all countries with the notable exception of Palestine.[61]

The last element of crumbling isolation was religion. In the 1870s, one commentator wrote of the situation in Russia, "the cornerstone that has supported the entire House of Israel throughout time was the Torah. She was the breath of life that revived his collapsing body, and in her he found salvation and consolation for all his sorrows".[62] But by 1916 in the US only 12 percent of American Jews belonged to synagogues.[63] By 1945 only a quarter of Jewish workmen on the Lower East Side, New York, observed the Sabbath, 60 percent of Jewish shops remained open, and *American Hebrew* magazine continued to complain bitterly about non-attendance at synagogues in New York.[64] A major injunction was that Jews could only marry other Jews. From the other side many states barred intermarriage, but that was changing: "From France the recognition of mixed marriages gradually extended to Belgium, Holland, Denmark, Great Britain, the Scandinavian countries, and the United States".[65] Germany followed in 1875, Hungary in 1895 and Russia in 1917. Once the door was open many stepped through. Between 1900 and 1930 the percentage of mixed marriages in Germany rose from 8 to 22 percent of all Jews who married. In Hungary it went from 3 to 17 percent, and so on.[66] In the USSR the figure was 42 percent.[67]

The function of the diaspora was also different now. The Jewish Marxist historian Eric Hobsbawm wrote that "the family was a network stretching across countries and oceans...shifting between countries was a normal part of life".[68] This feature had once set Jews apart and reinforced their community ties. Now integration into so many different countries created a new relationship. Radical Jews brought a sense of living class internationalism to those they interacted with at local level.

Together these cumulative changes did not mean being less Jewish but being Jewish in a different way. It was no longer inevitable that life was bounded within a carapace resistant to but moulded by oppression. The chance to positively interact with others was not a diminution of their human existence but an enhancement, and it encouraged a secular cultural renaissance. Many immersed themselves in the art forms of wider society (literature, music, and painting), sometimes imparting a distinctive character such as using Yiddish, or ethnic mottos as did Marc Chagall in painting. The contribution of Jews to music was particularly marked, from composers such as

Felix Mendelssohn and Fanny Mendelssohn[69] to Gustav Mahler and George Gershwin,[70] or performers such as Joseph Joachim, Jascha Heifetz and Arthur Rubinstein. This was not self-abasement but self-expression at the highest level. In *Jewishness in Music* Wagner was objecting to the mutual benefit gained by all from such flowering of world culture.

The new and exciting sense of how one could live was not something done *to* Jews. No policeman told them who to love, what to study, when to shop, or what to read or write. The decisions were made *by* Jews acting in what they judged their own interests. That did not sit well with Ruppin. He complained that Jews had "lost by now their national consciousness, or are losing it and are disappearing as a nation".[71] The political project founded on that concept seemed to be running out of time.

What kept it alive was the continuing pressure of antisemitism. Racism had not disappeared despite formal emancipation. From the Russian pogroms of 1881 to the Holocaust there was a dramatic and terrifying upswing in anti-Jewish violence. Would this emergency neutralise the centrifugal forces identified by Ruppin and restore the "national consciousness" he thought Jews should have? The answer to that question would be found in migration patterns.

Mapping the new Jewish identity

Though Jews had been on the move for millennia nothing matched the half century after 1881 when a quarter migrated abroad.[72] At the beginning only one in 30 lived in the US and other non-European countries; but in 1933 it was one in three out of a world population of 16 million.[73] Four fifths of those arriving in the US came from Eastern Europe,[74] the Russian sector providing by far the largest group.[75]

Jews were just one part of a wider spectrum of mass relocation. Ironically, despite nationalist insistence that individuals must identify with one place and its state, huge numbers were leaving for other countries. Assisted by the invention of modern steamships, 150 million people migrated in the hundred years after 1840, including 58 million Europeans.[76] Taking 1940 as the baseline, this amounted to 6.5 percent of the world population and 12 percent of all Europeans. For example, almost as many non-Jewish Poles emigrated to America as Jewish Poles.[7] Widespread movement was driven by economics—the birth pangs of capitalism and poverty—and Jews felt these too. Yet the ratio of Jewish migration was twice the average, so the additional push of ethnic oppression must have played a role.

If these were the motives for leaving, what determined the chosen destination? The answer can be seen as a vast natural opinion poll on Jewish self-image. Comparing data on migration to Palestine with elsewhere helps us weigh the appeal of ethnic separatism versus living alongside non-Jews to achieve the sort of progress Marx had talked about.

A contemporary observed that, "To other countries the Jews are attracted by the chance to better their economic condition. To Palestine, they have been and still are attracted by nationalistic and religious sentiments".[78] In 1914 just 94,000 Jews lived there after decades of inward migration.[79] By contrast, the US contingent alone had reached 3 million people.[80] Even after Palestine became a last resort for those fleeing Nazi Germany (because the US had restricted entry), the number was only 449,000 by 1939.

Palestine was easier to reach than the US. Yet between 1901 and 1925, 27 times as many Jews chose to take the lengthier and more expensive trip of around 7,000 km (the distance from Vilna to New York then costing 72 rubles), rather than go half that distance (Vilna to Jerusalem at 13 rubles).[81] As Chapter 8 will show, New York was no paradise for Jewish immigrants, and life in Palestine was hard too. David Ben Gurion, later the prime minister of Israel, reported in 1906 that wages there were lower than in Russia and most workers lacked secure employment.[82] But these concerns should have been of minor import if ineluctable nationhood and the imperative need to shun non-Jews applied. Palestine, with the highest Jewish density in the world (over six times greater than the US),[83] should have been the homeland of choice.

Herzl had acknowledged that ending what he called exile would "be gradual, continuous, and will cover many decades".[84] Yet dispersion was increasing not declining. New countries such as Australia, South Africa and Argentina were being added to the diaspora. Between the foundation of Zionism at the close of the 19th century and 1939, the

Jewish population increased by 5 million. Only one 13th of this growth occurred in the designated sanctuary.

Care needs to be taken with migration statistics. Destinations are not solely determined by refugees but also by government policies. Jacob Lestchinsky, the Zionist socialist, divided the worldwide pattern into two time periods: a) up to around 1926, "when Jewish migrants voluntarily sought out new countries"; and b) "the period of quotas and restrictions when Jewish emigrants were prepared to look for a haven anywhere in the world, so long as they fled Europe".[85] Accordingly, in the period of free choice 3.6 percent went to Palestine. When they would have to go to "anywhere in the world" that would take them, the proportion shot up to 33 percent.[86] Indeed, two thirds of those who went to Palestine between 1840 and 1942 did so in the 13 years after 1926.[87] Even then Palestine could still be far down the queue. In 1929, for example, more Jews arrived in Argentina, Brazil and Canada.[88] Nonetheless arrivals in Palestine were boosted by Hitler's accession, and from 1933 to the Second World War it challenged the US as a primary refuge.[89]

A sign of the coerced nature of phase b) was that during an economic downturn in the mid-1920s many recent arrivals left.[90] The US enjoyed greater loyalty from its Jewish visitors. Whereas one third of non-Jewish immigrants returned to their original countries,[91] Jewish immigrants saw it as their final and permanent home with 19 out of 20 staying indefinitely.[92] The high proportion of Jewish women and children arriving[93] also indicated an intention to resettle. Most Jews found self-imposed isolation in Palestine unattractive.

The role of class

When economic barriers came down, Jews became subject to the industrialisation and rapid class polarisation common everywhere.[94] Ruppin downplays this feature in his study, perhaps because it went beyond describing a community fraying at the edges to reveal diametrically opposed interests within it. Writing in 1918, Lestchinsky analysed changes: "At the beginning of the nineteenth century the working classes constituted no more than 10 percent to 12 percent of the Jewish population and now they are more than 50 percent".[95]

Though the pattern converged more and more with society in general, the economic structure was still unusual (see table 1).[96]

Table 1: Jewish occupations across the world in 1932

Sector	Absolute number	Percentage
Commerce (including transport, entertainment, trade and banking)	6,100,000	38.6
Industry (including mining and handicraft)	5,750,000	36.4
Professions and the civil service	1,000,000	6.3
Agriculture	625,000	4.0
Casual labourers and domestic servants	325,000	2.0
Unoccupied (living on private means, pensions, or in receipt of assistance)	2,000,000	12.7
TOTAL	15,800,000	100

Source: Ruppin, Arthur, 1934, p137.

Jewish employment statistics were skewed towards "commerce",[97] a deceptive term including many living a highly precarious existence. The Zionist leader Max Nordau called them *luftmenschen* (people floating in the air). At around 40 percent of Russian Jewry,[98] they were "without a sound economic basis, were dealers one day, traders the next, and teachers on the third".[99]

Another economic snapshot is provided by emigration statistics: the proportion of Jews writing "no occupation" on entry to the US was double that for immigrants in general.[100] Yet skilled Jews (at 68 percent) dwarfed the non-Jewish average of 20 percent. They worked in "sweated trades" such as clothing. A quarter of family breadwinners were tailors, compared to just 1 percent for non-Jews.[101]

Though clearly not an exact match, class divisions for Jews paralleled those elsewhere, leading to poorer members confronting its leading figures and to looking outside the community for allies.

Before the Second World War Jewish ethnic separatism was a minority current.[102] Though radicalism was a demanding and perilous individual choice, its aspirations chimed with significant and substantial tendencies in Jewish development. Oppression, emancipation and class polarisation had created a distinct mass of Jews who actively sought freedom and equality wherever they lived, in a social structure that offered neither. They bore a new self-identity to which the left could appeal. But this was no more than an objective possibility. The subjective choice would be determined by politics.

3

Jewish political currents

Although Jews were scattered around the globe, in 1900 five out of six European Jews lived in Russia, Austria-Hungary and Romania. Half of European and 45 percent of all Jewry lived in Russia alone, where most were confined to a western region called the Pale of Settlement.[1]

At this time the rise of global capitalism was stimulating the parallel growth of both proletarian socialism and nationalism. Workers everywhere were organising to further their interests. Under the Marxist banner of internationalism, Social Democracy spread rapidly after the foundation of the German party (the Social Democratic Party of Germany—SPD) in 1875. Here was a movement which working-class Jews, already part of a global community, could readily identify with.[2] Nationalism was also expanding. Popularised by the French Revolution, new states, or movements to create them, sprang up everywhere.[3] Sometimes this ideology served reactionary purposes, strengthening oppression and colonialism. Sometimes nationalism could represent the desire of the oppressed to break free; though even the most progressive form of nationalism saw change occurring within the existing economic and social framework.

In the face of heightened antisemitism in Eastern Europe, both nationalism and socialism were attractive, producing a spate of organisational efforts. The first Zionist Congress was held in August 1897. Six weeks later the Jewish Labour Bund was set up in Russian-ruled Vilna. Four months after that in nearby Minsk, the Russian Social Democratic Labour Party (RDSLP) was established. There were now several trends competing for Jewish allegiance, both old and new. Each in its own way represented a Jewish identity.

49

Rivals to the radical tradition

Conservative orthodoxy

Until the 19th century the community was wrapped in religion and its primary survival strategy was to stick defiantly to the "old Jewish political traditions of seeking a *modus vivendi* at all costs".[4] Many Jews avoided challenging the states where they resided by abstaining from politics altogether or by supporting mainstream parties.

The Lithuanian Hasidic leader Rabbi Shne'ur Zalman provided an insight into the accompanying mindset. When emancipation seemed possible due to France invading Russia in 1812, he said, "If Bonaparte were victorious, happiness in Israel would increase and the dignity of the Jewish people magnified" but that would cause a "parting and estrangement of the hearts of the Jews from their Father in heaven". He went on, "If on the other hand, our sovereign [Tsar] Alexander were victorious, the poverty of Israel would increase, and the dignity of Israel would be downtrodden. But the hearts of the Jews would be bound and attached and joined to their Father in heaven".[5] So tsarist oppression was preferable to emancipation!

Conservative orthodoxy was hostile to socialism not only because the left was frequently atheistic, but because Jewish activists associated with non-Jews. With a different social base to that of the left, it survived best in places where traditional social isolation held or modernisation and emancipation were recent. This meant there was often a generational divide between religious-minded parents and their more militant children.[6]

It seems surprising that Zionism was initially "anathema to the most illustrious and influential of Eastern European rabbis as a matter of course".[7] The foremost theologian of the time described Zionism as "the most terrible enemy that has ever risen against the Jewish nation"[8] for advocating return to Palestine. Religious teachings insisted that Jews would only go to Eretz Israel (the Land of Israel) when the Messiah arrived at the End of Days. There was a clash between Jews as defined by their religion and those defined by their nation in exile, as Zionists saw it. Religious Jews were committed to a form of internationalism while Zionist nationalism defied centuries of Jewish tradition!

With few exceptions Jews eventually accommodated their religion to Zionism. They shared common ground in opposing the left, whose desire for freedom and equality was interpreted as being "ready and willing to eradicate their own self [in] a dishonourable process that was to be resisted by all means".[9] Zionism cleverly invoked religious historical associations as justification for colonising Palestine.[10] The Mizrachi religious Zionist movement was established in 1902 and eventually all but a tiny minority of traditionalists made their peace with their most terrible enemy.[11] The words of "divine and eternal" holy texts may not change, but expediency demands their interpretation keeps up with the times. Nonetheless, that there had been initial discord shows that Zionism was not the culmination of a 2,000-year-old prophecy, as would be claimed in Israel's Declaration of Independence in 1948, but a cultural break.

Assimilationism

Assimilationism—fully identifying oneself with the surrounding society—was another important current. The hope was to achieve "a future of progress, including education, new occupations, and geographic, social, and economic mobility".[12] Assimilationism garnered support where emancipation had sunk its deepest roots and a sense of difference was least.

The strategy seemed most feasible to bourgeois elements. Integrating as wealthy individuals rather than as Jews, many were keen not to jeopardise their newly acquired membership of the elite. They proved their worthiness through exaggerated patriotism and support for secular centre or right-wing parties. A famous assimilationist was Benjamin Disraeli, British Conservative prime minister in the period 1860–1880. Despite his efforts and high status, he was not spared "the most virulent and repulsive antisemitism throughout his career".[13]

As the class divide between rich and poor Jews grew, the assimilationist bourgeoisie increasingly saw their lower-class brethren as embarrassing or as a threat. If it retained a connection with other Jews it tended to be advocacy via conformist institutions such as the Central Union of German Citizens of the Jewish Faith and the Board of Deputies of British Jews, which arrogated to themselves the right to speak for all. At best the wealthy might subscribe funds for suffering co-religionists as long as no taint of radicalism was suspected.

A significant example at the end of the 19th century was the rescue of bankrupt Jewish agricultural settlements in Palestine by Baron Edmond de Rothschild, an assimilated French Jew. He was alarmed:

> by the plight of the east European Jewish masses and favored their resettlement—though preferably not in France where an influx of poor Jews from the east might fan the flames of antisemitism and undermine the tenuous place which the Rothschilds, and later other assimilated Jews had secured.[14]

Hostility to immigration often accompanied philanthropy. Britain's Board of Deputies did not oppose the racist 1905 Aliens Act, designed explicitly to exclude Jewish refugees.

Some writers suggest that "socialism, in the same way as liberalism, regarded assimilation as the true end of emancipation",[15] with the effective dissolution of Jews and their culture being the goal. The Jewish socialist writer Isaac Deutscher gave some credence to this view when he wrote that Napoleon's plan to *make* Jews "submerge themselves in the gentile population was certainly sound".[16]

As *On the Jewish Question* showed, Marx rejected the destruction of one identity to be absorbed by another, because freedom and equality were not gained by submergence but by the power to choose. Socialism does not aim at blending into existing structures but at transcendence—a society without discrimination due to gender, sexual orientation, ethnicity, religion, or disability. Assimilationists hope legal reform will suffice, but the system's need for diversionary ideology continues regardless, so joining bourgeois society cannot end discrimination. Only socialism can do that. This lay behind Trotsky's sharp comment shortly before the Holocaust. He predicted "the fate of the Jewish people—not only their political but their physical fate—is indissolubly linked with the emancipating struggle of the international proletariat".[17] Because the working-class revolutionary wave after 1917 had been defeated by capitalism, millions of Jews would perish during the Second World War.

Political Zionism
Ilan Pappé explains the background to the emergence of Zionism in a break with religious orthodoxy.

The roots of modern-day Zionism can be found already in the eighteenth century in what was called the Jewish enlightenment movement. This was a group of writers, poets, and rabbis who revived the Hebrew language and pushed the boundaries of traditional and religious Jewish education into the more universal study of science, literature, and philosophy. Across Central and Eastern Europe, Hebrew newspapers and journals began to proliferate. Out of this group there emerged a few individuals, known in Zionist historiography as the "Harbingers of Zionism". [18]

Herzl's booklet, *The Jewish State*, launched Zionism at a time when modern antisemitism was visible in Russia, Germany, France, and Britain. Herzl therefore got a hearing for his plan for Jews to leave their current places of residence and reassemble in a "homeland". His was the first of many varieties of Zionism.

Before developing his ideas, Herzl was an assimilated German nationalist who believed Jews only need shed their feudal communal character to be welcomed into the new nation states. He even advocated Jewish conversion to Christianity at one point. [19] Herzl's turn to Zionism stemmed from a rude awakening to reality—particularly the election of a virulent antisemite, Karl Lueger, as mayor of Vienna in 1895 and restrictions on Jews that followed. [20]

Herzl's new approach was silent regarding conservative orthodoxy and did not criticise assimilationism, [21] but he recognised and countered the strength of Jewish radicalism: "Educated Jews without means are now rapidly becoming Socialists. Hence we are certain to suffer very severely". [22] The problem was that "When we sink, we become a revolutionary proletariat, the subordinate officers of all revolutionary parties". [23] "Universal brotherhood is not even a beautiful dream. Antagonism is essential to man's greatest efforts". [24]

Political Zionism's alternative was that Jews join the queue forming independent states. Leo Pinsker's *Autoemancipation* of 1882, the most important precursor to Herzl's work, says, "The *general* history of the present day seems called to be *our* ally. In a few decades we have seen rising into new life nations which at an earlier time would not have dared to dream of a resurrection". [25] If the nationalist tide was clear, there was a problem for Jews who wanted to swim with it.

The claim that Jews were a nation was no less valid than any other in principle.[26] But Jewish nationalism found it particularly difficult to make a plausible case.

Firstly, the accepted idea of a nation was of a geographically-based population. The convention for determining whether someone is Australian or British, for example, is simple: a passport will suffice. But Dubnov admitted Jews were "without a land, a people stripped of all the tangible accompaniments of nationality".[27] Alongside dispersal across the diaspora there was also dubiety about who was Jewish with talk of Jews "only in name" (Dubnov), "self-hating", or "not Jews any more" (Herzl). These show how slippery imposing a fixed category, an essentialist designation of "a people", could be for Jewish nationalists of all stripes. (Antisemites have no such problem because they use any arbitrary measure, just so long as a believable scapegoat is discovered.[28] Marxists see the issue as socially contingent.)

Jewish nationalists tried to get around the problem through either diaspora nationalism or Zionism. In place of territory both trends hoped that it would be sufficient to invoke the classic foundation used by all nationalisms, that "the people" is timeless. As a diaspora nationalist Dubnov believed in cultural autonomy rather than a specific homeland, writing that Jewry had been "successful in preserving its spiritual unity, its originality, complete and undiminished"[29] and possessed a "national spirit undergoing continuous evolution during thousands of years".[30]

The Zionist project required physical relocation and an invented continuity. This was put emphatically in the Declaration of the Establishment of the State of Israel in 1948:

> After being forcibly exiled from their land, the people kept faith with it throughout their Dispersion and never ceased to pray and hope for their return to it and for the restoration in it of their political freedom. Impelled by this historic and traditional attachment, Jews strove in every successive generation to re-establish themselves in their ancient homeland.[31]

Self-consciousness related to Judaism had indeed existed for thousands of years; but rabbinical hostility to Zionist thinking shows, as Shapira says, that it was "entirely different".[32] And there was little sign of the striving of "successive generations" since fewer than half of 1 percent of world Jewry had chosen to live in Palestine before the torrent of pogroms drove migration there.[33]

Secondly, "national spirit" based on religious affiliation was a weak card to play. Christianity, Buddhism or Islam do not define nationality even though they have holy places. Like Judaism they are international. Nor have more geographically circumscribed belief systems, such as Shintoism in Japan or Hinduism in India, provided the basis for independence movements.

Thirdly, the Zionists had a problem identifying a homeland in the first place. Palestine was by no means the only option floated. In 1896 Herzl himself posed Argentina as another potential candidate. A faction called Territorialism investigated possibilities in Angola, Libya, Texas, Mexico, Austria, Australia and Canada.[34] Arguments became toxic after 1903 when the British dangled the idea of a colonial settlement in Uganda. Some, desperate for an immediate haven, backed the idea; but others saw the symbolism of Palestine as indispensable. The issue split the sixth Zionist Congress and although Palestine won out, the movement risked imploding in bitter recriminations.

Even if a way round the lack of standard qualifications could be found, how would the homeland be won? In *The Jewish State*, Herzl disowned mass activity as dangerously subversive and hoped salvation would come from above: "All our material welfare has been brought about by men of enterprise".[35] He went on to say, "Politics must take shape in the upper strata and work downwards".[36] There was a difficulty with the upper strata, however. The nation is supposed to include everyone, but the most successful "men of enterprise", wealthier Jews, were assimilationists who disliked Jewish nationalism.[37] Caught between a grass-roots Jewry it feared and a summit that was unsympathetic, the social base of political Zionism remained narrow.

Herzl was therefore no inspiring nationalist figurehead like Simon Bolivar in Latin America or Giuseppe Garibaldi in Italy. He mobilised no forces, had no territory to operate on, and was without bargaining strength. At his death just 1 percent of world Jewry were affiliated to Zionism.[38] The only remaining option was a craven one. In a world of imperial powers, to obtain a Jewish state in Palestine, at that time a country under Ottoman rule, required "the friendly cooperation of interested Governments".[39] The incentive he offered them was the

prospect of ridding their countries of Jews. This must have been entic-
ing because despite Zionism's lack of a significant base, between its
launch in 1897 and his death in 1904 Herzl met the German Kaiser,
the Ottoman Sultan, the kings of Italy and Bulgaria, British foreign
and colonial secretaries, and the Pope.[40] His most controversial visit
was in 1903, the year of the notorious Kishinev pogrom. To the alarm
of many Zionists, Herzl sought to cut a deal with the mastermind of
the outrages, Plehve, tsarist Minister of the Interior.[41]

Abraham Ussishkin, right-wing leader of the strongest Zionist
Federation in Russia,[42] complained pointedly about Herzl's tactics on
practical grounds:

> On the one hand, the whole movement was dependent upon the diplo-
> matic progress of the given moment; on the other hand, the numerous
> members of the organisation, walking blindly behind their leaders,
> longed for active work, while such work really did not exist, for only
> the chosen ones, or more correctly, the chosen one, could occupy them-
> selves with diplomacy.[43]

Not only was Zionism politically feeble, its tactics rendered its few
supporters irrelevant.

The only glimmer of hope was the Balfour Declaration of 1917. In
the midst of the First World War, the British government declared
support for "a National Home for the Jewish people" in Palestine. This
was no "romantically sentimental" move by "Bible lovers",[44] as Arthur
Koestler alleged, but the cynical decision of an embattled imperialism desperate for allies. Britain offered a country it did not own to
the Arabs in 1915 and as a joint administration to the French in 1916.[45]
Touting Palestine to yet another customer was designed to solicit an
"enthusiastic message to us from American Zionists and prominent
non-Zionists".[46] Double-crossing everyone, the British were intrigued
by the prospect of a reliable military base ("a little loyal Jewish Ulster
in a sea of potentially hostile Arabism", according to the first British
governor of Jerusalem).[47] The British prime minister freely admitted
these mutually contradictory promises were thrown around like con-
fetti for "propagandist reasons".[48]

When, in 1922, Britain gained control under the League of Nations
Mandate, the Balfour Declaration eased the passage of Jews into

Palestine, but not many wished to go there and it failed to boost Zionist popularity. Walter Laqueur mourns that on the eve of Hitler's accession to power in 1933:

> How little had it achieved in more than three decades! The *leitmotif* of failure, even impotence, recurred frequently…we have not won over the Jewish masses to the Zionist idea. The movement was still weak by any standards: of four million American Jews, a mere eighty-eight thousand had voted in the elections for the Prague [World Zionist] congress and the membership of the American Zionist Federation had in fact declined since the late 1920s. In Rumania a mere forty thousand had voted, in Hungary only five thousand out of a Jewish community of half a million.[49]

Of German Jews "only a comparatively small minority joined the movement and…the majority was actively opposed".[50] In Britain "the majority of the community were…indifferent or even actively hostile".[51] Zionism did not naturally inherit the Jewish mantle.

Political Zionism's fundamental problem was that, as Shapira puts it, Herzl believed "there was no point in fighting antisemitism, in proving it misguided".[52] He wrote that "nothing effectual can really be done"[53] and, "Great exertions will hardly be necessary to spur on the [Zionist] movement. Antisemites provide the requisite impetus. They need only do what they did before".[54] This meant passivity before antisemitism and withdrawal from the surrounding society. While still a conventional Zionist, Vladimir Jabotinsky, future leader of the right-extremist Revisionist wing, wrote: "We turn our back on the external world which has turned its back on us a long time ago, and we turn ourselves to an internal, national Jewish policy. It is not necessary to write manifestos to Russian society".[55] Political Zionism was therefore of little comfort to Jews being persecuted there and then in the diaspora.

The Bundist Medem identified another weakness which followed from the social changes identified by Ruppin. The premise of a monolithic Jewish nation which needed a single homeland was flawed: "Worldwide Jewry has become a fiction. It is its individual components that are truly alive… Worldwide Jewry—this is an abstraction, and an obsolete one at that".[56] The real focus of Jews was where they lived and this meant "less dreaming by the moonlight... And more living work among living people!"[57]

Jewish radical politics

On many levels conservative orthodoxy, assimilationism and political Zionism were poles apart. However, each in their own way refused to question the system that scapegoated Jews. The first avoided entanglements with it, the second tried to blend in, and the third ran away. Jewish radicals challenged that system, but did so in very diverse ways.

Socialist Zionism

Nationalism and socialism are fundamentally different concepts. One advocates cross-class alliances, the other international working-class unity against exploiters irrespective of borders. This theoretical distinction was not always obvious for left-leaning Jews. Persecution of all Jews simply for being Jews was layered on top of class division between rich and poor Jews, and growing links with exploited non-Jews. In such circumstances a dual identity which frustrated neat categories could develop.

Socialist Zionism was proof of that. It appeared as early as the second annual World Zionist Congress in 1898. Nahman Syrkin spoke twice and each time the minutes record disorder and commotion. His crime was to criticise the number of rabbis on a particular commission and suggest some workers should be included instead.[58]

Syrkin remained a Zionist throughout his life, but that did not prevent him from wanting to join the Bolshevik Third International or penning a deathbed letter to Trotsky urging him "to fight for socialism as a son of his people".[59] Syrkin's *The Socialist Jewish State* was a direct response to Herzl's *The Jewish State*. It affirmed a connection between Jewish and non-Jewish workers: "In truth, Jewish socialism and proletarian socialism have a common source in human oppression and in the unjust distribution of power".[60] The two were embodied in the Jewish radical tradition: "The socialism of the Jewish proletariat contains a special Jewish protest, as well, which expresses itself along with its class consciousness".[61]

But Syrkin doubted the effectiveness of intercommunal solidarity because the pre-eminent socialist party of the Second International, the German SPD, exhibited an "opportunism [which] sometimes led it in a direction opposite to the basic principles of socialism".[62] Exiled from Russia in Berlin, Syrkin witnessed first-hand how one SPD leader, Eduard Bernstein, himself a Jew, led the party's degeneration, abandoning revolution in favour of limited reforms. This laid the ground for the SPD's disastrous capitulation to German chauvinism in 1914 when it forsook internationalist principles to back German imperialism in the First World War. *The Socialist Jewish State* expected SPD decay would spread:

> In Russia, where Jews are not emancipated, their condition will not be radically altered through an overthrow of the present political regime. No matter what new class gains control of the government, it will not be deeply interested in the emancipation of the Jews.[63]

The only remedy for the beleaguered Jewish worker was flight.[64]

> We are driven to the unhappy conclusion that unlike all the other oppressed, he has no real, immediate weapon with which to win an easing of his lot. His only alternative, as it was centuries ago, is emigration to other countries.[65] A separate homeland must be sought even if not all could reach it.[66]

Syrkin's outlook was vividly illustrated in his exchange with Alexander Parvus (original name Israel Gelfand). Parvus was instrumental in the development of Trotsky's theory of permanent revolution, which had internationalism at its core. Here is Parvus at a meeting speaking about global links between workers. He is using his coat as an example:

> It was spun in England; it was woven in Lodz; the buttons came from Germany, the thread from Austria; is it not clear to you that this world of ours is international, and even a miserable thing like a coat is made up of the labour of different races?... Hands were lifted to applaud... Syrkin, unable to contain himself, rose to his feet and shouted: 'And the rip in your sleeve comes from the pogrom in Kiev'.[67]

To Medem, socialist Zionism was built "on a foundation of despair".[68] Syrkin, however, painted it in left-wing colours:

The Jewish proletariat, however, is the class which will solve the Jewish question through the class struggle. It has a national interest in a territory because among alien surroundings it lacks the possibility for developing its powers for the class-struggle.[69]

The Socialist Jewish State finished with this programme:

1. Social-democratic movements must be joined in those countries where the Jewish masses live.

2. A Jewish socialist commonwealth must be founded in Palestine...

As there is no organic connection between political struggle in the Diaspora and the reconstruction of Palestine there must be two independent organisations for the concrete realisation of these two ideas...

Long live international socialism!

Long live Socialist-Zionism![70]

Syrkin avoided the contradiction between socialism and nationalism by separating them: left policies for the diaspora, and emigration to Palestine.

Borochov took a different tack. He inverted the class content of socialism and nationalism. In *The National Question and the Class Struggle* (1905), Borochov argued that capitalist globalisation meant "big business has long ago swept beyond the narrow borders of the national market and language. Now it strides, head raised high, over the broad extensive world market". He contrasted that with workers who were physically bound to a particular location: "The territory has likewise its importance for the proletariat, ie, the importance of a work-place". It followed that the proletariat "must develop a specific proletarian type of nationalism"[71] and for Jews this could only happen in Palestine.[72] Workers were nationalist; bosses were internationalist! This upside-down formulation confused capitalist economics—which trades internationally—with capitalist political ideology—which relies on nationalism.

While Borochov recognised the role of class, like Herzl he believed immigration itself caused racism, rather than ruling class divide and rule, meaning separatism was the solution:

The constant immigration of new workers into England and the United States of America is a threat to the security of the places of employment of the English and American workers, and as a result, the national consciousness of the latter is heightened, deterring the development of their class-consciousness.[73]

In 1906 Borochov set out the programme of the Jewish Social Democratic Workers' Party (Poale Zion), arguing that "colonising a territory [eg Palestine] is a prolonged process, during which we must also defend our needs" in exile.[74] His blend of left radicalism with nationalism, solidarity with separatism, was encapsulated in this formula: "Our ultimate aim, our maximum program, is socialism... Our immediate aim, our minimum program, is Zionism".[75] Borochov's ideas influenced people like Ben Gurion.

Borochov's Poale Zion Party disagreed with Syrkin's Zionist Socialist Workers' Party over the Uganda project, but both inhabited a topsy-turvy world blending nationalism and socialism (while the existence of the Arab majority in Palestine was ignored). This mixture of national and class identities was not as strange as it seems. In left reformism generally, resistance to the system coexists with acceptance of its idea of "national interest".

Lack of coherence notwithstanding, and however uncomfortable for "antisemitism of the left" theorists, Zionism itself depended upon a significant radical current to attract a popular base because it had something to offer the diaspora. By 1905, 43,000 leftist adherents were the majority of the 70,000 Russians constituting Zionism's largest federation.[76]

At the same time factionalism complicated matters for all Zionists. For a movement claiming Jewish unity there were "a bewildering number [of parties]...several varieties of socialist Zionism, Zionist Zionism, cultural Zionism, Mizrachi (Orthodox Zionism), Sejmism, territorialism, socialist territorialism, and Bundism".[77] In 1933 there were no fewer than six Zionist socialist parties in Poland alone![78] Jabotinsky's Revisionism would be a later addition on the far right. Splintering was a further sign of weakness in the national case. Class polarisation, different rates of breakdown of isolation, local variations across the vast diaspora, a chasm separating rich and poor, created a perfect storm of division in what was supposed to be a single people with a single self-image—"*ein* Volk" to use Herzl's description.[79]

After the 1929 Wall Street Crash world politics polarised and the move away from the political centre ground affected Jews as it did everyone else. Jabotinsky's extreme right-wing Revisionists detested socialism even more than Herzl. In *The Iron Wall*[80] he insisted on a "monist" programme of forcibly wresting Palestine into Zionist hands to the exclusion of all non-national questions. The left-right antagonism could be violent. In 1933 Chaim Arlosoroff, one of the leading left Zionists, was murdered and though never conclusively proved, the Revisionists were blamed. Between the two sat Weizmann's General Zionists (formerly the political Zionists).

Trends can be seen by comparing votes at the World Zionist Congresses of 1929 and 1933, held seven months after Hitler became German Chancellor (see table 2).

Table 2: Votes at the World Zionist Congresses, 1929 and 1933 according to political party

	1929	*1933*
Number of voters	211,000	700,000
General Zionists	47%	23%
Left Zionists	26%	44%
Revisionists	7%	16%
Mizrachi (religious)	16%	12%
Others	7%	7%

Source: Resolutions of the 16th Zionist Congress, Zurich, 28 July to 11 August 1929 and Resolutions of the 18th Zionist Congress, Prague, 21 August to 3 September 1933.

As the table shows, though still a miniscule force in the 16-million-strong community, the electorate had tripled. More Jews were turning to Zionism for salvation, but to which variety? The share of the inheritors of political Zionism (General Zionism) had halved, Revisionism took one sixth, but all were dwarfed by socialist growth.

This shift was not transient. David Ben-Gurion became chairman of the Zionist Executive, and Jewish Agency's Executive two years later.[81] Left Zionism would dominate world Zionism for 40 years. It only relinquished its grip when the Labour Party lost to Likud in Israel's Knesset in 1977. Zionists tend to forget their own history when they besmirch the left to deflect criticisms of the Israeli state. It was the left's appeal to a mass of Jews that saved Zionism from oblivion at a crucial moment in Jewish history.

However, the term "left" needs to be used with caution. The social-ist ideas of rank-and-file Communists were not equated with Stalin's labour camps, executions and extreme exploitation of workers. Equally, reformist voters were not responsible for the failures of reformist gov-ernments. In the same way, left Zionists suffering oppression in the diaspora were not at all the same as those practising it in Palestine.. There the Zionist current functioned in a very different way. A clear distinction must be drawn and each understood in its own context. (See Chapter 13.)

Bundism

Jewish populations across the world varied so there was no "average" community. If it was correct that only "individual components" were alive, then Eastern Europe was where the most vibrant would be found, and the Jewish Labour Bund was one of its most remarkable creations.

The nearest Marxist designation for the Bund is "centrist". A host of such parties emerged during the 1914 to 1920 interregnum separat-ing a single world socialist movement and the discrete reformist Social Democratic (or Second) International and the revolutionary Communist (or Third) International. But Bundism was precocious. Studying it gives an insight into the thought processes of a radical Jewish working class struggling to find a way through uncharted territory. Even if that cul-minated in a dead-end, tracing the journey is illuminating.

Bundism's attitude to nation and class was complex. Faced with the antagonism between lower and upper-class Jews, its leaders rejected the idea of a common Jewish national interest. Medem had a "sharply negative attitude toward nationalistic aspirations and appetites" and "passionately hated the very word 'nationalist'".[82] Yet at the same time he castigated the RSDLP for having "an extraordinarily feeble con-ception of the National Question. Totally unconcerned about it [they] constituted the most embittered opponents of the Jewish national idea [believing] the Jews weren't a nation".[83]

A modern author confirms Bund "disinterest in national questions"[84] while simultaneously noting a "crystallisation of a national program within the Bund between 1899 and 1901".[85] Such paradoxes were everywhere. For example, the Sixth Bund Congress distanced itself from the movement for Polish independence from tsarist Russia because this would "only divert the proletariat…obscure its class consciousness, and shatter the strength of the revolution".[86] Thirty years later the party "continued to oppose vehemently any manifestation of Jewish national separatism…however, the national issue became the main item on the Bund agenda".[87] These contradictions were not evidence of slapdash intellects. They arose from the unusual environment the Bund inhabited.

It prided itself on its *doykeit*—"hereness". Local particularism was encapsulated in its title of "Jewish Labour Bund of Lithuania, Poland and Russia". Instead of Zionist fantasies of reunification in the faraway vacant land of Palestine, the Bund grappled with the immediate reality of Jewish workers' lives in situ.

The Bund was founded in 1897 in Vilna, then under tsarist rule. The city had a complicated ethnography. Despite several communities living cheek by jowl, it was no melting pot. One commentator said they were "partitioned by an impenetrable wall, each nationality lived a separate life and had absolutely no contact with the other".[88] Eight different languages were spoken. Polish stood at 31 percent, Russian 20 percent while Belarusian and Lithuanian were among the others. But Yiddish was easily highest at 40 percent.[89] These proportions were reversed outside the city precincts. Yiddish speakers in the Empire were just 4 percent whereas Russian constituted 44 percent, Ukrainian 18 and so on. Even in the Pale of Settlement, to which 96 percent of Russia's Jews were confined, they were just 12 percent of the population.[90] The Bund was a popular organisation[91] but could only appeal to the minority of the minority—Jewish workers. The simultaneous push and pull of high concentration together with minority status, of co-location and separateness, was tremendous.

The pioneering Vilna group that established the Bund considered itself Marxist and was shaped by left politics at the moment of its inception. There was not even a theoretical awareness of the difference between reform and revolution, something which only emerged when Luxemburg and Bernstein debated the issue in 1900. Sitting dead centre, it saw no tension between efforts for gradual progressive change (the minimum programme) or the goal of overthrowing capitalism (the maximum programme). A mixed reformist/revolutionary content was also reflected in the Bund's activities. It did not demarcate between organising all Jewish workers to meet daily needs on the economic front, and the party-political task of toppling tsarism to achieve equality.

If this was its centrist socialist starting point, nationalist complications did not lag far behind. The founders "did not even dream of a special Jewish mass movement"[92] but very soon were "forced into all-night arguments on the question of whether the Jewish worker in fact needed a special central organisation".[93] One reason was that when the socialist intelligentsia arrived to organise Jewish workers, they discovered they could not talk to them. The radicalised daughters and sons of the middle class "had ceased to speak Yiddish long ago whereas Jewish workers hardly spoke any Russian".[94] So how were they to communicate literally and in policy terms? As one organiser explained, the solution was to incorporate "a completely new element…a kind of 'intermediate layer' [who could] speak Yiddish to the Jewish worker and unlike us, these new comrades had a national attitude".[95]

A case study of Łódź, "the Polish Manchester" and the second strongest centre of Bundism (after Warsaw), confirms the picture painted so far. The town had undergone stormy industrialisation, growing from just 33,000 inhabitants in 1865 to 314,000 30 years later[96] and had a proportion of Jews similar to Vilna.[97] Bundism was brought to Łódź by pioneers such as Central Committee member Abram Mutnikovich, who had a middle-class background, advanced education and was entrenched in Russian culture.[98] The "intermediate layer" consisted of two teachers, a midwife, a weaver and a shoemaker. The membership comprised weavers, painters, bookbinders, tailors, stocking-makers, bakers and carpenters. Their average age was 18 to 20.[99] The Bund therefore embodied,

> a fully shared, deeply felt and incessantly practiced ethos (more characteristic of youth movements and sects than of political parties) at the very heart of which stood the valiant and unceasing effort to get under the skin of the Jewish proletarian masses in the Pale of Settlement, the pariahs of the pariahs about whom no one else bothered or cared.[100]

Responding directly to both oppression and exploitation gave the Bund real cohesion. It was an impressive movement that was better organised than the Russian working class in general.[101] But this very strength risked a focus on what distinguished Jewish workers from others, leading to what today would be called "identity politics".

Yet with good reason the Bund feared nationalist independence movements in the Pale, home to many ethnic groups. If, as would happen after the First World War, this multicultural setup was replaced by a string of nationalist-minded states, the Jewish minority in each would suffer.[102]

The Bund also rejected Zionism's brand of Jewish independence. At the 1901 Congress it was argued:

> The final goal of political Zionism—the creation of a territory for the Jewish people—insofar as it could only accommodate *a small segment*... is a matter of little significance and cannot solve the "Jewish question"... It is a utopia incapable of realisation.

Four decades later Ehrlich, the Bund leader, was still making the same argument:

> The area of Palestine is approximately equal to that of the province of Warsaw... There are 300,000 Jews and approximately the same number of Arabs. The immigration of millions more to the Jewish state is not possible... Is this acceptable to the Arabs?[103]

A Jewish state in Palestine would "be yet another class-ridden society in which Jewish workers would have to fight their Jewish bosses".[104] Finally, to Bund ears calls for Jews to flee sounded like desertion. As Frankel puts it, "The battle was taking place day by day in the Pale of Settlement, in every town and *shtetl* [small Jewish town], here and now".[105] Jewish emigration was one response to antisemitism, but the Bund represented those who chose to stay and resist.

The paradox was that despite strongly objecting to nationalism, the milieu in which the Bund operated was predominantly Jewish. To square the circle the Bundist, John Mill, originated the idea of national cultural autonomy in a federated state. Otto Bauer and Karl Renner, who led Austrian Social Democracy, became its best-known exponents in the wider movement. They argued that "socialism would fully realise the national principle, where all members of society, not just its rulers, could feel part of a nation".[106] Demanding cultural autonomy neither challenged capitalism' nor the continuation of structures of existing empires such as Austria and Russia. Marxist academic Rick Kuhn notes that the federal structure of the Austrian party represented "a capitulation to nationalism within the workers' movement".[107]

Despite giving it a socialist tinge, in practice the Bund had espoused a left-wing version of bourgeois diaspora nationalism. Ahad Ha'am, an early advocate of this idea, wrote that Eastern European Jewry "needs not an independent state but only the creation in its native land of conditions favourable to its development". That would produce "a great national culture, the fruit of the unhampered activity of a people living according to its own spirit".[108] Dubnov was another adherent. Diaspora nationalism substituted cultural autonomy at home for a Zionist government in Palestine. The Bund took up the concept at its congress in 1901:

> Russia, which is made up of many different nations, will in the future be transformed into a federation of nationalities, and...each will have full autonomy independent of the territory in which it resides.[109]

The Bund was committed to the class struggle and fighting oppression. It also argued Jews should take a stand where they lived. As an exploited minority, Bundist workers viewed non-Jewish workers as allies, and collaborating with them was not only possible but essential. The Bund refuted the notion non-Jews were inherently antisemitic and to be feared. Yet tendencies towards ethnic separatism were also powerfully felt.

Ultimately, the Labour Bund's policy of simultaneously opposing, diluting, and accepting nationalism was inconsistent, yet it accurately reflected radicals torn between separatism and solidarity. It had, however, posed the crucial question about how struggles against oppression and against exploitation should interrelate.

Lenin and the Marxist tradition: the benefits of debating with the Bund

Since the publication of the *Communist Manifesto* in 1848 the motto of Marxists was "Workers of the World Unite! You have nothing to lose but your chains".[110] Such internationalism does not discriminate between atheists, Jews, Christians, Muslims or any other faiths, ethnicities or nationalities and stands for the liberation of all. While many individuals and parties have fallen short of the ideal, in some form its logic still informs the left today.

The "Workers" of the slogan represent a universal class with the social and economic potential to create a new society. The call to "unite" means sectoral, national and social divisions must be overcome to make this possible. The "chains" thrown off are those of exploitation and oppression. This described a preliminary strategy for the Jewish question but no more than that.

Anti-capitalist currents which did not rely on working-class internationalism could end up seeing matters in racial/national terms. The French anarchist Pierre-Joseph Proudhon wrote that Jews were a "race that poisons everything [and] must be sent back to Asia or be exterminated... The hatred of the Jew like the hatred of the English should be our first article of political faith".[111] After clashing with Marx in the First International, the Russian anarchist Mikhail Bakunin wrote off Jewish radicalism in these terms:

> There are Catholic, Protestant, pantheistic and atheistic Jews, reactionary, liberal, even democrats and socialists. Above all they are Jews, and this establishes between all the individuals...the sense of race, which links the kings of the Bank, the Rothschilds, or the most scientifically elevated intelligences, with the ignorant and superstitious Jews of Lithuania, Hungary, Rumenia, Africa and Asia.[112]

Conditions at the end of the 19th century were more opportune for developing a mature Marxist position on oppression, including Jewish oppression, than were available to Marx in 1843. The centre of world antisemitism was Russia and within the Pale the Bund led a militant Jewish workers' movement. Even if it found answers elusive, posing immediate questions around exploitation and oppression, solidarity and separatism, nationalism and socialism put these issues on the agenda.

Russian revolutionary socialism, with Lenin at the forefront, was able to use this to move from a formal commitment to fighting oppression to a theory and practice of how to achieve it. It was the most effective response to the Jewish question of any of the left's attempts, and its consequences would be far-reaching.

The Bund's activity is covered in the next chapter. Here we look only at its political relationship with the wider labour movement. It was the first Marxist group in the Empire to create a mass organisation and remained the largest up to 1905. It participated in the establishment of the RSDLP, a body for the entire working class under tsarism. Because its resources and organisational skills outstripped those of its Russian and Polish comrades, it was central to organising and hosting the First Congress at Minsk.

It was also the first organisation in Russia to implement many of the features we see today that are characteristic of the revolutionary party—the agitational paper, the professional revolutionary, and the need for the party to be rooted among workers. In the western part of the Russian Empire the Bund helped the RSDLP to produce and distribute their first publications.

The Bund was the largest body at the first RSDLP Congress and by the second it had 30,000 members compared to 8,400 in the rest of the RSDLP affiliates.[113] Before the 1905 Revolution one third of the prisoners in the Siberian labour camps were Bundists.[114] Its contribution was acknowledged by George Plekhanov, a non-Jew known as "the father of Russian Marxism". He had participated with Lenin and Martov (who was Jewish and played a formative role in the development of the Bund) in the *Iskra* group that led the early RSDLP. Plekhanov described Jewish workers as "the avant garde of the workers' army in Russia".[115]

At the Bund's founding conference, Arkady Kremer set the goal of overthrowing absolutism with the Bund having "the special task of defending the particular interests of Jewish workers, conducting a struggle for their civil rights, and, above all, waging a campaign against anti-Jewish legislation".[116] This formula was adopted at the RSDLP's founding congress. When all groups were "merged into a single organisation", the Bund continued to exist within it as "an autonomous organisation, independent only in questions especially concerning the Jewish proletariat".[117]

The arrangement was short-lived due to inherent tensions. Medem agonised over whether "to direct our greater attention…toward the class feeling of the proletarian or toward the awareness by the Jew of his essential Jewishness".[118] Another issue was whether to emphasise politics or economics. The economists argued for predominant focus on the latter and Medem defended them on the grounds that "they were most closely attuned to the life of the workers and they endeavoured to penetrate into the very souls of the working masses".[119] Impressive as Bundist strike action was, if the aim was only to win economic demands to the exclusion of, or in counterposition to, politics, then there was a problem. To make real progress the immediate fight over pay had to be linked to challenging tsarism, the source of antisemitism. Even on its own terms failure was likely because behind every hostile employer stood a tsarist policeman.

Lenin was critical of this approach:

> [S]triving to restrict political agitation and political struggle or to reduce them to petty activities, [is a] failure to understand that unless Social-Democrats take the leadership of the general democratic movement in *their own* hands, they will never be able to overthrow the autocracy.[120]

Mounting difficulties in the arena of economic struggle would force the Bund to reorient away from economic struggles in later years, but in so doing it would tend towards a reformist direction. Stress would be put on Jewish civil rights and culture, neither of which addressed the overriding question of tsarism. In 1901 the Bund proposed the adoption by the entire RSDLP of John Mill's policy of federated autonomous nationalities, defined not by territory but self-image. In 1901 it declared:

> [C]onsidering the RSDLP to be a united federation of social-democratic parties of all nations living with the Russian state, congress declares that the Bund, as the representative of the Jewish proletariat, enters it as a federative part.[121]

A year later the argument was put in even stronger fashion. The *Di Arbeyter Shtimme* newspaper wrote:

> As with the proletariat of *each* nation, so [the Bund] is also an *independent party* of the universal proletariat...the Jewish proletariat must build a separate revolutionary organisation, an independent revolutionary force.[122]

The issue came to a head in 1903 when the Bund proposed to the full RSDLP Congress that the Party constitution be changed.[123] A move from being "independent *only* in questions especially concerning the Jewish proletariat" to being independent in *all* questions, would create problems. The RSDLP was not a federation. It would fragment if each of the numerous national groups in the population had their own "separate revolutionary organisation". The RSDLP would disappear and centralised struggle against tsarism with it. This would have created serious problems not just for Jewish workers but for all workers. The RSDLP was fighting for a class and a population which suffered in many different ways at the hands of the tsarist regime. There was a common enemy.

The Second Congress of the RSDLP in 1903 is remembered mainly for the Bolshevik/Menshevik split into revolutionary and reformist organisations. But the Bund also broke away, after Lenin strongly resisted its proposals for federation. Medem interpreted his position as a sign of authoritarianism, writing that "the Bund was literally thrust out of the party" because its "demands had been poorly and incorrectly understood, and still worse were more incorrectly interpreted; and an atmosphere was generated marked by burning hostility and passionate polemicising".[124]

This was unfair. Lenin's approach was summed up by a resolution that restated the existing position. The RSDLP:

> can in no respect or manner restrict the independence of our Jewish comrades in conducting propaganda and agitation in one language or another, in publishing literature adapted to the needs of a given local or national movement, or in advancing such slogans for agitation and the direct political struggle that would be an application and development of the general and fundamental principles of the Social-Democratic programme regarding full equality and full freedom of language, national culture, etc, etc.

Lenin acknowledged the value of "the great, world-progressive features of Jewish culture…its internationalism, its responsiveness to the advance movements of the epoch (the percentage of Jews in the democratic and proletarian movements is everywhere higher than the percentage of Jews in the population as a whole)".[125] But for that very reason Jews were a vital part of the wider struggle and should not be cordoned off.

Shortly before the Congress he wrote that a Social Democratic leader's ideal was to be "*the tribune of the people*, who is able to react to every manifestation of tyranny and oppression, no matter where it appears, no matter what stratum or class of the people it affects".[126] Any party, Jewish or otherwise, which focussed on one specific oppression or sectional economic class issues alone, would fall short of the broad front needed to win. Therefore, Lenin rejected federalism because "the fullest and closest unity of the militant proletariat is absolutely essential for the purpose of the earliest achievement of its ultimate aim".

He insisted this approach was in the Jewish interest:

[C]omplete unity between the Jewish and non-Jewish proletariat is moreover especially necessary for a successful struggle against anti-Semitism, this despicable attempt of the government and the exploiting classes to exacerbate racial particularism and national enmity.[127]

Only through solidarity in action could the double-headed hydra of exploitation and oppression be defeated.

At one level the Bund would have agreed, but in practice it privileged autonomy over unity, ignoring the centralised nature of the enemy. The autocracy (literally "the rule of one") was the opposite of federal. The tsar could easily defeat any number of minorities if he fought one section at a time. Creating a barrier between the fight against oppression and exploitation, and between the minority and the majority, lessened the chances of success for everyone.

Lenin was not alone in the RSDLP to call for unity between the working class and the oppressed so as not to play into the hands of the enemy. Plekhanov moved a motion calling on members "to explain to the proletariat the reactionary and class inspiration of antisemitic and all other national-chauvinist incitements".[128] This motion was approved *after* the departure of the Bund from the 1903 Congress.

The 1903 debate has implications for all oppressions. Divide and rule impacts both the exploited and the oppressed, and in combating it each faces strategic challenges.

The group that experiences oppression may be radicalised and seek out united action with others. But, by definition, the deception and the deceiver are not immediately obvious. In this case Jewish workers could also feel singled out and alone, with some non-Jewish workers, who had fallen for the lies, appearing as the problem rather than the solution. If the oppressed focus solely on their own predicament to the exclusion of the conditions of other oppressed groups or the exploited majority, the result is self-defeating. The antidote to divide and rule is united struggle.

For the exploited, too, the deceiver may not be obvious, and some workers will believe the lies that scapegoats are the problem. This must be overcome. Solidarity is not merely an optional extra; unlike all previous classes, the proletariat can only succeed if it unites against its real enemy. The solitary peasant farmer could expand at the expense of another; the feudal lord could increase his dominions by acquiring other landowners' territory through force or marriage. The capitalist system is the quintessential juggernaut driven by blind competition between its separate parts. Yet the very existence of the working class is based on collaborative production involving many people in a vast integrated process. Progress cannot come by pursuing narrow interests but only through common endeavour. The trade union principle "unity is strength" and the picket line are evidence of this.

However, solidarity is not only vital in the economic sphere. To go beyond the limited trade union goal of pay and conditions to challenging the root of exploitation itself requires overcoming divisive ideology and supporting the very people workers have been encouraged to despise, just as an oppressed community depends on the power of the proletarian majority to effect the change it needs.

In "normal times" the prevailing ideas of the ruling class affect the exploited and the oppressed alike, and though each suffers in society, mutual distrust exists. In Russia recruits to the left wing were not inherently immune to antisemitism so it had to be challenged. By the same token the oppressed, Jews in this instance, had to be convinced of the need for solidarity with workers, even when some of these were prejudiced. A constant, organised, political argument for solidarity and against divide and rule was needed inside both camps. Such was the breakthrough hammered out in the debate with the Bund in 1903.

How representative was the radical tradition?

Having surveyed the various political currents, it is legitimate to ask how representative the radical tradition was amongst Jews overall. This is difficult to answer because in contrast to conservative orthodoxy, assimilationism and political Zionism, it was based on activism, which was a risky individual choice. Entire communities are rarely mobilised, and unlike the simple matter of counting ballots, marching, striking, and rebellion are inherently difficult to quantify.

The following description by Shlomo Szlein, a Jewish militant in the interwar years, sets out the complicated cross-currents:

> In [Polish] eastern Galicia where I lived…except for a small stratum of big entrepreneurs or businessmen, the Jews lived in indescribable poverty… The Ukrainians suffered discrimination along with the Jews… Younger Jews, in the late 1920s, had joined the communist movement… on a massive scale. The movement's power of attraction was that it seemed to promise to resolve both the social question and the national question in a short space of time. There was such a high proportion of Jewish youth in the communist movement here that you could almost say it was a Jewish national movement. In any case, the question of any stifling or denial of Jewish identity absolutely didn't arise.[129]

If Jews on the left were not real Jews, there were very many of them![130] But we must also be careful not to slip into thinking that the following comment from the Jewish novelist Grace Paley was true either: "To be Jewish was to be a socialist…that's what it meant to be Jewish".[131]

Perhaps this judgement, drawn from South Africa, captures the essence: "While perhaps one Jew in ten might be a [left] activist, out of ten activists, five or six would be Jewish".[132] Whatever the exact numbers, Jews and their interests were an integral part of the radical tradition and vice versa.

Section 2

Revolutionaries: The Jewish radical tradition in history

Tsars, pogroms and revolutionaries: Tsarist Empire 1880s–1906

The Pale of Settlement

During the Middle Ages, Poland was the most tolerant country in Europe and became a refuge for Jews persecuted in and expelled from other countries. As a result, by the middle of the 16th century, perhaps three quarters of the world's Jews lived there. The Habsburgs, Prussia and the Russian Empire partitioned Poland in the early 18th century, with Russia annexing the eastern part outright; the western part was retained as a distinct entity, known as the Congress Kingdom of Poland.[1]

Tsarist Russia thus ended up with the majority of the Jews in Europe under its jurisdiction. It certainly did not welcome them and until it was surpassed by the Holocaust, Russia was the site of the worst antisemitism.

Alongside religion and customs, language set the community apart from the local populations. Yiddish was the predominant language, although upper-class Jews often regarded Yiddish as debased and not suitable for sophisticated purposes. But, more importantly for our purposes, socialists also often regarded the working-class vernacular as "jargon" and promoted the use of Russian or Polish. In their early educational work, they usually commenced by teaching Jewish participants Russian.

Yiddish remained the primary language among Jews in Europe, the UK and the US until the First World War. It was still widely spoken in the interwar years: prior to the Holocaust, there were over 10 million Yiddish speakers worldwide.[2]

In 1826, Tsar Nicholas I launched a systematic plan to "de-Judaise" Russia. The first move was to restrict nearly 4.9 million Jews to the urban areas of the Pale of Settlement, which, as we have seen, comprised the western region of the Empire, the annexed parts of Poland and most of modern-day Ukraine, Lithuania and Belarus. Although they made up only 12 percent of the population overall, as we saw with Vilna, Jews now developed a large social weight in cities and small towns (*shtetls*); in nine provinces, they were the majority of the urban population.[3]

Nicholas also brought in restrictions on education, civil liberties and occupations, tightening them further in 1835 when almost all Jewish printing presses were closed and books were burnt.

The next tsar, Alexander II, had a reputation for liberalism, with his greatest reform being the abolition of serfdom in 1861. As the rigidities of the feudal economic structure were seen as obstacles in the drive to modernisation, there were even tentative steps towards reforming anti-Jewish measures.[4] However, his easing of restrictions was minor and limited to the upper echelons; and, after the Polish insurrection of 1863, official repression again increased. Most notorious was a pogrom in Odessa in 1871, in which an organised mob, with active or tacit approval from the authorities, rampaged through the Jewish quarter for three days.

Pogroms took on a whole new dimension when Tsar Alexander II was blown up by populists on 1 March 1881. This crisis meant a large-scale diversionary tactic was urgently needed. It took many decades in the West to transition from feudal scapegoating via emancipation to renewed scapegoating to defend modern capitalism. In Russia, both oppressions came to overlap overnight.

Many populists were put on trial over the tsar's death, but one of them was Jewish—Gesia Gelfman.[5] This was enough. The right-wing press went into overdrive announcing that an outraged population was bent on "spontaneous" anti-Jewish riots. Curiously they managed to pinpoint the city of Elisavetgrad (modern Kropyvnytskyi in Ukraine) as the venue along with the likely date. On 15 April a gang of 1,000 gathered: "Simultaneously, bands of about forty people each sprang up in different parts of the city led by strangers... The mob included women of high society... The military and the police...remained passive; some even accepted looted gifts". One historian concludes, "That day is responsible, in a sense, for the entire subsequent wave of pogroms in the Russian Empire. On that day was born the misguided conviction that the tsar's subjects had a duty to beat Jews".[6]

Trotsky explained the tactics of the instigators and psychology of perpetrators:

> That a pogrom is imminent—this all known beforehand…bloodthirsty articles appear… The military band keeps repeating tirelessly: "God save the tsar"—this being the martial hymn of pogroms. If there is no pretext, it is created… The barefoot ragamuffin rules. The trembling slave, who only an hour ago was himself hunted down by the police and by hunger, feels that he is an absolute despot now. He is allowed everything, he is omnipotent.[7]

Recently it has become fashionable to deny pogroms were encouraged by the establishment.[8] Reading Vital's account we end up feeling sorry for the tsar, who was "very sad",[9] while senior levels of government feared "*loss* of social control" in the face of "a permanent condition of social and political instability" driven by "ever higher levels of mindless and triumphant violence".[10]

The violence was not mindless, however. Whether sad or not the tsar's view was, "On the souls of the Jews, too, a sin is burning [of] exploiting the Christian population".[11] His adviser believed one third of Jews should be converted to Christianity, one third made to emigrate and the rest killed.[12] In just three years after 1881 more than 250 places experienced pogroms and antisemitic violence[13] and over 50 villages near Kiev "succumbed to the epidemic" over a two-month period in 1881 alone.[14] Simultaneously a panoply of anti-Jewish laws was also enacted in Alexander III's "Cold Pogrom".[15]

The authorities cynically presented the laws as generously responding to demands from the populace and addressing their needs. The government "must protect the Russian people against the Jews' injurious activities which, according to local reports, were responsible for the disorders".[16] A new law constricted the borders of the Pale further, forcing more than 1 million people to move. The lives of Russian Jewry were squeezed and regulated by some 650 separate statutes running to over 1,000 pages of petty detail.[17] Jews could not stand for the board of an orphan asylum, constitute more than 5 percent of military surgeons, or live or work in the Pale's rural areas. Outside the Pale artisans could not operate machinery[18] and only 2 percent of university places were open to Jews (with 10 percent inside the Pale). Vital lists further infringements on "midwives and lawyers, distillers and tavern-keepers, apothecaries and stockbrokers, domestic servants and political exiles, military conscripts and jurymen, schoolboys...holders of foreign university degrees and merchants".[19]

Thus, at a time of increasing political opposition and frustration among the Russian population, Jews were fashioned into a convenient political scapegoat, and the word "pogrom" came into the English language. This outbreak of violence and repression precipitated the first great wave of emigration; a quarter of a million Jews fled Russia between 1881 and 1882.

"Pariah among pariahs"

The popular image of the Russian Empire at this time is of vast steppes populated by backward and superstitious peasants. But the western border area, where the Jews were located, was a crossroads of exchange and influence. Industrialisation was taking off because the Romanovs needed an industrial sector that could compete economically and militarily with more developed neighbours and bolster its efforts to preserve the traditional policy of "orthodoxy, autocracy and [Russian] nationality".[20] According to one map, over half of all Russia's industrial clusters were located in the Pale, even though the area was just one fifth of European Russia itself.[21] Until the turn of the 20th century the total value of industrial production in Poland alone exceeded the rest of the Empire.[22]

The development of capitalism here led to crucial social transformations. In the early part of the century, most Jews in the region were petty traders and artisans—many in the countryside. But with the spread of the capitalist mode of production, social structure became dominated by urban manual labour, transforming traditional social relationships and customs. No longer was the typical Jew a narrow-minded, conservative country bumpkin like Tevye, the hero of *Fiddler on the Roof*. The new culture which was open to the modern world had arrived.[23]

Concentrated in the urban centres in the Pale of Settlement, the Jewish masses were now at the centre of this developing capitalism, and proletarianisation was very rapid; it was estimated that, by 1897, there were 105,000 Jewish workers, approximately one third of all economically active Jews.[24]

Some were employed in larger enterprises, such as textile factories in Bialystok and Łódź in Poland and match and cigarette factories in Belarus. But most Jews worked in small workshops in the low technology handicraft sector. Nonetheless, this was no longer the older post-medieval world of masters and apprentices; rather, the workshops were embedded in modern capitalist relationships of employers and workers, of capital and wages. In this way, this "wretched complex of workshops and petty industry" became the basis of the Jewish workers' movement. The resultant misery and isolation from the concurrent formation of the Russian-speaking proletariat led to a distinctive radicalism as well as the development of specifically Jewish organisations.[25]

Table 3 shows clearly how Jews were disproportionately represented in industry, while virtually absent from agriculture.

Table 3: Distribution of Jews and total population by occupations in the Pale, 1897 (%)

	Jews	Total population
Agriculture	2.5	53.0
Industry	36.2	14.6
Commerce and transport	34.6	7.4
Personal services	11.9	11.8
Professions, state services, social services	7.2	8.2
Rentiers, indeterminate unproductive occupations	7.6	5.2

Source: Weinstock, Nathan, 1979, p10.

The process of proletarianisation was accompanied by severe immiseration; overcrowding, disease and want were the norms.[26] Particularly characteristic of Jewish economic life were the *luftmenschen*, sorry individuals who existed by very petty trading and peddling, fiddling or charity, with perhaps an occasional paid job.

One could be forgiven for thinking at this stage that the "lachrymose" view of Jewish history was perhaps correct: a downtrodden and despised population, subject to systematic discrimination and violence, desperately poor and subjugated. German social democrat Karl Kautsky explained:

> If the Russian people suffer more than other peoples, if the Russian proletariat is more exploited than any other proletariat, there exists yet another class of workers who are still more oppressed, exploited and ill-treated than all the others; this pariah among pariahs is the Jewish proletariat in Russia.[27]

But capitalism generates its own gravediggers. Despite the overcrowding and squalor, the misery and disease, another process was developing.

The early Jewish labour movement

As Plekhanov said, the Jewish workers may be considered to have been the vanguard of the labour army in Russia.[28] As they proletarianised, they began to organise themselves collectively. The first known Jewish trade union was the Women's Tailors Association in Mogilev (modern Belarus) as early as 1864. By the 1870s and 1880s, textile workers were taking part in significant strikes. These early economic struggles were mostly defensive around such issues as wage cuts, working hours, fines and the like.[29]

Bialystok in north-east Poland was a centre of industry in the late 19th century. "In and around the town stood tall round factory chimneys, belching forth industrial smoke".[30]

It was also a centre of Jewish working-class activism. According to one socialist newspaper:

> In those quiet, still times, when Jewish workers throughout Russia were sound asleep, dreaming of the Messiah and the world to come, we Bialystok workers were already waging economic battles, beating up the industrialists, breaking looms, striking, struggling.[31]

During the Russo-Turkish war of 1877–8, the demand for uniforms for soldiers gave these workers leverage, and they won a wage rise following a "huge aggressive strike" of 15,000 workers—consisting of Jews (1,500), Germans and Poles.[32]

Over the course of 20 years, there were strikes, rapid technological changes and dramatic political developments, as shown in this list of events in Bialystok from a non-political source, the *Bialystoker Memorial Book*:

1876: Jewish wagon drivers' strike against new police regulations.

1882: The first weavers' strike occurs in Bialystok.

1882: A pogrom is threatened in Bialystok. Jewish butchers, wagon and coach drivers repel the attackers.

1890: The first spinning wheel is brought to Bialystok.

1890: Jakow Pat, writer and leader of the Bund, is born in Bialystok.

1895: A wildcat strike by weavers breaks out in Bialystok.

1897: Bialystok contains 41,905 Jews (the general population is 67,000). The financial status of the city is good.

1897: The Bund party is established in Bialystok.

1898: The first strike fund is established by the Bund.[33]

The 1882 strike was probably the first in Russia to demonstrate trade union organisation. It was exceptionally well organised for the period and gained financial support from other Jewish workers and ethnic German weavers.[34]

Łódź in Congress Poland, another industrial centre with a large Jewish population, became the main centre for textile production, with 23,000 workers in 1885. Socialists were active among them as early as 1878. On May Day 1892, a mass demonstration of 20,000 strikers and their supporters battled troops, resulting in 46 deaths.[35]

Borochov calls these early economic struggles the "pre-history" of the Jewish labour movement; generally lacking class consciousness and organisation, workers were still "blindly groping".[36]

"Men, women and children are talking about strikes"

A turning point came in 1887. The Jewish workers' movement began to move beyond spontaneous local activity and to take on a more planned and conscious character. A successful rolling strike by 2,000 Bialystok weavers led by a strike committee resisted the blandishments of the governor of the province and held firm for two months. This required organisation and discipline. In the same year, there were strikes of locksmiths in Minsk (Belarus) and women stocking-makers in Vilna (Lithuania). The following year, Leo Jogiches, later to become known for his leadership of Polish social democracy and then his role in the German socialist movement, led a strike of 30 Vilna printers. These actions often resulted in embryonic trade union structures.[37]

Militancy spread in the 1890s with the eruption of a strike wave. With workdays of 18 hours common, the demand for a 12-hour day exploded across the region as workers' impatience "could not be controlled" and the "pent-up hostilities workers had long been harboring towards their employers" were unleashed. In Vitebsk (Belarus), the movement "rapidly embraced almost all the crafts, strike followed strike". A general tailors' strike in Vilna was "an event of the first order".[38]

Agitation among Bialystok textile workers was almost non-stop. A three-week strike of 10,000 in 1894 saw weavers eject scabs from factories.[39] The following year, 8,500 weavers, both Jews and non-Jews, repeatedly broke factory windows.[40] Such actions "threw a scare into the manufacturers and the master weavers".[41] In 1900, in "a spectacular event", weavers and their wives protested against unemployment in the synagogue on a Saturday.[42]

Beginning among craft workers and artisans, the strike wave began to draw in unskilled workers such as the 800 women in Shereshevsky's cigarette factory in Grodno, who went on strike in 1899, "much to the alarm of local public opinion".[43]

This strike wave had a major impact on socialists. Arkady Kremer, later one of the founders of the Bund, and Martov, later a Menshevik leader, argued in a widely read pamphlet, *On Agitation* (1893), that the main task now was to move away from small circles and to turn attention towards masses of workers. Lenin subsequently embraced these arguments. The Vilna socialists formulated a new programme of agitation, which historian Ezra Mendelsohn considers "the greatest single contribution the Jewish Marxists of Belorussia-Lithuania made to the general Russian social democratic movement".[44]

Of course, Jews weren't the only ones making the turn to agitation. Martov acknowledged that the Jewish socialists were influenced by the example of the Polish labour movement, which began mass agitation among workers in the 1880s.[45]

But, as socialist activist and academic Sai Englert comments:

The consequence of the dual experience of rampant anti-Semitism and rapid proletarianisation of the Jewish masses was a particular openness from Jewish radicals to the arguments about the need to do away with oppression and exploitation.[46]

Consequently, Jewish workers rapidly outpaced Russians in terms of trade union organisation. As late as 1907, only 7 percent of St Petersburg workers were members of trade unions; by 1900, 20 percent of all the Jewish workers in Bialystok and up to 40 percent in other cities were organised.[47]

Brossat and Klingberg note:

Until the revolution of 1905, the lead taken by the Jewish workers' movement over that of its Russian, Polish, Baltic, Ukrainian and Caucasian counterparts was an evident and remarkable feature of the situation in the tsarist empire.[48]

Table 4 shows the growth of militancy among Jewish workers around the turn of the century.

Table 4: Strikes among Jewish workers in Lithuania and Poland 1895–1904

Year	Number of strikes	Approximate number of strikers	Number per strike
1895	83	4,700	57
1896	92	3,300	36
1897	150	23,800	159
1898	179	11,000	61
1899	223	18,000	81
1900	277	16,000	58
1901	453	22,000	49
1902	455	28,000	62
1903	340	41,000	121
1904	166	8,000	48
TOTAL	2,418	176,400	73

Source: Derived from Borochov, Ber, 1916b.

Many strikes involved only a small number of workers, but the sheer number of strikers in the pivotal years of 1897 and 1903 is impressive. This popular Yiddish song gives an idea of the atmosphere:

> *Everywhere you go, on every street*
> *You hear rumblings*
> *Men, women and children*
> *Are talking about strikes*
>
> *Brothers, enough of your drudgery*
> *Enough of borrowing and lending*
> *We're going on strike,*
> *Brothers, let us free ourselves!*[49]

Borochov concluded that this strike movement of Jewish workers in the Pale was more intense than any in the western world in the period.[50] Whether or not this is an exaggeration, the strike wave was certainly massive and deserves to be better known.

The core issue underlying the movement was the establishment of more modern labour relations: overwhelmingly, the small workshops operated under a pre-capitalist model of no fixed hours, irregular payment of wages and a patriarchal relationship between bosses and employees. The movement "was directed squarely against the anarchical, chaotic conditions" and demanded "uniform, well-regulated conditions of work", the most important being a 12-hour day. Thus, although the immediate demands were economic, the relations between workers and bosses were also being challenged.[51]

Socialists became very important in the movement. They helped to set up trade unions, planned actions and tried to teach strategy, for example, calling strikes when they would be most effective during the high season of demand. They also wanted the workers to think beyond the present and form long-term structures. This was difficult because spontaneous actions continually sprang up, and the socialists often had trouble preventing "unauthorised" strikes. This new, raw movement was often unable to see very far and made many mistakes.

Certain sectors, such as tanners and shop assistants, proved particularly successful, but the bristle workers (who processed pig hair into bristles to be used in brushes) were outstanding; theirs was the only organisation of the time to extend beyond local towns. They also took more far-sighted positions, such as the demand for better medical facilities and against child labour and overtime, declaring themselves to be a political organisation "which fights not only individual capitalists but the regime and the present order".[52]

This mass strike wave required funds, the collection of which built further solidarity. Women strikers at a match factory, for example, appealed for aid in the socialist press: "Help us, dear comrades, write to other cities, help us in our struggle". This was surprisingly successful. During the abovementioned strike at Shereshevsky's factory, money came from workers throughout the Pale and from Bundists in Azerbaijan, New York, London, Berlin and Lyon.[53]

How did the activists manage all this illegal activity? How do you sell newspapers, collect union dues and pass on information in a situation of illegality, when all activities have to be clandestine? The main strategy was to gather in specially designated streets called *birzhes*, where activists could walk and talk in the open. If one street became too dangerous, people just moved to another. Despite police spies and frequent raids, *birzhes* were a vital part of the movement. As we will see, this custom of organising in the streets appeared again in the countries of emigration even though there was no longer any illegality.

Class conflict, class solidarity

In small workshops, both the bosses and the workforce were Jewish, and this had been the basis for a particularly insidious form of super-exploitation—it was easy to appeal to the belief in a common interest when everyone attended the same synagogue and lived and worked apart from the non-Jews in separate Jewish quarters of the towns.

In Jewish-owned factories, however, the workforce included both Jews and non-Jews; and in industrial centres, such as Bialystok and Łódź, both groups lived in close proximity. Mendelsohn comments that, in these circumstances, "relations between Jewish and gentile workers often held the key to the success or failure of a given strike".[54]

Jewish bosses were often reluctant to hire Jewish workers:

Jewish workers were often hired last because they were considered to be too quick to organise, strike or revolt. A Jewish factory owner in Vilnius [Vilna] explained: "I prefer to hire Christians. The Jews are good workers, but they are capable of organising revolts against the boss, the regime and the Tsar himself".[55]

Mendelsohn gives many examples of how Jewish employers exploited intercommunal hostilities in conflicts with their employees. In Berdichev (now in Ukraine), "a factory owner made a speech in front of Christian workers…[saying] that the Jews were disloyal to the Christians…and that they should therefore break the strike".[56]

A Jewish factory owner in Bialystok "used all his eloquence to arouse a strong hatred on the part of the Christians for the Jews" to prevent them joining together in a strike, while in Łódź, a boss in a sock-making shop "instigated the Christians against the Jews and fomented quarrels between them".[57]

Non-Jews were particularly sought after as scabs. For example, one factory owner argued, "We must hire people, especially Christians, who will be able to give a good lesson to those strikers rising against their employers".[58]

Sometimes, workers were able to successfully resist the use of non-Jewish scabs. One example occurred in 1901 when a Bialystok cigarette factory owner fired 45 young Jewish women and replaced them with non-Jewish peasants. The union declared a boycott to "wage war against" the boss. After a month of announcements in the synagogues and the destruction of purchased tobacco, the factory owner conceded and rehired the Jewish women.[59]

The socialists did their best to argue against intercommunal hostility, trying to replace the tradition that all Jews were brothers with the new idea of class solidarity. They argued that "among us workers there exists no difference between a Jew and a Christian, we advance hand in hand against our oppressors" and "the wealthy Jews 'have their own God; their money, their capital, is their god', whereas 'our God [of the workers] is unity'".[60]

They distributed leaflets to non-Jewish workers, trying to promote greater militancy in an attempt to raise class consciousness and counter antisemitism, but with very little success.[61] Nonetheless, there were important examples of intercommunal cooperation. During a strike at a match factory in Latvia in 1903, non-Jewish workers from a nearby leather factory held a demonstration, urging the strikers "to stand firm". At the Shereshevsky cigarette factory in 1904, non-Jewish workers refused to act as scabs: "Here Jew and Pole do not exist, we are all workers".[62]

"Swear an oath of life and death"

Jewish socialists formed the first socialist circle in the Russian Empire in Vilna as early as 1874. It was one of the first to produce socialist literature in Yiddish.[63] By the 1890s, Jewish socialist groups of various political tendencies were active in many towns.

Several of these came together at a clandestine meeting in the attic of a Vilna worker's house in September 1897. It was there that 13 people (five intellectuals and eight workers) representing 3,500 members formed the Jewish Labour Bund. Later ideological differences and splits should not divert attention from the importance of the early Russian Bund to the whole revolutionary movement. As a revolutionary organisation under conditions of illegality, the Bund combined engagement with the economic struggles of the Yiddish-speaking working class with the spreading of socialist ideas.

American writer and artist Molly Crabapple gives an account of the experience of her great-grandfather, Sam Rothbort, an apprentice leatherworker and member of the Bund in Volkavisk (south-west Lithuania). The town was overwhelmingly Jewish, with 4,417 Jews and 834 Christians.[64]

> Under the Bundists' influence, the apprentices went on strike. The bosses brought in strikebreakers. Running battles spilled from the streets into the synagogue itself, where Bundists and the employers' goons went after each other with clubs... "I took part in strikes and sabotage," Sam later wrote, "I became a revolutionist." The violence won the apprentices a radical new right: Saturday evenings off work.[65]

This did not mean finishing work early. The workers had the daylight period of Saturday off for the Jewish sabbath but were often required to return in the evening and work through the night. The strike success meant Saturday was now work free.

The 80 members of the Bund in the town held secret gatherings in the forest where, under a red flag, they sang the Bundist anthem "The Oath":

> *Brothers and sisters in toil and struggle,*
> *All who are dispersed far and wide.*
> *Come together, the flag is ready,*
> *Waving in wrath, stained red with blood.*
> *Swear an oath of life and death![66]*

This small group of revolutionists showed enormous bravery and flair in their fight against the ruling class:

They robbed a government alcohol monopoly… During strikes, they slashed phone lines, smashed up factories, beat scabs. They ambushed prison convoys, threw powdered tobacco (like improvised pepper spray) into the faces of the drivers and liberated their arrested comrades. They sawed through the cell bars of their friend…and when the cops came looking for him at a comrade's house he stole out, dressed as an old woman.[67]

The memoirs of American communist Alexander Bittelman are also evocative.[68] As a 13-year-old in Berdichev near Kiev, he was present when a Bund agitator, one Isaak, met with his father and other shoemakers. Bittelman describes the scene: himself sitting on his parents' bed while about 20 people mostly sat on the floor in their two-room dwelling, lit by a single kerosene lamp.

Isaak helped them to form the first union in the town in 1902 and subsequently led their first strike. But they did more than talk about purely economic issues:

He spoke of all the injustice and brutalities of the entire existing social and political systems. He did so in plain words…but very feelingly. About the doings of the Czar's government to the workers, the Jews and all the people.

Bittelman was "intensely interested" in Isaak's talks:

From him I first heard elaborate explanation of the meaning of such words as socialism, revolution, democratic republic…class struggle, exploitation, capitalists and proletariat.

Isaak also talked about their specific situation as Jewish workers:

According to him, the Jewish workers in Czarist Russia were carrying a double burden: the burden of exploited workers which they shared with all other workers in Russia and the burden of an oppressed and discriminated and persecuted nationality. Never before have I seen the special Jewish miseries in the Czar's empire in quite that light.

At the town's first ever May Day parade in 1903, demonstrators converged on the square singing revolutionary songs in Yiddish. The police allowed speeches but hurtled into the crowd of some hundreds when the banner was raised. After a "sharp fight…between the police and the strong-arm comrades of the front several rows", the banner was saved, although police shot the bearer in the arm. "The demonstration was the talk of the town for weeks".[69]

As for Bittelman, so it was for thousands of others influenced by the Bund in that period. They became revolutionaries and conceived an intense loyalty to the Bund.

Living as they did in what Lenin called the "prison house of nations", and alongside many other ethnic groups with national aspirations, it is not surprising that nationalist sentiments arose among the Jews of the Tsarist Empire. As already noted, although they made up only a minority of the population in the regions they inhabited, they lived in their own districts in many cities and towns, where they were often a large plurality or even a majority. Set apart as they were by geography, language, customs and, above all, by discrimination and prejudice, nationalist concepts were bound to arise.

In 1903 the Bund's hostility to Zionism led it to adopt a resolution declaring membership of a Zionist organisation incompatible with membership of the Bund. Workers who retained their Zionist convictions had to leave Bund-affiliated trade unions.[70] This was further reason for the development of several small parties that attempted to combine active participation in local struggles in Russia with some form of support for the establishment of a Jewish state in Palestine, such as the Jewish Social Democratic Party, Poale Zion, in 1906.

Poale Zion was engaged with workers' economic struggles and joined in the self-defence against pogroms. But their nationalism coloured their activity as militants. Take, for example, Yehoshua Rojanski, a tanner who in 1913 led a successful strike in his factory as a member of Poale Zion. Afterwards, he addressed a clandestine meeting of the workers, arguing that it was time to move from the economic to the political struggle:

> Comrades, aren't we all Jews? Why do you follow the Bund…[which] refuses to see the Jews of the whole world as a single people, a nation. We, Poale Zion, defend the idea of the Jewish nation.[71]

Not surprisingly, the contradictory positions of the socialist Zionists led to intense political conflict, resulting in splits and fusions. The period of reaction after 1906 led to their almost complete demise in Russia, and their leaders either emigrated or were imprisoned or exiled. Out of an impressive membership of between 25,000 and 30,000 in 1905, only about 300 were left.[72]

"Down with the Russian ruling class!"

Although the 1905 Revolution was sparked by the Bloody Sunday massacre in faraway St Petersburg, many Jewish organisations and individuals in the Pale were inspired to action. In many respects the greatest heights of activity occurred in regions with Jewish concentrations. In Poland for instance, 93 percent of workers engaged in strikes (almost five times the rate in Moscow), and one third of all strikes in the empire occurred there.[73]

Liberal currents saw the 1905 Revolution as an opportunity for increased civil rights and cultural autonomy, and 12 Jews were elected to the first Duma (parliament) (although they proved ineffective because they didn't want to be "provocative"). Even the mainstream Zionists issued a public statement supporting fundamental political change.[74]

The *yeshivas* (religious seminaries) also became politicised. Many of their students attended only because of the strict limits on places for Jews in universities:

> Sizable numbers of yeshiva students turned to radicalism, staging demonstrations that were sometimes accompanied by violence… At the well-known yeshiva in Telz, student unrest was so intense that in 1905 administrators shut down the institution for several weeks, expelled suspected troublemakers, and then enrolled young men who were considered to be politically reliable.[75]

As the revolutionary wave engulfed Russia, the Bund responded with its entire organisation:

> Bundists fought with exceptional devotion, played the key role in most events of the revolution, and suffered the largest casualties during the clashes with the Russian army and police.[76]

Englert notes that "the Bund put itself at the centre of the revolution and was largely recognised for it". In one town, Łódź, membership grew from 100 to 1,600; across the region, membership exploded—to perhaps as many as 40,000.[77]

A popular song reflects the mood:

> *Brothers and sisters, let us join hands,*
> *Let's break down little Tsar Nikolai's walls!*
> *Hey, hey, down with the police!*
> *Down with the Russian ruling class!*
>
> *Brothers and sisters, let's all get together,*
> *Let's bury little Nikolai with his mother!*
> *Hey, hey, down with the police!*
> *Down with the Russian ruling class!*[78]

A feature of the 1905 Revolution in the Pale was that it was marked by united action: "From the first days of the revolution of 1905–7 in Łódź onwards, Jewish workers, along with their Polish and [ethnic] German counterparts, participated in street fights, demonstrations and rallies… They stood shoulder to shoulder beginning with the first street clashes." The bloodiest incident of the Revolution in Poland was the Łódź Uprising in which Jews placed a major role. Of 151 people killed 52 percent were Jews, over four times their proportion in the Łódź working class.[79]

Across Poland throughout 1905 the Bund worked closely with the nationalist-inclined Polish Socialists, Rosa Luxemburg's anti-nationalist Social Democrats (SDKPiL), and left Zionists. The Revolution was essentially a class movement in which Jews played a prominent role. This is reflected in a mass meeting in Warsaw after the tsar issued his October Manifesto establishing a parliament. The assembly resolved to "continue revolutionary work aimed at the overthrow of the tsarist government, the convocation of a constituent assembly, the achievement of complete equality for the Jews, and the introduction of Polish in schools, courts, and other public institutions".[80]

The 1905 Revolution ultimately failed to topple tsarism and when counter-revolution struck back Bund membership collapsed.[81] And, as the reactionary movement gained strength, so the Jews again became an immediate target. Scapegoating was part and parcel of counter-revolution with its slogan "Save Russia, beat the Jews".[82]

"Everyone prepared for self-defence"

Reading accounts of pogroms, one would think that there was little or no resistance: that Jews submitted themselves to their fate—with wailing and gnashing of teeth perhaps but doing little more than taking refuge in the synagogue. The rabbis only encouraged this attitude, that pogroms were the will of God to which Jews had to submit.

But this is not the case. Even in the early pogroms, there were some efforts at defence. But there was a turn towards organised resistance after the Kishinev (Moldova) violence that began on Easter Sunday 1903. The *New York Times* reported at the time:

> There was a well laid-out plan for the general massacre of Jews... The mob was led by priests, and the general cry, "Kill the Jews", was taken up all over the city... The scenes of horror attending this massacre are beyond description.[83]

The pre-planned and systematic poisoning of minds was typified by this entry from a government-subsidised local paper:

> Our great festival of the Resurrection of Christ draws near... The vile Jews are not content with having shed the blood of our Savior... They aspire to seize our beloved Russia. They issue proclamations inciting the people against the authorities even against our Little Father, the Tsar... Brothers, we need your help: let us massacre the Jews.[84]

Kishinev cost around 49 lives, with 600 wounded or raped. Government officials were complicit in the notorious forgery *The Protocols of the Elders of Zion* around this time.[85]

It was in this climate that the Bund took the lead and argued for armed self-defence to "answer force with force":

> [W]e must come out with arms in hand, organise ourselves and fight to our last drop of blood. Only when we show our strength will we force everyone to respect our honour.[86]

Bundists and socialist Zionists put this into practice later that year. Although only partially successful, they believed that the effort at self-defence "was good for the soul":

> There are no longer the former, downtrodden, timid Jews. A newborn unprecedented type appeared on the scene—a man who defends his dignity.[87]

Under the leadership of the Bund, defence units proliferated rapidly. Commonly, each group had a core membership and a reserve. Members were often manual workers such as stevedores and butchers, because of the need for physical strength. In 1903–4, defence units are known to have existed in one fifth of all pogroms, rising to one third a year later; there may well have been more that were not recorded. By 1906, there were up to 1,000 core members of defence units and perhaps 8-10,000 reserves spread across the empire from Bialystok to Odessa, Kishinev to Minsk.[88]

The units needed more than personnel: they needed weapons. By 1905, "the Bund had amassed an arsenal of…home-made bombs, knouts, clubs, knives and spring whips". But most important were revolvers, because they were small and easy to smuggle in. This was usually done by young women who reportedly would travel to the Browning factory in Liège (Belgium) and bring the weapons back hidden in their clothes.[89]

A wave of pogroms followed a series of defeats in the Russo-Japanese war in 1904, whipped up by the right-wing press, who blamed the Jews. But the Jewish population now responded differently. For example, in Berdichev:

> Under the influence of self-defence the mood of the Jews changed. There was no sign of fear. On the contrary, everyone prepared for self-defence.[90]

Initially, there was some hesitancy, but attitudes changed as the effectiveness of the self-defence was demonstrated. After a looting and pillaging spree in Derechin (modern Belarus), the self-defence group recovered and returned looted goods. One shopkeeper was very thankful, adding that "it doesn't matter that you travelled a little on the Shabbos".[91]

During the 1905 Uprising and in the period of reaction that followed, antisemitic newspapers blamed Jews for fomenting the Revolution. The notorious ultra-right Black Hundreds organisation, noted for its extreme nationalism and incitement to pogroms, was set up at this time.[92] A wave of pogroms and right-wing terror ensued—so severe that it appeared the empire had "descended into complete anarchy". The complicity of the authorities was notorious. In one instance, the mayor in Kerch in Crimea ordered the police to fire at the defenders rather than at the attackers, killing two, one of them a non-Jewish Ukrainian:[93]

> It became a battle against the organisers of the pogroms—the Russian government. The battle against the pogroms stripped the masks from the faces of their organisers.[94]

Self-defence activity intensified further. The Bund formed a coalition with radical socialist groups, leading to a significant increase in the number of non-Jewish defenders. Critically, the Bund did not see the issue as just about Jews. The struggle against antisemitism, they stated, was "also directed against the ruling class and for socialism. Thus the two struggles were one".[95]

Success was variable; but, in some places, the defenders were able to make a significant difference. For example, in the town of Zhitomir (modern Ukraine) in 1905, about 450 Bundists, local students, left Zionists and socialists, armed with guns, daggers, whips and homemade bombs, defeated the pogromists resoundingly. When soldiers fired on a peaceful demonstration in Łódź, the defence units reacted "with a tenacity that aroused the admiration of non-Jews". Pitched battles resulted in the deaths of 560 people (including 341 Jews); one correspondent noted that "legends...describe the Jewish workers as some kind of Samsons".[96]

The place of antisemitic violence in counter-revolutionary activity is clear from the pogrom in Odessa in October 1905, which resulted in extensive damage and saw up to 250 Jews killed. Right-wing forces had been agitating against Jews for weeks, blaming them for confrontations between authorities and anti-government activists, including students and workers:

Jewish youths, students, and workers filled the ranks of the crowds that attended the rallies at the university in September and October, and Jews actively participated in the wave of work stoppages, demonstrations, and street disorders that broke out in mid-October.

On one day of major conflict, Jews constituted 197 of 214 people arrested. On 16 October, the army stepped in to "restore order". Three days later, the pogrom started.[97]

Two self-defence groups, one consisting of students and workers and the other of Bundists and other socialists, were able to mitigate the extent of the damage. Having earlier stockpiled medical supplies, guns, ammunition and bombs, they ran first-aid stations and incarcerated suspected looters and pogromists at the university, who were then interrogated by students and members of the law faculty.[98]

It is not surprising, therefore, that by the end of 1905, many of the segments of the Jewish community who had hesitated initially had been won over. One Jewish lawyer commented, "We are all Bundists now".[99]

Antisemitic violence increased even further in 1906, with even greater government encouragement. The public outrage following a military pogrom in Bialystok in June extended to the liberal Jewish deputies in the Duma, who made "scathing attacks" on the government for failing to stop the bloodshed. The prime minister "conceded officials had made mistakes and assured the deputies that he was determined to root out lawlessness".[100]

Effectively conceding the authorities' complicity in pogroms, the Duma concluded that "the only means to prevent further pogroms are to be found in an immediate judicial investigation and the punishment of all officials, high and subordinate, without regard to their position, who were responsible.[101]

Words were easy. But the Bund-led self-defence group was able to save thousands of lives and a great deal of their property and to completely protect major working-class sections of the city:

At every corner of the poor section of Bialystok, patrols of the Jewish Self-Defence League were stationed with revolvers and grenades, each group under one leader. They guarded the streets and fired warning shots into the air. If a gentile went by carrying loot, these Jewish protectors would frighten him until he threw down the stolen package and fled.[102]

No doubt, this partial success in Bialystok was at least partly due to its already decades-long history of working-class action.

It is no accident that the Bund took the lead in organising self-defence. With the experience gained since its formation, members were able to bring organisational skills and experience. As socialists, they were committed to working together with other non-Jewish socialist organisations, including Russian, Lithuanian and Ukrainian socialists and radicals. In one such solidarity action, Polish and Russian Social Democrats and Bund members in Vileyka (Belarus) held a joint mass parade with banners and wreaths to honour the victims of a pogrom in 1905.[103]

The Bund did draw in other Jewish groups, including the Socialist Zionists, but this was more problematic. Members of Poale Zion viewed themselves as socialists and as activists and on this basis, wanted to be part of the self-defence. But, as Zionists, they saw no future for Jews in Russia. Their contradictory position led to being less than fully committed to defence, as can be seen from a pamphlet of theirs:

> What do we achieve with self-defence?... Self-defence cannot deliver us completely from the evil which causes these pogroms.[104]

This was indisputably true—as far as it went. But the question was precisely what *could* deliver Jews from the evil that caused pogroms? Poale Zion and other Zionists built their strategy on the establishment of a Jewish state in Palestine. They saw the local struggle and their long-term goals as separate. The Bund and other revolutionaries fought to overthrow capitalism and, with it, all forms of oppression. The 1905 pogroms turned out to be the worst yet, precisely because the regime was fighting off a full-scale revolution. In dismay at the scale of death and injury,[105] Dubnov wrote:

> thousands and tens of thousands of workers, peasants...across the length and breadth of Russia, from Odessa to Tomsk, broke Jewish heads, tore out children's eyes, raped women and cut them to pieces... [They] were doing what their fathers and brothers did in years past and will do again given favorable circumstances.[106]

Dubnov criticised the left for not doing enough to defend Jews, and without attribution accused the RSDLP of thinking "the blood of the Jew must serve as lubricating oil upon the wheels of the Russian Revolution".[107] Not only was this unfounded, the revolutionaries were also embattled after risings in over 30 cities during December 1905 were rebuffed. Six hundred were killed in Moscow alone. Thousands were executed.[108] Perhaps 14,000 in all died directly in the crushing of revolt. Under these blows Bund membership fell from its peak of around 30,000 members and was only 609 in 1910.[109] Failure of the Revolution brought disaster on the heads of Jews and non-Jews alike. The fight against antisemitism and the liberation of society as a whole were part of the same struggle.

Looking beyond the lachrymose way of life

In spite of the setbacks, the changes wrought by the Jewish workers' movement were profound. They failed to overthrow antisemitic laws or prevent violence and, after 1906, freedom in action was limited by the reaction, but the experience of class struggle and defence against pogroms offered a new freedom in thought and values. Old, tradition-bound Tevye, from *Fiddler on the Roof*, or at least his sons and daughters, were now exposed to a world and to possibilities that they had never previously experienced.

Among other changes, for many, the new politics and way of living meant abandoning religious practice. Mendelsohn quotes a comment from a workers' gathering in Vilna on Yom Kippur (Day of Atonement), the major Jewish day of fasting:

> We felt joy and pride in our newness: we eat and rejoice, while all Jews fast and cry.[110]

Thousands were now able to look beyond the lachrymose way of life:

> The socialists repudiated what they considered to be the traditional Jewish characteristics of indifference, apathy, and resignation. These… would be replaced by activism and struggle.[111]

The hard-fought strikes and protests, the self-defence units, the secret meetings and risks run were not just about immediate gains. The writer quoted above concludes, "The feeling of pride and exhilaration derived from the struggle was a permanent gain".

For the Bundists, continued survival was through focusing on legal activities. The Bund promoted a flowering of Jewish national culture in the form of Yiddish literature, plays, music, Yiddish-speaking schools, sanatoria and sports associations. With these at the core of its innumerable activities, positive though they were, the hold of reformist politics also became stronger. Jewish accomplishments in the cultural sphere risked becoming a substitute for political activity, a local escapist utopia as Palestine was for the Zionists.

The other solution was emigration. But wherever they went, the emigrants took with them their own particular characteristics and experiences—their Yiddish language and culture, their early experience of trade unionism, their combativeness and militancy, their experience of the fight against antisemitism, their socialist ideas and their organisations.

Russia: 1917 and beyond

Jews, socialists and the First World War

Between 1914 and 1918 Europe was a slaughterhouse for profit and conquest. Fighting between the imperialist blocs of the Entente (including
Russia and Britain) and Central Powers (including Germany and
Austria) killed vast numbers—2 million soldiers each from Germany
and Russia. War was particularly devastating for Jewish civilians
because in Eastern Europe the conflict ran right through their centres
of population, such as Ukraine.[1] By the time the guns fell silent more
than 70 percent of the world Jewish community had experienced a
change of regime.[2]

The Russian war effort was chaotic and poorly led so the government deflected dissatisfaction by intensifying antisemitic measures. The
authorities accused Jews of being German collaborators and banned
the use of written Yiddish and Hebrew.[3] Furthermore:

> it was deemed essential to drive hundreds of thousands of Jews from
> their homes both on the northern and southwestern fronts. This was
> usually done at a moment's notice, in many cases in the depth of winter.
> Even when the roads became hopelessly clogged, impeding military
> transport, the policy was considered too important to cancel... [A]bout
> a million Jews had been made homeless by the end of 1915.

By June that year between 60,000 and 80,000 perished.[4] The death
rate among Jews of Vilna in 1917 was five times that of 1914.[5]

It seems strange then that a community with less reason for allegiance to their home state than most mobilised to fight for one side or
the other at twice the ratio of the overall population.[6] Although barred
from officer rank, there were half a million Jews in the Russian army

fighting 100,000 of their equivalents in the German army.[7] This cannot be completely explained by conscription.

One motive for volunteering may have been to disprove accusations of disloyalty; but two types of nationalism also drove this waste of life. Firstly, assimilationist Jews did their bit to assist their respective imperialisms. Britain's *Jewish Chronicle* declared that "Jews are bound in loyalty to the country of which they are citizens. The Jew in Germany is no more German than the German, and the Jew in England is no less English than the English".[8] Embarrassed by memories of pogroms the *Chronicle* continued, "Place aside...the bitter feeling that this country in this titanic struggle is linked with Russia... Jews will be all they can be to England".[9]

Following the Orthodox dictum of "seeking a *modus vivendi* at all costs", Rabbi David Herzog reciprocated in kind for the Central Powers: "It is the holy duty of every man of culture to fight this barbaric [Russian] people".[10] The Jewish press carried this letter by an Austrian soldier: "It is a very sweet feeling...to be able to go to war against an enemy like Russia. Oh, may we be able to take revenge for the mutilated bodies of Kishinev".[11]

Surely Zionists, seeing all non-Jews in both camps as bound to antisemitism, would stand aside. Quite the contrary. They removed any obstacles to Jew killing Jew on behalf of the various governments. The Zionist Executive transferred its HQ from Berlin to neutral Copenhagen not to escape imperialism but so that Jews could more easily support the warmongers *on both sides*.[12] They were continuing Herzl's quest for "the friendly cooperation of interested Governments" and fawning took precedence over Jewish lives.

The official German Zionist weekly said, "We do know that our interest is exclusively on the side of Germany".[13] In the opposite camp Chaim Weizmann was closeted in with the British government developing plans for the Balfour Declaration. He wrote, "Though I was violently anti-Russian, I was just as violently anti-German and pro-British".[14] Meanwhile Ben Gurion backed the Central Powers. He gave up his Russian passport to apply for Ottoman citizenship, which he dubbed "our country". He hoped to become a Turkish Cabinet minister and lead a militia to defend Jerusalem.[15] If this had happened, he might well have shot at Jabotinsky, who enrolled in the British

Royal Fusiliers to officer the 800-strong 38th Regiment training to invade Palestine.[16]

Sadly, this enthusiasm for internecine strife was matched by most Social Democratic parties. In 1914 they abandoned commitments to oppose war, voted to fight "for their country" or, at best, not to impede the slaughter, and watched worker kill worker. Luxemburg summarised the SPD's betrayal:

[W]hat did we in Germany experience when the great historical test came? The most precipitous fall, the most violent collapse. Nowhere has the organisation of the proletariat been yoked so completely to the service of imperialism [or] the economic and political class struggle of the working class so totally surrendered as in Germany.[17]

Standing true to Marxism was an internationalist strand which rejected imperialist war and strove to end it. In Russia this was represented by the Bolsheviks, and in Germany by the Spartacus League (led by Luxemburg and Karl Liebknecht). Serbia and Bulgaria's Social Democrats, James Connolly's Irish Citizen Army, and John Maclean's small group in Britain (which included the Jewish Ukrainian Peter Petroff) were other sources of resistance. The general approach was outlined by Lenin in 1915:

We cannot tell whether a powerful revolutionary movement will develop immediately after this war, or during it, etc, but at all events, it is only work in this direction that deserves the name of socialist work. The slogan of a civil war is the one that summarises and directs this work, and helps unite and consolidate those who wish to aid the revolutionary struggle of the proletariat against its own government and its own bourgeoisie.[18]

The war pitted the interests of humanity—all humanity—against the imperatives of capitalist competition in its starkest form. Socialism or barbarism was the mantra of Luxemburg's outstanding anti-war *Junius Pamphlet*. Writing from her jail cell in 1915 she said:

Violated, dishonored, wading in blood, dripping filth—there stands bourgeois society. This is it. Not all spic and span and moral, with pretense to culture, philosophy, ethics, order, peace, and the rule of law—but the ravening beast, the witches' sabbath of anarchy, a plague to culture and humanity.[19]

She pointed out the hypocrisy of governments that were outraged now barbarity had come to Europe but had said nothing when they themselves perpetrated identical policies as colonial powers long before:

> This same "civilised world" looked on passively as the same imperialism ordained the cruel destruction of ten thousand Herero tribesmen and filled the sands of the Kalahari with the mad shrieks and death rattles of men dying of thirst;...as forty thousand men on the Putumayo River [Columbia] were tortured to death within ten years by a band of European captains of industry, while the rest of the people were made into cripples... Only today has this "civilised world" become aware that the bite of the imperialist beast brings death, that its very breath is infamy.[20]

However, Luxemburg is slated as antisemitic. Vital claims she refused a request to publicly oppose the persecution of East European Jews in 1916.[21] A prison letter (using identical examples to *The Junius Pamphlet*) to a friend is offered as proof:

> Why do you come to me with your special Jewish sorrows?... I feel just as sorry for the wretched Indian victims in Putumayo, the negroes in Africa... I cannot find a special corner in my heart for the ghetto. I feel at home in the entire world wherever there are clouds and birds and human tears.[22]

This passage lies behind Cesarini's claim her attitude to antisemitism was "notorious".[23] *The Jew in the Modern World*, a documentary collection, titles her letter "No Room in My Heart for Jewish Suffering".[24] Another says it shows she withdrew "solidarity from the other Jews".[25]

These accusations are false in general and in particular. Her Polish organisation, the SDKPiL (Social Democracy of the Kingdom of Poland and Lithuania), was "a multinational party able to unite Polish, German, and Jewish workers under one political-ideological roof through a variety of organisational, cultural, and linguistic vehicles".[26] She battled the antisemitic Polish National Democratic Party, which said "the Jew was the most dangerous enemy of Polish civilisation",[27] categorising it as "a volunteer of the [pogromist] Black Hundreds of Russian absolutism".[28] To her, persecuting "someone because of their beliefs" was "barbarism".[29] Though a critic of national self-determination as a policy, she supported "the *cultural* and *democratic* content of nationalism…in the spirit of solidarity and cooperation of various nationalities",[30] and on these grounds the SDKPiL had close relations with the Bund.[31]

Unlike the assimilationists, Zionists and reformist social democrats, who enthusiastically lined up with the oppressors on either side to continue the mass slaughter, as a member of the Marxist, internationalist left she was in jail for an anti-war stance extending solidarity towards *Jews and everyone else* ("the entire world wherever there are…human tears"). All human life was of equal value, European and non-European, Jew and non-Jew. Rejecting the cynical use of Jews as pawns to justify imperialist war she explicitly echoed *The Junius Pamphlet*'s indictment of governments for racially selecting who was worthy of sympathy.[32] Her prison letter does *not* say "I am less concerned about Jews" but "I am *just as much* concerned". She did *not* write there was "no room in my heart" but that she had no "special corner" privileging one group above others. Is it "notoriously antisemitic" to repudiate a hierarchy of oppressions[33] and believe in the equality of Jews, Africans and indigenous South Americans? Charges against her reveal more about the thinking of her detractors than that of Luxemburg herself.[34]

Losing the chains beyond the Pale

In the midst of the bloodletting, Russia's capital, Petrograd, rose in revolt. On International Women's Day, 23 February 1917, tsarism was toppled by "the most oppressed and downtrodden part of the proletariat—the women textile workers",[35] as Trotsky put it. A Provisional Government was set up on 3 March. The very next day age-old quotas on Jews in education were lifted and on 20 March all anti-Jewish laws were abolished.[36] Confirming Jewish bellwether status, ending the detestable restrictions which underpinned antisemitic ideology, assisted all the oppressed, since the repeal also benefitted Muslims and the nationalities of Russia's "prison-house of nations".

For generations the Russians had been told to choose between Jews and "our little Father, the Tsar", beating and massacring the one to preserve the other. Through their action Petrograd's workers had chosen Jews. This was a city 500 miles away from the Pale, with a factory workforce only 0.3 percent Jewish.[37] These events contradicted Herzl's assertion that the masses were irretrievably antisemitic. In two weeks, the revolutionary solidarity of the militant working class had achieved more for half of Europe's Jews than two decades of separatist agitation. This breakthrough did not come from the efforts of exclusive Jewish organisations, because Jews were a minority. They could play an important role in self-defence but when it came to stopping the engine of antisemitism, progress depended on a revolution spearheaded by working-class women. Solidarity linked all the oppressed and exploited together.

Why had support for racial equality arisen now among people susceptible to antisemitic manipulation in the past? Working women protested over bread, not atrocities in the Pale. Male workers who joined them acted due to intolerable conditions, not the persecution of Jews. Yet connection there was. It lay in the proletariat understanding through struggle who was the real enemy, how it used divide and rule, that unity was required for success, and that the working class had the economic and industrial power to transform society. The ground had been prepared by revolutionaries acting as the "tribune of the oppressed" over years of arduous and dangerous education and organisation.

The February events did not guarantee a final end to antisemitism. Workers can still be prey to divisive ideology even when they fight for their interests. Some Western trade unions, for example, barred membership to Black people, women or the unskilled, because they were seen as competitors despite all being members of the same class. Legal emancipation did not banish antisemitic attitudes and the Black Hundreds had not dissolved. The Provisional Government stood for capitalist class rule and that system would attempt to divide and rule when in peril.

The Provisional Government was not the only institution in play, however. Balancing its power was the Soviet, or "Workers and Soldiers Council", which organised the urban masses and army units. Its delegates were elected in regiments and factories and were directly answerable to their electors rather than in a poll once every few years. This made the Soviet more democratic and reflective of the grass roots than any parliament.[38] Trotsky led the first Soviet in St Petersburg in the 1905 Revolution and while it existed it prevented pogroms: "One deputy after another mounted the rostrum, raising their weapons high above their heads and transmitting their electors' solemn undertaking to suppress the pogrom as soon as it flared up".[39] Now, in 1917 the Soviets wanted to go further than the Provisional Government's abolition of anti-Jewish statutes.[40]

The approach was summed up at their First Congress in June 1917 in a six-point resolution moved by the Bolshevik Yevgeni Preobrazhensky. Its main points can be paraphrased as follows:

1. Noting the long history of Jewish persecution, antisemitism is one of the principal means used by tsarism to stay in power.
2. The regime uses the "dark prejudices of the masses" as a diversionary tactic to scapegoat Jews.
3. Antisemitic agitation masquerading as a radical slogan is a mortal danger to Jews.
4. Therefore, it is in the direct interest of the broad masses of the people and the revolution to demand energetic struggle against all manifestations of anti-Jewish sentiment.
5. The Congress calls on all Soviets to take measures to combat antisemitism.
6. Fraternal greetings of welcome are sent to working-class Jews in the ranks of the revolution.[41]

The resolution, moved by a non-Jew, was not a condescending act of charity. It confronted the organised antisemites but also challenged workers who might be harbouring their views. In moving the motion, Preobrazhensky stressed that antisemitism represented "an enormous threat to the Jewish people and the whole revolutionary movement".[42] Non-Jewish Soviet delegates were therefore much more than mere "allies" lending a hand. Though not subject to antisemitism themselves, inter-communal solidarity was as essential to their cause as it was to the oppressed. The vote was unanimous.

While compressed in time, revolutions are still a process. Once battle against the social system is unleashed, it will be fought out until one side wins. The possessing classes never give up meekly and not overthrowing them completely is fatal to the cause of the exploited, but also to the oppressed. As Louis de Saint-Just said during the French

Revolution, "Those who make revolutions by halves do nothing but dig their own graves". In 1917 not everyone shared this view. The left parties were divided over how far the revolution should go. The Bolsheviks wanted a Soviet state in place of the Provisional Government, but the majority of Soviet delegates, made up of Mensheviks and the Social Revolutionary (SR) peasant party, thought that replacing feudalism with capitalism was all that could be accomplished for now.

Given carte blanche by the Soviet majority, the Provisional Government's Foreign Minister, Paul Miliukov, intended to "carry the world war to a decisive victory".[43] On 7 April the Menshevik/SR-dominated Petrograd Soviet Executive backed a "Liberty Loan" to finance the army, but the fighting went disastrously. As discontent grew and support for Bolshevism rose, the establishment turned back to scapegoating. Miliukov now warned of "Chaos in the army, chaos in foreign policy, chaos in industry and chaos in the nationalist questions".[44] Jews were a target once more.

No antisemitic attacks were recorded in the days following the February revolt, but after 7 April pogroms returned. At least 235 anti-Jewish incidents followed that year[45] and right-wing forces regained momentum.[46] In the face of this resurgence, as McGeever shows convincingly, the Provisional Government was either unable or unwilling to act: "Not so with the soviets. [Their] remarkable display of solidarity shows how deeply engrained the fight against antisemitism was within sections of the organised socialist movement".[47]

In late August General Lavr Kornilov, recently appointed by the Provisional Government as supreme army commander, launched a military coup to destroy what he called the "army of maddened dark people" responsible for revolution. He appealed to "all in whose breast a Russian heart is beating, who believe in God, in the Church".[48] On his banner was written "private property, revival of the monarchy and an iron fist".[49] The leader of the Black Hundreds telegraphed Kornilov to say "I heartily pray God to help you save Russia. I put myself absolutely at your disposal".[50] Kornilov was defeated after the Bolsheviks roused all left forces to resist, but it was clear the only remaining options were further revolution or counter-revolution. Kornilov's action was a warning of what would happen to Jews if the latter succeeded.

By October the Bolshevik policy of "All power to the Soviets" gained a majority in the workers' councils and they moved to take power. The 25 October insurrection was not a self-interested plot by Lenin, but an expression of working-class willpower through the Soviet. The next day a decree on peace pulled Russia out of the war, the peasants were given the land, a "Workers' and Peasants'" Soviet government was established, and the following resolution was passed: "The honour...of the revolution demands that no pogroms take place".[51] Just how much importance was given to the Jewish question was shown by the priority it received in a flood of progressive legislation. It preceded the Decree on the Eight Hour Working Day by three days, workers' control and nationalisation of the banks by 19, decriminalising of homosexuality by 27, and emancipation of women through civil marriage by 53.

How was this achievement received in the Jewish community? Frankel writes that all the Jewish political parties "from the Bund, the Fareynikte and the Poale Zion on the left to the General Zionists and Vinaver's circle on the right...came out bitterly against the revolution".[52] While the opposition of middle and upper-class Jews fearful for their property is understandable, the unanimity of left-leaning Jewish nationalist forces seems harder to fathom. Besides being reformist, just as some workers needed convincing that they must be on the side of Jews, many Jews needed convincing that their interests lay with the workers. Oppression is no more guaranteed to educate victims about the causes of their woes than exploitation automatically turns workers into revolutionaries. The potential exists in both cases, but for pre-existing politics to surrender its grip, the experience of struggle and political argument are needed. This was not long in coming.

Such was the impact of the 1917 Revolution that belief in radical change expanded rapidly. Bolshevism proved a powerful pole of attraction because, as Salo Baron put it, "The victorious communist revolution in Russia, finally, for the first time in history outlawed all antisemitic activities, counting them among counter-revolutionary crimes".[53]

This conclusion was, and remains, highly contested. McGeever's book *Antisemitism and the Russian Revolution* is very informative but is also littered with dubious formulations such as "fear that revolution—and, in particular, a Bolshevik revolution—would exacerbate the threat of the pogroms was something that was felt across the socialist left".[54] If this is suggesting counter-revolutionaries would scapegoat Jews to defeat Bolshevik revolution, that is true but unsurprising. But if the insinuation is the Bolsheviks planned pogroms, that is false.

The same ambiguity applies to other phrases: "The Russian Revolution, a moment of emancipation and liberation, was for many Jews accompanied by racialised violence on an unprecedented scale".[55] The reason Jews encountered racialised violence was that counter-revolutionaries opposed emancipation and liberation, not that emancipation meant racialised violence. Then we are encouraged to think a Bolshevik statement against antisemitism is actually an admission of antisemitism:

> [T]he Bolshevik Vladimir Bonch-Bruevich also issued an appeal against antisemitism. Though he laid the blame squarely with the Black Hundreds, and not the Bolsheviks or their working-class supporters, the timing of his intervention reflected a widely held anxiety about the relationship between revolution and antisemitism.[56]

McGeever's "antisemitism of the left" argument portrays Bolsheviks as prey to antisemitism and needing correction by Bundist and Socialist Zionist interlopers in the Moscow Jewish Commissariat of the People's Commissariat of Nationalities (Evkom).[57] McGeever sees the latter as entrists with their own agenda rather than genuine converts. This makes little sense. Their involvement is better seen as a reversion to the position the Bund held before its 1903 breakaway.

To make his argument McGeever cites a decree issued on 27 July 1918 to which Lenin appended a sentence instructing "all Soviet institutions to take uncompromising measures to tear the antisemitic movement out by the roots. Pogromists and pogrom-agitators are to be placed outside the law".[58] McGeever says this line was added due to "demands tabled by Moscow Evkom activists back in April".[59] Why assume Lenin's call for merciless "struggle against anti-Semitism, this despicable attempt of the government and the exploiting classes", made not three months but *15 years before*, counted for nothing?[60]

Vital dispenses with subtlety. He writes the Bolsheviks practised what the tsars "would have understood and probably approved". Bolshevik measures "had marked affinities with what in Nazi Germany would be termed *Gleichschaltung*, the principal difference being that the Bolshevik version of *Gleichschaltung* was pushed through with greater efficacy".[61] *Gleichschaltung* ("coordination") meant absolute Nazification of society. Hitler would not have agreed with Vital. He declared war on Bolshevik commissars for being "the bearers of ideology directly opposed to National Socialism".[62] How does it benefit anyone, and Jews in particular, to suggest the regime behind Auschwitz was somehow better for Jews than the one which outlawed antisemitism?

Vital claims there is statistical proof the Bolsheviks were an unpopular rabble. He writes that in the November 1917 Constituency Assembly elections "half a million votes went to the Jewish parties: a little under 2.5 percent of all votes cast"[63] and has a table showing that "in some provinces the vote for Jewish parties was greater in absolute terms than *total* popular support for the Bolsheviks".[64]

Half a million Jewish votes came to 1.25 percent. If that is "a little under 2.5 percent" rather than half, so be it; the figure is well below the 4 percent of Jews in the population. And, of course, in some provinces the Bolsheviks did not do well. These were the ones he selects in Ukraine and Belarus where, owing to the history of Great Russian chauvinism, nationalist parties inevitably scooped up most votes. The Bolsheviks drew their votes from the urban proletariat in Russia itself.

Constituent Assembly data taken in the round yields the opposite conclusion to Vital's. Out of the 164 million in the Empire only around 2.6 million people (12 million if families are included) were proletarians, the rest being mostly peasants who voted Socialist Revolutionary. Moreover, 55 percent of the Empire's electorate was non-Russian. Given these obstacles Bolshevism did remarkably well. Its regular voting base should have yielded a maximum 6 percent (and that shared with the Mensheviks). Yet Bolshevism registered 24 percent, while Jewish parties gained less than one third of their natural constituency.[65]

Frankel gets closest to the truth in this fair summary:

The crucial issues were being decided…in the capital cities, in the central industrial areas and in the army. True at the hub of events a high percentage of the professional revolutionaries, socialists of various denominations, were of Jewish origin. Some represented Jewish parties; most did not. Some were Bolshevik; most anti-Bolshevik… The failure of the political center to hold, the rapid polarisation of forces pulled to the extremes of left and right…undermined faith in the Western system of parliamentary government. The greater the successes of the Communist movement were, the greater the anti-Communist hostility to the Jews became. And the higher the fires of antisemitism raged, the more the Jews on the left came to identify with Soviet Russia.[66]

The evolution of the Bund was revealing. Its eighth conference in December 1917 roundly condemned the October Revolution as "insanity" and "adventurism".[67] Yet by 1921, after a split, most of the Bund in Soviet Russia backed the Communist Party.[68] Among them was Moishe Rafes, who had been in the Petrograd Soviet and led its commission against antisemitism.[69] Another was Esther Frumkin, member of the Bund Central Committee and Minsk Soviet. Of her it has been written, "No woman was more admired or more hated by Jews under the first phase of Soviet rule; no woman in Eastern Europe achieved such stature in Jewish politics".[70] A separate Bund formed in newly independent Poland. Here, in true centrist fashion the majority stuck to a position of criticism but wavered about whether or not to join the Communist International.

Many left Zionists also joined the Communists. Examples include Zvi Fridland, who was a central committee member of Poale Zion. During the October Revolution he was a Red Guard before becoming a Bolshevik.[71] In Palestine Ben-Gurion described Bolshevik Russia as a "sacred revolt against the falsehood, dishonesty, deception and wickedness of the old, crumbling social order; against the dominion of greed that is decaying under the weight of its own sinful, evil violence".[72] He wanted Poale Zion to join the Communist International because "every socialist belongs to it".[73] A rival left Palestinian Zionist, Berl Katznelson, wrote, "There is no political movement anywhere to which masses of mankind, in their millions, looked with such messianic yearning as they did to the Russian Revolution".[74] Although these statements from left Zionist leaders may have been primarily intended to retain the allegiance of their followers, clearly the Revolution had traction. Ultimately, the Communist International leadership rejected applications from both the Polish Bund and left Zionists. This was not because of antisemitism but due to its disagreement with Jewish nationalism.

Jews had very different responses to the greatest single blow against antisemitism. These showed they were not an undifferentiated people isolated from society in general. The intersection of class and oppression encouraged a radical Jewish tradition, but that does not mean there was a unified response on key questions.

Counter-revolution, Stalin and the Jews

Despite the success of the October insurrection the Bolsheviks knew achievements for women, LGBT people, workers, peasants, oppressed nationalities, and Jews could not be secured without outside assistance. This was the crux of Trotsky's theory of permanent revolution. Workers collectively have enormous influence but they were a small minority of the Russian population. Due to economic backwardness peasants were numerically preponderant—which the devastation of war increased. This plus counter-revolutionary Civil War and foreign intervention meant the socialist cause totally depended on external backing. Nikolai Bukharin, the editor of the Party newspaper *Pravda*, wrote, "The final victory of the Russian Revolution is unthinkable without the victory of the international revolution" and "impossible without proletarian revolution in Europe". [75] For the same reason, final victory over antisemitism was unthinkable without the victory of the international revolution.

Hopes of success were not without foundation. Social upheavals were galvanised on a world scale, ranging from the German Revolution of 1918–1923, the Italian *biennio rosso* (two red years) 1919–20, the toppling of the Emperor in Austria, and a short-lived Hungarian revolutionary government, to Red Clydeside and the formation of soviets in Limerick (Ireland), Surabaya (Indonesia) and Seattle (US). Above all a world movement of mass revolutionary Communist parties was established. [76]

Yet capitalism fought back and the spread of revolution was thwarted, with disastrous consequences. For example, while Russian soldiers immediately stopped fighting, the Germans did not. In March 1918 the Soviet government had no choice but to sign the crippling Treaty of Brest-Litovsk, under which Russia lost 34 percent of its population, 89 percent of its coalfields, and 26 percent of its railways. In that same year countries ranging from Britain, US, France, Japan, Czechoslovakia,

Italy and Romania invaded to obliterate all the Revolution stood for. They also assisted the antisemitic White Army in their bitter civil war. That put Jews in mortal danger.

To defend the gains from that onslaught the Bolsheviks were forced to maintain 5.5 million soldiers along a 16,000-mile front. The government survived but at a tremendous material and human cost. There was a 180-fold decline in imports and a 2,000-fold fall in exports. Pig iron production fell to 1.5 percent of the 1913 level. The population of Petrograd, birthplace of Jewish emancipation, dropped from 2.4 million to 720,000. The counter-revolutionary offensive brought epidemics in its wake. Dysentery, typhus, typhoid and cholera took 3 million lives. Famine killed an additional 5 million.[7] One million Russians died fighting the counter-revolution against Bolshevism, but a disproportionate burden was borne by the working class, the core of the Revolution. One hundred and eighty thousand were killed and the class shrank by well over half.

The political cost was devastating too. The only way to repel the enemy was through marshalling all available resources via draconian top-down measures and a command economy. This entailed the complete destruction of workers' power from below, making Soviet democracy a hollow phrase. Opposition parties and factions within the Communist Party were banned and non-Bolshevik Jewish organisations were not exempt.[8] Pro-Zionist historians select only the latter aspect and portray the Bolshevik leadership's actions as antisemitic, but this was a tragedy for the Bolsheviks. Leaders such as Lenin and Trotsky continued to hold the banner of revolution aloft to aid the worldwide Communist movement and keep hopes alive, but beneath them the Russian foundations were dissolving away.

Given these costs, it is argued that it would have been better for Jews if the Bolsheviks had not challenged capitalism and its antisemitism in the first place. But what would have been the situation—for Jews and everyone else—if the working class had refrained from taking power in October 1917, permitting the likes of Kornilov to take over instead? Aside from the progressive reforms enacted inside Russia itself, the 1917 Revolution hastened the end of two other authoritarian imperial regimes—Austria and Germany—and a world war that had taken 20 million lives, and brought a flu pandemic that killed 50 million others. How many more victims of capitalism would there have been without October 1917?

Above all, the Bolsheviks' action came close to ending the racist system. Had they succeeded, the Holocaust and the Second World War would not have occurred. Luxemburg had criticisms but she was in no doubt that:

> Whatever a party could offer of courage, revolutionary far-sightedness and consistency in an historic hour, Lenin, Trotsky and all the other comrades have given in good measure. All the revolutionary honor and capacity which western Social-Democracy lacked was represented by the Bolsheviks. Their October uprising was not only the actual salvation of the Russian Revolution; it was also the salvation of the honor of international socialism.[79]

The most bitter fighting of the Civil War was in Ukraine. At the time of Kornilov's assault in 1917 the following statement appeared: "A short time ago the sun shone and the Russian Tsar used to visit Kiev. Now you find Jews everywhere! Let us throw off that yoke, we can no longer bear it!… Down with the Jews!"[80] Ukraine was home to two thirds of Soviet Jews (after post-war readjustment of borders) and what happened here presaged in miniature the fate of Jews had the Bolsheviks held back and allowed counter-revolution to prevail. The counter-revolutionary Whites were led by a series of tsarist generals, from General Kolchak to Wrangel and Denikin. Under Denikin 8,000 Jews were massacred in the summer of 1919 alone. Ukrainian nationalists joined in. One contemporary reported that the Ukrainian nationalist Simeon Petliura's entire edifice "rested upon their sufferance of the destruction of the Jewish people".[81] One historian writes of the Whites:

> In the thousands of reports and documents in the Volunteer archives, one cannot find a single denunciation of pogroms. The agents sending reports to their headquarters simply assumed that Jews were responsible for all miseries…anti-semitism was neither a peripheral nor accidental aspect of White ideology; it was a focal point of their world view.[82]

By the time the Bolsheviks finally defeated the Whites and stopped their killing, the loss of Jewish lives in Ukraine exceeded 50,000. Add others who died from wounds or indirect causes and about 10 percent of the community had perished.[83] Overall during their brief tenure the Whites were responsible for 200,000 Jewish dead, 700,000 maimed and 300,000 orphans.[84]

There is no space here to discuss Ukraine in great detail, but McGeever's book provides essential information. A horrific pogrom at Hlukhiv, perpetrated by the Red Army, gives a general picture of the Civil War. Between 7 and 10 March 1918 at least 100 Jews were killed. That such an outrage should have happened at all seems to contradict the account given of Bolshevism thus far.

However, this pogrom was not evidence of Communist Party decision-making. It was conducted by military units that had been hastily cobbled together and "rarely submitted themselves to centralised Bolshevik authority".[85] The killers at Hlukhiv were local peasants lacking the working-class tradition of solidarity. According to McGeever, when the Supreme Soviet Commander in Ukraine found out about Hlukhiv he dissolved the "autonomous Red units" and issued an order to execute anyone who ignored his instructions.[86]

Presenting context for Hlukhiv is certainly not to excuse the inexcusable; it is to understand the appalling situation created by counter-revolution. McGeever calculates 8.6 percent of pogroms in Ukraine were perpetrated by forces associated with the Reds,[87] while Gitelman ascribes 2.3 percent of those killed to them.[88] The fact that any atrocities occurred was tragic. Nonetheless, against enormous odds, in an isolated, backward and poverty-stricken Russia, the Bolsheviks defeated the antisemites militarily. Gitelman writes that Jews "came to regard the Red Army as their protector, and young Jews joined it in order to avenge the crimes against their families and people". A Zionist eye-witness in Ukraine wrote:

> In the Klinovka station I was surprised to see a Red Army company composed entirely of Jews and even including some wearing earlocks. These were yeshiva students from Proskurov who joined the Red Army after Petliura's riots in order to take revenge…and I, the Zionist opponent of Communism [which] I saw…as a fatal danger to Judaism—I was filled with pride seeing those Jewish fellows.[89]

As a result of Bolshevik efforts, the sort of genocidal antisemitism the Whites stood for was banished from the region until the Nazis arrived during the Second World War.[90] With some justice Trotsky would write that were it not for the taking and defending of workers' power, "the world would have had a Russian name for Fascism five years before the March on Rome".[91]

In the end the proletariat from which socialism drew its strength was atomised and decimated. By contrast, the state bureaucracy mushroomed in order to direct the military effort. In 1921 it numbered 5,880,000 people—five times the industrial proletariat.[92] By 1923 only 10 percent of Party members were rank-and-file workers and only 2 percent had joined before 1917.[93] State officialdom developed its own class logic, which found expression in the Party's general secretary, Stalin. After hope of assistance from a German revolution ended and Lenin's death in 1924, a faction fight erupted over party democracy and internationalism *versus* "socialism in one country". This eventually pitted Trotsky, Kamenev and Zinoviev (who, incidentally, were Jews) against Stalin's bureaucratic state machine.

As the radical internationalist left was driven back, so was the fight against antisemitism. The latter had been an important feature of Party life and as late as 1927 Stalin told the Party Congress, "This evil has to be combated with utmost ruthlessness".[94] His counter-revolution began the following year in a drive to compete with foreign imperialist powers on their own terms. Hectic industrialisation was pursued. Under Stalin's Five-Year Plans forced collectivisation led to some 10 million peasants dying, along with the super-exploitation of the population and enormous repression. Jews were scapegoated almost immediately, and the evil seeds of divide and rule originally planted by tsarism sprouted once more. A survey of Moscow trade unionists in 1929 found "Anti-Semitic feeling among workers is spreading chiefly in the backward section of the working class that has close ties with the peasantry, and among women... Talk of Jewish domination is particularly widespread".[95]

The USSR was now capitalist, though ownership was in the state's hands rather than private. Nonetheless the government retained the language of 1917 to claim legitimacy. But what was now "combated with utmost ruthlessness" was the egalitarian tradition of the Revolution and its adherents. In a process ably satirised by Orwell's *Animal Farm*, Soviet power, a byword for direct workers' democracy, became a vicious dictatorship over workers. Khrushchev's "secret speech" of 1956 revealed that "of the 139 members and candidates of the party's Central Committee 70 percent were arrested and shot". Most were "old Bolsheviks", people who had joined the Party in the crucial revolutionary period and were often working class in origin.[96]

The repressive apparatus that led to the Moscow Show Trials and the murder of Trotsky by a Stalinist assassin affected non-Communist Jewish organisations too.[97] Little matter that repression was conducted by Jews such as Genrikh Yagoda, director of the NKVD secret police. Ethnicity does not trump the imperatives of class. In 1930 the Jewish Commissariat was dissolved.[98] Internal passports which "effectively re-invented racial categories"[99] were reintroduced. Many Jews suffered repression[100] when Stalin signed a non-aggression pact with Hitler in 1939, which included the carving up of Poland between them.

Treacherous as ever, the Nazis breached the agreement and attacked. Jewish lives preserved by Bolshevik victory during the Civil War were again in jeopardy after Stalin bungled the initial Russian response to Nazi invasion. It required astonishing efforts by the Russian people, who suffered enormous casualties, to prevent a German victory.[101] Thanks to this heroic people's war, around three of Europe's 9.5 million pre-war Jewish population escaped the Holocaust behind Russian lines. Frankel notes that "it was the Red Army…that remained the only force strong enough to defeat the Wehrmacht, so saving the Jews in Europe—and indirectly in Palestine—from complete annihilation".[102] Though the Russian Revolution had degenerated into state capitalism, a continuing legacy of 1917 beyond the defeat of the Whites were the foreign Communist Parties who, despite their Stalinism, spearheaded anti-Nazi resistance movements across Europe. These were a lasting gain to Jews, something critics choose to ignore.

Stalin's regime did persecute Jews, however. During what he called the "Great Patriotic War" (1941–1945), the government nurtured the Russian Orthodox Church, eulogised earlier tsars, and stoked racism. As ever oppressions were linked. Increasing discrimination against Jews was accompanied by the expulsion of the entire Chechen and Crimean Tatar populations, while hundreds of thousands of other ethnic minority groups were forcibly evicted from their homes.[103]

For propaganda purposes abroad Stalin set up the Jewish Anti-Fascist Committee, which included leading Bundists.[104] But no sooner was Hitler gone than Stalin launched a "struggle against cosmopolitans" (for that read internationalist Jews), which led to the liquidation of the Jewish Anti-Fascist Committee. Its members were killed or sent to labour camps where they joined millions of other victims of repression.[105] Just before his death Stalin began a widespread anti-Jewish purge initiated after a phoney "Doctors' Plot", purportedly instigated by Zionists.[106] Counter-revolution outside and inside (masquerading in Marxist clothes) took a heavy toll.

The radical tradition reached its zenith in 1917 when revolution struck at the very heart of capitalism and its antisemitism, but it was unable to deliver the final blow. With the class system still intact, the muck of the past revived in Russia and elsewhere. With that, so would the threat to all Jews. Stalin's counter-revolution was consolidated by 1932. Hitler became German chancellor the following year.

A Jewish ghetto in London's East End: 1880s–1912

"Clearing house for the Jewish revolutionary labour movement"

About 140,000 (7 percent) of the Jewish emigrants from Eastern Europe in the period prior to the First World War settled in the UK, mostly in the East End of London near the docks where they came off the ships.[1]

There was no legal discrimination in the new home. Although Jews in the UK had received formal emancipation in the mid-19th century and divide and rule tactics were usually directed against the Irish, life was not very different.

Class remained a major divider of the community. The old Anglo-Jewish families—the likes of the Rothschilds and Montagus, whose native language was English and who were part of the ruling class—didn't welcome the influx of poor Jews with their outlandish costumes and customs and foreign language. They were prepared to support charitable works but were fearful of the socialist ideas that many of the newcomers, or "greeners", carried. Socialist Morris Winchevsky said, "They are ashamed of us, not as one is ashamed of poor relations, but as one is shamed by a leper, an outcast".[2]

Most immigrants continued in the occupations they had brought with them—tailors, carpenters, brush-makers or shoemakers—or worked in small sugar, metal and tobacco factories. But the clothing trades were overwhelmingly predominant. In what was a very profit-able process, large City and West End firms contracted work out via middlemen to small sweatshops in the East End.[3]

Living and working conditions for the newcomers were dire:

> In the narrow, crooked streets of Whitechapel, in the smelly and dirty holes and corners of the workshops working twelve to fourteen hours

a day for a paltry starvation wage...here have the Jewish workers of Poland, Russia, Germany, Austria...found their better life?[4]

The sweatshops were poorly ventilated and prone to fires and rodent infestation. Piecework at extremely low rates was the rule, with extremely long hours and fines for minor infringements. Above all, the seasonality of the work meant no job security; many workers were unemployed for a significant part of the year.[5]

But the inflow of refugees brought people with the drive to act upon the problems.

Aron Lieberman, a leading early socialist, started the Hebrew Socialist Union in 1876. At an early meeting, Jewish and non-Jewish speakers addressed a packed hall. Here is one (Jewish) speaker, a tailor:

The underlying class struggle exists also amongst Jews... Therefore Jewish workers must unite among themselves against the other spurious unity—that with the masters![6]

The bosses weren't their only intracommunal enemies. At a subsequent meeting, "masters gathered on one side and synagogue wardens on the other".[7] When Lieberman rose to speak, a *shamus* (a synagogue functionary) jumped on to the stage, shoving Lieberman aside. Then, as we might say today, all hell broke loose:

Everybody started fighting: *cupals* [skullcaps], glasses, hats and sticks flew... [Those near the *shamus*] went for him and beat him up from head to toe. "No", cried the shamus, cowering beneath the blows... "Beat him, brothers!" cried the crowd in unison. During the melee [Lieberman] was rendered black and blue as people beat the hell out of each other. Bodies were pulled out like casualties from the field of battle. Then the police arrived.[8]

The Hebrew Socialist Union collaborated with local socialists and the English-speaking trade unions. They even attempted to agitate among the militant Irish, known for anti-immigrant feelings, and set up an all-Workmen's Society. Although this body only lasted a year, it set the pattern for future solidarity.[9]

In March 1889, conflict with communal authorities recurred around the issue of unemployment. Between two and three thousand Jewish workers joined in a "synagogue parade"—a march to the Great Synagogue (frequented by the Jewish bourgeoisie) on a Saturday (the Jewish sabbath) to demand "work, bread and the eight-hour day".[10] An editorial in the anti-immigrant *Jewish Chronicle* entitled "A Hebrew Hubbub in Whitechapel" commented that "[a] more abject and miserable set of men it would have been impossible to have seen anywhere".[11] Speakers attacked the indifference of rich Jews and called upon workers "not to depend upon the rich classes but to organise in a strong body for the abolition of the capitalist ruling class".[12] The day ended with a police riot where property was destroyed and comrades beaten with batons "until the blood streamed, three were dragged to the station, again beaten and then charged with assaulting police".[13]

Three years later, a deputation representing nine local Jewish unions approached the Chief Rabbi demanding he take a stand against unemployment and sweating. With working days of 18 hours not uncommon, the workers were desperate. The rabbi declined, saying that he himself worked harder than they did. In 1894, a group of unemployed invaded the Jewish Board of Guardians (a charitable organisation). A few days later, 500 barged into the Great Synagogue, where they sat in until dispersed by police truncheons.[14]

The radicals who agitated in the Jewish East End in the late 19th century were a peripatetic lot who lived in a multilingual, internationalist environment. Many had come from Russia, had lived in Paris or Switzerland, were on their way to the US or had already been there. With the constant influx and outflow, London became "the clearing house for the Jewish revolutionary labour movement":[15]

> London had become a training centre for Jewish socialists, the majority of whom went on to the States to assume top leadership in the radical movements which were developing there. [London was also] a base for the accumulation of political experience and literature that could be fed back into Russia.[16]

The words of Bertolt Brecht, written 50 years later, are an apt description of these early Jewish socialists:

> *I came to the cities in a time of unrest*
> *When hunger reigned.*

In a time of rebellion, I came to the people
And I rebelled with them…

For we lived, changing our countries more often than our shoes,
Through a war of classes, despairing
When there was only injustice, no rebellion.[17]

In 1885, a group of radicals took over a house in Berner Street (now Henriques Street) and established a club called the International Workingmen's Educational Association. Led by William Wess, a Lithuanian Jewish anarchist, the club became a centre for radical and trade union activities throughout London. "Invariably, on a Saturday or Sunday, there was a truly international gathering of Russian, Jewish, British, French, Italian, Czech, Polish and other radicals".[18]

Another crucial method of organising was through newspapers. The short lived *Poilisher Yidl* (*Polish Jew*), founded in 1884, was Britain's first socialist paper targeting an immigrant audience. The *Arbeter Fraind* (*Workers' Friend*), established by Winchevsky in 1886, became a crucial contributor to the movement. Addressing its audience of workers, "it reflected their harsh daily lives but also told them that they could become agents of change".[19] The newspaper was a major influence upon the growing socialist and trade union forces in several British and European centres. By 1905, it was printing 5,000 copies weekly and was the most popular Yiddish radical newspaper in London.[20]

The *Arbeter Fraind* and other Yiddish-language newspapers were not parochial; they reported international events and were sold overseas. One newspaper, *Germinal* (not to be confused with the novel by Emile Zola), had an extraordinarily wide readership, ranging from most of the larger cities of the US to Paris, Berlin, Bucharest and Sofia in Europe and to Cairo, Alexandria, Johannesburg, Cape Town and Buenos Aires. Such newspapers enabled Jewish workers in different countries to share ideas and support each other. For example, several local immigrant unions sent funds to Bialystok strikers in 1898. The Yiddish newspapers also reported on the pogroms in Russia, which the mainstream newspapers rarely did. The Bund in London even distributed an information sheet called *Pogromen Blat* (*Pogrom Sheet*) giving news of both attacks and defence actions.[21]

Strike fever—1889

The late 1880s were tempestuous years for the British working class. The old traditional craft unions were uninterested in the increasing masses of unskilled workers in the new industries. The famous match girls' strike in July 1888 (another instance of an oppressed group launching workers' action) set a precedent for the new movement of industrial unionism. One of the leaders of the East End Jewish tailors, Lewis Lyons, participated in this dispute. When he was arrested, pickets demonstrated outside the police station until he was released—an early example of cooperation and solidarity in the East End.[22]

The Great Dock Strike of 1889 galvanised workers throughout the East End as "coal men; match girls; parcels postmen; car men... employees in jam, biscuit, rope, iron, screw, clothing and railway works" became infected with "strike fever".[23] In the first mass immigrant strike, around 6,000 tailors from 120 workshops joined in the fever. This took its own brand of courage, because many of their bosses were also Jewish—sometimes from the same town, sometimes family members. William Wess chaired the strike committee, and there was strong support from the Berner Street group.[24]

Crucial to the success of this strike was the support the strikers built outside their own community. Wess, Lyons and their comrades built on the existing links with William Morris's Socialist League, anarchists and others, and non-Jewish speakers often addressed the mass meetings.[25]

After a month, with the strike fund virtually empty, it seemed that the tailors would be starved back to work. At first glance, the largely Irish Catholic dockers were not very promising as a source of support. Their leader, Ben Tillett, was an important militant who unfortunately had antisemitic tendencies—he had earlier described Jewish immigrants as "the dregs and scum of the continent" who made the slums even more "putrid and congested". Nonetheless, the tailors approached the Docks Strike Committee. In a wonderful gesture, although themselves short of funds, the Committee donated £100, by far the largest single donation the tailors received. Reinvigorated, they were able to stay out until the employers caved in. This marvellous display of working-class and cross-community solidarity from the Irish Catholic dockers meant victory for immigrant Jewish tailors. Lieberman's instinct in 1876 to link up with Irish Catholics was vindicated.[26]

After their victory, the tailors' union declared its hope that the "grand lesson of solidarity from the Dock Labourers' Strike" and the other strikes would "mark a new and splendid epoch in the history of Labour".[27] The Federation of East London Labour Unions, launched two months later, was a fruit of this new comradeship.[28] Nearly 3,000 people listened as non-Jewish union leaders, including Tom Mann and Tillett himself, spoke alongside Jewish militants from many trades. The Chair, cabinetmaker Charles Adams, said: "If ever labour is to rise successfully…it must rise as a whole… This new organisation must be composed of people of all creeds and of all nations"; it must never let employers "exploit one against the other".[29]

The new organisation was not to survive long. But belief that solidarity across trade and community lines was essential for the working class was growing. The basis for action founded upon such solidarity was being built.

Socialists and anarchists: 1890s–1908

There were many links between the immigrant Jewish radicals and home-grown socialists. By the third London May Day march in 1893, Jews had a visible presence, with a contingent of over 800 joining in with socialists and trade unionists of all varieties.

One socialist who consciously engaged with Jewish immigrants was Eleanor Marx. In November 1890, she spoke at a mass rally to condemn persecution of Jews in Russia. This event had been forced to move to an outdoor venue when the Chief Rabbi and Jewish MP Samuel Montagu pressured the owner into cancelling the booking of a hall. Marx responded to the invitation to speak: "I shall be very glad to speak at the meeting of November; the more glad, that my father was a Jew".[30]

Other speakers included Cunninghame Graham and William Morris from the Social Democratic Federation, Russian revolutionaries Felix Volkhovsky and Sergius Stepniak, and local Jewish leaders.

Marx became involved with East End Jewish women workers, even learning Yiddish in order to be able to communicate better. Addressing a meeting of the United Ladies Tailors' Association in 1891, she appealed for unity between English and Jewish workers, emphasising their common enemy, capitalism. At another gathering, she spoke in German, while Stepniak spoke in Russian, Abraham Cahan (a well-known Bundist visiting from New York) in Yiddish, and others in English. Despite "the babel of tongues", there was complete harmony because "the spirit of Socialism, which heals all divisions of nationalities, animated every man and woman present".[31]

Marx worked closely with Morris Winchevsky, and both were among the 65 British delegates at the International Congress in Zurich in 1893. At a large parade through Zurich on the first day, she invited Winchevsky to march beside her next to Will Thorne and Edward Aveling, saying: "We Jews must stick together". Winchevsky mentioned to her his fear that many socialists were unaware that there was such a thing as a Jewish worker, "let alone organised Jewish workers", but it was unlikely that the British delegation would choose him to address the congress. To bypass this, Marx herself announced in three languages that he was there to represent eight trade unions with some 600 Jewish members. "The information was received in each language with tumultuous applause. Eleanor's face was radiant with pride".

In 1895, when the Cardiff Trade Union Council passed a resolution advocating control of immigration, ten London Jewish trade unions held a mass protest meeting chaired by Edward Aveling. Marx joined Jewish and non-Jewish socialists and trade union leaders on the platform to denounce the act. Partly as a result of her active involvement with East End Jews and the explicit politicisation of the Jewish question, she saw it as important to publicly emphasise being Jewish more than her father had; she took an open and definitive stance around the time of the Dreyfus affair in 1894, announcing "I am a Jewess".[32]

The *Arbeter Fraind* had been founded by a range of socialists, including Marxists; but, by the 1890s, it became dominated by anarchists. They built links with non-Jews such as Charles Mowbray, exiled revolutionaries Peter Kropotkin and Errico Malatesta, and visitors such as Emma Goldman and Louise Michel.

Most important of the East End anarchists was the German Rudolf Rocker, who came to London in 1893. Although he was not Jewish, Rocker learned Yiddish and immersed himself in the Jewish East End trade union struggles and propaganda ventures. The anarchists' club in

Jubilee Street provided the headquarters for many activities that went well beyond anarchist circles, including strike committees, cultural activities and political meetings. Up until the First World War, Rocker was an inspiration to many people in the East End.

As a political current, however, the anarchists remained a small elitist group. Their particularly strong promotion of causes that challenged conventions, such as atheism and free love, may have prevented wider support.[33]

The Kishinev pogroms in April 1903 caused a wave of outrage around the world. There were protest events in London, including a huge demonstration in Hyde Park organised by socialists and radicals. A grouping of Jewish trade unions, anarchists and socialists (including the Polish Socialist Party) also called a mass demonstration. Held against the opposition of the mainstream, middle-class Yiddish press and the rabbinate, the largest gathering of Jews ever seen in London marched from the Mile End Waste (a large area of open land where political meetings were held), to Hyde Park, where 25,000 people listened to Jewish and non-Jewish speakers in English, Russian, Yiddish and Polish.[34]

Rudolph Rocker recorded delightedly, "The demonstration succeeded beyond our expectations", noting that the opposition feared the linkage between Jews and socialists.[35]

The marchers sang a Yiddish song by David Edelshtat:

> *We have been shot and hanged,*
> *Robbed of our livelihood and rights;*
> *And only because we clearly demand*
> *Freedom for those enslaved in poverty.*[36]

Edelshtat, who emigrated from Russia to New York in 1882 as a teenager, was a famous poet of the sweatshops. His songs were very popular and sung on May Day and other occasions in different continents. We will encounter him again.

Bundists from the Russian Empire set up an association in London in 1900. Although they held May Day parades and joined in local events, their main focus was on campaigns to support their comrades back home. They also printed leaflets and periodicals to be smuggled into Russia. In 1905, they sent £106 from 325 local donors to help self-defence groups in Russia to buy guns.[37]

"Down with the sweating system!"

By 1902, there were 32 Jewish trade unions in London—although many were short lived. But the success of the 1903 demonstration against the Kishinev pogroms motivated the Jewish radicals to renew the economic struggle and, in particular, to attack sweating again. They began the campaign in 1904 with a packed hall of 5,000 people listening to Jewish and non-Jewish speakers argue for a general strike.[38]

But little happened until 1906 brought a new wave of immigrants who were "fresh from the scenes of heroic struggle for liberty" in Russia—the 1905 Revolution. As a result, "the Jewish workers of the East End of London appear to have undergone a process of transformation", and activists thought that the time had come: an "assault on sweating by collective action was imperative".[39]

The workers were ready. Makers of walking sticks and cabinet-makers went on strike as early as February, and the *Jewish Chronicle* commented, "Hardly a week passes without a fresh strike breaking out in one or other of the trades". Again, the main thrust was among the tailors. Actions in individual shops and mass meetings reached a climax in June, with a spontaneous mass walkout. "Hoisting improvised banners and shouting slogans, they marched off through the streets, stopping at each workshop and calling the workers inside to come out". Two days later, strikers packed a local theatre. "Speakers advocating caution were shouted down".[40]

> There was unanimous acclaim at the vote to strike with shouts of Long live the strike! Down with the Sweating System! The War is on!, culminating in the singing of the Marseillaise.[41]

It was a major showdown between workers and bosses, simultaneously a strike and a lockout:

> Each party has entered in the fight with grim determination not to lay down its arms until the other party is vanquished.

The anarchists played a major role in running the strike, with Rocker addressing meetings at their club in Jubilee Street and open-air meetings all over Stepney. Pickets dealt with scabs, who were "forcibly seized and frogmarched to headquarters", where they were put in a room "apportioned as a gaol for blacklegs". Family members could bail the prisoner by paying a fine, which went into strike funds. Fundraising included house-to-house collections, and Jews throughout the East End "responded magnificently". There was also a "continuous flow of donors, mostly shawled housewives, bringing bagels, brown herring, fruits, and home-made *gefilte* and fried fish".[42]

The master tailors dug their heels in, refusing to negotiate with the Jewish strike committee and insisting that they would only meet with English trade union leaders "authorised with sufficient authority to enforce any decision arrived at". They transferred work to other cities and waited for the strike funds to be exhausted. By the end of June, the strike had fizzled out. A mood of despondency led to a significant drop in union membership; but, as Fishman notes, there "remained a staunch minority of workers, experienced in the field of labour struggles who were dedicated to rebuild the union and renew the strike".[43]

This bore fruit six years later. The year 1912 was one of bitter labour disputes in the UK, with hard-fought strikes by miners, railwaymen and dockers. When (non-Jewish) West End tailors went on strike over pay and conditions in April, there was major concern that the strike would be undercut by subcontracts with (Jewish) East End sweatshops. Rocker and his fellow anarchists not only promoted solidarity but argued that this was the time to also go on strike, to again challenge the sweating system. A mass meeting of 8,000 tailors overwhelmingly agreed.

With their members dispersed in small workshops, enforcing a total strike was a mammoth task. Rocker's organisational and fundraising skills proved crucial, and his leadership was a major contributor to the ultimate success.

The strike found overwhelming support throughout the Jewish community. Bakers and cigarette makers gave free supplies; Yiddish theatres gave benefit performances. After three weeks, the West End employers offered some concessions and settled with their workers. But the East End workshops held out for a full victory. When the employers agreed to every demand except one—the right to a union—Rocker addressed a meeting to consider the offer:

I saw those pale, pinched, hungry faces…of people who had come together at midnight to decide what to do about the strike for which they had sacrificed so much… I said if they decided to go back now the Masters would make them feel they had lost… You must decide for yourselves. There was an outburst of applause and from all sides came the cry: "the strike goes on".[44]

The employers settled the very next day.

The strike showed that the most exploited and vulnerable workers could organise themselves to win, give solidarity beyond their own community and locality, and gain esteem among workers who regarded immigrant unions as a weak link.[45]

Although the outcome did not mean the end of the sweating system:

it certainly dealt it a severe blow, which no act of parliament could have rendered. For the practical necessity of unionisation was now firmly embedded among the immigrants; and recognised by the masters as a force.[46]

With the strike won, Rocker now mobilised the Jewish tailors in support of the recently commenced dockers' strike. Huge joint meetings were held on the Mile End Waste. Jewish trade unions and local anarchists organised a support committee, and gifts poured in from Jewish workers and retailers. Famously, Jewish families welcomed more than 300 dockers' children into their homes. This act did more than help the dockers in their immediate struggle. According to Fishman, "it laid the foundations of many friendships which neither time nor circumstance could erase".[47]

The dockland slogan "No Jews allowed down Wapping" might persist. But it was the dockers of Wapping and St George's who constituted the militant vanguard of the movement which, in 1936, forcibly prevented the Mosleyite incursion into East London.[48]

Debate and dances

Crucial to the functioning of radicals before the First World War were the centres and clubs they established. As well as organising hubs, they were social centres, meeting halls, educational institutions and propaganda outlets.

The earlier Berner Street club, set up by Jewish socialists in 1885, had played an important role as a base for trade unionists and radicals from across London. We have already seen its value during strikes; but it was also a centre for lectures, theatre and literary events. William Morris, the famous textile designer, poet and socialist activist, gave poetry readings there frequently. When printers succumbed to pressure from Anglo-Jews not to print the *Arbeter Fraind*, the club provided premises for a printing press. This independence gave the newspaper the opportunity to attack upper-class Anglo-Jewry, Chief Rabbi Nathan Adler and Jewish MPs.

Atheism was a popular lecture topic, and speakers on such topics as "The absurdity of religion" and "Is there a god?" drew substantial audiences. On one occasion, the speaker took out his watch and declaimed, "If there is a God…I give him just two minutes' time to kill me on the spot". After a tense wait, with the speaker still alive, "a thunder of applause echoed through the hall", the band struck up "La Marseillaise" (then regarded as the most revolutionary anthem), and the audience joined in the Yom Kippur ball.[49]

The club encountered difficulties in 1888 when the building became implicated in a Jack the Ripper murder. The relationship between the Social Democrats and anarchists subsequently deteriorated, and the club folded in 1892. Several temporary buildings in the East End served in the following years until the anarchists set up the Jubilee Street Club in 1906. During strikes, it served as an organising centre but was also open at other times. It offered a bar (non-alcoholic) and food; dances, plays and concerts; chess competitions; and English lessons. Lectures on political and cultural topics, which were not restricted to Jewish themes or authors, opened the eyes of many workers to the wider world. Importantly, the club was open to all, Jewish and non-Jewish. It attracted "the young…and old, the political and apolitical, the informed and the ignorant".[50]

Above all, there was debate and argument and:

> discussion would go on far into the night between Bundists, Zionists, Anarchists and Social Democrats who argued excitedly together.[51]

The club hosted visiting revolutionaries from many countries. Millie Sabel, a volunteer, recalled:

> I occasionally saw a small, intense man who sat alone at a table in the corner. He had slant eyes, balding reddish hair, drank Russian tea and spoke little. He was Lenin.[52]

The radicals were naturally all atheists and tried to win the Jewish workers away from their beliefs—or at least from their adherence to the synagogues, which had consistently played a conservative role. Apart from arguing with them at every opportunity they carried out stunts such as eating ham sandwiches outside the synagogues on Yom Kippur, simultaneously breaking rules against eating on a fast day and the consumption of pork. This was certainly sectarian and probably counterproductive. Less publicly, but nonetheless tellingly, some attendees of the synagogue would "creep furtively into the Club to snatch a meal with their *talusim* [religious items] under their arms". Not only were these people breaking the rule on fasting, they were also eating non-kosher food. The volunteers "were kept really busy preparing extra food, while [an anarchist leader] took advantage of the situation to lecture the invaders on the falsity of religion".[53]

The social environment among the radicals was very open for the period. Many women were active, and young girls could come to the freer atmosphere in the clubs. Rudolph Rocker and Milly Witkop lived together unmarried. This caused some raised eyebrows and even led to headlines in the US press when the couple visited the country. The parents of another woman, "Red" Rose Robins, forbade her to attend lectures at the Sugar Loaf, a pub popular among anarchists, where "free love" was one of the topics. Returning home late one night, she had to sleep in the street because her parents had locked her out.[54]

EastEnders was and remains a very popular TV show. An *EastEnders* based in the pre-First World War Jewish East End would provide a glimpse into a world of harsh living conditions, but also of comradeship, struggle and hope, that remains inspiring today.

Fascists and the fight back: interwar London East End

In the 1930s approximately 330,000 Jews lived in Britain, which had a population at that time of about 45 million. One hundred and eighty-three thousand lived in London, with an estimated 60 percent of those in East London, half in the borough of Stepney. Thus, despite generational and other changes, working-class Jews were still largely concentrated in a relatively small area, where they lived alongside cockneys, Irish Catholics and other working-class communities in an area with continuing poverty, overcrowding and unemployment.[1]

The sons and daughters of immigrant Jews were still mostly workers and poor traders. David Rosenberg notes that this so-called "new community" were often collectively characterised as "Jewish labour and Jewish youth"; they basically shared the outlook and culture of their social environment. He argued that there was:

> so much in common between the young post-war English cockney and the young East End Jew...[that] what goes under the name of the East End Jew is in reality no specific Jewish type at all, but a general East London labour type.[2]

Whether this was strictly true is not so important; it is clear that, despite conflicts, there was an underlying sense of commonality. This was an important change from the pre-war period, when the Jewish community lived in some ways in a virtual ghetto, separated by language, customs and religion. Now that the younger generation, at least, spoke English and felt themselves to be British (not Russian or Polish), it was much easier for socialists and Communists to overcome antagonisms and build solidarity. This was to stand them in good stead in the fight against fascism and other struggles.

The upper-class Jewish Rothschilds and Montefiores, meanwhile, were content with their status as a powerful elite living in much more salubrious surroundings. Lionel Rothschild lived on an estate in Hampshire. Nor did most of the bosses and landlords live in the East End. Similarly, as the threat of fascism grew after 1933, the president of the Jewish Board of Deputies was mostly concerned with his status; he advocated an "overriding consideration of duty and loyalty"[3] to the UK. Their fear of the "general East London labour type" overrode any anxiety about danger from the right.[4]

British Brothers' League

Britain had earlier been a place of refuge for Europe's persecuted, such as the Huguenots. Legislation in 1753 made it easier for Jews to settle, although they did not receive full political equality until 1858.[5] By the late 19th century, Anglo-Jews had lived in the UK for many generations, largely as an accepted and respected part of the community.

However, with rising inter-imperialist competition and the growth of nationalism in the 1890s, antisemitism gained strength in Britain as it had internationally. Many left-wing opponents of the second Boer War (1899–1902) blamed "Jewish capitalists" who were "behind the war and imperialism in general",[6] including Keir Hardie and the Independent Labour Party (ILP).[7] The Trade Union Congress concurred but went even further, passing resolutions calling for immigration control three times during the 1890s.[8]

Driven by economic crises and rising working-class struggle, conservatives and right wingers exploited antisemitic strategies to divert attention to immigrants, particularly Jews. Typical is the 1893 parliamentary debate, where Tories blathered on about the growth of the "Jewish race" and the country being "overrun" by "destitute foreign immigrants".[9] In 1895 under Joseph Chamberlain, they adopted a policy of immigration controls. It is interesting to note that, at the same time, Chamberlain supported the Zionist project. He met Herzl in 1903 and supported the establishment of settlements in the Sinai or Uganda, both at the time under British control. This engagement with Britain was a major breakthrough for the Zionists.[10]

Thus, when unemployment rose sharply after the turn of the century, the ground was ready for anti-alien sentiment to be expressed in more virulent ways.

The British Brothers' League (BBL) was founded in 1900 as an explicitly anti-immigration campaign group. While its office was in the City, the financial and business centre of London, and its leadership was middle class, its strategic orientation was the working-class East End, where it could mobilise support by rehashing old charges: that Jews were ousting locals from jobs and houses and that they were the cause of crime.

BBL membership reached 6,000 very quickly. In 1902, they held a large rally in a hall in Mile End:

> Four simultaneous marches led by drummers converged on the building. The marchers held Union Jacks and placards saying "British Homes for British Workers". Inside the hall, where 4,000 had gathered, an organ played There's No Place Like Home.[11]

Speakers railed against Britain being "the dumping ground for the scum of Europe". When one claimed that they were not persecuted refugees but came because "they want our money", supporters shouted "Wipe them out!"[12]

Anti-immigration sentiment was now concretised in a local antisemitic organisation. But counteraction could not come from Anglo-Jewish leaders, who had joined the chorus against immigration, declaring that they shared the Tories' fears. Some elements of the Jewish communal leadership were even willing to associate themselves with BBL campaigns.[13] Sir Henry Samuel, President of the Board of Jewish Deputies, "took an out-spokenly active role" in the BBL. Another leading member was on the Executive of the National Vigilance Association.[14] The London branch of the Board told those in Russia, "It is better to live a life of hardship" there than to come here.[15] "England is overcrowded" was the message sent to Odessa.[16]

It was radical East Enders who organised against the BBL, setting up the Aliens Defence League. Drawing in Jewish and non-Jewish socialists, anarchists and progressives, they held rallies and public meetings and heckled at BBL events.[17] Their work was cut out for them. A BBL petition with 45,000 signatures added to the political pressure for restricted immigration. A royal commission in 1903 was followed by the *Aliens Act 1905*. It introduced the categorisation of migrants into "desirable" and "undesirable", establishing "the invidious value system that still dominates today's immigration discussion".[18]

For Jews, the Act was particularly pernicious. While it seemed to restrict immigration in general, and the word Jew did not appear anywhere, the legislation in practice drastically reduced Jewish access to the UK at the time of mass emigration following the wave of pogroms in 1905–6 and even led to deportations. The *Aliens Act* was steered through parliament by none other than Arthur Balfour, of Balfour Declaration fame. He argued for restrictions on Jews entering the UK because "they are not to the advantage of the civilisation of this country".[19] One person who gave evidence to the Royal Commission was Herzl. Although his contribution was fairly anodyne, by participating he was complicit in this antisemitic piece of legislation.[20]

The marches and rallies of the BBL prefigured the actions of Mosley's British Union of Fascists (BUF) in the 1930s and the National Front in the 1970s. Although the target of the latter was the more recent immigration from the Indian sub-continent, the dynamic and strategy were similar.

Many of the characteristics of this campaign were to appear later: right-wing agitators focusing on the East End; the attempt to drive wedges between different ethnic groups; traditional antisemitic tropes; absence of support—and even active opposition—from the established and wealthy local Jews. The preparedness to fight the fascists and solidarity from non-Jews and socialists also reappeared later. And the base issues that underlay the events in this early period—poverty, unemployment, housing and rent—played out into the 1930s.

The British Union of Fascists

Although the BBL declined into insignificance, antisemitic attitudes did not. Rather, they had become normalised by the 1930s. Mainstream newspapers, the clergy and even well-known authors such as H G Wells, George Bernard Shaw and J B Priestley disseminated antisemitic tropes such as the "international Jewish conspiracy". Insurance companies classified Jews as "bad risks" or "untrustworthy individuals". Houses to let displayed signs with the words "no dogs, no Jews", and job advertisements often specified that applicants must be gentiles.[21]

This non-systematic antisemitic climate set the stage for an organised antisemitic force. Enter the BUF.

Formed in 1932, the BUF did not initially focus on Jews. Its core ideas at the start were nationalism, corporatism and anti-communism, and it attracted considerable mainstream interest. The BUF first gained notoriety following large public meetings in 1934. The first one at the Albert Hall in April won "enthusiastic plaudits" from the conservative media, who said that leader Oswald Mosley's "peroration was perfect" and the event "a notable triumph".[22] But the subsequent mass rally in June at Olympia played a significant role both in the public attitude to the fascists and for the forces organising against them and also in the development of the antisemitic theme. MPs and other prominent political figures, some of them wearing black shirts, joined 15,000 people to hear Mosley speak, flanked by 56 Union Jacks and 24 microphones. While stewards savagely beat hecklers from the Communist Party (CPGB) and the ILP in the body of the hall, police perpetrated their own violence on demonstrators outside the building. The *Daily Mail* commented that this "mob" was "largely composed of aliens" while Mosley himself, somehow claiming self-defence, pointed out the prominence of Jews among the counter-demonstrators.[23]

The violence of Mosley's Blackshirts shocked many people, including several of his wealthy backers. People were pummelled, kicked, clawed "as though an animal had attacked them" and there were smashed faces, damaged breasts and dangling legs. One observer commented that "the most revolting part of the meeting was the blood lust on the faces of those around me [in the audience inside]... It made the tales I had heard of Austria and Germany become real".[24]

David Rosenberg notes that, at Olympia, "the fascists won the physical war but the anti-fascists largely won the propaganda war". Despite, or maybe because of, the serious violence, they found it easier to campaign and mobilise the numbers. The *Daily Worker*, the main CP newspaper, remarked that "Mosley might have the millionaires but he hasn't the millions".[25]

The fascists then changed tactics and planned the next rally for outdoors. In September in Hyde Park a wide range of forces lined up to oppose them in a counter-demonstration. The *Jewish Chronicle* urged Jews to "stay away and refrain from adding to the sufficiently heavy anxieties of the police". The labour and liberal press and trade union leaders urged anti-fascists to ignore the event. But leafletting and workplace organisation by Communists and rank-and-file trade unionists led to a spectacular result: a crowd of 100,000 workers and anti-fascists overwhelmed the 5,000 fascists at the event.[26]

Following this setback, the BUF lost most mainstream support and changed tack. Having now developed a comprehensive antisemitic propaganda push, in 1935 it turned to building a "belligerent street-level populist movement of agitation and provocation in predominantly working-class areas surrounding Jewish populations": the battle for the East End had begun.[27]

It is important to emphasise that continued anti-communism was entwined with antisemitism; contemporary writer William Zukerman argued "for fascists, Jewish and non-Jewish East End labour equally represented the 'alien nation'":[28]

> Fundamentally the British Fascists' outburst against the Jews is an out-burst against British Labour, "Reds", Socialists and Communists. It is more political and economic than national and racial. Its anti-Semitism is a guise under which its profounder class feeling is hidden.[29]

Mosley constantly referred to the East End in his speeches as "alien territory" and a "Communist stronghold", and the party propaganda increasingly equated Communist with Jew.[30] Modern historians also agree that the left and Jews were equally the targets of the BUF. This is important in understanding the fascist movement: the BUF was founded primarily as an anti-communist movement, and it never lost this goal. It turned to antisemitism as a way of building support by inflaming hostilities, but also because it could characterise Jews as Communists, and thus kill two birds with the one stone.[31]

Cable Street: "the great epic of the Jewish East End"

From the summer of 1936, the BUF intensified its antisemitic campaign with racist abuse, assaults on individuals in the street, fire-bombings and attacks on Jewish premises. By the end of September, they were ready for a show of strength. By marching openly through Stepney, they hoped to intimidate the organised working class and the Jewish community and to swing workers to their arguments.

The climax of the struggle occurred in Cable Street in Stepney on 4 October 1936. That otherwise unremarkable street was the scene of events that marked a generation. Let's look at this event and why it created such a lasting impact in the minds of participants then and continues to do so today:

> No English-speaking city has ever seen anything like the scenes which marked this attempted demonstration… Those who like myself had the privilege of taking part in the event will never forget it. For this was one of those great communal acts of a mass of people aroused by a profound emotion or by a sense of outraged justice, which makes history… It was indeed the great epic of the Jewish East End.[32]

When the BUF's plans became known, anti-fascists had just one week to organise. Their success was not due to leadership from mainstream Jewish organisations or the labour leaders.

It was as though they had all received the same memo: the Jewish Board of Deputies and the Labour leadership urged people to stay away. Labour MP George Lansbury avoided mention even of antisemitism and called on the home secretary to re-route the BUF through "less congested" areas. Stating that he wanted to "maintain peace and order", Lansbury advised "those people who are opposed to Fascism to keep away from the demonstration". Calling this "sound advice", the official labour movement paper, the *Daily Herald*, produced arguments of a type that continue to be heard to this day: "Fascist meetings are in themselves dull… The only attraction is the prospect of disturbances. Withdraw that attraction and Fascist meetings would die on the organisers' hands". The Labour Mayor of Stepney appealed to all East Londoners "most earnestly to stay away".[33]

The CPGB tends to take credit for the counter-demonstration, but it also initially opposed any action. Despite a good record on fighting fascists locally, national policy was to prioritise the Spanish Civil War. They continued to push their rally in solidarity with Spain that had been called for that day in a different location.

It was local activists and Jewish groups, rank-and-file trade unionists, community activists and socialist organisations that swung into action, and it was their efforts that led to the mass show of resistance that has become known as the Battle of Cable Street.

Rank-and-file Communists were appalled by the Party line and lobbied desperately within the Party for it to change. Many members even attended organising meetings under the auspices of other organisations. CP activist Joe Jacobs noted that the "pressure from the people of Stepney who went ahead with their own efforts to oppose Mosley left no doubt in our minds that the CP would be finished in Stepney if this was allowed to go through as planned by our London leaders".[34]

Only after several days did the CPGB cancel the Trafalgar Square demonstration and support the call for a mass protest in the East End. The CP newspaper, the *Daily Worker*, printed a special supplement calling for the biggest rally against fascism that has yet been seen in Britain. Aiming to deny the fascists entry to the East End, the Spanish slogan "they shall not pass" became an English mantra.

The ILP also played an important role in building the demonstration, so much so that one local East End newspaper actually referred to the "ILP demonstration against the fascists".[35]

Without modern technology, the event was built by local activists:

Few people had telephones or access to them... There was no TV. Radio was still almost a novelty. So our communications were through knocks on doors, notes through letter boxes, the post, meetings in the street, or at work, and by word of mouth.[36]

Newspapers such as the CPGB's *Daily Worker* were read by thousands in the factories and workplaces:

On the Sunday morning we took this round the streets of the small council estates in Southgate. We sold them at almost every other house. Our main propaganda medium then was by chalking slogans on walls and in the roads...we chalked thoroughly all the entrances to the great Standard Telephones cable factory in New Southgate where 10,000 went to work every day.[37]

On the day, up to 300,000 people participated. With the local population numbering approximately 60,000, it is clear that an enormous number of people from elsewhere joined in. They were young and old; men, women and children; Jews and Catholics; socialists and communists; dockworkers and housewives—no distinction of age, gender, work, religion or ethnicity.

Alice Hitchen describes what it was like:

> There were so many of us that you couldn't move. I can remember the elation in the crowd that so many people were there. The dockers came from Limehouse and Poplar—to my amazement, because they had a reputation for being antisemitic. There were cabinet-makers from Bethnal Green and tailors from Whitechapel. There were so many different accents. Miners came from Wales and Communists from all over Britain. "They shall not pass" was on everybody's lips.[38]

The local Irish dockers played a pivotal role. Max Levitas, a Jewish Communist who had grown up in Dublin, stood at the barricades with his father and brother, both of whom had worked with the socialist trade union leader Jim Larkin:

> We knew the Irish would stand with us. When [the dockers] went out on strike in 1912, it was a terrible time. Jewish families took in hundreds of their children. They were starving. We knew [the Irish dockers] wouldn't forget. They wanted to repay the debt...
>
> There were huge crowds, the dockers were shouting: "Come on lads, we're going to go out and stop them! They want to march, we won't let them!"[39]

The crowd was so enormous and so dense that the battle was between the anti-fascists and 10,000 police, while approximately 3,000 fascists stood aside under police protection. People chanted slogans and raised clenched fists behind barricades. Broken glass and marbles in the street helped deter mounted police:

> In Leman Street police drew their truncheons and charged when a section of the crowd attempted to rescue a man who was being escorted by a policeman. Stones and other missiles were thrown and a bag of pepper was burst in front of the policeman's horse. In Cable Street a crowd seized materials from a builder's yard and began to construct a barricade. They used corrugated iron, barrels, coal, and glass to construct

a barrier, even pulling up paving-stones. When the police intervened they were greeted with a shower of stones, and reinforcements had to be sent and a charge made before order could be restored and the barricade removed.[40]

In a surprise action, women, mostly Irish Catholics, leaned out of upper storeys and threw rubbish, rotten vegetables and the contents of chamber pots at the police:

From the roofs and the upper floors, people, ordinary housewives, and elderly women too, were throwing down milk bottles and other weapons and all kinds of refuse…onto the police.[41]

Despite many injuries and about 150 arrests, the crowd refused to give way. Eventually, the police realised that they would never be able to clear the way and told Mosley to give up. "They shall not pass" prevailed, and the fascists were prevented from entering the East End.

The anti-fascists celebrated with an impromptu march in the streets and partied in the pubs until early morning. Participants reveal a level of euphoria over much more than the achievement of the immediate goals.

Max Levitas: "You should have been there to hear the cry, and see people jumping and shouting in joy. People who had never drunk beer in their lives, drank a glass of beer. We had won".[42]

Alice Hitchen: "Everyone was cheering. Where I was, people were dancing and singing and throwing their arms around one another".[43]

Bill Fishman: "There were parties, there was dancing in the streets. The cafés were full, the pubs were full. And there was a feeling of elation, a feeling of relief, particularly amongst the immigrant Jews".[44]

This jubilation has remained within the memory of the labour movement to this day, 85 years later: the intense feeling derived from the creation, even for a short time, of a radical united movement of the working class in its broadest sense, together with its allies. The people present could feel the possibilities and strengths that unity brings, and that feeling has been passed on to later generations.

Bill Fishman, who was only 15 at the time, described it this way:

I was moved to tears to see bearded Jews and Irish Catholic dock-ers standing up to stop Mosley. I shall never forget that as long as I live—how working-class people could get together to oppose the evil of fascism.[45]

Where did this unity come from? Firstly, we need to recognise the extraordinary organising effort by local militants and activists, carried out against the opposition of bureaucratic leaders. But looking further back, we can see that the East End community drew on its experience and tradition of combined struggle and solidarity: the mutual support in 1889 between the tailors and the dockers; and 1912, when Jewish families cared for dockers' children. The latter, little more than 20 years previously, lived in the local memory. So it is no coincidence that dockers were the militant vanguard of the fight against the BUF.

The Labour Party and the Communist Party

As we have seen, the leaderships of the Labour Party and the unions failed to take the BUF seriously, arguing that antisemitism was a passing phenomenon and need not be directly fought. They refused to support anti-fascist actions and even called on their members to stay away, claiming that, if they weren't "provoked", the fascists would somehow disappear.[46]

An anti-immigrant posture, however, often underlay this stance:

> The official Labour Party position...suggests that Jews were a separate category of the working class...seen as immigrant, rather than indigenous.[47]

There was a different story at the rank-and-file level. Throughout the country, discontent with the Party was increasing because of Labour government betrayals from 1929 to 1931.[48]

In the East London trade union and Labour Party branches, where Jews and non-Jews had worked together over many years, there was a passionate desire for direct action against the BUF. A significant number of rank-and-file members defied the local right-wing leadership and the Party line, working alongside Communists to organise defiance. A Labour official noted that "we have a great difficulty in the Labour Movement in persuading our people that all is being done that ought to be done to deal with what they consider to be a very serious situation". At the massive Hyde Park action in 1934, many participants were Labour members. "Many were out for their first demonstration, but they had shown that their loyalty was not to party tags but to their class".[49]

Stepney was a firmly Labour borough by the mid-1930s, with seats on the council equally divided between Irish, English and Jewish members. Within the branch there were major conflicts between left and right. In 1938, two former Jewish mayors of the borough raised complaints about the Labour council's failure to act on rent control, its hostility to the CPGB and other issues. As they were evicted from a council meeting, one shouted, "It is with pleasure that I leave this session of the Reichstag".[50]

Other nearby Labour branches were also active. The Hackney branch, which had a massive Jewish membership, carried out many street meetings at the Ridley Road market, where Mosley repeatedly tried to march. It is probable that many branch members were absent from the Cable Street demonstration because of the Party's official lack of support; nonetheless, their activism contributed to building the movement which provided the basis for the mass action.[51]

Labour continued to condemn the Cable Street demonstration even after the event. Its commitment to anti-communist politics outweighed any concept of the need to fight fascism, even equating the two—"[we] have no sympathy with red Communism or black Fascism".[52]

A number of left and revolutionary groups did support confrontations with the fascists, including the CPGB, Trotskyists and others. But the weaknesses within the Labour Party and consequent loss of support created space for the CPGB, which became the most important organisation in the anti-fascist struggle in the East End.

This did not happen automatically. During the so-called Third Period (1928–1933) of the Communist International, when policy was based on the expectation that capitalism was about to collapse and revolution was around the corner, the CPGB maintained a rigidly sectarian attitude towards reformist organisations and rejected work among other class forces outside the working class. The Labour Party was their main target of hostility and anti-fascist activity a lower priority. With the adoption of the Popular Front strategy in 1934 and the concomitant orientation to non-working-class layers, the CPGB backed further away from confrontations with the fascists, arguing that violence would detract from the image it was trying to build.[53]

This did not go down well with the membership. According to well-known Stepney Party member (at the time) Joe Jacobs, "The majority view, certainly among the youth, was that Mosley should be met everywhere with the maximum force available".[54] Notwithstanding their foot-dragging, the CPGB were happy to take the credit for the fight against the fascists.[55]

But Jacobs maintained that the:

local antifascist initiatives owed more to the sustained, independent efforts of the grassroots fighting for a unified approach in the local branches and local trade unions initially, than wrenching support from the London District Committee and the party nationally.[56]

Local activists were at the heart of the social movements in the East End in the period and formed the links between the political groups, the communities and the workplaces which underlay the solidarity shown at Cable Street.

One of the less well known is Sarah Wesker, a Communist. As a machinist at Goodman's trouser factory in 1926, she led the all-female workforce in a walkout, demanding a farthing a pair.[57] She became a formidable union organiser, leading strikes at several textile factories.[58] Sarah was fluent in English and Yiddish and so could communicate well with the mostly older women factory workers. Under five feet tall, she was "a ferocious speaker, as if the energy of five men was balled up inside that miniature frame of hers". Wesker was "a real inspiration to all of us" at Cable Street.[59]

A large majority of the 500 members of the Stepney branch of the CPGB was Jewish. One attraction was the way Party membership broadened their horizons through social and cultural activities as well as political actions. It "introduced young Jews to a wider world, as they campaigned outside the old boundaries and sang Irish songs with their Catholic comrades". Lectures on a range of subjects were very popular, with even BUF members turning up.[60]

Thus, despite the opposition from both Labour and, initially, the CPGB, Jewish and non-Jewish rank-and-file Communists and Labour Party members, along with local union leaders and activists, forged bonds of solidarity, forming almost a de facto united front. The anti-fascist struggle and other local issues merged into a larger, community-based movement, which was the foundation upon which the mass participation at Cable Street was built:

Just from the family stories you get the sense of how Jewish socialists, of whatever stripe, pulled non-Jewish people into anti-fascist activity as they fought alongside each other on housing, wages, public health and all the other revolutionary and reformist issues of the day.[61]

Beating back the landlords

The fight against fascism and the fight for better housing boosted each other. People were drawn into the Communist Party by the fight against fascism and, through the Party, they helped to organise the attack on housing conditions. The fight for better housing brought everyone together, Jew and non-Jew, to attack the social and economic causes on which fascism thrives. It was a virtuous cycle.[62]

Stepney, as one of the most overcrowded districts in London, was practically all a slum, and the situation of tenants deteriorated further after partial reduction of rent control in 1933.

Phil Piratin, a young Jewish Communist resident of Spitalfields, was looking for local issues for the Party to campaign around. One evening in 1934, he noticed the open gas flares on the staircases of a housing block. He knocked on a nearby door and asked the woman how she felt about this. "Immediately I received a torrent of information, and a cursing of the landlord. *I had found an issue!*"[63]

Piratin coordinated a successful tenant letter-writing campaign, and the landlord installed electric lighting. Writing later, Piratin himself was quite critical of how he ran this first campaign: he failed to get the tenants "to feel that they were doing something for themselves". He and other Communists, however, developed better strategies when they decided to make a serious effort to win over Mosley's local working-class supporters by focusing on housing.[64]

There were sporadic rent strikes from 1935, but the campaign really got off the ground in June 1937 with action around the eviction of two families in Paragon Mansions in Mile End; they were actually members of the BUF, which had declined to help them. Having involved other tenants in resistance, Piratin and his comrades were able to get the two BUF families to join in also.

Tenants set up barricades, with people armed with mouldy flour and water standing on balconies from which anyone trying to get in "could be bombarded with ease". They made full use of their "ammunition" when the police arrived. "Some of the women had to be persuaded... that it was inadvisable to use anything more than the flour and water. Some were disappointed." During the subsequent standoff, Piratin addressed passing factory workers from a soapbox.[65]

News of the action spread very quickly. "The lessons did not require being pressed home. BUF membership cards were destroyed voluntarily".[66]

As the movement grew, more tenants set up committees and formed a coordinating body, the Stepney Tenants Defence League (STDL). Its leader, Michael Shapiro, recalled:

> It was a genuine united movement of the people, drawing together Jews and Christians at a time when anti-Semitic propaganda was being stepped up, helping to isolate and expose both fascists and right-wing local Labour leaders.[67]

Activity increased further after the abolition of rent controls and massive rent increases in early 1938. Some strikes were won easily, but others were bitter affairs.

The tenants on Flower and Dean Streets, most of whom were Jewish, "turned their building into a 'fortress'" in order to avoid bailiffs and eviction. They guarded all entrances, picketed continually and held street marches. The children demonstrated in front of the home of the landlord in well-to-do Golders Green. The owner caved in after five weeks.[68]

Many Jewish Communists lived in the Brady Street Mansions, including Max Levitas, who had been heavily involved at Cable Street. They carried out a joint strike with tenants at Langdale Mansions directed at their common landlords, two clothing manufacturers. With barricades and barbed wire around the buildings and guards patrolling the entrances, there was a virtual state of siege, even the milkman had to get a permit to enter. The tenants' committee, all women, ran a very active campaign including demonstrations outside the landlords' West End business premises and the comfortable Hampstead home of one of them.

When police broke through the barricades at Langdale Mansions at the end of June, "a fierce struggle ensued with the tenants, who armed themselves with sticks, shovels and saucepans, and there were several injuries".[69] A mass demonstration of 15,000 people, including rabbis, church dignitaries and the mayor, also faced the police. Finally, under pressure from the council and even parliament, the landlords capitulated, resulting in a clear victory for the tenants.[70]

By mid-summer, the strikes and campaigns had "beaten back the landlords who have for years sucked the lifeblood of the people of Stepney",[71] and there was a large victory parade in July.

One important aspect of the CPGB strategy was to link rent strikes to the anti-fascist struggle. For example, the activists deliberately targeted Quinn Square in Bethnal Green, a block in the heart of the area where fascists were active. A rent strike in August 1938 involving many BUF members was won after two weeks.

From the beginning of 1939, a new campaign aimed at rent control for all working-class houses, with rent strikes "in street after street in rapid succession". With the STDL membership nearly 5,000 and with 2,000 tenants refusing to pay rent, the big landlords "were on the run". Two months later, the tenants had recovered £10,000 in overcharged rent, had won massive rent reductions and had forced landlords to carry out repairs. About 10,000 people joined in a celebratory May Day march, with columns converging from five centres of recent strikes.[72]

The success of the movement was due to the responsiveness and militancy of the residents. One commentator was amazed by "the speed with which people came together, organised, and threw up their own leaders... They ran great risks".[73] In particular, the role of women has been described in terms strikingly reminiscent of the 1984–85 miners' strike, a more recent event which is famous for the way in which women were in the forefront of the struggle:[74]

> [I]t was the women who did the picketing, women who often dominated the committees making up the [STDL], women who came out on demonstrations.[75]
>
> Outstanding were the women... There was nothing that the men could do that could not be equalled by the women, and, in fact, they were mostly more enthusiastic and hence more reliable.[76]

Piratin gave examples of how the experience transformed the women's consciousness:

They are shy, they lack confidence. Oh, no! they cannot be a secretary, they cannot write too well! Speak on a platform? Never!... But so rapidly did the campaign develop, so many things needed to be done, so many people were required, that [one woman] soon found herself doing many of the things she had hitherto thought beyond her powers.[77]

Academic Henry Srebrnik argues that the movement's success was primarily due to housewives' networks. But while they did serve as "resources of resistance",[78] the networks did not operate in a vacuum. Housewives were married to male workers and trade union members; many would have had experience of militancy in the workplace; and many were also involved in left-wing organisations. The links were the same as occurred in the New York rent strikes.

The fact that the rent strikes mostly occurred in the Jewish community also demonstrates that more was at work than women's networks. The STDL made "strenuous efforts" to engage the Irish community, but with little success. The Irish women no doubt had as strong networks, but the dynamic there was different, with the local Catholic hierarchy fiercely anti-communist. Mosley's Blackshirts were also able to manipulate anti-landlord sentiment to provide material for anti-semitism, because many landlords were Jewish.

The Jewish women, on the other hand, came from a culture "with a well-developed ethic of social justice" that encouraged militancy in both sexes.[79] The tenants' movement carried on the tradition of struggle and resistance that many of their parents and grandparents had engaged in earlier in Europe and then in the East End.

Piratin stresses that the keynote was the "over-all solidarity [which] was tremendous".[80] He gives us a very telling story. In Langdale Street Mansions, there was a mixture of Jewish and non-Jewish families. The picketers, all women who were also responsible for the daily shopping, had a novel way of carrying out both responsibilities:

Without any hesitation, and with lots of fun, Mrs Smith would go to the Jewish butcher-shop to buy meat for Mrs Cohen on the picket line, and the next day Mrs Cohen (who would never have thought of doing it in all her life) would go to buy meat at the local general butcher for Mrs Smith.[81]

The CPGB played a leading role in the movement, but Piratin acknowledges that rank-and-file Labour Party members and supporters were also heavily engaged. On the other hand, while Stepney Trades Council gave full support, several trade unions failed to respond in any way; much more could have been done to involve the whole labour movement.[82]

Nonetheless, in spite of limitations:

> Tens of thousands of working-class men and women had organised themselves for common struggle. There was a common bond between them…[and] this was indeed an achievement. Committees were formed and hundreds of people who…had no experience of organisation or politics learned these things and learned them well.[83]

Bermondsey against fascism

A year after the events at Cable Street, the fascists tried again. "Smarting with disbelief that the East End Irish dockers had supported the Jews the previous year", the Blackshirts decided in October 1937 to attack another London dockers' area south of the river in Bermondsey with another provocative march. Again under pressure from their members, the local CPGB branch announced a counter-march, which gained wide support from the local labour movement, including the ILP and the local Trades and Labour Council. Several Labour Party branches also defied the London executive and declared support for a militant counter-protest.[84]

The counter-demonstration used tactics similar to the previous year:

> Barricades of costers' barrows, fences with barbed wire, with red flags flying at the top, were flung up with incredible speed; when police tore them down, others were erected a few yards further on… Mounted and foot police, with lashing batons, swept…into the crowds… Missiles were hurled from roofs: eggs, stones and fireworks were flung at the marchers and at police horses.[85]

The police diverted the fascists' march, but they could not avoid a final barricade of "men, women and children from the great flats that Labour has built in Bermondsey", with banners proclaiming "Socialism builds. Fascism destroys. Bermondsey Against Fascism".[86] A CPGB speaker at the concluding rally deliberately referenced Cable Street:

> The 100 percent cockney borough of Bermondsey has given the same answer to Mosley as the Jewish lads and girls did in Stepney just twelve months ago.[87]

Although the protest was smaller, it was just as militant. The police struck a man on the head with a baton and were taking him away when he was rescued by 40 dockers. Several East End Jews were among the 111 people arrested. One magistrate commented, "It is extraordinary how many of the population of Whitechapel and the East End seemed to choose Bermondsey for a Sunday afternoon walk".[88] The magistrates were much harsher than at Cable Street, with 23 custodial sentences handed out. But one Betsy Malone was only fined after taking a running kick at a policeman and telling him to arrest someone his own size!

This was the last major street confrontation. The attempt by the Blackshirts to make inroads into working-class areas declined; and, most importantly, the BUF was never able to get a real hold in the East End working class. They did not pass.

Yearning to be free: United States
1880s–1914

"Huddled masses yearning to be free"

In 1883 Emma Lazarus wrote a poem which was to become a founda-
tional myth of America's self-image. Herself Jewish, Lazarus carried
out welfare work with Jewish immigrants. "The New Colossus",
inscribed on the iconic Statue of Liberty at the entrance to New York
harbour, is viewed by millions of people each year. But, as one commentator says, the poem is "almost universally underread".[1]

Everyone knows the last couple of lines, but let's look at the
whole stanza:

> *"Keep, ancient lands, your storied pomp!" cries she*
> *With silent lips. "Give me your tired, your poor,*
> *Your huddled masses yearning to breathe free,*
> *The wretched refuse of your teeming shore.*
> *Send these, the homeless, tempest-tost to me,*
> *I lift my lamp beside the golden door!"*[2]

The poet is not just saying that refugees are welcome; she says clearly
that poor and homeless people are *preferred* over the rich and aristocratic. This radical and even class-conscious element is usually ignored.
The core image of the US as a land of refuge is tied up with *Jewish
working-class* immigration.

Between 1880 and 1924, 2.5 million Jews from Eastern Europe
sought refuge from persecution and poverty in the US. New York
was the point of arrival, and nearly three quarters of the total settled
in the Lower East Side, partly because of restrictive rental practices in
other areas. The city was transformed from a middle-class, conservative
community into a radical, working-class, multilingual melting pot. By

1914, there were more than 1.75 million Jewish New Yorkers, constituting nearly one third of the city's population.[3]

For the incoming migrants, the watchword was the "*goldene medinah*"—the land where the streets were paved with gold, the "golden door".

Certainly, the gold was there for some. Known as the Gilded Age, the period from 1870 to 1900 was one of rapid economic growth, monopolisation and concentration of power and wealth. The *New York Times* gleefully prophesied that, soon, "Millionaires will be commonplace".[4] The dazzling riches of the robber barons have provided endless material for television shows, books and monuments.[5]

But what did the immigrants find?

> Many exchanged the stagnation of a feudal society for the bondage of an industrial system. The riches of the new world were frequently a miracle mirage, and the dream of American opportunity led often to the sweatshop, where laborers slept on unswept floors littered with work refuse while their worktables doubled as dining tables. They labored fantastically long hours; a 4 am to 10 pm day was not uncommon... Immigrant workers cried out in despair: "We worked, worked, and our profits went into the hands of others".[6]

The disparity between the wealth of the robber barons and the poor immigrants with barely the clothes on their backs is shocking. In 1900, Andrew Carnegie's annual income was $23,000,000 (equivalent to $748,000,000 today)—on which he paid no income tax. Coal miners averaged an annual income of $240—approximately $4.60 per week. Meanwhile, New York women clothing workers earning 30 cents a day sang, "*with a great lament/Why was I born to be a seamstress*".[7]

Arriving in New York from Ellis Island, the immigrants desperately searched for food, shelter and a job in the new land. No gold paving was to be found in Hester Street, the centre of the Jewish community on the Lower East Side. In his memoirs, Bernard Weinstein pictures the usual dwelling of the 1880s as resembling "prison cells, lacking sun, air or light...overlooking a tiny courtyard or a filthy, narrow alley". Plagues of cockroaches and bedbugs were the norm, as were fires from kerosene cookers. To escape the vermin and summer heat, people slept in the streets or on the roofs. Diseases such as tuberculosis were rife, and mortality was high, particularly among children.[8]

Many ended up working in sweatshops, denounced as a "system of making clothes under filthy and inhuman conditions" and a "process of grinding the faces of the poor". But, in typical victim-blaming fashion, investigators saw these conditions as somehow introduced by the immigrants: "Some even declared the sweatshop a special Jewish institution explicable by the 'racial' and 'national' characteristics of the Jewish workers". One official wrote that Russian Jews "evidently prefer filth to cleanliness". Another concluded that the "factory system with its discipline and regular hours" was "distasteful to the Jew's individualism" and that the Jewish worker preferred "the sweatshop with its going and coming".[9]

As in the UK, the Jewish immigrants found co-religionists already living in the new country.

German nationals were the most numerous immigrant group to the US between 1840 and 1890. Among them were German Jews, many of whom were comfortable businessmen by the end of the century. Some, such as Levi Strauss, later became household names. Others, such as Goldman Sachs, Lehmann Brothers, Kuhn Loeb and Salomon Brothers, founded investment banking firms that became mainstays of industry and were at the core of modern US capitalism. They epitomised the American dream, having risen from humble positions to extraordinary economic power. Known as "our crowd", they were a self-conscious group whose lives differed in every respect from those of the poor immigrants.[10]

Like the British Anglo-Jews, the German Jews in the US considered themselves superior to the newcomers:

Buttressed by their higher class status, social exclusivity...they separated themselves socially from the Yiddish-speaking, differently mannered newcomers.[11]

In his memoir, Paul Jacobs describes how:

the atmosphere in our house was as much German as it was Jewish... I said my nightly prayers in German [and] my parents didn't observe the kosher dietary laws... So although we were Jewish, we weren't "Jews," like the men with beards and earlocks or the women with brown wigs who embarrassed me when I saw them on the street or the subway reading Yiddish newspapers...

The gap between families like mine and the Eastern European Jews was nearly as great as the one separating my parents from their Christian friends… In the Gentile world, a "kike" may have been descriptive of any Jews, but to my parents and their friends it was any East European Jew, especially the noisy ones. "Stop acting like a kike" was a frequent admonition to noisy, badly behaved children—or adults as well.[12]

German Jews were also prominent as bosses in the small tailoring and other workshops in New York where the Eastern European refugees provided a convenient workforce.

But Germans, mostly non-Jews, played another important role—that of bearer of radical ideas. Many had fled from the 1880s anti-socialist law in Germany. The majority were social democrats or Marxists, with anarchism also a significant current. They found a responsive audience among the newcomers and helped to link immigrants to local labour and socialist organisations.

Take, for example, Jewish immigrant cloakmaker Abraham Bisno, who was 20 years old during the massive national strike wave of 1886–87. One day, he heard the German anarchist August Spies[13] speak about class struggle, bosses and wage labour:

On that night when I went home I was aflame; the whole argument struck me like lightning and went all through me. I had heard ideas that I had never heard before in my life and they seemed to express the very thoughts that were in my inner consciousness…we are disinherited, the property of the country does belong to the rich; all we get out of it is a bare living for very hard work; there must be a chance to improve conditions; there are so many of us…we ought to all unite, all the working people from all trades.[14]

Some immigrants, as we have seen, were already experienced trade unionists or socialists. But those who had not previously been exposed to such ideas in Europe now had another opportunity.

"Fight together like mighty lions"

A capmakers' strike in 1874 and cigar makers' strike in 1877 were among early militant actions by Jewish workers in New York.[15]

Given their existing skills, the newcomers naturally gravitated to light industry, which was undergoing rapid expansion in the US at the time. Foremost was the garment industry, which covered a wide range of occupations, including men's and women's clothing, millinery and hats, neckwear and corsets. The last two decades of the 19th century saw production respond to urbanisation and the development of a national market by moving out of the household to the factories. The workforce surged from 39,000 in 1898 to 150,000 in 1905. By 1921, nearly three quarters of national clothing output was in New York.[16]

Occupations ranged from highly skilled, such as cutters, through semi-skilled sewing machine operators to a range of roles regarded as unskilled. Early in the period, skilled male tailors making suits and coats predominated; but, as manufacture of women's and children's clothing grew and mechanisation increased, employment of relatively unskilled women operatives expanded. They were generally very young—the majority under 25, and many only teenagers. The move from small workshops to an industrial structure laid the basis for organising efforts; the demand for union recognition was vital during the first two decades of the 20th century as initially local and spontaneous collective action grew to industry-wide dimensions.[17]

The main American trade union organisation, the American Federation of Labor (AFL), was craft based. It tended to stand aloof from unskilled workers, immigrants and women, and spearheaded the movement for restricted immigration, arguing for "racial purity" and exclusion of Italians, Japanese and others. In a clear combination of antisemitism and conservatism, the AFL was particularly hostile to "alien groups bearing the taint of European radicalism".[18] This was despite the fact that Sam Gompers, head of the AFL, was himself Jewish, as were many leaders and members.

Consequently, Jewish socialists and trade unionists in New York felt the AFL could not be relied upon; they looked to themselves. In 1888, they formed an umbrella organisation, the United Hebrew Trades (UHT), modelled after a similar grouping of German trade unions. Within two years, there were 22 affiliated union locals with predominantly Jewish memberships, especially within the garment industry. In 1910, the UHT had 61 unions with 65,000 members; in 1914, it had 104 unions with almost 250,000 members.[19]

At a time when unions in the US were dominated by white, skilled males, the UHT engaged with women, most importantly through the International Ladies' Garment Workers' Union (ILGWU), founded in 1900.[20] Another important member of the UHT was the Amalgamated Clothing Workers of America (ACW), founded in 1914, whose members made men's clothing. Many of its officers and members were socialists. Both these unions were industrial unions at a time when most were craft unions.

Not surprisingly, the AFL opposed the UHT, which it denounced as "a bogus labor body" that exerted "a disruptive socialistic influence upon American labor".[21]

The UHT was formed on the back of nearly constant unrest among Jewish workers in New York. Typical were strikes by knee-pants makers in 1890. At one point, police armed with clubs charged into a packed mass meeting which:

> turned into a terrible riot… A bold female striker treated a policeman to a ringing slap in the face, which caused a stir in all the New York newspapers.[22]

There were sometimes more personal reasons for striking, as one young woman indicated:

> Please brothers of the strike committee, do not allow my boss to sign the agreement until he also agrees in writing to stop his wife from beating me with a broom.[23]

Six months into a strike by 3,000 garment workers the same year, with funds virtually exhausted, the bosses attempted to divide the workers by offering male cutters a separate deal. When a mass meeting rejected this:

> The enthusiasm [to continue] was indescribable. Men and women jumped on the tables. Their voices could be heard ten blocks away.[24]

With donated watches and jewellery, the strike continued to a successful conclusion, including union recognition.[25]

These and other struggles inspired a Yiddish song by David Edelshtat, written in 1891 as a call to women workers to join in the struggle and "help build a temple of freedom, of human happiness". Popular in the US, it was also sung by striking workers in Russia and Poland:

Help us carry the red banner
Forward, through the storm, through dark nights!...

Help us raise the world from its squalor
To sacrifice everything we hold dear;
Fight together like mighty lions
For freedom, equality and our ideals![26]

The scale of struggle escalated dramatically in the 1890s. One massive year for the US labour movement was 1894, with the pivotal Pullman railway workers' strike and other major disputes. More than 12,000 tailors in New York State (4,000 in New York City) went on strike against sweatshop conditions and for a ten-hour day. Starting in September, they picketed through the autumn and winter, eventually gaining a partial victory. Although the employers soon reneged and the union was too weak to renew the struggle, this strike laid the foundation for many US labour laws today and led to the establishment of the September Labor Day public holiday.[27]

Bernard Weinstein gives a fascinating picture of how this early movement floundered and struggled, sometimes winning, more often failing, but building a culture and tradition of working-class resistance:

It sometimes happened that, by the time we decided to call a general strike in a certain trade, spontaneous strikes had already broken out at individual shops, because the workers couldn't take it any longer and wouldn't wait for a general strike. Strikers would often walk out and go to a beer hall, rent a meeting room, and then look for Jewish labor leaders, who did not have their own offices at the time. The Socialist union activists would come into the beer hall, ask the strikers for the details that had led to the strike, and organise the strike in an orderly fashion.[28]

But there was a snag:

Although it was easy to have Jewish workers go on strike, it was very difficult to actually win a strike...

The bosses would usually hire toughs, hoodlums [and the] police and the detectives would also beat up the strikers, drag them off to jail or to court, and frame them. The judges at that time were in cahoots with the pack of politicians from the East Side, so they obliged them by sentencing the strikers to months in the workhouse. In addition, the workers were very poor, so when they went on strike they had nothing to live on. When…they didn't have the money for the rent, the landlords would threaten to throw their furniture out on the street—and some actually did. You can well imagine what an awful responsibility it was for those organisers of the first Jewish unions and the strike leaders.[29]

The efforts of these socialists, trying to raise the consciousness of the masses of workers and help them to organise, are captured in another popular song from David Edelshtat, calling on workers to "recognise your own strength!":

> Awake!
> How long will you remain slaves
> And wear degrading chains?
> How long will you produce splendid riches
> For those who rob you of your bread?
> We must become free![30]

"Bravo, bravo, bravo, Jewish women!"

After the turn of the century, the locus of action moved into the community. Home and workplace were, in any case, very intertwined; outwork and sweatshops, peddlers and street shopfronts, seasonal work and a strong sense of community show how important it is to see the Jewish labour movement in New York primarily in terms of the class as a whole, not according to employment status.

The workplace militancy of the 1890s flowed into the meat boycotts and rent strikes of the first decade of the 20th century. Calling them "great folk struggles", the radical Yiddish-language newspaper *The Forward* drew attention to the links: "The meat strike was a child of the trade strikes…and the rent strike, in turn, comes from the same source".[31]

An increase in the retail price of kosher meat from 12 to 18 cents per pound in May 1902 outraged housewives. A poorly organised boycott by butchers caused Fanny Levy, the wife of a unionised cloakmaker, to respond, "This is their strike? Look at the good it has brought! Now, if we women make a strike, then it will be a strike".[32] She and another woman mobilised in the neighbourhood. A few days later, a crowd of 20,000 women set out. "They raided butcher's shops, tore the meat to pieces, flung some into ash barrels, and what they could not carry they sprinkled with kerosene".[33] One newspaper reported that "an excitable and aroused crowd [mostly of women] roamed the streets...armed with sticks, vocabularies and well-sharpened nails".[34]

Police arrested 85 people for disorderly conduct. The *Herald* reported that the women "were pushed and hustled about [by the police], thrown to the pavement...and trampled upon". The police didn't have it all their own way however—one woman retaliated by slapping a cop in the face with a moist piece of liver![35]

The Forward welcomed the protest with the headline, "Bravo, bravo, bravo, Jewish women!" By contrast, the *New York Times* called for the repression of this "dangerous class...especially the women [who] are very ignorant [and]...mostly speak a foreign language".[36]

When a magistrate asked one woman why they were rioting, she replied:

> We don't riot. But if all we did was to weep at home, nobody would notice it, so we have to do something to help ourselves.[37]

The mainstream press denounced the women as "a pack of wolves". The *New York Times* positively frothed at the mouth:

> The class of people...who are engaged in this matter have many elements of a dangerous class... The instant they take the law into their own hands, the instant they begin the destruction of property... They should be handled in a way that they can understand... Let the blow fall instantly and effectually... They did not get treatment nearly severe enough.[38]

Circulars in both English and Yiddish called upon consumers not to buy meat: "Patience will win the battle".[39] Although women in synagogues are supposed to be neither seen nor heard, a group stormed the podium during services and lectured the congregation on the boycott.[40]

The boycott spread to other towns. The *New York Times* screamed, "Brooklyn mob loots butcher shops. Rioters, led by women, wreck a dozen stores. Dance around bonfires of oil-drenched meat piled in the street—fierce fight with the police":

The mob ran through the street, howling in their peculiar Russian and Polish dialects, wrecking with stones and other missiles, every butcher's shop in their path.

[When the police arrived the] women threw bottles, stones and whatever they could place their hands on at the policemen. Women shook their fists in the faces of policemen and tore off their shields and buttons from their coats. There was a charge on the mob and night sticks were used freely.[41]

The boycotts drew in widespread participation, with perhaps 50,000 families abstaining from meat. After about three weeks, there was partial success: the price of meat was reduced to 14 cents per pound. Many of the women involved in these boycotts were the wives of union activists. Their daughters were involved in the major fights in the garment trades in 1909 and later. But, before that, they turned their attention to the other major cost of living—rent.

The great rent wars: 1904–8

With immense pressure on housing in the slums of the Lower East Side, landlords simply increased rent at will, hoping to exploit the downtrodden and submissive foreigners. In 1904, they were to be disappointed. Following rent increases of 20-30 percent, protest spread "like an angry wave". The Jewish newspaper *The Forward* declared, "this strike can be as great as the meat strikes" and advised Jewish housewives "to take the rent question into their hands as they did the meat question".[42]

Many of the tenant activists were garment workers and socialists. Class consciousness is evident even in the language they used—words such as strike, scab and calling their associations tenants' unions. *The Forward* editor Abe Cahan commented:

The trade union movement in the Jewish quarter has been growing apace… The spirit which impels one to struggle for his rights, to combat robbery, has imbedded itself in the hearts of our workingmen… This is the case with the present rent strikes. They are the outcome of the same spirit, the offspring of that same struggle against Capital.[43]

As with the meat boycotts, women were the main activists. They discussed strategy at meetings, picketed buildings, organised building-level tenant unions and campaigned through the neighbourhood:

> Local Jewish women…began the rent strike and through their efforts and enthusiasm, they spread it. Through their strength, even the blackest strike was won and without their remarkable activities, the strike would not have been possible.[44]

Within weeks, tenant protest had grown so large that the Lower East Side was "seething with activity and protest".[45]

This first strike did achieve some success in preventing rent increases and evictions, although the formal organisations could not be sustained. Rent strikes occurred over the next several years, coming to a climax with the "greatest rent wars" that New York City had seen, from December 1907 to January 1908. Led by 16-year-old Pauline Newman, the strike involved 10,000 families in Lower Manhattan and is remarkable for the way it combined women factory workers and neighbourhood networks of housewives. Support from the Socialist Party meant that this strike was also better organised.[46]

Strikers hung their landlords in effigy and flew red flags (actually petticoats dyed red) from windows. Landlords hit back by shutting off water, and magistrates issued several thousand eviction notices, saying that a "rent strike cannot be entertained as an excuse for not paying rent". This time, there was much more violence, with the police forcibly disbanding gatherings.[47]

The strike spread to Brooklyn, Harlem and Newark (New Jersey). While strikers received support from socialist unions, the members of the "Hebrew local" of the Teamsters Union refused to dispossess striking tenants. On the other hand, the mainstream media were generally unsupportive. The *American Hebrew*, a middle-class Jewish newspaper, criticised the rent strikers for "not acting wisely" and called the strike "a typical example of how not to do things".[48]

Most accounts of the rent strikes conclude that they failed. In terms of their immediate goals, the outcome was very limited; but, viewing them as part of the larger picture, we can see how the community-based action and workplace militancy fed off and reinforced each other. Working-class people gained experience and the confidence to take action. American socialist and feminist Rose Pastor Stokes commented,

"The fight itself must result in great good. It makes [the tenants] conscious of the common interests of their class, this fighting together".[49]

As so often happens in the class struggle, participants learnt lessons and took them into the next struggle. The issue of housing and rent strikes did not go away. Rent strikers in the 1930s no doubt had memories of the pre-First World War tenants' actions and this has in fact been a recurring theme in New York's working-class history right up to recent times.[50]

The waistmakers' revolt: 1909

The very year after the 1908 rent strike, the fight returned to the workplace.

The most important sector of women's garment production was the manufacture of shirtwaists, a type of blouse worn by the rapidly increasing numbers of women office workers in the early 20th century. Five hundred shirtwaist factories in New York employed approximately 30,000 workers at the time of the strike. The workforce was 80 percent young women between 16 and 25, most unmarried. Most of the employers were Jewish.[51]

Although production was in factories, conditions were no better than in the sweatshops. All sorts of mean devices reduced pitifully low wages even further. Workers paid for their own needles, for electric power and even for the boxes they sat on. Bosses used fines and tricks to avoid paying for all the work done. The work day could be up to 20 hours, and the women were subjected to personal humiliations. One of them said, "In the shops we don't have names, we have numbers".[52]

Momentum for strike action built through 1908. The rent strikes stoked militancy, and Pauline Newman and other garment workers went around workplaces building support for action. Walkouts and confrontations over issues such as piece rates became increasingly frequent.

A large parade on 8 May 1908 was part of the campaign. Socialists chose the date to honour an 1857 demonstration of New York garment workers, which police had attacked and dispersed. The 1908 march of 15,000 women garment workers demanded better pay, shorter hours, voting rights and an end to child labour. It was so successful that the Socialist Party declared an annual Women's Day, with the first occurring in 1909. The famous German socialist Clara Zetkin, inspired by this idea, proposed the establishment of an International Working Women's Day in 1910. This was celebrated for the first time in March of the following year, with rallies of more than a million men and women in many countries. Thus, when we celebrate International Women's Day today, we can trace its roots back to the women garment workers of New York in 1857 and 1908-9.[53]

The period of intensifying conflict came to a head in September 1909. Variously known as the Uprising of the 20,000 or 30,000 or even 40,000, the industry-wide strike of New York shirtwaist workers in 1909 is an icon of American women's labour history. It was the largest strike by female workers in the US up to that time and has been called "women's most significant struggle for unionism in the nation's history".[54] It is also one of the most significant events of the US Jewish labour movement.

The participants were approximately 21,000 Russian Jewish women, 6,000 Jewish men, 2,000 Italian women and approximately 1,000 who were born in the US. The Jewish women were the militant core of the strike.

The battle started when the Triangle Waist Company locked out their entire workforce of 500 over union membership. The Waistmakers Local of the ILGWU, in a parlous state at the start of the strike with approximately 100 members and $4 in the treasury, started an organising drive. For a month, picketers endured attacks from police and thugs, with dozens fined or sentenced to the workhouse.

Then came a critical mass meeting at which a well-known incident occurred. After two hours of lukewarm speeches from union officials, five-foot tall Clara Lemlich, who had already been on strike for 11 weeks and had just returned from hospital after a brutal beating, was lifted on to the stage where she made an impassioned speech in Yiddish:

> I have listened to all the speakers, and I have no further patience for talk. I am one who feels and suffers from the things pictured. I move we go on a general strike.[55]

Phillip Foner, a leading historian of the US labour movement, describes the response:

> Instantly, the crowd was on its feet—adult women, men and teenagers—cheering, stamping, crying approval. [The chairman] called for a vote.

Three thousand voices shouted their unanimous approval, waving hats, handkerchiefs, and other objects.[56]

The union secretary was astonished by the reaction to the strike call:

I shall never again see such a sight. Out of every shirtwaist factory…the workers poured and the halls…were quickly filled.[57]

So overwhelming was the response that confusion reigned for the first few days. "Women walked out of shops uncertain where to go or what to do".[58]

About half of the employers settled quickly, but the rest formed an association and "declared open war against the union". They recruited scabs and played the race card by "exploiting Jewish and Italian antagonisms" and keeping Black workers on the job where possible. But their major strategy was brute force, arrests and convictions. Magistrates told picketers that they would get what was coming to them and handed out sentences of weeks of hard labour for minor offences such as yelling "scab".[59] One magistrate told a "group of bruised and bleeding girls":

You are on strike against God and nature, whose prime law is that man shall earn his bread in the sweat of his brow.[60]

George Bernard Shaw's famous comment on this was "Delightful. Medieval America is always in the most intimate personal confidence of the Almighty".[61]

That winter of 1909–10 was exceptionally cold and snowy. Although there were men in the strike, the women did most of the picketing, hoping that the police would be a bit easier on them.[62] But the "gorillas", as the strikers called them, who attacked the picketers had no mercy. And the employers had no end of devices. One company hired sex workers to join the thugs. One woman picketer:

was arrested for speaking to one of [the sex workers]. The officer pinched her arm black and blue as he dragged [her] to court…

The hiring of women thugs ended dramatically. Six of them attacked two young pickets, threw them to the ground and beat them until their faces streamed with blood… [This] was too much to endure and the whole street [all the factories on the block] went on sympathetic strike. In less than two days the prostitutes were removed.[63]

The struggle galvanised the whole left, and there was extensive support action, including from the UHT. The Women's Trade Union League, an organisation of middle-class women which provided legal help and publicity, extended the support network into suffragist circles.[64] The campaign climax was an enormous rally at Carnegie Hall.

Some accounts emphasise the inter-ethnic conflicts but the Jewish strike leaders made a conscious effort to engage other language groups:

> The initial response of young Italian women to the call for picketing was strong. But the bosses put enormous pressure on these strikers… In one instance, Jewish manufacturers…brought an Italian Catholic priest in to tell striking women that they would go to hell if they continued to strike.[65]

Unionists responded by holding Italian language meetings and social events. But perhaps even more important was the fact that these women had brought their own culture of struggle from Italy.

The relationship with the small number of Black women is also interesting. According to historian Daniel Katz, Mary White Ovington, a white socialist who cofounded the National Association for the Advancement of Colored People, noted how friendly the young Jewish women were to Black co-workers, and the strikers consciously reached out to the Black people of Brooklyn.[66]

This strike has become a major benchmark in US labour history, particularly as an example of unskilled women surging into struggle, and has inspired generations of clothing workers and others. The strike had a strongly Jewish presence, but as we have noted, many other ethnic groups were drawn in. Its international character is also remarkable. One socialist publication called it the "Strike of the Singers of Shirts", a reference to an 1843 poem by the English poet Thomas Hood that was popular among Russian revolutionaries.[67]

The strike officially ended in February 1910 with partial success—339 shops settled with the union, 19 remained open. Over 300 shops had achieved most of their demands.[68]

"But we'll fight as hard as we can to win strong union victory"

The struggle had an enormous impact on workers in other trades around them:

Hail the waistmakers of nineteen-nine
Making their stand on the picket line,
Breaking the power of those who reign,
Pointing the way, smashing the chain.
And we gave new courage to the men
Who carried through in nineteen-ten
And shoulder to shoulder we'll win through
Led by the ILGWU.[69]

Inspired by the shirtwaist workers, 60,000 cloak and suitmakers walked off the job in July 1910.

This time, most of the strikers were men. The strike was well prepared and planned, a key factor being the work done beforehand among the Italian workers, who constituted about one third of the labour force in the sector. Having been involved in all stages of preparation, the Italians joined the Jewish workers on strike.

Again, police protected thugs who terrorised the strikers, and magistrates fined and sentenced picketers. But the workers defied injunctions with mass picketing and an enormous demonstration against "judicial tyranny" supported by the Socialist Party. After nine weeks of bitter struggle, an agreement gave important gains in wages, hours and conditions but failed to deliver the closed shop.[70]

The movement moved to yet another sector in 1912. Furriers worked between 56 and 60 hours a week in "filthy, disease-breeding sweatshops, usually located in ancient, broken-down wooden tenements or in basements":

In one or two small rooms, without even a pretense of ventilation, about twenty fur workers would labor. Stairs, hallways, rooms, and closets were packed with dust-saturated fur pieces and cuttings. Stench and dust blanketed everything. Hair, dust and poisonous dyes ate at the workers' eyes, noses, skin, and lungs as they toiled at the bench or machine.[71]

A strike of furriers in 1904 had collapsed because of the union's failure to organise the Jewish workers. A subsequent organising drive by the UHT laid the basis for a major struggle. The strike call, printed in red and known as the "red special", was posted on 20 June 1912 and brought out 10,000 strikers, three quarters of whom were Jewish. The battle of the "Fighting Furriers" was long and bitter. Within three weeks, the union's funds were virtually exhausted; but the strikers were not:

> Women pickets marched around the buildings that housed the fur shops, carrying signs in Yiddish and English that read: "Masters! Starvation is your weapon. We are used to starving. We will fight on 'til victory!"[72]

Once again, gangsters and police attacked picketers, with more than 800 arrests and 215 serious injuries.

The leader of the 2,000 women strikers was Jewish-Russian Esther Polansky, who was legendary among the strikers for her militancy:

> She never stopped before any danger. This the workers appreciated so much that not only did she win their admiration but also their willingness to sacrifice if she ordered them to do so.[73]

After 13 weeks, the furriers gained a major victory, winning nearly all their demands—including union recognition. *The Forward* declared, "The power of unity and solidarity triumphed over the power of money, the power of police attacks and hunger and want".[74]

At the end of 1912, inspired by the waistmakers, cloakmakers and furriers, workers in the men's clothing sector voted overwhelmingly for a general strike. By one week into 1913, more than 100,000 workers were on strike in the largest of the series in the garment industry. The majority were Jewish, the second-largest group Italians, and one third of the total were women. *The Forward* reported that the vitality of the Italians "was wonderful, their energy is simply incredible, their devotion exceeds everything".[75]

Describing a parade of workers in one factory heading to their strike headquarters, *The Forward* reported:

> Here there went arm in arm an old Jew with a young Italian. A little farther on there marched an old Italian worker, gesticulating to the young Jewish worker who was his partner on the line.[76]

An astonishingly large picketing committee of 10,000 strikers led mass picketing. Again, there were insufficient funds, it was freezing, and the picketers faced the daily ferocity of scabs, thugs and police:[77]

Blood flowed freely, skulls were cracked, ribs were broken, eyes black-
ened, teeth knocked out and many persons were otherwise wounded in
a brutal assault on the garment strikers and pickets.[78]

Again, magistrates supported the manufacturers. There were hundreds of arrests. Eventually, the union president bypassed the rank
and file and settled. This sellout meant that this was the only one
of the garment industry strikes not to achieve at least some form of
union recognition.[79]

The struggles heated up even further in 1913 as many sections of
the garment industry went out in what Foner calls "tremendous labor
uprisings".[80] At one point, more than 150,000 workers were on strike
at the same time, with disputes among men's tailors and a range of
women's clothing workers. "The local needle industries have been
practically paralysed by one of the most gigantic and general uprisings
which Greater New York has ever witnessed", declared one newspaper.[81]

Early in the year, in one of the biggest parades ever in the city, up to
80,000 strikers in the men's and boys' garment industry marched through
Manhattan and Brooklyn to protest against police and thug brutality:

> One of the remarkable features of the parade was the number of nation-
> alities represented. Workers from 15 countries were pointed out and
> they all marched shoulder to shoulder, seemingly on the best of terms.[82]

Meanwhile, militant disputes continued in the women's garment
industry, including a walkout of 7,000 teenage girls who made under-
wear and had the worst conditions and were the most poorly paid. The
bosses added a new tactic to the usual attacks:

> Into the battle came the gangsters' "molls". They filled their pocketbooks
> with stones, and when a skirmish began, they swung their loaded bags
> against the pickets' heads. They also carried concealed scissors, and at
> an opportune moment they would cut the strikers' long braided hair.[83]

But the pickets fought back. When a boss threatened a young picketer, she retaliated:

> I gave the boss such a smash with my umbrella that it flew into two
> pieces. He was so surprised he fell down... I was arrested, but I was so
> little and he so big and fat, the Judge said "Go on home," and he let me

off. And from that day he [the boss] found out he was fighting with someone who wasn't afraid.[84]

To give themselves strength, the 15-year-old girls sang:

> *We're getting beaten by policemen,*
> *With their heavy clubs of hickory,*
> *But we'll fight as hard as we can*
> *To win "Strong Union Victory".*[85]

The strikers may have been uneducated young women, but they articulated very clearly to interviewers why they were prepared to fight so hard. "My heart and soul is just with the union. It makes you feel so big instead of like a piece of dirt in the world", said one. Another said that, when she had lived in Russia, she had believed that there was liberty in America:

> [B]ut now I know the workers must fight for liberty in this country, too. It's the same fight everywhere. In Russia it is the Czar. In America it is the boss and the boss's money.[86]

By the end of that year, every branch of the women's garment industry in New York had an agreement with the ILGWU, and women had become members in unprecedented numbers. Between 1910 and 1913, union membership in the garment industry increased by 66,000, a 68 percent increase. This was greater even than miners with their 60 percent increase.[87]

"We gathered to make revolution": socialists and the American Jewish labour movement

Dwellings in the working-class areas of New York were small and were often simultaneously workshops; social life centred on the streets and so did much of political life, as it had in Russia. According to an article in the *New York Times*, "The Jews talk and walk in their several districts" and New York "is the talkiest city in the world":[88]

> Little groups of [people] dot the sidewalk all Summer long, strolling up and down, discussing art, literature, drama, Socialism, Anarchy, woman's suffrage, child labor…

The rich man has his clubs in which he may discuss Wall Street...
The clubless poor man has the streets wherein to talk of wages and that
part of the social structure which concerns him and his.[89]

Union Square was the locals' mecca:

We gathered to make revolution and stayed to talk. And how we talked—
anarchism, atheism, against the military, for birth control, against
injustice, for socialism, for the rights of workers to organise.

Up to 20,000 people would gather there, over "almost any issue". A
demonstration in the square was "a holiday, an escape from the long
hours of drudgery and the grim realities of a dull, crowded tenement
life". The rallies were:

frequently preceded by scores of community meetings, a clustering around
street corners...the heart of the assembly was that of the labor force,
working people, registering their awareness of the troubles of the world. [90]

Cafés also provided places to meet and talk. The Café Metropole in
downtown New York was a hub for East Side intelligentsia:

They gossiped and chattered; but most of all they argued. They sat at
their tables consuming enormous quantities of Russian tea and lemon
and stared and were...stared at in turn.

Men and women of every conceivable political complexion gathered
here: single taxers, Marxists, Veblenites, Revisionists, Kropotkinites,
Fabians, syndicalists and pacifists. They sat throughout the night
destroying and reconstructing entire social systems.[91]

One person who frequented the Metropole in early 1917 was Trotsky:

a man with an unusually broad and high forehead topped by a tempestuous shock of black hair. Behind the thick lenses of his pince-nez flashed
eyes of magnetic and restless power.[92]

Although Trotsky insisted that his being Jewish was of no importance,
in New York he moved in Jewish circles, addressed Jewish audiences and
frequented their cafés. He also wrote for *The Forward* until a dispute
about US entry into the First World War put an end to the alliance.
Historian Tony Michels suggests Trotsky's Jewish activism was because

"the Left and the Jews were so thoroughly enmeshed that one could not necessarily discern where one ended and the other began".[93]

Jews formed the backbone of New York socialism at a time when the Jewish labour movement reached mass proportions in the period before the First World War. It encompassed trade unions, political parties and welfare organisations and was active across the country but centred in New York. At its high point in 1914, the socialist-led UHT had a membership of a quarter of a million. We have already seen the importance of Jewish unionists in the garment trades. The Workmen's Circle (*Arbeter Ring*), a welfare body which aided striking unions and socialist causes and had 87,000 members at its peak, eventually came under the control of the Bund.[94]

Newspapers were also a crucial means of communication in the days before electronic media. The most important Yiddish-language newspaper was *The Forward* (*Forverts*), later *The Jewish Daily Forward*. Started in 1897 by a group of about 50 socialists, its name and political orientation were based on the German Social Democratic Party and its organ *Vorwärts*. Politically close to the Bund, it was one of the first national newspapers in the US. It had more readers than any other Yiddish daily in the world or socialist daily in the country, with a circulation of more than 275,000 in the 1920s.[95] It was the "primary voice of Jewish immigrant Socialism".[96]

With all this talking and writing, the languages used are significant. Yiddish was crucial to the mass struggles in New York up to the First World War and gave the struggles there a unique flavour. The early immigrant agitators had spoken German or Russian; but, in 1882, Abraham Cahan asked organisers of a workers' meeting:

[W]hy they did not use the language of the people they were trying to reach. The radicals laughed at the thought and contemptuously suggested that he try it himself.

A week later, in a packed meeting room, Cahan explained the Marxist theory of surplus value in Yiddish. Bernard Weinstein, who was to become secretary of the United Hebrew Trades…later wrote in his memoirs that this was the first time he really understood the doctrine of Socialism.[97]

Apart from formal organisations:

an untold number of individuals marched in parades, participated in rent strikes and consumer boycotts, crowded around soapboxes, and flocked to celebrations and fund-raisers for one cause or another.[98]

Outside their own community, many Jews were members of, or supported, American socialist organisations. The main socialist party in the late 19th century was the Socialist Labor Party and later the Socialist Party. In New York, between 1908 and 1912, 39 percent of the Socialist Party were Jews; in 1904, 60 percent of the New York Jewish electorate voted for its candidates.[99]

Anarchism was another important current, Emma Goldman being a prominent example. As in the UK, the anarchists were busy attacking religion, and their parties on Yom Kippur (Jewish Day of Atonement, the most important religious festival where fasting for 24 hours was required) were famous: "Revellers danced, ate, drank, sang revolutionary songs, and performed skits, all in a gesture of contempt for Jewish religious practice".[100]

The immigrants retained strong international links. "Organisations, publications, individuals, and ideas moved from country to country, following Jewish migration patterns".[101] New Yorkers contributed to revolutionary activities in Russia by sending money and thousands of publications. During the 1905 Russian Revolution, for example, American Bundists raised $5,000 each week for several months.[102] This all reinforced the ties between Jewish and non-Jewish socialists and labour movement activists across national boundaries.

The period of open immigration came to an end with the First World War and the passage of restrictive laws in 1921 and 1924. But, during the four decades of mass immigration, the Jewish labour movement in the US established patterns, standards and ideas which endured in the subsequent decades. Although, by the postwar generation, New York Jews spoke English, Yiddish remained an active language for decades, and the garment industry and its Jewish workers remained a major focal point for socialism and working-class struggle.

Roaring and battling: interwar United States

The year 1919 saw mass working-class struggle in the US. An article in *The Nation* commented:

> The most extraordinary phenomenon of the present time…is the unprecedented revolt of the rank and file.[1]

This revolt expressed itself in a country-wide strike wave including four regional general strikes and masses of local ones. Immediate issues such as inflation and the rising cost of living were coupled with rising expectations for the post-war world after the privations of the war, and above all the example of the revolution in Russia.[2] When a police strike in Boston led to looting and minor disorders, the *Wall Street Journal* proclaimed, "Lenin and Trotsky are on their way".[3]

New York was no minor participant in this mass movement, with many of the Jewish-dominated industries playing a major role:

> In a small way New York City has lately been through a general labor crisis. To unemployment, daily growing more acute, have been added strikes following one another in rapid succession. [Men's clothing workers] after several months of struggle, have won a substantial victory…the 44-hour week. The hotel workers are still on strike and 8,000 furriers have voted to go out… The most immediate and crucial symptom…is the strike of some 35,000 ladies' garment workers for a 44-hour week, a 15 percent increase in wages and permission [for] a representative of the union to visit the shops once a month.[4]

During the great steel strike of this year, Jewish garment unions contributed $175,000. This was not only an enormous sum, but was half of the total given by all unions in the country.[5]

But the AFL looked in a different direction, pushing a no-strike

policy and a corporatist strategy orientated to labour banks and investment houses known in the US at the time as New Unionism.[6] Most
of the major strikes of 1919 were defeated, setting the tone for the
new decade.

The Roaring Twenties

It is a widely held view that society enjoyed "general prosperity during
the golden perfection of the boom days of the 1920s".[7] The Roaring
Twenties was a decade "characterized by economic prosperity, rapid
social and cultural change, and a mood of exuberant optimism" in
which the US was transformed into a global economic power, and the
"economy continued to accelerate" due to electrification, the advent of
mass production methods such as the assembly line and the increased
use of cars. "The technological and manufacturing boom ushered in a
modern consumer culture".[8]

We are expected to believe that this was a time of generalised afflu-
ence, of capitalism functioning well and in the interests of the mass
of the population.

But this fantasy does not reflect the reality for many living through
the "Golden Twenties". In 1929, the richest year up till then in all US
history, almost 60 percent of the population did not receive sufficient
income to buy the basic necessities of life.[9] Foreign born and Black
workers received about half the average wage of white American-born
workers. Together the two groups "did the hardest work for the least
pay...while living in the worst housing".[10]

Of course, prosperity for the upper echelons was predicated on
keeping the working class subjugated. The government, employers
and the union officials of the AFL joined in an unholy alliance aimed
at stamping out working-class combativity. Promulgating the slogan
"Not Marx but Ford"[11] they used an eclectic strategy: a combination
of red scare, moves to drive the unions out of workplaces, increasing
bureaucratisation and gangsterism in the union movement, speedup
and piecework. Al Capone, whose underworld was as much a business
as any other, said, "Bolshevism is knocking at our gates... We must
keep the worker away from red literature and red ruses".[12] William
Green, president of the AFL, declared strikes were outmoded and

the head of the Locomotive Engineers Bank of New York declared, "Who wants to be a Bolshevik when he can be a capitalist instead?".[13]

It is not surprising that all these pro- and proto-capitalists referenced Marx and Bolshevism. The successful workers' revolution in Russia had an enormous impact on US political life. As well as putting the frighteners on the capitalists, it shook up the labour movement, transformed the political landscape on the left, and set the government in motion to attempt to head off the threat. The "Red Scare", a wave of rampant anti-radicalism and nativism, swept the country.

Linking immigration and radicalism, the government claimed that foreign communists and anarchists were plotting to overthrow the government and in the Palmer raids of 1919–20 they arrested 10,000 radicals with the utmost brutality and held them in virtual concentration camp conditions. Ultimately 556 foreign-born were deported, among them many Russian Jews, including Emma Goldman, Alexander Berkman and Mollie Steimer.

Despite a public backlash the raids largely served their real purpose: they frightened people, dampened militancy and weakened union activism. The real target of the raids was homegrown radicalism: workers' demands such as "union recognition, shorter hours, higher wages, regulation of child labour and the wages and hours of women and children in industry".[14] The burgeoning tenant movement in New York also became the target of widespread red-baiting and harassment in the courts and on the picket line.[15] And Jews were inextricably linked with radicalism. "Socialism had made Jews more conspicuous, so much so that many people viewed it as a specifically Jewish trait".[16]

Following on from the anti-foreign scare, legislation limited immigration dramatically in 1924. What became known as the Johnson-Reed Act barred the entry of Asians and set country quotas to reflect the American population of 1890, when there were low numbers of Eastern Europeans, Italians, and Jews. This same act was later used to limit admission of refugees from the Holocaust.[17]

It was a seminal moment. A *New York Times* headline declared "America of the melting pot comes to an end".[18]

This then was the environment that the US labour movement and Jewish radicals inherited after the First World War.

The Jewish community

Most sources on the topic of the Jewish community in this period harp on the same theme—how Jews moved "upward in status, but also outward beyond the ghettos".[19] In so doing they supposedly abandoned their working-class and immigrant roots and in acclimatising themselves to American life also left their supposed outdated radicalism behind. For example, ex-communist William Herberg maintains that early Jewish radicalism was simply the result of "the dreadful anomy of early immigrant life" and disappeared as Jews moved upward in society. "Originally almost entirely proletarian in composition, they became with the years increasingly middle class, reflecting the de-proletarianisation of the Jewish workers".[20]

Rachel Cohen castigates this "rags-to-riches tale of rising up the economic ladder", whereby Jews are all supposed to have embraced the American dream.[21] Radical Jewish historian Tony Michels comments that "in the success story that American Jewish history has become, the radical experience has been made irrelevant".[22]

One objection to this type of analysis is that "middle class" is used with typical looseness. In fact, white-collar workers such as teachers and office workers are a very important component of the modern working class. Another is the almost universal underlying distinction between "foreign born" and "American", an oxymoron if ever there was one in a society built on immigration, but a term which serves the purpose of emphasising differences and redirecting working-class attention away from class.

While there were indisputably social and geographical changes among the second generation of Jews as they learned English and became acculturated, there was no universal class transformation and abandonment of radicalism. The immigration flow which had partly fuelled the pre-war radicalism paused during the First World War but resumed after it. Between 1919 and 1924 more than a quarter of a million Jews arrived, predominantly from Russia and the new Eastern European states, wracked as they were with civil war and conflict. As had happened after the 1905 Russian Revolution, many of these new immigrants had participated in revolutionary movements.

As one union official noted:

The great majority of them come from Russia; a large number of them have been engaged at home in fighting autocracy, in fighting ukases [decrees] of the Czar.[23]

This brought a revival of the radicalism associated with the Jewish communities, most of all the garment unions, which "kept these organisations politically astir with their radical activities and rhetoric for years afterward".[24]

And another wave of Jewish immigration occurred in the late 1930s as Jews fled fascism in Europe, with a peak of 43,450 in 1939, and this again contributed to continuing radicalism in the community in the US.[25]

Certainly, some Jewish radicals left their early convictions behind as they developed new careers and dedicated their skills to personal achievement and right-wing politics. But the Jewish communities which were the basis of the earlier radicalism did not in fact disappear as they became "Americanised". In any case, the onset of the Depression largely put a halt to the movement into the middle class with many losing jobs and homes.[26]

Poverty, activism, political passions and struggle continued to mark the Jewish labour movement in the interwar period just as it had earlier on.

One very significant current was the group that later became known as the New York intellectuals. This group of writers, with a largely Jewish composition, became famous for its literary innovation. For our purposes, however, these writers are more important for their attempt to build an anti-Stalinist Marxist alternative to the CP in the 1930s. The Jewish component was crucial. Starting out in the 1920s with the aim of building a Jewish cultural movement, they "found themselves propelled first toward Communism and then toward Trotskyism",[27] as they shed ambivalence about their ethnic background and moved towards a revolutionary universalist internationalism under the impact of the Depression. They were heavily influenced by Trotsky:

Trotskyism made it possible for these rebellious intellectuals to declare themselves on the side of the revolution…and yet also to denounce Stalin from the left as the arch betrayer of Lenin's heritage.[28]

They included figures such as Elliot Cohen, Lionel Trilling, Herbert Solow, George Novack, Max Shachtman and many others. Alan Ward emphasises that by 1933, the intellectuals were dissident communists, not socialists or liberals.[29] Shachtman for instance was a leading member of the CP in the 1920s; by the 1930s he was a leading political figure of the New York intellectuals.

One member of the group, Maurice Hindus, argued that "Jews had a predisposition to radicalism that stemmed from their ancient heritage, a predisposition that could be stimulated by certain conditions".[30]

Wald makes an interesting comment on the application of this observation:

> The pattern of radicalisation among Jewish intellectuals in the United States appears to be halfway between the eastern European and western European models. In Russia and Poland, where anti-Semitism was the official state policy and the majority of Jews tended to be workers and paupers, there was a massive movement of Jewish intellectuals into labor, revolutionary, and socialist movements of all types. In England and France, where anti-Semitism was not official and where there had been a considerable integration of Jews into the middle and upper classes since the eighteenth and nineteenth centuries, the Jewish intelligentsia tended to be liberal, conformist, and, at best, moderately reformist; radical intellectuals were relatively exceptional.[31]

Wald notes that in the US, the intellectuals were neither outcasts nor deeply embedded, and that the interwar years:

> were marked by potentially radicalising factors, such as the existence of a substantial Jewish working class and the persistence of a virulent anti-Semitism. Thus all wings of the radical movement in the United States experienced a considerable influx of Jewish intellectuals in the 1930s.[32]

Wald goes on to point out that Jews could be found in many of the political currents of the time. But this does not remove their importance for radicals and the anti-Stalinist revolutionary movement of the period. New York is the only place in the world where large numbers of intellectuals went over to revolutionary socialism and Trotskyism (as opposed to Stalinism). The fact that they were Jewish is relevant here—their opposition to Stalinism was rooted in the disaster of the

Comintern's Third Period politics, which was a major factor in the rise of the Nazis in Germany.[33]

Zionism was not an important political current in the US until after the Second World War. Before 1914 there was very little support and most Jewish organisations were either lukewarm or openly opposed. By 1917 the American Zionist movement had 200,000 members nationally, very small compared to the proportion of Jews in the various socialist organisations. Although the official goal of the Zionists was the establishment of a state in Palestine, the main focus of activity was philanthropy within the US Jewish community and welfare projects for the Jews in Palestine itself. Thoroughly settled in the US, Zionists there had to make up a new way of being a Zionist, "a Zionism for the Jew who would never live in Palestine".[34]

That the movement was essentially middle class can be seen by the women's organisation Hadassah, which was modelled on "a heritage of Jewish philanthropy as well as upon the charitable and organisational model provided by the US women's club movement of the Progressive Era". There was nothing radical about this movement. "The humanitarian and social concerns these organisations addressed were viewed as logical public extensions of traditional female domestic responsibilities".[35]

Given the lack of a strong political goal relevant to most US Jews, it is perhaps not surprising that Zionism remained a minor current in the broader community. Given they were middle class, conservative and conventional they certainly had little appeal to working-class Jews. By the 1930s, national membership had shrunk to a mere 13,000 and even by 1941 was still only 46,000.[36]

The Battle of the Bronx

By the 1930s, new concentrations of Eastern European Jews had grown up in boroughs of New York outside Manhattan such as Brooklyn, the Bronx and Williamsburg. But the movement out of the Lower East Side did not automatically lead to the end of the old living conditions.

Irving Howe gives an impression of what these neighbourhoods were like:

The East Bronx…formed a thick tangle of streets crammed with Jewish immigrants from Eastern Europe, almost all of them poor. We lived in narrow, five story tenements, wall flush against wall… There was never enough space [and] the apartments in the buildings were packed with relatives and children, many of them fugitives from unpaid rent. Those tenements had first gone up during the early years of the century, and if not so grimy as those of the Lower East Side in Manhattan or the Brownsville section of Brooklyn, they were bad enough… Hardly a day passed but someone was moving in or out. Often you could see a family's entire belongings: furniture, pots, bedding, a tricycle, piled upon the sidewalks because they had been dispossessed.[37]

The Jews that moved out of Manhattan took the pre-war radical networks and affiliations with them. Many had grown up in environments in which "socialism and trade unionism provided models…and more than a few had extensive activist backgrounds, whether in bitter garment strikes in New York City or clandestine revolutionary struggle in Europe".[38]

The onset of the Depression hit the community hard, causing wage cuts, job losses and evictions, but they "were not about to sink quietly into poverty and despair".[39] No doubt many remembered the Lower East Side tenants' struggles of 25 years before. They were a potentially receptive audience for the new orientation of the Communist Party.

A Comintern directive of February 1930 called for "mass revolutionary actions of the proletariat—strikes, demonstrations, etc". Communists were now expected to go on the offensive and "fight for the streets".[40] In the eight months ending June 1932, 185,794 families in New York City were served with dispossession notices, with a similar pattern throughout the country.[41] The Unemployed Councils founded by the Communist Party USA (CPUSA) included a strategy to "develop mass struggles against…evictions".[42]

The campaign of rent strikes and resistance to evictions in 1932, which became known as the Battle of the Bronx, "perplexed and enraged landlords and city officials".[43] The first wave of evictions resulted in a "rent riot" involving over 4,000 people, with tenants posted on the roofs and at the windows of buildings and supporters ready outside. They fought the police with "fists, stones and sticks" accompanied by chants against the police, the landlords and capitalism in general. The *New York Times* noted that "the women were the most militant"—they were the majority of the crowds, the arrests and of those fighting the police.[44]

When a landlord gave in, the crowd "promptly began chanting the Internationale and waving their copies of the *Daily Worker*".[45]

In the Bronx alone tenants in more than 200 buildings went on strike.[46] The campaign was for a time quite successful with nearly half of dispossessed families in New York (77,000) moving back into their homes.[47] Activists organised "electric squads" and "gas squads", which became expert at reconnecting cut off electricity or gas lines:[48]

> Using the networks they possessed in fraternal organisations, women's clubs, and left wing trade unions, aided by younger comrades from the high schools and colleges, Communists were able to mobilise formidable support for buildings that were on strike and to force police to empty out the station houses to carry out evictions.[49]

Subsequent waves of evictions saw many thousands of protestors confronting the police and numerous arrests and injuries:

> The police have set up a temporary police station outside one of the buildings. Cops patrol the street all day. The entire territory is under semi-martial law. People are driven around the streets, off the corners, and away from the houses.[50]

But overall gains were limited as the landlords were organised and had considerable ties with the authorities and political and legal influence.

During the second campaign in the winter of 1932–33, the battles were even more ferocious. "News of the impending eviction…spread like wildfire", wrote one newspaper:

> Jeers and epithets were hurled at the police as they were jostled, shoved and manhandled… A woman tenant appeared on a fire escape and screamed to the crowd to do something. This time, the efforts of Sergeant Maloney and his small force were unavailing… For more than an hour, the battle raged. Policemen were scratched, bitten, kicked and their uniforms torn. Many of the strike sympathisers received

rough handling and displayed the scars of battle when order was again restored.[51]

Women were again at the forefront of the affray:

> When the police went for the men, the women rushed to protect them… While the men were busy looking for work, the women were on the job.
>
> On the day of the evictions we would tell all the men to leave the building. We knew that the police were rough and would beat them up. It was the women who remained in the apartments, in order to resist. We went out onto the fire escapes and spoke through bullhorns to the crowd gathered below.[52]

Although a majority of participants in this second wave were Jewish (based on names of evicted tenants and arrested protestors), there were also Italians and other ethnic groups, but "despite the foreign accents and sectarian slogans the movement had considerable force". With rent strikes and even the threat of strikes, the campaign won substantial reductions in rent. As one landlord complained, "the entire East Bronx is full of fire". Another compared the movement to a flu epidemic and complained that "some landlords have been forced to reduce their rent a number of times".[53]

While the militancy was fierce and the demonstrators committed, the CP's Third Period tactic of excluding any alliance with reformists, and thus reducing participation by working-class people who followed reformist organisations, meant that these struggles were more narrowly based than necessary and so susceptible to being undermined. This ultra-leftism can be seen in the rhetoric:

> Orators delivered blistering speeches from the fire escapes in denunciation of the policemen, the landlords, the marshal!…the capitalist system, the vested interests, and the imperialist designs of Japan in the Far East.[54]

But militancy did not translate into immediate revolution. The tenants' successes themselves were short lived and the party was unable to build sustained organisation. An unholy alliance of landlords' associations, city authorities, municipal judges, the police and the financial institutions intimidated activists with legal rulings.[55] With New Deal work programmes and a change of CP tactics as they turned to the Popular Front policy in 1935, the focus moved away from grass-roots-based militancy.

Naison and others draw attention to these limitations and complain the campaign was only a qualified success due to the failure of Communist policy.[56] Certainly it was true that the policy of the CPUSA was distorted by Stalinism, Third Period ultra-leftism and growing party bureaucratism.

The focus on physically fighting the police in these eviction actions does seem ultra-left, based as it is on the assumption that they were preparing for imminent revolution. But it is worth noting that the police and the government also saw the conflict in the same light:

> [They] jailed and clubbed the unemployed with an almost unprecedented ferocity, justifying their actions on the grounds that the jobless were trying to overthrow the government.[57]

It is important to see the pattern of state violence and militant response in the Battle of the Bronx as not just an expression of Third Period excess, but a continuance of pre-First World War struggles and those of the 1920s. The battles over rent eventually forced the city to introduce rent control at the start of the Second World War.[58]

But, also, what is important about the rent strikes and eviction resistance is not the violence or the failures in policy or limitations in strategy. It is the fighting spirit, the preparedness to engage in struggle, the response to the idea that change is possible that was found in rank-and-file party members and the broader members of the local Jewish and non-Jewish population. The anti-eviction fights in the new Jewish community in the Bronx were part of the national wave of struggles of 1932 that changed the country and "transformed America from a place of despair to a country of struggle".[59]

This is the spirit that broke out later in other communities and in other parts of the country, with the high points of the San Francisco general strike and the teamsters' strike in Minneapolis in 1934 and the sit-down strikes in the later 1930s. In this sense, Communist or not, these local tenants' campaigns remain wonderful examples of the possibility of community organisation and social power within the radical Jewish tradition.

The Socialist Party and the unions

> The unions that the Russian-Jewish immigrant established in the United States in the late 1800s and early 1900s were socialist unions.[60]

This plain statement describes a state of affairs that is fundamental. Not only were the leaders and a large proportion of members socialists, they themselves were core institutional bulwarks of the socialist movement until the mid-1930s. As late as 1932, "being a Socialist was apparently a basic requirement for becoming president of the ILGWU"[61] and the situation was similar in the other Jewish garment unions.

But while the lip service remained in the language, the radicalism among the union leadership with which it was inextricably linked in the pre-First World War period was in the process of disappearing. The "Americanisation" of the unions was much lauded—by which was meant they moved into the mainstream. While previously being a socialist had been about struggling for radical social change, it now increasingly became about building careers for the individual and organisations that would be accepted in American political and social life. This was called being "realistic". As Irving Howe notes, this transformation was a common one, but provided a particularly convenient route for some Jewish socialists: "Political training enabled careers venturing not only upward, in status, but also outward, beyond the ghetto".[62]

The leaders of the garment unions were more interested in maintaining themselves in positions of influence and pushing pragmatic alliances with manufacturers. While continuing to pay lip service to socialism, such as by supporting socialist candidates in elections, they increasingly treated the unions as "a businesslike institution requiring efficiency and meriting honesty, while leaving the rhetoric of socialism to nostalgic banquets and the Sunday pages of *The Forward*".[63]

But a different tendency operated among the rank and file. The radicalism and socialist commitment continued and was reinforced by new arrivals from Europe in the 1920s, as we have seen.

The massive strike waves in the New York garment trades in the pre-war years came to an end as the war began. But through the 1920s the garment centre of New York remained a Jewish working-class radical stronghold. Many of them women, and working alongside Greek, Hungarian, Slav, Italian and Black workers, the clothing workers fought gangsters and police in some of the most important strikes of the period.[64]

Many of the accounts of these strikes argue that they were primarily the product of Communist policy or conflict between socialist and Communist factions. But mass radical action cannot be manufactured artificially. The actions of the workers themselves show that there was still a strong commitment to militancy and to following a leadership which advocated it.

Moreover, structural changes in the industry itself were the main motivation behind the struggles of the 1920s. Sub-manufacturing, the system of contracting out, and changes in fashion away from suits to more informal clothing led to unemployment and also to outwork, which was more difficult for unions to organise. In 1923 a general strike of dressmakers won a 40-hour week.[65] In 1925 a mass meeting of 40,000 cloakmakers and dressmakers filled Yankee Stadium, followed by a work stoppage of 30,000 which filled 17 halls to listen to speakers.[66] The following year the ILGWU called a general strike among cloakmakers. Virtually the entire New York Jewish community supported the strike, "despite the leftist character of their leadership", as Irving Howe puts it.[67]

The furriers' union (International Fur and Leather Workers Union, IFLWU) is, however, the prime example of continuing militancy. In the early 1920s, the leadership were right-wing socialists in liaison with the most reactionary of the AFL leadership.[68] Gangsters enforced sell-out contracts and "slugged anyone who objected or questioned union policy".[69]

A typical incident occurred when union activist and Communist Ben Gold asked about details of a contract that had just been signed. The president responded, "Whoever asks questions tonight will pay for it with his blood".[70] They were not joking. When Gold persisted, "the goons jumped into action with knives, chairs, and the butt end of revolvers".[71] Gold needed eleven stitches but was nonetheless arrested for assault.

Ben Gold was a powerful and effective orator. A small man, when he opened his mouth a "stream of fire came pouring out of him, not always as grammatical speech, either in Yiddish or in English…and not always elegant either, but a flood of rage".[72]

Gold was part of a rank-and-file takeover of the union in 1925. Under the new leadership, a strike by 10,000 furriers in New York in 1926 faced police violence from day one:

> The police lunged into the mass of workers and beat down hundreds of strikers… The workers fought back. Frail girls leaped up as fearlessly and returned blows squarely in policemen's faces…police in patrol cars drove with breakneck speed into the large numbers of workers on the sidewalk. Still the mass of strikers did not budge. Finally the great mass of pickets broke through completely and marched triumphantly to the strike halls.[73]

After 17 gruelling weeks with thousands injured, hundreds arrested and scores in prison, the workers won a wage rise and a five-day-week, unprecedented for the time. This latter was a critical demand for the Jewish workers, who wanted Saturday (the Sabbath) off. But the AFL actually induced the bosses to break the contract, ousted Gold and the other progressive leaders, and the wins were reversed. The workers had to fight all over again in 1927.

In the years following, Gold went on to lead further fights among fur workers and other unions, with strikes, pickets and street marches, and facing violent encounters with the police, imprisonment and the machinations of the conservative leaders of the AFL. Once the Depression hit, with unemployment and under-employment, the struggle was no longer to reduce the working week but to increase it. A fur workers' strike in 1931, considered madness by almost all labour leaders, nonetheless successfully won a guaranteed 40-hour week; this achievement was important in the establishment of the standard work week.[74]

The furriers' union was dominated by the Communist Party, and Ben Gold himself was a committed member. But unlike the belief of right wingers, Communists do not manipulate people into action. A militant lead will only produce struggle if the rank and file are themselves militant and want to engage in struggle. As Richard Boyer and Herbert Marais argue, "such struggles as these were the reality of American life behind all the golden froth of the Golden Twenties. It was men and women fighting for a better life amid conditions that would have discouraged those less brave that was remarkable".[75]

The onset of the Depression in 1929 saw the union movement in disarray, but by 1933 they had found their feet again with what they saw as the opportunities presented by the New Deal. The union leaderships, which were by now significantly bureaucratised, now approached strikes not as a way of mobilising for socialist goals but as a way to regain the loyalty of the membership. This strategy paid off and the Jewish unions in the garment trades grew rapidly. In 1933 the right wing split off, officially dumped the socialist goal and entered the New Deal coalition. In this way, the union bureaucracies were able to pursue their own separate interests as mediators between rank-and-file workers and the bosses.

Sidney Hillman, a Jewish leader of the Amalgamated Clothing Workers of America (ACW), although still a self-defined socialist, declared in 1939, "Certainly I believe in collaborating with employers! That is what a union is for". Elaborating on another occasion, "Class collaboration does not necessarily conflict with a socialist position. It is simply making the best of what is indisputably a fact, that…we are likely to live for some time to come in a capitalist system, and it is just as well to get as much return as possible for the workers meanwhile".[76]

One interesting illustration of the political deterioration of the union leadership can be seen in the trajectory of the musical comedy revue *Pins and Needles*, staged by the ILGWU between 1937 and 1941. Starting out as a local production, the show was extraordinarily popular and became a Broadway hit. When it opened, virtually all of the actors were politically conscious unionist garment workers, who were used to having a say. In an early production they complained that the production was too light and demanded that it express class consciousness more openly. But progressively, professional actors replaced the garment workers and the content changed to a more moderate political focus. It now "served to illustrate a new image of organised labor less concerned with workplace confrontation and more with achieving security through cooperation with the state".[77] Alongside these structural changes there were other indicators. On a national tour in 1938, management capitulated to local segregationist customs in hotels and restaurants, although the cast members resisted this. There was also pressure to distract attention from the Jewish preponderance within the cast and the union. The management persuaded Jews to change their names, pressured women to get nose jobs and replaced "Jewish looking" actors.[78] By the time the Second World War began, *Pins and Needles* had clearly joined the trend of the union leaders and the Socialist Party of abandoning socialism and promoting a liberal agenda.

Despite the bureaucratisation and political deterioration of the leadership, it is important to recognise the contribution of the Jewish unions to the fundamental structural transformation that occurred in the union movement in the US in the 1930s. Until that period, craft-based unions were the rule, and the only significant industrial unions were the Jewish ILGWU and ACW together with the United Mine Workers. These three unions were on the organising committee for the formation of the industrial union organisation the Congress of Industrial Unions. Thus, two Jewish unions played a historic role in the whole US working class, and this contribution remains a cornerstone of US trade union history.

Nonetheless, the political trajectory of these two unions was clear. Following a well-worn path, they had become dependent on the state and the administration of President Franklin Roosevelt and from there moved on to support the Democratic Party.[79]

A sad end for a great socialist radical tradition.

The Communist Party

The revolutions in Russia in 1917, which sent a shock wave around the world, had an enormous impact in New York. "The whole of immigrant Jewry welcomed the February Revolution; an end to the hated czars and the government-arranged pogroms!"[80]

As in other countries, existing organisations debated and struggled with the political lessons of the Revolution and the disputes led to splits and new bodies. To the detriment of the communist movement in the US, two organisations were set up and then immediately went underground. It was not until 1923 that a single above-ground party came into existence, but at 15,000 it was much smaller than its membership of perhaps 50,000 in 1919 and it continued to shrink until late in the 1920s.[81]

The numbers, however, belie its effectiveness and reach. It is clear that the membership was expected to maintain an extraordinarily high level of activity. And even in its sectarian phase of the late 1920s, membership activity reached out in many different directions.

Consider the activities announced in the New York edition of *The Daily Worker* on a single day, 16 February 1928. An impressive total of 25 events included two conferences, three protests and mass meetings, seven lectures, three party members' meetings and ten social events (dances, concerts, etc). One intriguing announcement was all party members were instructed "to report at 11am today at 108 E 14th St, for important Party work".[82] One wonders what the significance of that day was.

The story of the formation of the CPUSA, the factions and splits and personalities and directives from the Comintern, is well covered elsewhere. But all are agreed on one thing—the central role played by Jews.

Tony Michels goes so far as to claim that Jews formed the Communist Party's most important base of support.[83] The Jewish Socialist Federation was one of its founding bodies and contributed a significant number of members. Many Jews were members of the other foreign language federations such as the Russian one.[84] In 1931 the percentage had risen and was estimated to be at least 19 percent.[85] The Jewish component went beyond bare numbers. A large proportion of the leadership was Jewish: between 1921 and 1938, the proportion in the Central Committee was between a third and 40 percent and even higher in the second level cadre. Their women's body was virtually a Jewish monopoly with 97 percent.[86] The Party's largest district was in overwhelmingly Jewish New York, and its headquarters and most auxiliaries were based there. There were a number of ethnic committees in the Party, but the Jewish Bureau with 4,000 members was by far the largest.[87]

Many writers try to minimise the influence of the CP in the Jewish community by noting that CP members were only a very small percentage of the total Jewish population. This is disingenuous. The CP was in fact a mass phenomenon within the largest and most important Jewish communities, the most obvious being New York, with influence well beyond formal Party membership. With its social, welfare, trade union and fraternal organisations, it had access to a broad audience. For instance, the Jewish section of the International Workers' Order had 38,000 members and the Jewish Bureau sponsored 50 workers' choruses.[88] Communists also had significant influence among students, with Jewish students in turn playing a significant role in the Young Communist League.[89] *Morgen Freiheit* (*Morning Freedom*), the Communist Yiddish daily newspaper based in New York, with a circulation of 22,000 in 1925, had a larger circulation than the official CP paper the *Daily Worker*.[90]

This Jewish preponderance was seen at the time as a major problem. The Comintern was justified in recognising the need to organise workers outside the groups of recent immigrants, but the focus on the percentage of Jews as compared to "Americans" is a sign of Stalinist deterioration. As one commentator states, the "CPUSA owed much of its energy, drive and idealism to first and second generation Jews".[91] It was not the Jews' fault that the Party could not extend its forces into other important areas of the political life of the country.

The Party did have difficulty in its early years sinking roots into the blue-collar working class, with the needle trades of New York in fact being one of the most important exceptions.[92] As late as 1929, ten years after the Party's formation, the Comintern was still complaining that as "an organisation of foreign workers [the Party was] not much connected with the political life of the country".[93] The watch-word was "Americanisation"—a push to engage with and recruit the native born.

The push for Americanisation was a component of Third Period Stalinism in the US (1928–1933) and included elements that were deeply problematical. It seems that there was a belief that visibility of the Jewish element would deter potential (non-Jewish) recruits and they therefore ensured the head of the national Party was not Jewish, effectively promoted the adoption of Americanised names and repeatedly sent Jewish organisers into districts with small Jewish populations. "The party appeared to act as if Jewish support could be taken almost for granted or the disproportionate number of Jews within it were an embarrassment".[94] This led to the perceived tendency to devalue Jews relative to other ethnic groups, and to Jews themselves repressing and even hiding their background and trying to establish an "identity more in line with the idealised notion of what a Communist should be".

With the adoption of the Popular Front Strategy in the mid-1930s, the Jewish proportion became even higher, possibly up to 50 percent of the total, and about half of the Party's strength was in New York. Jews were particularly preponderant among students, youth groups and Party intellectuals, and were noted to lead all the Communist demonstrations at Union Square. Liebman provides many further estimates and examples to underscore the central role of Jews in the Party.[95]

But with the Popular Front policy there came a new attitude. Jews, or the proportion of them in the Party, ceased to be perceived as a problem. The new policy for broad coalitions led now to a new orientation to the Jewish community and other ethnic groups. In a new definition of Americanisation, one CP leader stated that Jews were "among the largest and most important" national groups the Party had to reach.[96] The secretary of the New York State Jewish Bureau of the Party drew attention in 1937 to problems of antisemitism and social and economic discrimination and concluded that they were an oppressed minority[97]—a very different approach from the pressure to anglicise names applied under Third Period policies.

The Party had always been opposed to antisemitism, but the policy was brought to the fore in the second half of the decade. It became the only US party to advocate making the propagation of antisemitism illegal.[98] This was an important position in a period of growing fascism and antisemitism and in its opposition to Nazis, "the CP may have been the most militant public force in the Jewish community" as they focussed on street mobilisations while others oriented to boycotts, petitions and prayer days.[99]

This is not to say that the Popular Front period is to be preferred over Third Period Stalinism. Both were Stalinist distortions and neither offered a genuine revolutionary path in the US. But the activism of the CP in both periods attracted serious rank-and-file militants. As one Jewish Communist later commented about the years of Herbert Hoover's presidency 1929–1933:

> These were "desperate days when nothing worked". There was a vacuum of ideas and of action… [The Communists] alone seemed to have a program… Only the Communists were able to infuse youth with idealism, missionary zeal and a crusading spirit. With these, they invoked a willingness to undergo any hardship, to sacrifice life itself if need be, for the cause of the socialist revolution.[100]

This is the spirit that survived through the interwar years among rank-and-file Jewish Communists and which carried the Jewish radical tradition through this period.

The "Negro-Jewish Alliance"

The large number of Jews in the Communist Party and the left in general meant that Jews were not only active in causes relating to their own interests as workers and in their communities. They also played a special role as activists around many other issues. Of particular interest is relations between Black people and Jews in this period.

The CP made the fight against white chauvinism a central plank of Party policy following a resolution of the Comintern in 1930. In what Mark Naison calls a "landmark in American race relations", the Party "tried to create an interracial community…and defined participation… as a political duty".[101] This campaign was enthusiastically taken up by the younger generation of Party activists, particularly those of Jewish ancestry, although many other ethnic groups also participated. The impact of this campaign was particularly evident in Harlem, a neighbourhood in Upper Manhattan, New York City, with an overwhelming preponderance of Black residents by the 1930s.

While official statistics are not available, Naison provides evidence that the majority of whites active in Black parts of Harlem in the 1930s were Jewish. In a period where there was considerable tension within the broader Black and Jewish communities in the neighbourhood, virtually none was evident within the CP and the left in general. This may have been partly due to the Jews downplaying their ethnic background. But antisemitic feeling in Black Harlem centred on the image of Jews as neighbourhood exploiters—small businessmen and landlords—whereas the white Jewish Communist activists were "young, poor, and willing to take substantial physical risks on behalf of black neighbourhood residents or black victims of injustice".[102]

An early manifestation was the Scottsboro struggle when, in 1931, nine Black boys and young men in Alabama were accused of raping two white women. According to some historians, Jews provided "the shock troops for Harlem protests around this issue".[103] Adam Clayton Powell Jnr wrote in 1945 that Jewish participation in radical causes had helped counter antisemitic agitation of some Black nationalists:

> The Scottsboro case was the first successful refutation of the antisemitic propaganda with which the Negro had been bombarded.[104]

In the depths of the Depression in 1934, Black people and Jews challenged discrimination in relief agencies in Harlem. The CP ran a campaign that combined the trade union of the relief workers, which was heavily Jewish dominated, and the Black clients and employees, who, following demonstrations and delegations, gained a number of concessions.

Another example of combined action was the campaign against high meat prices in New York in 1935. Instigated by the CP, the campaign started in Jewish neighbourhoods with a strike by "rebellious house-wives and belligerent butchers".[105]

The action quickly spread to hundreds of "aroused Negro women" in Harlem:[106]

> More than a thousand consumers formed a flying squad and moved down Lenox Avenue holding meetings in front of all open [butcher] stores... So great was the sense of power of the workers that when butchers agreed to cut prices, housewives jumped up on tables in front of stores and tore down old price signs... No store held out for more than five minutes after the picketers arrived.[107]

The Party was not strong enough to sustain the actions outside the Black and Jewish neighbourhoods. Nonetheless their combined forces were able to achieve prices lower than before the protests.

Harlem was one of the localities that participated in rental strikes and resistance to evictions led by the CP and its associated organisations in the early 1930s. While Jews are not specifically named in the accounts it is very likely they were as active in this arena as in the other community campaigns.

The novelist Ralph Ellison describes a crowd returning an old woman's furniture that had been put out on the street. "We rushed into the little apartment...and put the pieces down and returned for more. Men, women and children seized articles and dashed inside shouting, laughing".[108] The narrator was surprised to see white people helping and "cheering whenever another piece of furniture was returned". The novel is based on the real-life Communists, mostly white, who were often involved in these neighbourhood protests. The identification was so close that it has been claimed that a resident about to be evicted immediately told her children, "Run quick and find the Reds!"[109]

The logic of the Popular Front led to a change in the party's attitude to its Jewish members in the latter part of the decade and to promotion of the concept of a progressive Jewish identity. This had an impact on the public pronouncements of Black Communists in Harlem. They began to speak of a "distinctive Jewish contribution to labor and civil rights and call for 'unity of the Negro people and the Jewish people in the struggle against fascism'".[110]

[I]n the long struggle to build a progressive movement...which has brought more than 500,000 Negroes into the ranks of organised labor... who more than the Jews have been instrumental in aiding this development...the Jewish people have played a prominent role in every progressive movement, in every struggle for Negro rights.[111]

The Party subsequently repeatedly talked about the "Negro-Jewish alliance" in Harlem and across the country.

Naison demonstrates that despite individual anti-Jewish feeling in some quarters, the 1930s was a high point of relatively favourable mutual relationships. But he also documents a few antisemitic comments from Black people in private communications. Naison has to dig deep into archives to find these whisperings, but his purpose seems to be to show that the post-Second World War increase in intercommunal conflict had its roots in this earlier period.

However, there is in fact no necessary connection between individual thoughts in the 1930s and later events. When Communists were a leading influence, with their determined opposition to racism and antisemitism, the Black and Jewish communities in Harlem lived not just in relative harmony but were active in joint struggle. The post-Second World War world was changed in a multitude of ways, not least of which was the decline of CP influence and the massive swing to the right in political life in the country.

Naison himself points to one of these political considerations:

Rising nationalist feeling among Jews, coming at a time of rising nationalist feeling among blacks, inevitably evoked a drama of conflicting claims which Communists had avoided in the 1930s.[112]

For "nationalist feeling among Jews" read Zionism. The conclusion is clear.

Fighting fascism

In coming to the US, the Jewish immigrants entered a country with no official state-sanctioned Jew-hating or pogroms and no restrictions on formal legal rights. But although it wasn't official government policy, antisemitism was rife in the years prior to the First World War, and continued to be widespread after that.[113] At a senate committee hearing in 1919 aimed at investigating Bolshevism, one witness claimed that the Bolsheviks were Jews and that "the conspiracy to overthrow the tsar was hatched in New York's Lower East Side ghetto".[114] This type of propaganda about the evil of the "Jew-Bolshevik" helped provide the justification for the aforementioned Palmer raids and subsequent deportations.

Industrialist Henry Ford took the propaganda campaign to a new level. Drawing on *The Protocols of the Elders of Zion* and other conspiracy theories, he "poured out an uninterrupted stream of uninhibited antisemitism into millions of American homes" via his newspaper *The Dearborn Independent*.[115] As well as the well-worn theme of financial control, Ford blamed Jews for starting the First World War. He railed against jazz as "a Jewish creation". "The mush, slush, the sly suggestion, the abandoned sensuousness of sliding notes, are of Jewish origin." He poured money into the promotion of square dancing and old-time music as supposedly more white and more gentile.[116] Ford even vented his spleen on popular sport: "If fans wish to know the trouble with American baseball they have it in three words—too much Jew".[117]

Ford was openly pro-Hitler and the favour was returned. Until organised by the United Auto Workers union in the 1940s, no Jews were hired, although some did work there secretly.[118]

Ford's seven-year hate campaign did not go unopposed. Various public figures made statements, including President Wilson, but much more effective was a mass boycott of Ford cars, resulting in a big slump in sales eventually forcing Ford to recant his views, at least nominally.[119]

After Hitler came to power in 1933 many Jewish and non-Jewish organisations organised rallies and protests. In March a crowd packed Madison Square Garden to hear speeches from trade union leaders, politicians and prominent Christian and Jewish speakers. Among the last was Rabbi Stephen Wise, who warned that "what is happening today in Germany may happen tomorrow in any other land on earth unless it is challenged and rebuked". Similar protests occurred in more than 65 places nationwide.[120]

Wise was pressured by the State Department and the German embassy to call off the meeting. The hundreds of thousands who attended vindicated his refusal. When Hitler announced book burning in May, the US government refused to comment. But Wise organised a mass street parade, arguing, "We went ahead pressed forward by the Jewish masses who could not be expected to understand such silence".[121]

The Jewish War Veterans and others initiated a boycott of German goods, which did find some response among consumers and also workers such as the furriers who refused to work on materials imported from Germany.[122] The campaign did not, however, become a really sustained national movement.[123]

Actions and campaigns continued through the 1930s. One internationally publicised incident occurred in 1935 when about 4,500 people demonstrated on a dock against a German ship moored in the Hudson River. One participant managed to get on board and ripped the swastika flag from the flagpole, throwing it overboard.[124]

Ford was not a weird eccentric or outlier. He was a prominent and visible figure in the broad setting of social antisemitism, an informal system of exclusion, which intensified in the chauvinist atmosphere after the First World War.[125] Traditional stereotypes continued, although this was of course also true of other immigrants such as Italians and Irish. Jews were shut out of upper-class country clubs and the like, a restriction that only affected a tiny minority. But the imposition of quotas in major universities was more serious. Some did this indirectly. Columbia University instituted regional quotas, and as most Jews came from the east, the proportion of Jewish students was halved. Harvard, the most liberal of the Ivy League universities, openly imposed a quota to deal with the "problem" of Jewish students, while at Yale, the Dean instructed the admissions office, "Never admit more than five Jews, take only two Italian Catholics, and take no blacks at all".[126]

This seriously affected the second generation of Jewish immigrants, many of whom wanted to become doctors, lawyers, teachers and academics.

Government policies and social antisemitism cross-fertilised each other in the immigration situation. Despite desperate need during the 1930s, Jews were particularly affected because the US did not recognise refugees as a category. They had to wait in line with migrants in general for admission under regular national quotas. By 1937 the authorities were congratulating themselves on how tightened restrictions meant "approximately one million aliens who might have been admitted during normal times did not enter". In the face of daily atrocities in Germany, the argument was made that the Nazis might perceive granting Jews refugee status as a criticism, and that "would not be aimed to promote international good will"![127]

Attitudes such as this continued to promote anti-Jewish sentiments in the population. By 1938, a poll found that 60 percent of respondents had a low opinion of Jews, and 45 percent agreed that Jews had "too much power".[128]

In this environment it is no surprise that fascist organisations and movements grew in the US during the 1930s. This was accompanied by the growth of other radical right organisations such as the Ku Klux Klan. The two most important were the followers of the fascist priest Charles Coughlin and the German-American Bund.

Coughlin gained an audience of tens of millions of radio listeners through the 1930s. He openly supported Hitler and Mussolini and promoted the standard linkage between Jews, atheists and communists, while claiming that Jewish bankers were behind the Russian Revolution.[129] At his famous broadcast following the Kristallnacht pogrom of 1938, Coughlin defended Nazis and attacked communists and Jewish financiers, and indirectly called for the death of Jews in Germany.[130] He followed this up with, "When we get through with the Jews of America, they'll think the treatment they received in Germany was nothing".[131]

The German-American Bund (not to be confused with the Jewish Labour Bund) was based in the German immigrant community in the US. By the late 1930s it had emerged as "the largest and best-financed Nazi group operating in America".[132] Its leader, Fritz Kuhn, called himself the "American Fuhrer", and members sang the Nazi anthem, the "Horst Wessel" song, gave the fascist salute and shouted, "Heil Hitler, Heil America".[133] And true to form, the Bund also consciously linked communists and Jews, its stated purpose being "to combat the Moscow-directed madness of the red world menace and its Jewish bacillus-carriers".

By 1938, increasing numbers of people wanted to confront these fascists openly. Thousands protested a Bund rally in New Jersey following the annexation of Sudetenland and "sent Kuhn running into the night for his life".[134] Similar counter protests occurred again in New Jersey and Chicago and teamsters were able to run another fascist organisation, the Silver Shirts, out of Minneapolis. But the most important counter demonstration occurred when the Bund planned a show of strength in February 1939 with a rally in New York's Madison Square Garden, nominally "pro-American" but in actuality pro-Nazi.

During this period there were at least 1,765,000 Jews in New York, 30 percent of the population, plus hundreds of thousands in nearby suburbs. Yet not one Jewish organisation planned a counter-demonstration. Both Yiddish daily papers actually opposed such an action and called on their readers to stay away from the venue. Labour Zionist youth organisation Hashomer Hatzair refused the invitation to join in a protest, saying "sorry we can't join you… Our Zionist policy is to take no part in politics outside Palestine".[135]

Perhaps this is not surprising. But the Communist Party, who at first glance would appear to be mostly in the running to organise a protest, also did nothing. More than that, they took the position that there should be no such thing: "The Communists could not undertake to forcibly prevent such a meeting once the City Administration had allowed it". They even ruled out peaceful picketing.[136]

In the event it was the much smaller Socialist Workers Party (SWP)[137] that set themselves the task. With only 300 members in New York, the party threw itself into the challenge of mobilising a mass response, printing 200,000 flyers declaring "Don't wait for the concentration camps—Act now!".[138]

Many government figures called for people to stay away, as did many Jewish bodies, including the newspaper *The Forward*. Meanwhile the SWP focussed on preparing for the expected more than 1,700 police, many on horseback. The New York Police Department, predominantly Irish Catholic, were sympathetic to the Coughlinites.

On the day, with the inside of the Garden looking like a Nazi party rally, 50,000 people gathered immediately outside, with a similar number of onlookers nearby.[139] Of the actual protestors most were Jews, but there were very significant additions such as a contingent from Harlem of the Universal Negro Improvement Association, followers of Marcus Garvey, a Jamaican political activist whose ideas about Black nationalism and Pan-Africanism were very influential in the US in the 1930s. Many rank and file Communists also participated in defiance of their leadership.[140]

According to the Trotskyist newspaper *Socialist Appeal* protestors included:

> Spanish and Latin American workers, aching to strike the blow at fascism which had failed to strike down Franco; Negroes standing up against the racial myths of the Nazis... German American workers... Italian anti-fascists singing "Bandera Rossa"... Irish Republicans conscious of the struggle for the freedom of all peoples if Ireland is to be free.[141]

A furious five-hour battle ensued. Reminiscent of Cable Street in London, the fight was between the protestors and the police protectors of the fascists. Although the demonstrators couldn't break through the police line and the rally took place inside the hall, the counter-protest was considered "an overwhelming success, beyond the wildest dreams of the organisers".[142] After that day, the Bund's offensive ground to a halt and they had to cancel scheduled rallies in San Francisco and Philadelphia.

The Jewish radical tradition in the US

Writing about this period, authors make a range of related arguments: that the pre-war Jewish working class in New York was on the wane due to upward social mobility; that the strife and violence that occurred between adherents of the Socialist Party and the CP was somehow inherent in socialist organisation; that the militant actions during Third Period Stalinism were inherently ultra left and/or a failure. They all tend to the same conclusion—the pre-First World War period of working-class Jewish militant socialist struggles was a short lived "heroic" era. That Jewish socialists came to their senses and faced reality in the interwar period—they made their peace with capitalism and moved on from radical socialist ideas.

But we have shown here that the Jewish radical tradition not only remained a strong current, in many ways it extended its influence in a period marked by violence and class struggle, the growth of fascism and increasingly threatening war clouds. In spite of demographic changes and political conflicts, Jewish workers continued to fight for union rights, and CP activists at the rank-and-file level forged links of solidarity and struggle which were to carry through into the postwar period.

Take the link between Black and Jewish people that was created in that period. Abel Meeropol is an interesting example. Born to Russian Jewish immigrants, he grew up in the Bronx and became a Communist and a teacher union activist. James Baldwin was one of his students. In response to a wave of lynchings of Black people in the south, Meeropol published a poem in the magazine of the teachers' union and later set it to music. This song became Billie Holiday's signature number, "Strange Fruit".[143]

The radical Jewish tradition in the US was grounded in the late 19th century and grew through struggle up to the Second World War. It had an indelible impact on left-wing, socialist and radical movements in the whole country, and particularly in New York. Before the Second World War, there was a social layer clearly identifiable as the Jewish working class, with a concentration in certain industries and localities, their own culture, language and history, and a specific relationship to the rest of society and within capitalism. Since then, with demographic changes, upward social mobility and assimilation into mainstream US society and politics, the sector of the class is no longer identifiable in the same way, although in New York at least a strong sense of this community has remained to this day. There does remain a strong Jewish component among white-collar workers such as teachers, although to some extent their presence may be more evident in the union leadership than the rank and file. As one author puts it, "'Jewish labor movement' transitioned to 'Jews in the labor movement'".[144]

However, an identifiable strong legacy of rank-and-file engagement in political movements persisted through the decades after the Second World War. Jewish Communists, for example, campaigned in the late

1940s to remove the colour bar in baseball, regularly picketing and leafletting baseball stadiums.[145] Continuing their parents' tradition of social activism, Jews were prominent among the Freedom Riders in the Civil Rights Movement of the 1960s. Jewish "red diaper babies" played leading roles in the New Left and the burgeoning social movements, including Women's Liberation, Gay Liberation (as the movement then called itself) and the anti-Vietnam War movement.[146]

We have seen how the combination of oppression (antisemitism) and exploitation was an explosive mixture in the European context. Yet when Jews were transplanted to the US, into a society which lacked that medieval legacy, that radicalism did not disappear. Although antisemitism existed in the new country, the general context for Jews was a different one. In the US a very successful, growing and aggressive capitalist class set out to maximise their exploitation of a largely immigrant working class. The Jewish fightback was just as radical and central to the wider movement but was more class driven and much less dependent on a sense of ethnic oppression than in Europe.

Antisemitism intensifies: interwar Poland

The revived Polish state that came into being in 1918 comprised Congress Poland, East Prussia, parts of Galicia (formerly in the Austro-Hungarian empire) and territories from several bordering countries. The 1921 census counted nearly 2.8 million Jews and many other ethnic minorities, including Ukrainians, Belarusians and Lithuanians. Of the population of 27 million, 10 million (30.8 percent) were non-Poles.[1]

The Polish national movement had long debated the role of the minorities in a united Poland. Proposals varied, but none anticipated that Jews would receive any form of national autonomy. Even the more liberal Polish nationalists regarded Jews as outsiders; they emphasised cultural differences and worried about their numbers.[2]

The right-wing National Democrats, commonly called Endecja, did more than view Jews as an alien force. As the prime proponents of modern antisemitism in Poland, they advocated mass emigration and began economic boycotts of Jewish businesses as early as 1912. In the post-First World War period, they participated in a wave of pogroms which was only ended by the intervention of the Allies, who forced a minority rights clause in the new Polish constitution.[3]

The first government after independence based itself on a pro-gramme of anti-Bolshevism and Polish nationalism—not a good outlook for Jews or the other minorities. The country they inherited was in a parlous economic condition. The First World War had destroyed a considerable amount of economic capacity, which deteriorated further with border wars. After a period of political chaos and multiple governments of various complexions, Joseph Pilsudski took power in a military coup in 1926, supported by most political currents. Pilsudski, once a member of the Polish Socialist Party (PPS), was now a right-wing reactionary. Although he was not an antisemite—and under his rule the police suppressed pogroms—by 1930, his regime had become a police state, with brutal treatment of political prisoners and rigged elections; in 1934, he signed a peace pact with Hitler.

Jewish bourgeoisie and Jewish working class

While the non-Jewish population in Poland was overwhelmingly agricultural, the Jews were more than 90 percent urban by 1865. By the end of the century, 462 towns had a Jewish majority population, including 116 with more than 80 percent. Having grown considerably in the 19th century, the Jewish plutocracy of Warsaw and other large cities dominated business and commercial life. By 1897, Jews owned nearly 60 percent of Warsaw's major private banks and up to 90 percent in other Polish cities. The ethnic Polish bourgeoisie resented the competition—and so complained about "Jewish business practices".[4]

Estimated at no more than 5 percent of Warsaw Jewry, the social weight of the Jewish bourgeoisie was more important than their numbers. Calling themselves "Poles of the Mosaic Faith", this wealthy and socially prominent layer was a visible target in a world of poverty and want.[5]

The contrast with the vast majority, the increasingly immiserated lower classes, could not have been greater. Words like "wretched" and "abyss of darkness" are frequent in descriptions of the living conditions of the poor Jewish workers, artisans and petty traders in independent Poland. In 1926, half of the Jewish workers and eight out of ten craftsmen were unemployed, and an estimated 40 percent of Polish Jews needed welfare support to survive. Diseases such as tuberculosis were rife. As the "safety valve" of emigration became less available, with quotas in the US from the early 1920s and tight restrictions in other countries such as Australia in the 1930s, many sank deeper into poverty.[6]

When the new regime "Polonised" the economy, thousands of Jews lost their jobs as the government took over many industries—including railways, cigarette factories and distilleries—and dismissed them from public sector jobs. The government policy of prioritising agriculture over trade and industry disadvantaged the highly urbanised Jews. Polish employers would generally not hire Jews, and nor would many large Jewish-owned companies, viewing them as "agitators and fomenters of strikes". The pressure of unemployment made it particularly difficult to organise workers into trade unions.[7]

Thus, the Jewish bourgeoisie and the Jewish working class entered the newly independent state in very different social circumstances. The "Poles of Mosaic Faith", living comfortable lives, wealthy and assimilationist, looked forward to their future as part of a revived Polish ruling class while hoping to continue to dominate Jewish communal life, while:

> Jewish workers and their movement were confronted…with a double adversary: a chauvinist Polish bourgeoisie incapable of giving any consistency to the "miracle" of renewed independence, and the Jewish capitalist bourgeoisie.[8]

"We had no spirit of animosity"

The Zionists were the dominant political current within the Jewish community at the time of independence. In the early 1920s there were 47 Jews in the Sejm (the Polish parliament), 32 of them Zionists. At first, they tried various manoeuvres within the Sejm; but after Hitler's accession to power in Germany in 1933, they gave uncritical support to Pilsudski.[9]

The proto-fascist right-wing Revisionist Zionists, led by Jabotinsky, strenuously asserted that Jewish life in Poland was doomed to fail and that it was pointless to counter antisemitism; they certainly made no effort do so. Quite the opposite: their youth group Betar, one of the most popular Zionist youth movements in Poland with 40,000 members, actively promoted Polish nationalism, for example by laying wreaths at Polish war memorials. The organisation was vehemently anti-communist and often brawled with Jewish socialists, when they could be heard singing the Polish national anthem.[10]

Betar, who were planning a military invasion of Palestine, carried out military training but never fought the right wing unless they were themselves attacked. According to the leader of their international organisation:

> It is absolutely correct that only the Bund waged an organised fight against the anti-Semites. We did not consider that we had to fight in

Poland. We believed the way to ease the situation was to take the Jews out of Poland. We had no spirit of animosity.[11]

There was another confounding factor for the Zionists. The Endeks (members of Endecja) and the fascists of the National Radical Camp (Nara) continued to declare that Jews had no place in Poland and to call for their mass emigration to Palestine. The post-Pilsudski government supported Britain's plan for partition of Palestine for similar reasons. When Jewish deputies spoke in the Sejm, they would be interrupted by shouts of "go to Palestine". Antisemitic boycott pickets carried placards with the slogan "Kikes to Palestine".[12]

The Zionists found themselves in a cleft stick. Here were violent, fascist antisemites lining up with their political programme of emigration to Palestine!

The position of the Zionists was incomprehensible to other political observers. The leader of the Peasant Party in the Sejm:

denounced the anti-Jewish attitude of Hitler Germany. The crime which is being committed against the German Jews is a world crime, he said… He could not understand…how Jewish politicians who are fighting against German dictatorship can reconcile with their conscience the support they are giving in Poland to the Polish dictatorship. It is not a good thing…for the Polish masses to bear in mind how the Jews are supporting their oppressors.[13]

All of this was not only embarrassing; it also undercut their political stance. As the dangers within and outside Poland visibly increased, and the British cut immigration to Palestine, the Zionists experienced constant disputes and splits; they seemed to have little to offer, and membership shrank.

"We were always demonstrating"

The "lost world" of Jewish life in interwar Poland is very often invoked with nostalgia. The romanticised image of the *shtetl* (small town) focusing on food, family warmth and traditional customs, is deeply conservative. But there is another side to the story. Arnold Zable describes his father's memories of Warsaw's political life:

Warsaw whirls into a frenzy of activity as the hub, the headquarters of political movements left, right, and indifferent. Bundists, Zionists, assimilationists, the orthodox, and freethinkers fought each other for communal control and allegiance…circles of aspiring artists and writers gathered in cafes and meeting rooms to argue, exchange ideas.[14]

And there wasn't just talk. This Yiddish song by Shmerke Kaczerginski, written when he was only 15 years old, is about a major strike in Łódź in 1926 and shows how whole families were caught up in action. A writer, poet and activist from Vilna, Kaczerginski was a member of the Communist Party, for which he was regularly beaten by the police and imprisoned.[15]

> Fathers, mothers and little children,
> Are building barricades,
> The workers' brigades are out
> Patrolling all the streets…
>
> The barricade is up,
> There's no one in the house,
> The police run past
> The children throw stones.[16]

Approximately 100,000 workers were organised in the Jewish trade unions in the 1930s, about one-quarter of all trade unionists in the country. Trade unions were organised in the European manner, being set up by, and affiliated to, political organisations. Immediately after the First World War, about 12,000 Jewish workers were members of unions led by socialist Zionists, whereas Bundist trade unions had more than 20,000 members in Warsaw alone. Bund-affiliated unions remained the largest and most important Jewish unions in Poland throughout the interwar period.[17]

Many of the socialist leaders from the pre-war period were still active in the 1930s, while the new generation renewed the tradition of militancy. This small but significant layer demonstrated a massive commitment to the working-class movement. "Militancy was the key word in [their] existence…the centre of gravity of their lives"[18] and "We were always demonstrating, whether on educational issues, or economic and political questions".[19]

We get a wonderful picture of the Jewish working-class environment in Bernard Goldstein's memoir, *Twenty Years with the Jewish Labor Bund*.[20] He writes about slaughterers and porters, food workers and bagel bakers, peddlers and fruit sellers. Many led a precarious existence, sometimes linked to gangsters and the underworld, living in slums and barely making a living. Goldstein and others worked among them to establish unions, to engage them politically and to motivate them to join in meetings and demonstrations.

Communists and socialists

The major parties of the left engaged in this milieu were the Polish Communist Party (KPP), the Socialist Party, the Bund and left Zionists such as Hashomer Hatzair and Poale Zion.

The prestige of the successful Russian Revolution meant that the KPP was a major pole of attraction. Despite the Party's twists and turns as it attempted to simultaneously develop its own programme for Poland while adhering to Stalin's instructions, it did attract significant numbers of young Jews. According to one member, Leo Lev:

> A broad debate took place in the [Polish] workers' movement of the
> 1920s: what perspective was most favourable for Jews? The petty bour-
> geois leaned in the direction of Poale Zion; but among the youth,
> communism was dominant, so great was the prestige of the USSR.[21]

Being a Communist in interwar Poland required a major commitment. The Party was illegal. Arrest was to be expected at some point, and the majority of left-wing political prisoners were Communists. In the earlier years, prisoners were well organised: they shared food and ran classes in Marxism, communicating in code by tapping on the walls.[22] Later, prison conditions deteriorated. The concentration camp of Bereza Kartuzka was openly intended for Jews, and humiliation, exhausting and pointless work, very little and very poor food, inhumane treatment and torture were the standard.

Despite the risks, there are many inspiring stories of militants who gave everything to the workers' struggle.

Bronia Zelmanowicz, imprisoned for activity in the International Red Aid (set up by the Third International) shared her cell with 13 other young women, all militants or communist sympathisers, of whom 12 were Jewish. After her release, she was active with a group of Jewish clothing workers.[23]

Yaakov Greenstein, a Łódź textile worker, was chosen as the workers' spokesperson during a strike. He was arrested for the first time in 1935 when his group demonstrated with red flags and banners, speeches and leaflets outside a factory. He was not yet 15.[24]

Shlomo Szlein took part in a large demonstration against unemployment in April 1936 in Lwów (now Lviv in Ukraine). When police killed a participant and then tried to smuggle the coffin away at the funeral, tens of thousands rioted. Up to a hundred died in the fighting, which lasted for hours, and agitation over the issue continued for weeks.[25]

Greenstein's reason for joining the KPP rather than the Bund was typical. He was "attracted by communism because it proposed global solutions…the emancipation that [the Bund] proposed was not bound up with that of other peoples. That did not satisfy me".[26]

According to Brossart and Klingberg, the Jewish members of the KPP in the 1930s "participated as Jews, drawing Jewish workers into the great movement of universal emancipation". Szlein notes that young Jews joined the Communist movement in Galicia (southern Poland and part of what is now Ukraine) on a massive scale. As noted previously, "there was such a high proportion of Jewish youth…that you could almost say it was a Jewish national movement".[27]

Although the convergence did not go so far everywhere, the tendency underlay the propaganda of the nationalist right wing, who merged "communist plot" with "Jewish plot" and coined the term "Judaeo-Bolshevism".[28]

The KPP never became the majority influence among the Jewish left, partly because of its sectarianism during the Third Period. The Bund was a particular target. Not only were they social democrats; being very combative, they also presented serious competition. Communists routinely physically attacked Bund events and individuals, requiring the Bund to employ their defence militias against the KPP as well as against the right. They even smashed up the Medem Sanatorium for children in 1931. They also carried out ultra-leftist actions such as calling unjustified wildcat strikes and physically attacking uncooperative workers in an attempt to split Bundist unions. After the turn to the Popular Front, potential cooperation could not be tested because the Polish party became a victim of the paranoia and suspicion that engulfed the Stalinist movement. Many KPP members were purged, sent into Russian exile or murdered, and the Party was dissolved in 1938. The Stalinists continued their war with the Bund for years, including causing the deaths of two of its leaders, Henryk Erlich and Victor Alter.[29]

So committed were the KPP rank and file to the struggle, however, that many members continued to be active after the Party was dissolved. By now, with Third Period policy in the past, the rank and file had established relationships on a local level with the PPS, the Bund and the left Zionists. Yaakov Greenstein records that "after the dissolution we kept these contacts and established cultural clubs that served as a façade; we continued to organise strikes".[30]

The PPS welcomed Jews and had assimilated Jewish leaders, but it was imbued historically with Polish nationalism, and this limited its appeal to the Jewish community. It had a chequered relationship with the Bund. As the 1930s drew on, the two groups grew closer together in practice. In 1931, the PPS and the Bund held a joint May Day demonstration, precisely at a time when the PPS was under attack from the Pilsudski regime. In anticipation of antisemitic attacks, the PPS bent over backwards in its offers of protection for the Jewish contingent, including proposing that their militia protect the Jewish marchers while the Bund militia protected the PPS. While recognising the value of the offer, the Bund turned it down on the grounds that they "wanted to march openly, without fear".[31] In the following years there were electoral alliances, further joint May Day activities and, most importantly, joint actions in the struggle against the right and antisemitism.

By the 1930s, Poale Zion internationally had undergone many internal fights and splits; the only remaining sizeable organisation was in Poland. Presenting themselves as Jewish communists, they had some success among radical youth. The left faction of Poale Zion peaked in the late 1920s when the Party received about 50,000 votes and elected 40 delegates to various city councils. In some smaller cities, it was the dominant Jewish party. But it lost ground to the Bund in the 1930s, probably at least partly because of renewed focus on settlement in Palestine:[32]

We could see on the one hand that conditions for Jewish workers in Poland were deteriorating, and on the other hand that something was amiss in the USSR... We thought, therefore, that our best chance was to make Eretz Israel a communist country.[33]

The leftist Hashomer Hatzair had 26,600 members in 300 branches in Poland by 1939. Although it claimed at its inception to be a Marxist party, it was a middle-class youth movement always attached to the World Zionist Organisation (WZO). It moved in a more radical direction in the late 1920s, partly through pressure from the communist movement. While the Party made references to socialism, it had a virtually negligible presence in the working class. During the 1930s, Hashomer focused on youth activities such as camping and support for their settlements in Palestine[34].

Left Zionists played an important role in resistance to the Nazis during the Second World War. Mordechai Tenenbaum (Josef Tamaroff), a member of Poale Zion, organised the resistance underground in the Bialystok ghetto which included members of Hashomer and Dror, another socialist Zionist organisation. Most notable is Mordechai Anielewicz, the leader of the Jewish Fighting Organisation in the Warsaw Ghetto, who was a member of Hashomer Hatzair.[35]

The Polish Bund

The Polish Bund separated from the Russian party after the First World War and continued an independent existence in Poland. The urgent political issues exposed by the Russian Revolution caused the Party to be riven with divisions. Englert succinctly notes that they were "caught between revolutionary ideals and reformist organisation". Some sections joined their local Communist parties. After splits and losses, the remaining Party organisation shifted away from direct struggle for a period in the 1920s and focused more on cultural activities, sports and youth groups and the promotion of Yiddish. It also engaged in electoral work, but with little success. This decline matched the international decline in revolutionary prospects and the triumph of Stalinism in Russia and elsewhere.[36]

The Bund revived in the 1930s, becoming embedded in the life of the Jewish working-class quarters of the cities and towns and was the dominant party of the Jewish labour movement.

The colourful annual May Day marches, opportunities for shows of strength, were replete with banners, pennants, marching bands and serried rows of marchers. All Bund union members knocked off work for the occasion, as did school student members of its youth organisations. The Party held May Day marches throughout the 1930s, quite provocatively parading through upper-class Warsaw districts. Frequently, the event was co-organised with the PPS, with generally separate contingents and march routes converging on a square and a joint speakers' platform. By 1938, the march reached 20,000 participants, with a 2,000-person militia. Thousands more watched from the side.[37]

One important component of the Bund was its militia, which explodes the Zionist myth that "contrasts brave Israeli warriors with meek and submissive Eastern European Jews".[38] At the first May Day march in Warsaw in 1923:

> A furious struggle soon was on between our militia guards and the hooligans and plainclothesmen over the flag of the Central Committee… Our guards, armed with sticks, fought back, and also our demonstrators fought back.[39]

At the subsequent indoor gathering, the packed audience included "many a bandaged head". The militia had a range of responsibilities. Notified of an impending eviction, they:

> would gather in the courtyard of the building…[and] quietly lose themselves in the crowd of [onlookers]…as the police and the superintendent, under the eyes of the bailiff…carried the few poor possessions of the tenant out onto the street. As soon as the bailiff and the police were gone, our Militiamen went to work. If the apartment was on the ground floor, they tore open a window and put the tenant's things back into the apartment.[40]

The focus of the Bund was trade unionism. It made extraordinary efforts to organise not only mainstream workers, but many groups on the periphery of the economy. Each small sub-group in an industry had its own union: porters who transported goods on their backs, tripe workers, bagel bakers and bootmakers. All the Bund-affiliated unions were Jewish only; it argued that "each union in any city with a large Jewish component should be required to form a separate Jewish affiliate". This was perhaps necessary to some extent, given the systematic discrimination Jewish workers faced. However, under these circumstances, cooperation with non-Jewish unions was essential, and in practice much of the Bund's trade union activity was in collaboration with the PPS.[41]

By 1939, 100,000 Jewish workers belonged to unions, giving the Bund the leadership of one quarter of all unionised workers in Poland—a substantial power source. Much larger than the Party itself, this union membership served as a major reserve of Bundist strength in elections and elsewhere.[42]

As the political situation deteriorated and the antisemitic right grew during the 1930s, the Bund ramped up its activities. Its membership doubled and then continued to grow through the decade, becoming the biggest Jewish organisation in Poland, with 20,000 members in 1939. This gave it the basis for electoral gains, with victories in several Jewish communal and city council elections in large cities in the late 1930s. Electoral success reached a peak in 1938 when the Bund gained 17 of the 21 seats taken by Jewish parties in Warsaw City Council.[43]

Much of this success was due to improved relations with the PPS. Although some writers portray the relationship as essentially weak and a failure,[44] and while there were ups and downs, a practical working relationship did develop. This was partly due to the increasingly obvious dangers of fascism internationally as well as in Poland, and partly due to the Bund being by then a committed reformist party, having joined the Second International in 1930. It was thus not difficult to find common ground with the Polish reformist party.

Although the Bund was no longer a revolutionary organisation, its experience in interwar Poland remains an inspiration. Englert says:

> It gave confidence to Jewish workers across Poland that it was possible to organise and fight while the world seemed to crumble around their ears.[45]

"Pogroms will not remain unpunished": self-defence

After Pilsudski's death in 1935, the new proto-fascist ruling group (known as the "colonels") pandered to the right, and conditions for

Jews, workers and the left in general deteriorated. The concentration camp of Bereza Kartuska followed Nazi Germany's example and incarcerated Communists, social democrats, radical intellectuals and Jews. The antisemitic populism of the right wing found a ready response in the traditional anti-Jewish prejudice of the Polish middle class, resulting in boycotts of Jewish stores, street assaults and a major wave of pogroms. Again, antisemitism was wielded as a deliberate tool, with the ruling regime aiming to present "solutions" to the Jewish question as "the panacea for the country's main socio-economic and political difficulties".[46]

Now the Bund militias came into their own. Originally for the defence of the Bund itself, they broadened to undertake the general defence of Jews. A Bund leader told a rally in 1937:

> Today, the Jewish working class is saying to the fascist and anti-Semitic hoodlums: the time has passed when Jews could be subject to pogroms with impunity. There exist a mass of workers raised in the Bund tradition of struggle and self-defense... Pogroms [will not] remain unpunished.[47]

There were two defence bodies: one was based on the Bund youth group and the other, the Ordenergrupe (marshals' group), drew in Bundists, Jewish trade unionists and PPS members. The support from non-Jews was crucial; for example, PPS sources were often able to give tip-offs about planned attacks.

In Warsaw, 24-hour flying squads would turn up wherever there was trouble. They dispersed picketers at Jewish stores, patrolled areas where attacks were occurring and responded to the fascist assaults in the universities. On hearing of an attack, the Ordenergrupe would rush out, sticks, pipes and iron gloves (but not guns which were deemed too risky) in hand. At times there were hundreds of Bundists, Jewish unionists and the PPS militia engaged in pitched battles with the "Polish Hitlerites".[48]

Perhaps the most important battle occurred in 1938 in the Saxonian Garden, a famous Warsaw park. Bernard Goldstein describes how, not wishing the battle to be between Poles and Jews but between fascists and anti-fascists, the Bundists deliberately drew in non-Jewish meatworkers to help. Then:

We prepared a large contingent of resistors who concentrated themselves in and around the square in front of the Iron Gate... Our plan
was to entice the hooligans into the square enclosed on three sides,
block their path on the fourth side, and, as soon as we had them
trapped, to engage them in battle and give them a lesson... When
we had a goodly number of [Nara] hooligans inside the square...we
emerged from the surrounding hiding places, surrounded them on all
sides... Again we demonstrated that...we can offer the antisemites
effective resistance.[49]

On occasions when they were too late to deal with attacks, the
defence groups organised retaliations. When Nara thugs bombed the
Bund headquarters in 1937, a group of ten Bundists, ten members
of Left Poale Zion and ten members of PPS headed for the Nara's
headquarters. The Poles pretended to be repairmen, went in first and
cut the phone wires. Then the rest of the group:

attacked them in blitzkrieg fashion. We really ruined the place and beat
them up quite badly... It was really an extraordinary piece of work.[50]

Pogroms and defence actions occurred throughout the country. A
major pogrom in 1936 in the town of Minsk-Mazowiecki followed
"all the 'rules' of this 'art': broken windows in Jewish homes, plun-
dered Jewish shops, bloodied and beaten Jews". Goldstein dashed
there to set up a defence group. When hooligans set a Jewish house
on fire and it spread to a neighbouring non-Jewish house, Goldstein
ran inside and rescued an old woman. The defence group grabbed
the opportunity and ran through the crowd calling out "A Jew is
saving a Polish house", then mobilised the crowd into an anti-
Endek demonstration.[51]

In 1937, the Jewish folk poet and songwriter Mordecai Gebirtig
wrote a famous protest song. Gebirtig was born in Krakow (at that
time part of the Austro-Hungarian Empire) in 1877 and was murdered
by the Nazis in June 1942. A member of both the PPS and the Bund,
he wrote numerous songs and poems which were, and remain, highly
popular in Jewish communities. "S'brent" (It burns) was widely known
in Poland before the war and was subsequently sung in many ghettos
and concentration camps.[52]

It burns! Brothers, it burns!
Oh, our poor shtetl, brothers, burns!
Evil winds are fanning the wild flames
And furiously tearing,
Destroying and scattering everything.
All around, all is burning

And you just stand there staring
With your folded hands…
And you just stand there staring
While our shtetl burns.

It burns! Brothers, it burns!
And help can only be from you alone!
If our shtetl is dear to you,
Grab the buckets, douse the fire!
Douse it with your own blood
Show us that you can![53]

The poem is generally stated to have been a response to a pogrom in the small town of Przytyk in April 1936, but one wonders whether the less well-known house fire mentioned above did not contribute to the imagery. It is also often suggested that Gebirtig somehow predicted the Holocaust. But the words are clearly a call to fight against the present danger of growing fascism.

The universities were an important site of antisemitic violence. Many of them introduced limits on the number of Jewish students (*numerus clausus*); those admitted were forced to sit in segregated seating, called "ghetto benches". As a gesture of defiance, the Jewish students would often stand in their places. Antisemitic students often attempted to force them to sit, which "led to dreadful scenes…culminating in frequent fights. They fell upon and beat the Jewish students, even women, till the blood flowed". Jewish student Isaac Sifrin gives this account:

Right-wing students were constantly provoking us. In January 1936 Endecy militants started physically expelling us from lecture halls. Fights broke out… Often blood flowed, when the fascists tried to start pogroms at the university. We called for support from Jewish porters and carters who came and gave the anti-Semites a lesson.[54]

Socialists and others also joined in their defence:

> Whenever the anti-Semitic "Endek"…students start one of their riots in the Universities…they meet with the resistance of considerable numbers of Socialist and Liberal students.[55]

Many staff and academics did nothing, but some professors who "had the courage to speak out against the attacks were subjected to insults, abuse, and even physical attacks".[56] When segregated seating was first introduced at Lwów Polytechnic, some Polish students joined Jews standing in their places. When ghetto benches were legislated throughout Poland in 1937, at least two university rectors resigned in protest, and over 50 professors signed a protest petition and tried to refuse to implement the measure. In Vilna and Lwów, Belarusian and Ukrainian students (also minorities) joined the anti-ghetto bench actions.[57]

The support that did occur, however, was most strongly grounded in the political Left. One Zionist source noted (with surprise):

> the strong and determined stand which a considerable portion of Polish Liberal and Socialist Society has taken in defence of the Jews. Not only has [their] Press come out strongly against the excesses; not only have there been remarkable…public meetings on behalf of the Jews, but the Polish Socialists and Liberals have actually come out into the streets in defence of the Jews.[58]

Throughout the late 1930s, there were numerous street demonstrations. Smaller, almost spontaneous, actions were often broken up by police, but there were also larger, better organised protests about which the police could do little.

On 16 March 1936, a half-day national general strike, originally called by the Bund to protest against the Przytyk pogrom, turned into a mass protest against antisemitic violence:

> Three and a half million Jews went out on strike. At noon all Jewish stores shut down, Jewish people walked out of school. The streets of Poland were filled with a fiery people, proud and battle ready.[59]

The PPS supported the action, and some Polish workers—mostly socialists—joined in; much of Poland was shut down.

A year later, the pattern was repeated when a massive crowd demonstrated against the failure to punish the instigators of a pogrom. And in October 1937, a two-day mass strike included an enormous protest in Warsaw against the ghetto seats and the terror at the universities. A Jewish high school student wrote:

> The whole Jewish community chose to protest against this injustice... We know that after the university ghetto will come ghettos in other aspects of life... The streets were filled with [protesters]. Jewish stores were closed. The whole community showed its solidarity.[60]

PPS unions, academics and many others also joined in, and the large crowd was able to drive off fascist attacks.

The Bund was able to lead such impressive mobilisations not just because they had the will; the need was great and the threat clear. The Bund had a base in the working class that it had built up over decades. A layer of strong, militant workers was ready to respond to the call to action and provided an organising base. Beyond their own ranks, they were able to mobilise the broader trade union movement and students.

But even these strengths would not have been sufficient. Crucially, the Bund was able to draw on support from outside the Jewish community. Its ties with Polish socialists made successful self-defence possible.

"The workers have not been contaminated"

It is a widespread belief that Poles are somehow inherently antisemitic and that hatred of Jews was unalterably endemic in Polish society. In fact, antisemitism in Poland in this period was primarily a middle-class phenomenon. To a lesser extent, it also existed among the peasants, but most commonly among the richer ones. The bulk of the Polish working class supported the PPS, which had demonstrated throughout the 1930s that it recognised that the fight against antisemitism and the fascists was its fight.

One Zionist source acknowledged that the increasing support in 1936:

> shows that even in those countries which have been infested with anti-Semitism for generations, the curse is not by far universal; the intellectual

and progressive elements of society are opposed to Jew-baiting even at a time like the present when Jew-baiting has become fashionable.[61]

Jacob Lestchinsky, a leading Zionist scholar, also recognised this:

The Polish labor party may justly boast that it has successfully immunised the workers against the anti-Jewish virus, even in the poisoned atmosphere of Poland. Their stand on the subject has become almost traditional. Even in cities and districts that seem to have been thoroughly infected by the most revolting type of anti-Semitism the workers have not been contaminated.[62]

This is not to say that the PPS was above criticism. It was hostile to Yiddish, and no doubt its members were not completely immune from prevailing attitudes. The Party certainly prevaricated in its relationship with the Bund, sometimes supporting electoral alliances and other times not. Both the PPS and the Bund had their commitment to reformism to thank for the inadequacy of their policies in staving off the ultimate tragedy. But they did at least fight the fascists.

Although peasants were divided in their attitude to antisemitism, many did join in the fight against it. As we have seen, the leader of the Peasant Party denounced Hitler's actions against the German Jews as a world crime in 1933. By 1937, the Peasant Party argued that the antisemitic campaign in Poland was a ruse to divert attention from real political issues such as land reform. During a mass ten-day general strike of peasants in August 1937, police killed 50 demonstrators. Jews supported the strike, and a Bund youth leader reported, "you could see bearded Chassidim [ultra-orthodox Jews] on the picket lines together with peasants".[63]

The growing working-class alliance between Jews and non-Jews reached its peak just as the whole era came to an end in September 1939. Poland was again dismembered as Russia and Germany invaded from the east and the west, arresting the leaderships of most political organisations and crushing the entire labour movement.

At this critical moment, Jewish confidence in the working class was vindicated. According to the Labour Zionist Emmanuel Ringelblum, Jews tried desperately to find hiding places in the homes of workers:

Polish workers had long before the war grasped the class aspect of anti-Semitism, the power-tool of the native bourgeoisie, and during the war they redoubled their efforts to fight anti-Semitism… There were only limited possibilities for workers to hide Jews in their home…[but] many Jews did find shelter in the flats of workers.[64]

The relationship between the Bund and the PPS continued on into the war period and contributed to resistance during the Nazi occupation of Poland and the Holocaust. But that is another story.

Section 3

Resistance fighters:
The Holocaust

Germany: counter-revolution unleashed

The Nazi Holocaust was a gruesome contrast to the October 1917 Revolution, but it was not the inevitable result of German history. Jewish status there fluctuated wildly, showing it depended on social relations rather than a fixed human condition. Before 1789 it was "the most squalid and abject in all Europe".[1] Yet by the start of the 20th century, Jews "had been assimilated and integrated more successfully than anywhere else in the world".[2] Then from 1933 came the unbridled persecution that ended in Auschwitz. These variations cannot be pinned on anything that Jews did. As Klaus Fischer puts it, "Never well organised politically and seeing themselves, in fact, acculturated as Germans, the Jews posed no real threat... The Jewish question was really a German question".[3]

The history of Jewish-German interaction was one of strong cultural connections well beyond the Yiddish and German languages. Family names were related to German and even in the Tsarist Empire 43 percent had that origin.[4] Medieval Germans and Jews had a parallel tradition of east European migration and minority status.[5] Alongside Jews, non-Jewish German traders of the *Ostsiedlung* (eastern settlement) came to inhabit towns right across Eastern Europe when the surrounding rural population was overwhelmingly Slavic or Romanian. Centuries later the cultural overlap was reflected in Zionism itself. Herzl's *The Jewish State* was written in German; early Zionist congresses were conducted in German; the early presidents and vice presidents were all German speakers; and the headquarters were there until the First World War.[6]

Oppression was not determined from the bottom up—through the culture or traditions of either community. During the Black Death (1348–1350) it was the ideology of Christianity that made non-Christians the scapegoat for disease. Seventy-two percent of towns with Jewish populations experienced pogroms.[7] This spurred mass migration eastwards.[8]

German backwardness was prolonged by the Thirty Years War between Catholicism and Lutheranism (1618–1648).[9] It wiped out one third of the total population and shattered what was then the Holy Roman Empire into multiple independent principalities. "Except for World War II, there has been no instance in modern warfare when the population suffered as much." The result was "the triumph of the petty or princely nobility and of political absolutism, sanctified by religious authority".[10] The twin pillars of aristocracy and priesthood meant Jews were saddled with crippling impositions such as the *Leibzoll* body tax paid by Jews crossing any one of the hundreds of internal borders.[11] *Betteljuden* (beggars) were a common sight:

> Gaunt and emaciated, they trudged with their wives and children from city to city, from state to state, ragged and destitute. There was nowhere they could find shelter. The extent of this social evil was unparalleled.[12]

Progress would have to come from outside. After the French army invaded, bringing emancipation in its train,[13] aristocratic rulers modernised their economies, sometimes including Jewish emancipation, to repel the onslaught. The changes were solely intended to prolong feudal rule, in line with Macaulay's dictum "reform that you may preserve". For example, Prussia, the largest statelet and home to half of German Jews,[14] brought in the most liberal version of Jewish emancipation as part of the 1812 Stein-Hardenburg reforms.[15] These saved the reactionary Junkers, a landowning aristocracy wedded to feudal anti-Jewish attitudes, who went on to unite all Germany under its hegemony in 1871. Significantly, emancipation in civil society did not bring entry to the state. Jews remained excluded from teaching, local government, or civil service posts.[16]

Germany therefore had a peculiar combination of forward-looking and extremely reactionary tendencies in what has been called the *Sonderweg* (special path). Economic growth produced a rising capitalist class wanting liberal national unification and freedom from the old system and its prejudices, a sentiment expressed in Schiller's "Ode to Joy", which has the line "all men should be friends and brothers".

The aristocracy was happy to co-opt bourgeois wealth and weaponry, but it detested equality and its agenda was antisemitic. It developed a counter-revolutionary "blood and soil" version of nationalism that lacked any positive connotations. Ernst Moritz Arndt wrote, "The highest form of religion was to love the fatherland... Cursed be that Jewish one-worldism".[17] We have seen how Wagner slid from one to the other.

The effect of giving Jews equality in civil society, at least in the eyes of the law, put paid to pogroms with two significant exceptions.[18] The first was the Hep Hep riots of 1819, a time of famine and organised reaction after Napoleon's defeat.[19] Turning the political clock back to pre-1789 encouraged attacks on Jews as economic competitors with an unfair advantage: "While the Christian with heartfelt love clings to his fatherland the Jew has the whole world as home".[20] The second set of pogroms was during 1848-9 and had clear counter-revolutionary intent. As the editor of a Jewish newspaper put it at the time, "Everyone blames us that we act against the regime...they say the Jews are rebels, all Jews must suffer for one".[21] But such moments were unusual.

After the bourgeois bid failed to unify Germany in 1848, Prussia's Junkers and King, led by Chancellor Otto von Bismarck, pursued unification on their own account. It relied on what Bismarck called the "marriage of iron and rye"—industrial capitalism and aristocracy. The Kaiserreich (German Empire) of 1871 established Jewish emancipation throughout the realm as part of its economic liberalism. But there was a sting in the tail, for as one historian puts it, "The bourgeoisie was able to share in the political and social rule of the aristocracy [only through] a renunciation of all liberal principles of freedom".[22]

So emancipation accompanied entrenchment of anti-Jewish reaction at state level. The *Sonderweg* path meant potential for a divide and rule strategy with Jews as bait lay just beneath the surface while German capitalism boomed.

German Jewry responds

German Jews could choose continuing isolation or take advantage of new openings and they made their preference clear. They adopted the

German language as standard early in the 19th century.[23] By 1929 the rate of marriage to non-Jews was 23 percent annually and the highest in Europe,[24] whereas in the Pale, Belarus was at 3 percent and Ukraine at 5 percent.[25] The degree to which German Jews felt relatively comfortable is indicated by their comparatively lower emigration pattern (see table 5).

Table 5: Country of origin of immigrants to the US 1899–1924, and proportion of community emigrating

Country	Percentage of immigrants from each country	Numbers (in thousands)	Proportion of Jewish population in country of origin emigrating
Canada	3.1	57	1 out of 3
Austria-Hungary	14.2	260	1 out of 4
Russia/Poland	67.7	1,243	1 out of 4
UK	4.0	73	1 out of 4
Romania	5.6	103	1 out of 8
Germany	0.8	15	1 out of 33

Sources: compiled from Ruppin, Arthur, 1934, p26 and Hersh, Liebman, 1931

The Israeli historian Shulamit Volkov says, "The vast majority of German Jews in *fin de siècle* Germany had lovingly accepted the combination of legal emancipation and economic cum cultural success".[26] So many benefitted from economic prosperity that "within two or three generations [they] could be considered part of the German bourgeoisie".[27] Ironically their success was helped by the severity of earlier persecution. Near total exclusion from land, and forced dependence on commerce and urban occupations, meant Jews were well placed to benefit from the industrial revolution when it arrived.

The unintended by-product of oppression plus emancipation was that Frankfurt's Jews became eligible to pay four times more tax than Protestants and eight times more than Catholics in the pre-First World War period. In Berlin, Jews were 15 percent of taxpayers but contributed 30 percent of municipal revenues.[28] Well below one percent of the overall population, in Prussian universities Jewish students formed a quarter of law and medicine, and a third of the philosophy faculties.[29] After the First World War this atypical occupational pattern continued as the German Marxist historian Horst Haenisch explains:

> While 25 percent of employed non-Jewish Germans worked in trade, banking and as independent doctors or lawyers, they were 75 percent of Jewish people. Jewish entrepreneurs owned 40 percent of all textile companies, 60 percent of retail clothing, 25 percent of agricultural wholesale, 79 percent of all department stores and half of all private banks.[30]

This was twisted to claim there was a cabal of powerful controlling Jews, which was false for several reasons. Firstly, economic developments had also catapulted non-Jews into advantageous positions in the rest of the German economy. Economic opportunity not ethnicity was the relevant factor in this. Secondly, whatever the bourgeois status some enjoyed in civil society, Jews were almost totally excluded from levers of state power and administrative roles.[31] During the 1919–1933 Weimar period (that Hitler termed the "Jew Republic"), just three out of 387 ministers were Jewish, one of whom—Foreign Minister Walther Rathenau—was assassinated by the right. Of 500 top-ranking officials only 15 were of Jewish descent.[32]

The German Jewish community comprised two elements at opposite ends of the economic, social, and cultural spectrum, sometimes categorised as "the caftan and the cravat". Alongside the acculturated grouping stood the *Ostjuden* or eastern Jews, many from the area of Poland seized by Prussia during its partition. They moved westwards during the economic boom. Between 1871 and 1925 numbers in the east halved while in Berlin they increased from 47,000 to 181,000.[33] After 1880 Germany also became a transit point on the migration route to the Americas and beyond. In the decade before the First World War 700,000 passed through[34] and 90,000 stayed on.[35]

It is depressing to note the hostility of some wealthy German Jews. A well-known Jewish scientist who later emigrated to Palestine wrote, "These Jews are a disaster for us…they constantly create new barriers, bring in old ghetto air, and are the greatest danger". A famous Jewish novelist felt the Polish or Galician Jew "was totally alien to me, alien in every utterance, in every breath, and when he failed to arouse my sympathy for him as a human being he even repelled me".[36]

Oddly, for all the Zionist belief in *"ein* Volk",[37] the leader of German Zionism, Max Nordau, saw its role as being to hasten onward passage to Palestine of "the impudent, crawling beggar in caftan".[38] Heinrich von Treitschke, a highly influential antisemite, had said little different: "Year after year, out of the inexhaustible Polish cradle there streams over our eastern border a host of hustling, pants-peddling youth... this alien people".[39]

Not all wealthy Jews dissociated themselves from their community. Sigmund Freud wrote:

> My language is German. My culture, my attainments are German. I considered myself German intellectually, until I noticed the growth of anti-Semitic prejudice in Germany and German Austria. Since that time, I prefer to call myself a Jew.[40]

Despite running AEG, a vast electrical company, Rathenau recognised the limitations of assimilation:

> In the life of every young German Jew there comes a moment he shall never forget. It is the moment in which he first becomes aware of the fact that he has come into this world a second-class citizen, and that no talent or accomplishment could ever change this fact.[41]

Notwithstanding substantial progress, Germany proved that full parity under capitalism was not possible. Jewish efforts to fit in were not an equal trade, and sometimes involuntary (as with Marx's father who had to convert to Christianity to keep his job). Germans did not reciprocate by adopting Jewish culture, but Jews had to subordinate theirs.

Anti-socialism and the birth of modern antisemitism

After unification Germany industrialised rapidly. In 1871, 64 percent of people lived in the countryside; by 1914, 60 percent lived in towns.[42] The working class more than doubled in size and was under the thumb of authoritarian employers backed by a repressive state. This stimulated working-class organisation on an unrivalled scale. In 1875 the Social Democratic Party (SPD) was established. Its programme proclaimed "religion as a private matter" and aimed to "abolish social and political inequality".[43] From 1890 until 1930 it received the most votes of any party at each election.[44] The ruling class was so alarmed that a "Law against the danger of Social Democratic endeavours" was passed in October 1878. Although sentences amounting to 1,244 years in prison were issued, and many socialists were forced to emigrate,[45] it was abandoned as futile in 1890.

Just months after the Anti-Socialist Law was inaugurated a new word entered the lexicon—"antisemitism". Richard Levy writes:

> Antisemitism is a modern phenomenon, the origins of which can be dated precisely. The word *antisemite*, and the abstraction "antisemitism" first appeared in Germany in 1879...a new word was needed to describe the new sort of...long-term activity against Jews...its politicisation and embodiment in permanent political parties, voluntary associations and publishing ventures—in short, its institutionalisation.[46]

A plethora of organisations were indeed established in short order beginning with a body set up by the court chaplain, Adolf Stöcker. His Christian Social Workers Party appeared in the same year as the Anti-Socialist Law. A year later came Wilhelm Marr's League of Antisemites (1879), the Union of German Students (1880), and Otto Glagau's International Anti-Jewish Congress (1882).

Marr introduced the term antisemitism in his awkwardly titled book, *The Victory of Judaism over Germanism Viewed from a Non-denominational Point of View*. "Non-denominational" meant basing hatred on race rather than religion and was a significant departure from the feudal approach because conversion to Christianity was no longer an escape. Its opening chapter states, "Without exception from the very beginning the Jews were hated by all peoples".[47] This sounds remarkably like something we have heard from Zionists: "Throughout their history, Jews have regarded Jew-hatred as an inevitable consequence of their Jewishness".[48]

The converse was true. Renewed targeting in 1879 had nothing to do with long-term factors but current capitalist needs. Shapira explains how the new antisemitism functioned in Germany's context of high assimilation:

The old hatred of Jews had been aimed at the alien, different Jew, whereas antisemitism targeted the Jew who looked like anyone else, who spoke the local language, whose appearance and behavior was middle class, who took part in and even created national culture.[49]

So, whether a Jew was devout or atheist, Orthodox or assimilationist, left-wing or conservative, lumping them together as a racial enemy provided a new catch-all means of distracting from social and class realities. The racial stereotype applied to Jews drew on remote history to seemingly make sense of the modern era with its focus on money. Contemporary, non-denominational capitalism was masking its negative impact on society.

Jews were not the cause and it had nothing to do with anything they did (as Herzl believed). As proof, there could hardly have been a greater difference between integrated German Jews and Russia's community with its separate language, geography and culture. They were targeted purely for political expediency. As the SPD put it in 1881, "Hatred of Socialism and of Jews has the same roots…the intention to divert general unhappiness".[50]

To perform the trick the elite operated a division of labour. Chancellor Bismarck legislated against socialism and Stöcker, close at hand as court chaplain, agitated against Jews on the streets. To assist, the bourgeois press attacked the left and called for a boycott of Jewish businesses.[51]

Some of the more reflective proponents pursued divide and rule for conscious instrumental reasons, while others were unthinking mouthpieces. The balance between cold calculation and gullible belief in racist nonsense can be debated,[52] but that was incidental. For what it is worth Bismarck may have consciously and "scrupulously used the antisemitic movement for his own electoral ends"[53] while Hitler was a true believer who arrived as an outsider to the ruling class having swallowed the deception wholesale. Kaiser Wilhelm II seems to have been a combination of both. He waxed lyrical about his "massive primeval Aryan Germanic feeling", declaring "our aim must certainly be firmly to exclude Jewish influence"[54] but only expressed these ideas after antisemitism's instrumental value became clear.[55] While still Crown Prince he wrote, "the Jews—and behind them the Socialists and the Progressives—are trying everything to get Stöcker sacked" because "he has personally and alone won over 60,000 workers" from the left.[56] Zionism also figured in his calculations when he became Kaiser. He concluded that in Palestine, Jews "would be diverted to worthier goals than the sucking dry of Christians, and many an oppositional Semite now supporting the Social Democrats would go off to the East".[57]

Stöcker originally gave his party the name Christian Social Workers' Party when it was set up in 1878. He hoped to foment hostility against non-Christians (ie Jews) among the SPD-voting working class.[58] But his outfit received fewer than the 1 percent of the votes needed for a Reichstag seat. Since workers were relatively immune to cheap diversionary tactics,[59] other class forces would have to be marshalled to counterbalance the left. The word "Worker" was duly removed from the Party's title and the petty bourgeoisie was targeted with its antisemitic message.[60] As Stöcker put it, his newly named Christian Social Party (CSP) aimed to "forge a powerful movement out of the complaints of the middle class, out of fear of Social Democracy and the hatred of Jewish capital [to] sweep Social Democracy away".[61]

The apparent enemy was Jews, but half of one percent of the population was being attacked in the hope of controlling the rest. Though Stöcker was a pastor, as he said himself, he did not target Jews out of "religious intolerance but because of social concern… Social evils are visible in all the limbs of the body politic, and social enmity is never without a cause".[62] Glagau launched his campaign in 1878 with the catchphrase "the social question is the Jewish question".[63] Word order was important. They did not mean that persecution of Jews was the result of problematic social relations but the opposite—that problematic social relations were created by the Jewish race. August Bebel's phrase "the socialism of fools" was apposite.

Marr added the spectre of revolution to the mix: "Who can blame the Jews for welcoming the revolution of 1789 as well as the 1848 Revolution with joy and that they zealously participated in it?… The happy and contented do not revolt in this world".[64] The best-known voice in this dismal chorus was that of right-wing Reichstag deputy and historian von Treitschke, whose first article on the subject was written in 1879.[65] He came up with the phrase much echoed by the

Nazis, "The Jews are our misfortune". He also backed the Anti-Socialist Law, writing that the SPD were "a party of moral degeneration, political demoralisation and social dissension".[66]

Antisemitism was a novel fabrication for several reasons. Firstly, the very word had a racist fiction as its foundation. The term Semite (instead of Jew) is a linguistic category referring to a family of languages including Arabic and Hebrew. Marr wanted to infer that "Aryans" use a separate family of languages—the Indo-European, which includes English, German, French, and so on. To suggest speaking a language determines race (even as conceived at the time) was nonsense.

Secondly, its racial wrapping combined successive layers of Jew-hatred. Under feudalism Jews were portrayed as a religious foe. Later the rising bourgeoisie saw them as competitors to be pushed aside and so Jews were cast as an economic foe. This was now supplemented with the Jew as the political foe of capitalism itself.

Thirdly, antisemitism was facilitated by a ruling class in the most advanced and culturally integrated European country using science as justification. The philosopher Eugen Dühring claimed hatred of Jews was a "natural judgment" based on "natural grounds".[67] (It is noteworthy that Engels wrote a 508-page book devoted to refuting Dühring's entire philosophy.)[68]

Finally, workers were not fooled because their experience of direct exploitation pointed to the real cause of social misery. So the movement turned to wooing the middle class instead. This was a variation in the method of divide and rule but achieved the original purpose because it set subordinate classes against each other.

The Social Democratic Party based its outlook on a class analysis of society. It therefore stood for equality and rejected the antisemitic explanation for social ills. However, that did not mean it had a strong understanding of the new phenomenon. Its leader, Bebel, wrote that:

> social democracy is the most decided enemy of capitalism, regardless of whether Jews or Christians are its bearers, and since it has the goal of eliminating bourgeois society by transformation into socialist society, whereby all domination of man, all exploitation of man by man is put to an end, social democracy refuses to divide its forces in

the struggle against the existing state and social order by false and wasteful battles.[69]

Mechanically separating the fight against capitalism—which is irrespective of the ethnic background of the capitalist—with the fight against capitalist ideas—that uses ethnic differences—was a mistake as the two are connected. Therefore, fighting racism and oppression is not a "wasteful battle" or distraction, but a necessary step towards achieving socialism through united class struggle. Compare Bebel to the Bolshevik position that fighting antisemitism was an essential component for winning socialism.

Bebel regarded Jew-hatred as a time-limited hangover from feudalism. As the new economy developed, anti-Jewish prejudice would wither away naturally because "the capitalist knows no other goal than profit. Whether the capitalist is Jewish or Christian feelings of race, nationality or religion are entirely secondary".[70] This ignored the class system's continuing ideological need for social control through divide and rule.[71] While the SPD's approach was inferior to the Bolsheviks', it cannot be labelled antisemitic and was far in advance of rival political forces in Germany.

Given this weak analysis there was a risk that some SPD members might fall for clumsy stereotyping because many German Jews were politically conservative and wealthy.[72] But Rosemarie Leuschen-Seppel notes that "in practice, the party developed a great deal of activity through numerous publications in the press and brochures dealing with antisemitism"[73] as well as mass meetings and demonstrations. A good example was what happened in 1883 during intense CSP agitation when Paul Singer, a Jew, was purposefully selected as the lead SPD candidate in Berlin. His view was that:

It is completely irrelevant whether one works for Jews or Christians. The proof is thousands of workers have Jewish employers who are more humane towards their workers than those who daily babble about love for their neighbour and other beautiful things and call themselves Christians.[74]

An election meeting was disrupted by antisemites shouting "Jewish Paul" again and again. The mass of SPD supporters shouted back "Bravo Jewish Paul", hoisted him on their shoulders, and marched out to the street. Singer won a resounding victory.[75] As a percentage of Reichstag SPD deputies Jews were over-represented some ten times over compared to their share of the German population.[76]

Such facts do not sit well with writers who accuse the left of anti-semitism. Lars Fischer has written a large monograph proving an SPD link to the Holocaust:

> While standing firm in their party-political opposition to party-political antisemitism, Social Democrats thus helped maintain and extend an increasingly universal consensus throughout German society that a significant "Jewish Question" existed and they generally shared the dream of a future without Jews... To the extent that Social Democrats shared this dream they also share the responsibility for rendering German society susceptible to Nazi antisemitism and preparing the ideological seedbed from which the Shoah could grow.[77]

If fighting antisemitism contributed to awareness that a "'Jewish Question' existed", so did Herzl's *The Jewish State*, subtitled "Proposal of a modern solution for the Jewish question". He raised the issue wherever he could, including Germany. Did Herzl also lay the ideological seedbed for the Holocaust? The SPD policy of social equality did not mean "a future without Jews". Those who attained this in Germany would still be Jews but live better lives. It was Zionism that promoted a Germany without Jews through emigration to Palestine. Recall the Kaiser's response to meeting Herzl. Whether fight or flight, ultimately Fischer implies the very best way to prevent the Holocaust was to do nothing at all—a very odd argument.

Despite elite backing, political antisemitism failed to make inroads into the left vote (see table 6). That briefly dipped at the start of the Anti-Socialist Law[78] and when all parties rallied against the SPD to justify slaughtering the Herero people in South-West Africa during the 1907 "Hottentot" election. Otherwise Kaiserreich ballots saw SPD votes increase while antisemitic parties flatlined. Furthermore, far from the Jewish presence itself provoking antisemitism, an analysis of the 1893 election broken down into local results indicates the opposite. Places where antisemites polled better tended to have declining numbers of Jews, while they frequently did worst in regions where Jews (particularly Ostjuden) were on the increase.[79]

Table 6: Reichstag elections 1878–1912: percent of total vote by party

Party	1878	1884	1887	1890	1893	1898	1903	1907	1912
SPD	8.00	10.00	10.00	20.00	23.00	27.00	32.00	29.00	35.00
CSP	0.06				0.02	0.63	0.40	0.50	0.85
IAS		0.15	0.15	0.07	0.15	0.35	0.07	0.14	0.01
GSRP				0.60	3.00	3.00	1.50	2.00	1.10

SPD = Social Democratic Party of Germany; CSP = Christian Social Party;
IAS = Independent Antisemites; GSRP = German Social Reform Party.

Source: Heilbronner, Oded, 2000, p569.

In the face of SPD opposition, the antisemitic movement fractured. The death of Stöcker in 1909 was "synonymous with the death of political antisemitism"[80] in the era prior to the First World War.

Political antisemitism in the period before 1914 was very ineffective in civil society,[81] and this restricted the degree to which it could be used. Marr even recanted and denounced the movement he had started. Though the state establishment remained deeply antisemitic, people such as Wilhelm II worried that publicising their anti-Jewish views or acting upon them would damage Germany's status and set back the economy.[82]

Revolution, counter-revolution, and its consequences

Extrapolating back from the Holocaust to cast Germans as uniformly and eternally "exterminationist" (as historian Daniel Goldhagen does) is therefore profoundly mistaken. As one writer puts it, "Surveying European society in 1914, it would have taken a great leap of imagination to nominate Germany as the future perpetrator of genocide against the Jews".[83] Integration had only been marginally interrupted when the German ruling class felt the pressure to divide and rule.

But everything changed in 1914. Extreme pressure became a permanent condition with a near unbroken sequence of existential crises—the First World War, revolution, the Wall Street Crash, and the Second World War. In urgent need of a method of social control, the failed instrument of antisemitism was dredged up and placed into violent centre stage.

As this was again driven from the top, the structure of German society and its state must be considered. The *Sonderweg* special path had resulted in a strong civil society with a high level of Jewish integration, a large well-organised left, and little popular antisemitism. But alongside this was a German state about which Wheeler-Bennett writes there was "no parallel to the status which the Army occupied".[84] Civil society could exercise few democratic restraints on an administration closely linked to captains of heavy industry and a military-industrial complex.

This elite structure was imbued with "blood and soil" nationalism and antisemitism, sharpened by the rise of the SPD. Even before the war a widely circulated War Ministry memo stated that "Social Democracy is truthfully nothing more than the brainchild of the Jews".[85] Contingency plans were drawn up to deal with the left "coolly and with an iron fist".[86] (Ironically these very measures would be enacted by the SPD itself after the war against the Communists.) Naval and Army Leagues were founded spouting blood and soil nationalism. They included prominent industrialists who became Hitler's fellow travellers and funders such as Hugenburg, Krupp and Thyssen.[87]

The First World War extended the reach of reactionary state power still further because it "allowed the military to stretch its tentacles into…control over policing, security, censorship, food distribution, education, transport and every other aspect of government".[88] After an initial relaxation when all were needed for the national effort, no sooner did it face deadlock at Verdun and the Somme than it sought to shift responsibility on to Jews,[89] despite the patriotic protestations of German Zionism. A pamphlet for the 19th Infantry Division read:

> Open your eyes! Who sat at home profiting from war industries? Who sat in the casinos and at writing desks? The Jews. Which doctors protected their own from the trenches? Who had us, no matter how badly we were shot, always proclaimed fit for duty?[90]

A "Jew census" was conducted which sought (unsuccessfully) to prove Jews were shirking frontline duty.

By 1918 Germany was approaching its final toll of 1.7 million dead and 4.2 million wounded. Inflation raged and food supplies were failing. In the midst of this disaster came the 1917 Russian Revolution, which created hopes of peace through mass revolt. Huge engineering strikes swept Germany in April 1917 and January 1918. *Arbeiterräte*, workers' councils modelled on Soviets, were formed. Then on 2 November 1918 sailors at Kiel mutinied and when this spread to the army, the High Command lost control. The uprising reached Berlin on 9 November 1918 and two days later, after the Kaiser's overthrow, the First World War ended.

While antisemitism grew more concentrated at the top, at the base hope of radical change led millions of citizens leftwards and away from it. In 1912 Stöcker's CSP had won 104,219 votes. In 1919 it received 664! Running from the sinking ship, many CSP supporters had joined the German National Liberal Party (DNVP), an amalgam of several right-wing parties. But compared to the 25 percent share its constituent parts had gained in 1912, the DNVP could only attract 10 percent of voters in 1919.

The corresponding vote for the left parties (labelled by antisemites as Jewish-controlled) went from 4 million in 1912 to 14 million in 1919.[91] This exceeded Hitler's July 1932 peak from an electorate almost 10 percent larger. The 1919 election also included polling of soldiers. While the generals were antisemitic 75 percent of the rank and file voted left.[92] On this showing revolution had ensured most Germans were philosemitic!

As was the case in Russia, the battle between revolution and reaction was not decided by voting for the Reichstag, though that was a gauge of shifting opinions. The outcome would determine the fate of Jews. On 9 November 1918 two conceptions of the future were laid out before the German public massed in the centre of Berlin. On one platform stood the anti-war Reichstag deputy Liebknecht calling for communism and internationalism—the kind of society that would outlaw antisemitism. On the other platform was the SPD leadership, which declared in favour of parliamentary democracy which meant preserving the existing capitalist economic framework.

To pull that off required cooperation with what remained of the old state machine. In a secret conclave Friedrich Ebert (who led the SPD) and General Wilhelm Groener of the Army General Staff struck a fatal deal. The Party had moved a long way from its revolutionary Marxist roots. To counter communism the SPD leadership pledged itself to politically defend its former enemy, the German military caste. This did not make the SPD antisemitic (and so the "left antisemitism" argument still did not apply to it), but it was inadvertently assisting antisemitic and anti-democratic forces. The social system that regularly used divide and rule tactics therefore survived behind a façade of democracy. Because the Revolution stopped halfway, as Saint Just predicted, the SPD leaders were digging their own graves, but also those of European Jewry.

Just how antisemitic the German military was is shown by the fact that Groener was regarded as a "moderate" in army circles. This was what he told his officers: "The Jews are hostile toward us… They fear us, the bearers of order, the bearers of reaction, and the destroyers… of the Bolshevik Revolution". "Crafty Jews" were the "string-pullers" of both the German and Russian Revolutions and controlled Berlin's workers' and soldiers' councils.[93] In a blaze of publicity the First World War leaders, Field Marshal Hindenburg and Quartermaster General Erich Ludendorff (the man who fronted Hitler's Beer Hall Putsch in 1923), blamed defeat in the war on a Marxist "stab in the back". Kershaw writes this was "a pure invention of the Right, a legend the Nazis would adopt as a central element of their propaganda armoury"[94] to prove a Jewish-Bolshevik conspiracy.

Pre-war antisemitism was an electoral intervention designed to weaken the SPD without interfering with what Borochov called "the law and order that are so necessary for the proper development of capitalism. Open violence and public scandals are not in the interests of the ruling bourgeoisie".[95] It failed because the SPD-supporting working class proved an unbeatable bulwark. In the inter-war crisis, all restraint was jettisoned and antisemitism was weaponised with the aim of aggressively crushing the revolutionary threat.

Nonetheless, those in the German ruling class had serious problems. The consent upon which the system relied had evaporated in the First World War's killing fields. The force and fraud upon which it relied were now weak and would need to be reconstituted from scratch. Let us consider each in turn.

Military ranks were depleted since soldiers were mutinous, and those who were not were reduced in number by the 1919 Treaty of Versailles. Coercive force began with the creation of an extreme right-wing militia. It comprised discharged soldiers out of which Jews, leftists and workers[96] were screened, though it was fronted by a Social Democrat, Gustav Noske. The Free Corps, or Freikorps, was 400,000 strong and commanded by officers drawn from the nobility. Dissolved in the mid-1920s, as Klaus Fischer explains, they went on to form "the vanguard of Nazism and…produced the Judeophobic mentality that subsequently defined Hitler's political foot soldiers".[97]

The Freikorps' first major engagement was in January 1919 when it crushed an ill-conceived rising in Berlin into which the recently formed Communist Party (Spartakists) were drawn. Afterwards right-wing soldiers murdered Luxemburg and Liebknecht. A few months later the short-lived Bavarian Soviet republic, which included a number of Jewish leaders such as Kurt Eisner and Eugen Leviné, became another scene of slaughter.

This does not mean the Ebert-Groener marriage of convenience was harmonious. In 1920 the Ehrhardt Brigade, a 6,000 strong Freikorps unit freshly returned from Bavaria, drove the SPD-led government out of Berlin and installed a retired civil servant, Wolfgang Kapp. The insurgents wore the swastika emblem of antisemitism on their helmets and had the backing of Ludendorff.[98] This galvanised the left and a militant mass strike from below dislodged the putschists, further radicalising the German population. The masses had the power to stop reaction and its antisemitism.

Kapp's failure proved that even with its militia the elite still lacked the ability to reimpose its dominance. As Müller puts it, "The old elites were no longer capable of maintaining their traditional position alone… They lacked the necessary social base".[99] This is where fraud, as a component of force and fraud, entered the scene. Though it had sown the ideological seeds, the reputation of the establishment was so damaged that the "necessary social base" had to come from outside its ranks.

The one place where the political appointments made during the Putsch were not reversed was Bavaria. Gustav Ritter von Kahr, its minister-president, allowed Munich to become a breeding ground for populist antisemitism. There an ex-soldier, Adolf Hitler, was "launched by the Army on his political career"[100] when he was employed as education officer to a regiment. He soon established his National Socialist German Workers' Party (NSDAP). The Bavarian authorities allowed it to evade the federal ban on right-wing extremism instituted after Rathenau was murdered.

Hitler was not of the ruling class but had thoroughly imbibed its explanation for the origins of social problems. This would be evident from his first political statements, which date from 1919. He wrote, "It was solely to save Germany from the oppression of Marxism that I founded and organised a movement", and "Only a knowledge of the Jews provides the key with which to comprehend the inner, and consequently real, aims of Social Democracy".[101]

In November 1923 the NSDAP made a bid for state power. Munich's Beer Hall Putsch was to be the prelude to the installation of Ludendorff as head of a military dictatorship. It failed because the army command was nervous about reigniting the working class so soon after the Kapp Putsch debacle. Hitler's Putsch was stopped, 16 Nazis were killed, and his hopes were dashed. But as he explained afterwards, "We never thought to carry through a revolt against the army: it was with it that we believed we should succeed".[102]

A flavour of the relationship between the Nazis and the establishment is given by this speech of the state prosecutor at Hitler's trial for treason following the Beer Hall Putsch:

> As a brave soldier he showed a German spirit, and afterward, beginning from scratch and working hard he created a great party, the National Socialist German Workers' Party, which is pledged to fighting international Marxism and Jewry...he has made a significant contribution.[103]

Hitler was no court chaplain, but Bavaria's army chief echoed Wilhelm II's words about Stöcker 50 years before. He told the court, "There was a healthy kernel in the Hitler movement. [It] possessed the power to make converts among the workers".[104]

Failure in 1923 led Hitler to conclude that to gain power he must take the electoral road previously trodden by the CSP: "We shall have to hold our noses and enter the Reichstag".[105] Before the 1929 Wall Street Crash, voting patterns did not suggest his attempt would prove more successful. The NSDAP attracted 2.6 percent in 1928. Yet just two years later the Party gained the second largest number of votes.

Was this a sudden revelation of a universal underlying hatred of Jews or proof of the Marxist analysis of the Jewish question? Three points need to be considered: 1) Who voted for the Nazis?; 2) The degree to which their appeal relied on antisemitism; 3) What drove electoral fluctuations?

Voting choices were clearly determined by class location. Table 7 shows how much the share of votes for the various parties deviated from the share of each class in the population. They are from July 1932, the Nazis' greatest success in a free election.

Table 7: July 1932 Reichstag election results showing deviation of party share of the vote from overall population (%)

	Workers	New middle class— white-collar workers, professionals, etc	Old middle class—farmers, shopkeepers, etc
Class share of general population (percent)	48	18	32
SPD voters	+9	+10	-17
KPD voters	+33	-5	-26
DDP/DVP (Liberals) voters	-15	+12	+5
DNVP (Tories) voters	-10	+9	+3
NSDAP voters	-9	+1	+10

Note: The Catholic Centre Party vote is excluded because it was a cross-class vote.

Source: Based on statistics in Gluckstein, Donny 1999, p86.

Old middle-class backing for the Nazis is striking. The further from workers' collective working experience (and ideas of social solidarity), the greater the support for right-wing ideas and ultimately the Nazis. Equally, the closer to the working class (which mostly voted SPD or KPD) the more the immunity to Nazism. This was evident across all Reichstag elections till 1933. Faced with this, Hitler ended up following Stöcker and others in attracting mainly traditional middle-class forces.[106]

If class location generally explains voting patterns, it does not follow that the old middle class voted Nazi en bloc because of its antisemitism. Consider what image the NSDAP projected. Party publicity was famously unscrupulous. Goebbels, who ran the operation, said,

"Propaganda has only one aim, to win the masses. And any means that serve this end are good".[107] Therefore the minimal coverage antisemitism received in Nazi propaganda shows they themselves doubted it was a vote-winner. For example, the most spectacular advance the NSDAP ever made was at the 1930 election when its vote increased seven-fold. Its manifesto did not even once refer to Jews.[108] Nazi newspapers and posters confirm the overall picture (see table 8). Phoney radicalism and counter-revolution were the predominant feature of Nazi propaganda in sharp contrast to modern neo-Nazis who foreground their racism.

Table 8: Nazi targeting of enemy groups in newspaper headlines and posters (%)

Enemy groups targeted	Newspaper headlines	Posters
The "system"	51.7	32.2
SPD/KPD/Marxism	24.1	36.3
Jews	3.4	4.8
Miscellaneous	33	26.7

Newspaper headlines: *Volkische Beobachter*, Berlin edition, 1 August 1932 to 30 January 1933; Posters 1928–1932.

Source: Gluckstein, Donny 1999, p76.

The millions of votes which catapulted the NSDAP from obscurity were due to class and economic discontent. Hyperinflation in 1923 wiped out middle-class savings. Subsequently these voters supported a sequence of parties each successively more right-wing than the previous, but not the Nazis. It was only after having tried every other right-wing alternative that the Wall Street Crash finally drove the middle-class voters into the Nazis' arms en masse. The first election after 1929 saw the Nazi vote increase from 2.6 to 18.3 percent. It peaked at 37 percent in July 1932 but fell back to 33 percent in November when economic recovery began.

As Childers explains, in voting terms the Nazis were "a catch-all protest movement".[109] "Electoral support for National Socialism represents a pristine pattern of protest voting, surging in periods of economic distress, subsiding upon the return of 'normal' times".[110] When people were asked why they joined the NSDAP, 60 percent made no reference to antisemitism. Four percent even disapproved in terms such as this: "Only their statements about Jews I could not swallow".[111]

If the root of Nazi electoral success was not antisemitism, Jewish racial incompatibility or human nature, that did not by any means make antisemitism unimportant. Those who voted NSDAP mostly did so to protest *against* mainstream parties, but that says nothing about the motives of confirmed Nazis themselves. The two constituencies were not the same. Thus, in 1926, when the NSDAP vote was collapsing (during the mid-1920s boom), its membership more than doubled.[112] Though hatred of Jews was not a primary reason for joining, once initiated into the ranks, antisemitism was inculcated systematically. When members of various parties were asked who had "real power in the state today?", the differences were striking (see table 9). The SPD and the KPD named capitalists, Nazis named Jews.

Table 9: Party members' attitudes towards Jews: percentage allocating perceived source of power in society (%)

Group considered to have power	Party		
	SPD	KPD	NSDAP
Capitalists	68	83	26
Jews	1	1	50
Other	31	16	24

SPD = Socialist Party of Germany; KPD = Communist Party of Germany; NSDAP = Nazi Party.

Source: Gluckstein, Donny 1999, p90.

Members of the old middle class were not only the most likely to vote NSDAP. If they joined, they proved most susceptible to antisemitic indoctrination.[113] This classic petty bourgeois layer consisted of people such as farmers, self-employed and shopkeepers. Their intermediate social position and economic independence made them receptive to portrayals of Jewish responsibility for their financial troubles *and* the sinister force controlling the socialist movement threatening their property. The conspiracy theory was packaged as follows: "How wonderfully the stock exchange Jew and the leader of the workers...

cooperate. Moses Kohn on the one side encourages his association to refuse the workers' demands, while his brother Isaac in the factory incites the masses".[114]

The antisemitic conspiracy myth was the glue binding the Nazi cadre. If Jews caused capitalist crisis in order to stir up the workers, there was a warped rationale for fighting "Jewish Marxism"—ie the organised German working class. No direct appeal by the discredited ruling class could have achieved such perverse wizardry.

The establishment's ideas were the NSDAP's *raison d'être*, but it prospered precisely because it appeared untainted by that establishment. It was the living embodiment of a top-down divide and rule strategy, yet was organisationally independent, a mass instrument of counter-revolution untrammelled by the niceties of established procedure. Disseminated fraud gave birth to a force at one remove, an ideological excrescence in the physical form of fists and boots.

Hitler could have been stopped. Working class collective power had been demonstrated in the November 1918 Revolution and when mass strikes repelled the Kapp Putsch—thereby also dissuading the army from backing Hitler's Beer Hall Putsch in 1923. Electorally the NSDAP never gained much beyond a third of votes and was outstripped by the left vote (SPD plus KPD) in every Weimar election except July 1932. Jews recognised the left as their best ally. The SPD received the largest share of Jewish votes, rising from 42 percent in 1924 to 62 percent on the eve of Hitler's accession.[115] If the champions of the "antisemitism of the left" argument are correct, then German Jews must have been very blind when they backed a Marxist party.

SPD socialists and KPD communists had every reason to unite against Hitler, who declared, "If we are victorious Marxism will be destroyed, and completely destroyed…the last organisation liquidated… the last Marxist converted or exterminated".[116] Unfortunately, they were disastrously led, underplayed the Nazi threat, and squabbled amongst themselves.[117] German Zionists were no better, saying, "The defense against anti-Semitism is not our main task, it does not concern us to the same extent and is not of the same importance for us as is the work for Palestine".[118] Observing developments from Palestine, Ben Gurion was seriously alarmed, but he too argued for escape rather than resistance:

[S]ome Zionists have joined the chorus of the assimilationists: a "war" against anti-Semitism. But we must give a Zionist response to the catastrophe faced by German Jewry—to turn this disaster into an opportunity to develop our country, to save the lives and property of the Jews of Germany for the sake of Zion. This rescue takes priority over all else.[119]

In contrast to these currents, Trotsky, the best-known defender of the internationalist tradition after Lenin's death, warned of the dangers: "Should fascism come to power, it will ride over your skulls and spines like a terrific tank". His prescription was unequivocal. "Your salvation lies in merciless struggle".[120] Alas, German Trotskyism was minuscule.

Though the left disunity did not help, it was not responsible for Hitler coming to power. That happened because the ruling class appointed him chancellor. Neither did this decision come from below. Whatever the Nazi vote, after 1930 ballots ceased to determine governments because they were selected by President Hindenburg using emergency powers. Hitler was not favoured at first. In July 1932 Hindenburg refused him the chancellorship, despite the strong NSDAP showing, because the Austrian posed as an opponent of the ruling class to win support and was an outsider greedy for his own rule.

Hindenburg's rebuff threw the NSDAP into disarray. It was bankrupt and its vote shrank in the November 1932 election. At the end of the year Goebbels wrote in his diary about "eternal misfortune. Everything is smashed... The past was hard, and the future looks dark and gloomy; all prospects and hopes have quite disappeared".[121] Yet at that very moment the governing clique appointed Hitler! As Trotsky put it, "Such are the times now that there is no guaranteeing property except with fists. There is no way of dispensing with the Nazis".[122] They had to act before the Party's internal crisis became terminal and the fists became disorganised. As General Kurt von Schleicher, the chancellor who preceded Hitler and decided on his appointment, said, "If there were no Nazis it would be necessary to invent them".[123]

He decided on Hitler's appointment in early 1933 after discussion with the army commander. Their reasoning was unequivocal: "The only possible future Reich chancellor was Hitler" because he alone could ward off "a general strike, if not a civil war".[124] They were backed by heavy industrialists for whom hatred of Jews was not a prime motivation. Hitler had promised to crush their class enemy at home and his plans for conquering an Eastern empire held out the prospect of lucrative military contracts and profit opportunities. Imperialist hegemony in Mitteleuropa (Central Europe) with Russia's border pushed back far to the east had been a German war aim since the First World War. The Führer would duly oblige and from the first day of his rule planned to overturn the defeat of 1918.

It was not the antisemitism of the German public or NSDAP strength, but the self-interested calculations of the elite that put Hitler into power. The facile equations—antisemitism made Hitler chancellor, proving Jews need an ethnic state in Palestine, or that ruling class responsibility "cannot be dispelled vigorously enough" (as quoted by Aly)[125]—disintegrate when the evidence is looked at.

Counter-revolution and resistance

Once in post Hitler rigged the March 1933 election and drove through an "Enabling Act" granting him his own emergency powers. Though sharing the same basic ideology as his rivals, Hitler had won the competition for state control and was bent on taking full advantage. Delivered from close supervision by the traditional elite, Hitler pursued a course based on his interpretation of its ideology. Although the means of manipulation had broken free and gained a life of its own, Hitler took care to remain securely within the capitalist economic framework, as evidenced by the notorious "Night of the Long Knives" in 1934. This was a blood purge of his own Nazi stormtroopers for daring to demand their share of the spoils. At the same time Hitler demonstrated organisational independence by slaughtering rivals in the ruling class such as Schleicher. The one certain element was the joint Nazi/ruling class goal of counter-revolution. So began ferocious repression of swathes of the German population, Jews and others.

With his slogan *Ein Volk, ein Reich, ein Führer*, Hitler claimed that under him Germany was a monolithic *Volksgemeinschaft* (racial community). This "single community" was a myth not only because it was internally divided between an enslaved population and exploiters, but because Hitler's racial obsession was unpopular. William Sheridan

Allen's masterful study of a typical German city (given the pseudonym Northeim) demonstrates this:

> Social discrimination was practically non-existent in the town. Jews were integrated along class lines: the two wealthy Jewish families belonged to upper-class circles and clubs. Jews of middling income belonged to the middle-class social organisations, and working class Jews were in the Socialist community… Anti-Semitism in the form of jokes…was prevalent, approximately to the extent that these things existed in America in the 1930s.[126]

Jews "were accepted as a normal part of the town's life" but "the Nazis were determined to change this". The book tracks Nazi *Gleichschaltung*, the means by which Nazi control was driven into every institution and discrimination was enforced.[127] Encouragement of active hatred had to come from above—Nazi party zealots pressured the general population.

Across Germany people from a variety of political persuasions actively opposed the regime. Reference is usually made to the "conservative resistance" and Operation Valkyrie, the July 1944 plot to blow up the Führer. It came so late in the day because its supporters, having tolerated and participated in Nazi rule, wanted to escape the consequences of losing the war.[128] In contrast, principled opposition to Nazism by liberal students, youth movements and so on began much earlier. But as a mass phenomenon the left parties stood out from the very start. It is a travesty to claim that the Marxist movement, which risked life and limb to combat the Nazi programme, was a link between Luther and Hitler (Carlebach).[129]

Haenisch points out that during the Weimar period both the SPD and KPD operated the previous mechanistic Marxism, which was unprejudiced and undiscriminating between ethnicities, but ignored ideology and the dangers of the divide and rule tactic. Both parties issued press articles which mentioned that capitalists could be Jewish or Christian, or recognised the counter-revolutionary and pro-capitalist function of the Nazis but underestimated its antisemitism. But these were not antisemitic. Blindness to the danger of antisemitism, while regrettable, cannot be equated with reactionary divide and rule.[130]

The proof is that Communist Anti-Fascist Action engaged in hand-to-hand combat with Nazi stormtroopers. In Prussia between 1 June and 20 July 1932, street fighting between them killed 30 Communists and 38 Nazis.[131] The fightback continued after Hitler's chancellorship began. Secret police (Gestapo) reports said, "We employ the expression 'Communist danger' with all seriousness",[132] and admitted the "self-sacrificing readiness of all the supporters of the illegal KPD who were on every occasion ready to fill any gap which occurred in the ranks".[133] The KPD called for people to, "Help our tormented Jewish fellow-citizens in whatever way possible. Wall into isolation the deeply despised anti-Semitic rabble… Show solidarity through sympathy and help for our Jewish comrades".[134] The 1939 KPD conference declared there must not be the slightest concession to the "contemptible persecution of Jews… The struggle against antisemitism is inseparably united with the struggle against the war and the liberation of the entire people from the yoke of the Hitler dictatorship".[135] At great risk the SPD kept going an illegal newspaper with a readership of up to 300,000[136] and organised underground trade union agitation, especially among metalworkers. A recent estimate suggests two thirds of resisters killed were from the workers' movement.[137]

The machinery of repression was manned by the Blackshirts (SS) and Gestapo. A high proportion of the top SS echelon were aristocrats, while the Gestapo was almost exclusively middle class.[138] Their target was the lower classes, and the order of their actions shows how the relative roles of counter-revolution and antisemitism interacted within the Nazi approach. A definite pattern can be discerned, one which shows that it was not only German Jews who did not believe in the "antisemitism of the left" thesis spouted today; neither did Hitler.

If the left shared his views, why were Communists systematically repressed first and Jews, the most defenceless group, last? The answer is he had to destroy the left before advancing his full antisemitic programme.[139] The campaign began on 28 February 1933, when the Communists were framed for burning down the Reichstag. This brought in the first wave of concentration camp prisoners, seized under what Heinrich Himmler (SS leader) called an operation against "Jewish-Communist asocial organisation". Ten thousand of the 200,000 people seized were Jewish left-wing activists.[140] Next came the trade unions, eliminated on 2 May 1933. In June it was the turn of the SPD. Three thousand SPD members were arrested in the last week alone.[141]

For the first five years of the Nazi regime Jews remained just one in 20 of the concentration camp population,[142] though the community was still harassed. Raul Hilberg's *Destruction of the European Jews* meticulously documents the steps, from boycott of businesses of 1 April 1933, followed by the Nuremburg race laws in 1935 and beyond. The ramping up of wider Jewish arrests (not associated with the left *per se*) and liquidation of German Zionism came with Kristallnacht in 1938. This event was orchestrated by Goebbels rather than reflecting spontaneous popular action, as claimed. In Northeim, for example, stormtroopers threw stones at Jewish shops, "but the reaction of Northeimers to this (as was the case all over Germany) was so openly negative that it was the last public anti-Semitic incident in the town".[143] Haenisch notes that the Nazis spent six long years launching tirades of hate through their media monopoly, laws and concentration camps, but completely failed to achieve the spontaneous pogrom they wanted. "This was the service that social-democracy had provided to the struggle against antisemitism".[144] After Kristallnacht, however, "never before had there been as many Jews [in the camps]. Now they were suddenly in the majority".[145]

Martin Niemoeller's famous poem was therefore accurate in its sequencing.

> *First they came for the Communists and I did not speak out—*
> *Because I was not a Communist*
>
> *Then they came for the Socialists and I did not speak out—*
> *Because I was not a Socialist*
>
> *Then they came for the trade unionists and I did not speak out—*
> *Because I was not a trade unionist*
>
> *Then they came for the Jews.*

The people who did this were no longer the original deceivers who conceived antisemitism to divide and rule. The Nazis were the deceived acting out the lie which had become an end in itself. In that sense the Holocaust of the Jews was the apotheosis of oppression, mythology unchained, the purest expression of an ideological social control mechanism acting with autonomy. The Marxist writer, Alex Callinicos describes how the thinking was articulated:

It was the Jewish "virus" as Hitler called it, that represented the most deadly danger to the health of the German *Volk*... Thus when it came to devising actual policies for the "final solution of the Jewish question," murder was the Nazis' default position, set by an ideology that identified the Jews as a deadly threat. The Holocaust was the outcome of a bureaucratic problem-solving process over-determined by the biological racism that constituted the ideological cement of National Socialism... Biological racism...played a crucial role in motivating the perpetrators.[146]

Yet there was a backdrop to this grotesque performance. Just as the existence of Nazi rule was the outcome of a specific set of conditions, Nazi actions in power did not operate in a vacuum. They unfolded as part of a totality. The mindset of the perpetrators was motivated by German nationalism, imperialism, and counter-revolution, all utterly fused with biological racism. The Holocaust unfolded during the Second World War and the German invasion of Russia, then seen (wrongly) as the bastion of world socialism.

In 1938 Hitler described Jews as "the advance troops for the bolshevisation of the world".[147] As the war progressed, Reinhard Heydrich, the architect of the Holocaust, said, "Judaism in the east was the source of Bolshevism and must therefore be wiped out". General Keitel saw Jews as "the main carriers of Bolshevism".[148] For General von Reichenau, the war was "against the Jewish-Bolshevistic system". General von Manstein added, "The Jewish-Bolshevist system must be exterminated once and for all. The soldier must appreciate the necessity for harsh punishment of Jewry, the spiritual bearer of the Bolshevist terror".[149] The quotes could go on *ad nauseam*. The Nazi leadership and core saw a Jewish conspiracy behind every foe, defeat and obstacle, not just in Russia. They believed there was Jewish financing of the war and Jewish control over Churchill and Roosevelt.

On 6 June 1941 the infamous Commissar Order instructing the Wehrmacht to shoot Soviet officials on sight was issued. Operation Barbarossa, a colossal invasion, began on 22 June 1941 and victory was expected within eight weeks. The German siege of Moscow began in September 1941. When enemy defeat failed to materialise, concentrating on Jewish civilians became a surrogate. What had been an ad hoc affair became planned genocide. Auschwitz began the assembly line slaughter of Jews at the end of 1941, and the Wannsee Conference, which set out the complete Final Solution, opened in January 1942. It was easier to exterminate ghettos than the Red Army. The community became victims of the ghastly delusion that through their incineration lay imperialist success and counter-revolution.

It was militarily counter-productive for the Nazis to doggedly indulge their preposterous fantasies to the last day of fighting in 1945. Such irrationality does not prove the primacy of antisemitic obsession over class-driven counter-revolution, but the inter-penetration of both. What began with a rational purpose consisted of peddling a pack of falsehoods. That these were believed and produced an irrational outcome may not have been intended originally, but the chain of cause and effect was unbroken.

Dubnov contended that Jewish history is "not isolated, not severed from the history of mankind. Rather is it most intimately interwoven with world-affairs at every point throughout its whole extent".[150] We saw how progress for Jews was linked to progress in general in 1789 and 1917. The Jewish Holocaust again shows the community's bellwether status, but this time in the opposite direction. The persecution of Jews and crushing of other groups were linked. The Nazi hierarchy of oppression had Jews at the bottom, but its broader Holocaust included the euthanasia of tens of thousands of disabled German children. Zyklon B poison gas was first tested on Russian prisoners of war, gays, Roma and people with mental health issues. Three hundred and sixty thousand German women were forcibly sterilised and 30,000 suffered forcible abortions as part of a programme under which 20 percent were judged "unfit to reproduce".[151] In addition, deciding "millions of people will become superfluous" in order to allow colonial settlement of the East by Germany, brought about the death of vast numbers of Slavic civilians.[152]

Between 1939 and 1945, mass murder, as seen in Auschwitz and Treblinka, stretched across the globe to the US A-bombs dropped on Hiroshima and Nagasaki, to Japan's "rape of Nanjing", the 2 million victims of famine in French/Japanese controlled Vietnam, the 3 million Bengali victims of famine engineered by Britain and its firestorm of Dresden. Perpetrated by politically contrasting regimes on either side, these demonstrated the inhuman depravity capitalism is capable of in its competitive struggle.

But the impact of the Holocaust on general Jewish thinking could not have been greater. Precisely because Germany enjoyed one of the highest levels of integration in the world, genocide of the Jews appeared to confirm the Zionist argument that an exclusive homeland was the only solution. For the majority of Jews, hopes of human solidarity, which had been embodied in the radical Jewish tradition, perished in the furnaces of Poland's killing centres.

Jewish resistance to the Nazis in Eastern Europe

What did the international community do?

When Hitler came to power in 1933 there were 600,000 Jews under Nazi rule, to which would be added 230,000 in Austria (from March 1938) and 360,000 in former Czechoslovakia (October 1938–March 1939). Although such numbers of potential refugees were far lower than the 89 million in the world today, the language used by governments was identical: "unbearable influx", "deluge", "tidal wave" and so on.

States moved quickly to turn words into actions. In 1935 the right-wing government in France banned entry to women fleeing forced sterilisation even if visa holders. Border police were told to "oppose by all means possible the entry of these individuals". Soon "women were throwing themselves under trucks to avoid being sent back, and several police officers deserted their posts, sickened by the heartrending scenes".[1] When mass opposition to an attempted fascist coup in 1934 and a general strike brought a left Popular Front government to power in 1936, the hard-line measures were lifted. But plans to provide refugees with social benefits and the right to education and work ended when the Popular Front government fell after a year.

British policy was summed up by Britain's foreign secretary, who was horrified by the prospect of being able to rescue 70,000 Romanian Jews—fully funded by the US community: "If we do that, then the Jews of the world will be wanting us to make similar offers in Poland and Germany. Hitler might well take us up".[2]

Holland's government complained the country was "overrun by foreigners who are competing unfairly". Denmark, apparently buckling under the burden of just 845 Jewish refugees from its southern neighbour, refused entry to victims of the Nuremburg laws (which banned marriage between Jews and non-Jews) alongside Jews and those fleeing forced sterilisation.[3]

Latin American countries such as Cuba, the Dominican Republic, Colombia, Ecuador, Bolivia and Paraguay all cut back on immigration in the early 1930s,[4] as did Uruguay in 1936 and Chile in 1940. Though it had a poor record towards Jews overall, Mexico, with its 1910–20 Revolution behind it, stood out from the other Latin American states in recognising refugees as a category. Trotsky benefitted alongside thousands of others.[5] Shanghai was an escape route until, in 1939, the British chair of the municipality called on the authorities to "take any steps in your power to prevent any further arrival of Jewish refugees".[6]

A turning point came on 13 March 1938. When Germany annexed Austria, its antisemitic policies were extended abroad for the first time and five years of accumulated oppressive measures were applied overnight. Far from this evoking sympathy for Jewish refugees, governments became even more reluctant to help. First out of the gate were the Dutch on 22 March, who demanded visas from Austrians where none had been required before. On 12 April France banned visas to Austrians. Britain demanded visas from May "in order to assist refugees",[7] but by the outbreak of war only 70,000 of the 600,000 applications had been accepted.[8] Switzerland, Sweden, Norway and Denmark also slapped on visa requirements. The Belgian government planned to restrict refugee intake and remove Jewish refugees, but a public protest by socialist Emile Vandervelde prevented the expulsions.[9] Italy brought in anti-Jewish laws, while Poland and Hungary devised schemes to prevent their Jewish citizens returning. Argentina, which per capita had taken the greatest number of refugees from Nazism, closed its border and stopped issuing visas. So did Brazil.

Finally in July the US President Franklin Roosevelt initiated a conference at Evian-les-Bains, France, supposedly to help Jewish refugees. At that time about 450,000 Jews had left German control out of a total of 950,000. But the conference did nothing. The US delegates offered no place to settle Jews fleeing Hitler and passed the buck to the South American states. One by one, the South Americans said no.

The Australian representative announced, "As we have no real racial problem, we are not desirous of importing one".[10] This was the culminating decision of a series of curious proposals that the Kimberley in north-west Australia be a resettlement area for European Jews fleeing Nazism. The first efforts came from Melekh Ravitsh, a Polish Yiddish poet who travelled the area in 1933. Although motivated by a desire to find a refuge for Jews, Ravitsh was not free from the Zionist "disease" of seeing the land as empty and the visible Indigenous occupants as belonging to "the very lowest level of human civilisation".[11] He supported his proposal by arguing that German Jews would not contravene the White Australia policy (racist immigration legislation that kept non-whites from Australia). However, the government decided against the proposal, arguing that it "would not contemplate imperilling British relations with Germany".[12]

Six years later, one Dr Isaac Steinberg, a visiting representative of the Territorialist Zionists, renewed the idea with a vision of Jewish settlers in the Kimberley "writing poetry about kangaroos and laughing kookaburras".[13] Amazingly many church groups, unions, business people and the premier of Western Australia supported him. Again, the Indigenous population were ignored. The government of conservative Prime Minister Robert Menzies blocked the proposal because an isolated single ethnic community was "contrary to the Government's assimilation aims".[14]

Although the proposals to rescue Jews by expropriating Indigenous people were misguided, it is nonetheless true that Australia could have accommodated a large number of refugees. As a lawyer who currently represents the local Indigenous community commented, "In my view the antisemitism that was in Europe at the time would have been reflective of some of the anti-Aboriginal thought processes that were going on in Australia".[15]

Leaving aside the proposals for the Kimberley, Australian policy restrictions on admitting Jewish refugees were no different from European countries and showed that the authorities "were unable to free themselves from the racist shackles of their cultural heritage".[16]

> For a country which perceived immigration as a prerequisite both for economic development and for strategic defence, the admission of less than 7000 refugees in the nine years between the rise of Hitler and...1941 is almost incomprehensible.[17]

Thus, in an unprecedented show of international capitalist solidarity, each country sought to match the other to ensure that none became a haven for desperate people. One thinks of the 1939 poem by W H Auden about the plight of German Jewish refugees:

> *The consul banged the table and said:*
> *"If you've got no passport, you're officially dead";*
> *But we are still alive, my dear, but we are still alive...*
>
> *Came to a public meeting; the speaker got up and said:*
> *"If we let them in, they will steal our daily bread";*
> *He was talking of you and me, my dear, he was talking of you*
> *   and me.*
>
> *Thought I heard the thunder rumbling in the sky;*
> *It was Hitler over Europe, saying: "They must die";*
> *O we were in his mind, my dear, O we were in his mind.*[18]

Outbreak of war

Following the Hitler-Stalin Pact in August 1939, Germany invaded western Poland. Russia did likewise from the east two weeks later and it was all over by 27 September. The spoils were divided almost equally. The Nazis annexed outright the western part of Poland, which became a part of "greater Germany", and controlled the remainder of the occupied area through a regime called the General Government. Later a third region was added when Germany occupied the area previously occupied by Russia.

Immediately following the invasion, Jews were subject to attacks and atrocities, but following the Wannsee Conference in January 1942, the extermination camps at Auschwitz and Treblinka operated at full capacity. From July 1942, Operation Reinhard developed the systematic annihilation of the Jewish population. Hitler's "Final Solution" meant genocide for Europe's Jewish population: 6 million Jews died in the Holocaust, 3 million of them in Poland. Only 5 percent of the Jewish population of Poland survived. Antisemitism could take no more dreadful form.

The Holocaust was incidental to Allied imperialism, which was fighting Hitler's battalions solely to maintain its hegemony. The British and US governments, far from being unaware of the situation, actually received detailed information of death camps such as Auschwitz and Treblinka but did nothing. When Jan Karski, the Polish resistance fighter, escaped to the West, he brought detailed information about the situation under the Nazi occupation, including the Holocaust. Karski met political leaders including UK Foreign Secretary Anthony Eden and President Roosevelt. None of the political leaders took him seriously. Roosevelt reportedly asked about the condition of horses in Poland but did not ask a single question about Jews.[19] Karski concluded that the Jews "were abandoned by all world governments".[20]

From March 1943, there were calls for the Allies to bomb the rails leading to the Auschwitz death camp. US military chiefs refused, arguing this would divert resources from the war effort and that the rails were hard to hit. Undersecretary of War John J McCloy fretted that such bombings might "provoke more vindictive actions by the Germans"—as if there was any worse fate than the death camps.[21] The tone was set in Allied refugee policy by the US but Britain followed closely behind, "putting self-interest first".[22] A measure of the desperation was that appeals came from within Auschwitz itself for the camp to be bombed to stop the agony. These too were ignored.

By late 1944 Allied air forces were dominant in the skies over Poland and between July and October "2,700 bombers travelled along or within easy reach [of] targets in the Auschwitz region". No bombs were targeted on the rail lines or crematoria. According to David Wyman, 437,000 lives could have been saved in Auschwitz had these been put out of action.[23]

European governments were rewarded by German invasion for their failure to take a principled stand against Nazism and its victims. Even then local ruling classes usually collaborated with the invaders rather than resist them. Germany's allies in Italy, Hungary, Romania and Bulgaria were joined by the Vichy regime and the Belgian King. Collaboration in Holland meant the extermination of three quarters of Dutch Jews, "a higher percentage than any other western European country".[24] In other places, such as Greece and Yugoslavia, the establishment carried on business as usual with Nazism while keeping a government in exile as an insurance policy in case the Allies won.

However, Switzerland, Britain and the US were still free to act. When news of the Holocaust reached Switzerland, it closed its borders to incoming Jews because, with around 10,000 Jews (less than 0.5 percent of population), the "lifeboat was full". Perhaps the fact that "Switzerland's establishment was haunted by the nightmare of a bolshevist takeover orchestrated from abroad"[25] was the real reason. But the Swiss government had a problem. The lifeboat could still find room for German traders who brought the loot from Nazi-forced expropriation of Jewish businesses to be deposited in its banks. How to distinguish "good Germans" from Jewish Germans? At Swiss behest the Nazis agreed to stamp "J" on relevant passports. Thanks to this charming scheme now every country in the world could easily spot "undesirables" and block their passage.

In sum the western governments displayed a shocking indifference to the fate of the Jews. Walter Laqueur concluded that, despite knowing about the "Final Solution" from an early date, the US, the UK and the Soviet Union showed no concern for the fate of the Jews.[26] US intelligence, for example, took notice of the movements of forced labour teams because they were a factor in the German war effort. But according to Richard Breitman in *US Intelligence and the Nazis*, the CIA's predecessor organisation, the Office of Strategic Services (OSS), "does not seem to have taken much detailed interest in German camps as they concerned the extermination of Jews".[27] Michael Neufeld, introducing a collection of essays on prospects for bombing Auschwitz, concludes that, "The Holocaust simply was not an important issue on the public or military agenda of World War II".[28]

Belief in solidarity was fundamental to the Jewish left tradition, but that was shaken by the callous behaviour of the so-called international community. In 1943 Shmuel Zygelboym, a Bundist and member of the Polish government in exile, committed suicide. The note he left said:

> The responsibility for this crime of murdering the entire Jewish population of Poland falls in the first instance on the perpetrators, but…by the passive observation of the murder of defenceless millions and the maltreatment of children, women and old men [the Allied states] have become the criminal accomplices… As I was unable to do anything during my life, perhaps by my death I shall contribute to breaking down the indifference.[29]

There was never a real prospect that the imperialist powers before the war or the Allies and the official war effort would help Jews because divide and rule was their tactic of choice. The fate of Jews depended on their own endeavours and the relationships built during the previous decades with opponents of the system.

"Never say there's only death for you"

> *Never say there's only death for you*
> *Though leaden skies may be concealing days of blue*
> *Because the hour we have hungered for is near;*
> *Beneath our tread the earth shall tremble: We are here!*[30]

There is a widespread misconception that the Jews themselves went passively to the gas chambers.[31] Henri Michel, a historian of the Resistance in Europe states:

Hundreds of thousands of Jews allowed themselves to be torn unprotestingly from their work and their homes, stripped of their possessions and taken they knew not where; finally they climbed docilely and apparently without fear into the trucks which took them to the door of the simulated "bath-houses"; when to their horror, they discovered the fearful truth that they were in a gas chamber, it was too late either to escape or to sell their lives dear.[32]

This is a chilling and inhuman image that comes very close to blaming the Jews themselves for their extermination. But it is only part of the story. Widespread resistance did occur. Furthermore, overwhelmingly the organised resistance was the work of socialists, communists and left Zionists. Despite the overwhelmingly difficult circumstances, the Jewish radical tradition continued into the war period.

The participation of Jews in the organised Resistance movements in France, Belgium, the Netherlands and Germany itself is generally recognised. Here we focus on the less well-known actions in Eastern Europe, where the population was concentrated and which was the epicentre of the Holocaust.

The establishment of the ghettos was the first step in the Nazis' plans to annihilate the Jews. Descriptions of life in these hundreds of walled, isolated and tightly controlled communities defy the imagination. For example, in Minsk a living space of 1.5 square metres was allotted per adult; no space at all was allotted for children. The food ration was 400 calories a day. In Warsaw, people returning home with their tiny bread ration had to ignore children dying in the street.

Jan Karski commented after a secret visit to the Warsaw Ghetto, "Everything there seemed polluted by death, the stench of rotting corpses, filth and decay".[33] Marek Edelman, a leader of the Warsaw Ghetto Uprising, described the terrible atmosphere:

> The Jews, beaten, stepped upon, slaughtered without the slightest cause—lived in constant fear. There was only one punishment for failure to obey regulations—death—while careful obedience...did not protect against a thousand and one fantastic degradations... [The] conviction that one was never treated as an individual human being caused a lack of self-confidence and stunted the desire to work... To overcome our own terrifying apathy, to fight against our own acceptance of the generally prevailing feeling of panic, even small tasks...required truly gigantic efforts on our part.[34]

Such an atmosphere is extremely corrupting. To obtain even the basic necessities of life the ordinary population had to bribe, steal or lie. With shortages of everything and survival at the centre of everyone's mind, some used their positions for additional personal advantage such as to avoid forced labour. The Jewish police were notorious for supporting the Nazis in their actions and there are horrifying examples of Jews spying for the Gestapo.[35] But this was not only true of the Jewish population. They were divided like all others.

Concentrating the Jews in ghettos served the Nazis strategically, but there was also an ideological function. In order to commit atrocities it is necessary to first dehumanise the victims and the ghetto environment facilitated this process. After a visit to the Warsaw Ghetto the Nazi governor of Krakow commented, "A German would not be able to live under such conditions" because they were a civilised people with a high culture and the state of the children of the ghetto was due to Jews being a diseased race.[36] As Chaim Kaplan put it, "We are segregated and separated from the world...driven out of the society of the human race".[37]

In all ghettos the Nazis created a special body, the Judenrat (Jewish Council), to act as an intermediary.[38] The Nazis carefully analysed existing community relationships and selected the membership of the councils from "authoritative personalities and rabbis", wealthy people and those they saw as likely to cooperate. In no sense were they community organisations: the basis of their power was the German oppressors.[39] The members of the Judenräte often saw their function as primarily welfare, running soup kitchens and so on. The confusion of roles was exacerbated by the fact that many Judenräte were created from pre-existing welfare bodies known as the Kehilla, which the community were accustomed to looking up to. Warsaw Ghetto survivor Hillel Seidman, for example, repeatedly uses the term Kehilla when referring to the Nazi-sponsored Judenräte.[40]

But to the Nazis these activities were irrelevant. The Nazis used the Judenrat to control the population, to provide manpower for the slave labour factories and finally, and chillingly, to process deportations to death camps.

Jewish leaders who served in the Judenräte clearly did not cause the Holocaust; it is crucial to distinguish between the oppressors and the oppressed. But the one thing that Jews could take responsibility for was their own response. Would they submit or would they resist? The responses of the Judenräte varied greatly. Many argued that compliance would limit the damage the Nazis did or that by making themselves economically useful at least some Jews would survive. They argued that resistance could not be successful so it was futile.

This is a much disputed field and perhaps the differences are easier to see in retrospect. Yehuda Bauer discusses the research of Aharon Weiss into the behaviour of the Judenräte. Weiss drew a "red line"— active collaboration "meant handing over Jews to the Germans at the latter's request".[41] Some, such as Joseph Parnes in Lwów and Adam Czerniakow in Warsaw, refused; the former was killed and the latter committed suicide.[42] At the other extreme was the Łódź Ghetto, where the head of the Judenrat, Mordechai Rumkowski, was, in Bauer's words, "without any doubt a brutal dictator",[43] who handed the children of the ghetto over to the Nazis and turned the ghetto into a slave labour camp.

Active collaboration is one thing. More significant for our general argument are the Judenräte who were not active collaborators but who failed to support the underground groupings and opposed active resistance to the Nazis. This was the case in several large and important ghettos such as Vilna, Bialystok and Warsaw. Their attitude affected the populations in the ghettos; it exacerbated the feeling of hopelessness and made the building of resistance organisations even more difficult.

Feelings of hopelessness are understandable. Militarily the situation *was* hopeless. Nechama Tec argues that there are five conditions upon which the possibility of successful armed resistance is predicated: time to prepare; a strategic base of operations; leadership; arms; and allies.[44] Overwhelmingly these conditions were lacking. As Lucjan Dobroszycki put it, "Has anyone seen an army without arms; an army scattered over 200 isolated ghettos; an army of infants, old people, the sick; an army whose soldiers are denied the right even to surrender?"[45]

Yet there was resistance—and on a scale that has somehow disappeared from historical awareness. The Warsaw Ghetto Uprising is not the only case; Jewish resistance occurred right across Nazi-occupied Eastern Europe.[46]

Definitions of resistance tend to divide into two groups. The first group focuses on an active ideological component:

> [Resistance] could develop only from an active ideology which presented its holders in opposition to the existing circumstances and believed in the possibility of changing the cultural and political ecology. Therefore the resisters usually had a previous history as members of anti-establishment groups.[47]

This type of definition applies readily enough to members of formally structured resistance organisations. The political parties, and above all their youth groups, formed the core of the underground. Overwhelmingly it was young people who were able to recognise the true intentions of the Nazis and to organise against them, particularly Labour Zionists, the socialist Zionists Hashomer Hatzair, the Bund youth group Tsukunft and Communist youth groups.[48]

However, the Jewish population as a whole faced a situation where almost all normal activities were banned by an enemy determined to exterminate them. In such circumstances even staying alive is at least defiance and even efforts to hide or flee must be regarded as opposition. In this broader context the definition offered by Nehama Tec sits better: "Activities motivated by the desire to thwart, limit, undermine, or end the exercise of oppression over the oppressed".[49]

Consider the case of the Jews in the small eastern Polish town of Biala Podlaska who gave bread to Soviet POWs marching through the town under guard in June 1941. Sent to Auschwitz, they were among the first Jewish victims to perish there.[50] Ideology does not enter into such acts of courageous defiant humanity that occurred in everyday activities. Even simple survival activities such as soup kitchens required a defiant attitude. As one Vilna Ghetto inmate said, "The resistance of the anonymous masses must be affirmed in terms of how they held on to their humanity, of their manifestation of solidarity, of mutual help and self-sacrifice".[51]

Sometimes defiant acts occurred at the moment of final extremity. In Lubliniec in the autumn of 1942, the Nazis had ordered all the Jews to gather together and undress while they stood over them brandishing whips and sticks and tore the clothes off the women. Suddenly the naked women reacted—they attacked the officers, scratching and biting, and throwing stones. The panicked Nazis ran off.[52]

Astonishingly, this incident made it into a newspaper report in New York, headlined "Jewish resistance in Poland: Women trample Nazi soldiers".

Defiance can also be seen in the extraordinary range of cultural activities that occurred including music, theatre and art.[53] In addition, "people kept their sense of humour, albeit grotesque, amidst the most appalling and unspeakable atrocities. We were always singing and telling vulgar jokes about our predicament". A song in one concentration camp sung every evening contained the lyrics, "It's already nine o'clock, All the camp is going to sleep, The latrines are locked up now, You're no longer allowed to shit".[54]

A very Jewish joke:

A Jewish teacher asks his pupil, "Tell me Moshe, what would you like to be if you were Hitler's son?" "An orphan", answers the pupil.[55]

The remainder of this chapter focuses on collective and organised active resistance within this wider context.[56]

Rising up against their destroyers

The most famous example of resistance by Jews is the Warsaw Ghetto Uprising.[57]

Nearly 400,000 people were sealed into the Warsaw Ghetto in 1940. The Judenrat and much of the population tended to rationalise what was happening. But some of the Zionist youth groups recognised the Nazis' intentions as early as March 1942 and called for the creation of a self-defence organisation but without success.[58] The Nazis started mass deportations to Treblinka in July 1942 in the so-called Gross-Aktion Warschau. By then over 100,000 had already died due to starvation, disease or random killings. With another 250,000–300,000 people transported, the political groups finally faced up to the need for a united armed response.

Finally, at the end of October 1942, three political groupings—the Bund, the Labour Zionists and the Communists—formed the Jewish Fighting Organisation (Żydowska Organizacja Bojowa, ZOB) under the command of the Labour Zionist Mordechai Anielewicz.

When a second wave of deportations commenced on 18 January 1943, ZOB members fought back. The subsequent four days saw the first street fighting in occupied Poland. Despite the almost complete lack of arms and resources, the ghetto fighters were able to force the Nazis to retreat and to limit the number of deportations.

Marek Edelman, a member of the Bund and the five-person command group of the ZOB, wrote:

> For the first time German plans were frustrated. For the first time
> the halo of omnipotence and invincibility was torn from the Germans'
> heads. For the first time the Jew in the street realised that it was pos-
> sible to do something against the Germans' will and power... [It was]
> a psychological turning point.[59]

The ZOB then took effective control of the ghetto. With a very different approach to the typical Judenrat, they executed Jewish police, Nazi agents and spies and prepared for military resistance. They also oversaw all aspects of ghetto life, including the publication of newspapers and taxing wealthy residents.

On 19 April the German forces tried to resume deportations with a view to finally liquidating the ghetto. At this point the ZOB had perhaps 500 fighters armed with some handguns (many barely functional), grenades and Molotov cocktails, a few rifles, two land mines and a submachine gun. They were aged 20–25 and a third were women. Also part of the uprising, but not operating under the direction of the ZOB, was the Jewish Military Union (Żydowski Związek Wojskowy, ZZW) with approximately 500 fighters consisting of former Jewish officers of the Polish army plus right-wing Zionists.[60]

The German side consisted of more than 2,000 soldiers with heavy weapons, including artillery, mine throwers and machine guns. With their overwhelming military superiority, they anticipated an action of only three days. But the Nazi commander General Stroop was forced to report after a week, "The resistance put up by the Jews and bandits could be broken only by relentlessly using all our force and energy by day and night".[61]

None were more surprised than the defenders themselves. They expected to last no more than a few days. But:

> After the first five days of fighting…the ZOB was left with a shocking result: most everyone was alive. This was, of course, good news, but it also presented a challenge. Because they had been prepared to die, they hadn't planned any escape routes or…survival plans, and they had no hideout and barely any food… [There was] a new, wholly unexpected, discussion: How would they keep going?[62]

The stories of personal bravery are inspiring and heartbreaking. Edelman describes a young boy, Dawid Hochberg, blocking a narrow passage way. Once killed by the Germans, his wedged in body took some time to remove, allowing the escape of fighters and civilians.[63] Batalion describes the response of Nazis to women who threw acid or grenades: "Look, a woman! A woman fighter!"[64]

A number of captured fighters—especially the women—threw hidden grenades or fired concealed handguns after surrendering, killing themselves with their captors. Some Polish resistance members fought alongside the Jews inside the ghetto. Polish resistance groups also engaged the Nazis at six different locations outside the ghetto walls to help divert the German forces.

The Nazis had to fight from building to building. Defeating the uprising took six weeks and necessitated setting fire to the ghetto. As Edelman says, the insurgents "were beaten by the flames, not the Germans".[65] Organised resistance was over by the end of April but localised resistance continued until June. Many people hid in bunkers and were only forced out by smoke bombs.

Anielewicz noted in his last letter, "What took place exceeded all expectations. In our opposition to the Germans we did more than our strength allowed".[66] Even Goebbels (unintentionally) paid the resistance tribute: "The Jews have actually succeeded in making a defensive position of the ghetto... It shows what is to be expected of Jews when they are in possession of arms. Unfortunately, some of their weapons were good German ones".[67]

The ghetto uprising was a military failure. But as Yitzhak Zuckerman, second in command of the ZOB, said:

> I don't think there is any need to analyse the uprising in military terms... [N]o one doubted how it was likely to turn out... The really important things were...in the force shown by Jewish youths...to rise up against their destroyers and determine what death they would choose: Treblinka or Uprising.[68]

The uprising had an enormous impact on the Polish population as well as the Jews and intensified resistance throughout the country. Many of the other uprisings were directly or indirectly inspired by the ghetto insurgents.

"We should have raised them in the spirit of revenge"

When the Nazis set up the Warsaw Judenrat in August 1939, it was argued that at least one Bund member should participate and Shmuel Zygelboym reluctantly joined. However, the demands of the position soon came into conflict with his politics. When the Nazis attempted to set up the ghetto in Warsaw in October of that year, Zygelboym refused to help. Instead, he addressed Jews gathered outside the organisation's headquarters waiting for news and told them not to cooperate but to remain in their houses and make the Nazis take them by force. This single call for resistance succeeded in having the order to establish the ghetto cancelled for several months.[69]

The leader of the Warsaw Judenrat, Adam Czerniaków (a general

Zionist), behaved differently. He carried out Nazi instructions, including providing lists of people to be deported, even though he knew their fate. In this he was supported by the Jewish police. Marek Edelman comments about a Judenrat meeting in July 1942 in response to the German demand that all "non-productive" Jews be deported in the Gross-Aktion Warschau.

> Not a single councilman stopped to consider the basic question—whether the Jewish Council should undertake to carry out the order at all... There was no debate on the implications of the order, only on the...procedure for its execution... Thus the Germans made the Jewish Council itself condemn over 300,000 ghetto inhabitants to death.[70]

The role of the youth in the creation of a fighting organisation was central. Immediately following the Nazi invasion of Poland, most of the top leaders of the Zionist organisations left the country to go into exile, leaving secondary leaders and the youth groups to lead their response. Similarly, the Bund leadership largely departed, leaving their youth group Tsukunft to play a leading role in the party's underground activities.[71]

The remaining Bund leaders were reluctant to unite in an underground organisation with the Zionists. When the ZOB was formed in July it was without the participation of the Bund. Nazi attacks in the meantime resulted in a very high attrition rate and by this time only a few dozen Bundists remained in the ghetto out of an original strength of more than 500.[72]

For virtually their entire history they had opposed Zionism. But the situation faced by the population of the ghetto was beyond normal political conflicts. The Nazis planned to annihilate Jews of all political currents, and military action required unity with anyone who was prepared to take up arms. It took the efforts of the youth group, in particular its leader Abrasha Blum, to convince the adults of the Bund to join in a united fighting organisation. Even then the decision to join in October was taken with a majority of just one vote.[73]

The Zionists in the ghetto on the other hand were hamstrung by their politics in a different way. In the first period even the youth groups mainly engaged in communal activities. Emmanuel Ringelblum described how Anielewicz regretted the delays and failure to face up to the necessity of armed resistance and felt that they "had wasted three war years on cultural and educational work".

> We had not understood that new side of Hitler that is emerging, Mordechai lamented. We should have trained the youth in the use of live and cold ammunition. We should have raised them in the spirit of revenge against the greatest enemy of the Jews, of all mankind, and of all times.[74]

Yitzhak Zuckerman, a founder of the ZOB and later a major historian of the Warsaw Ghetto Uprising, stated baldly, "The Jewish Fighting Organisation arose without the parties and against the wish of the parties".[75]

The failure of the ZOB to unite with the ZZW may also have weakened them, although they did fight together. Politically the ZZW were associated with the right-wing Revisionist Zionists, to whom the ZOB remained hostile. Their role was played down by the post-war Polish government and their actual contribution remains contentious.

Underground organisation and uprisings

In June 1942 the head of the Jewish Social Relief Organisation in Biala Podlaska expressed the views of many when he angrily asked, "How much longer will we go as sheep to the slaughter? Why do we keep quiet? Why is there no call to escape to the forests? No call to resist?"[76]

There was never going to be a general call to resist. But in spite of the almost hopeless situation, Jews did fight back against the Nazis far more extensively than is currently recognised. They did not go like lambs to the slaughter.

The Warsaw Ghetto Uprising is well known but it was not the only expression of resistance. There were underground resistance movements in approximately 100 ghettos in Nazi-occupied Eastern Europe (about a quarter of all ghettos) and uprisings occurred in five major ghettos and 45 smaller ones. In addition, there were uprisings in three extermination camps and 18 forced labour camps. Some 20,000–30,000 Jewish partisans fought in approximately 30 Jewish partisan groups and 21 mixed groups while some 10,000 people survived in family camps in the forest.[77]

There can be no strict division between the various means of resistance. Ghetto underground organisations communicated with partisans and provided them with information or supplies; carried out non-military sabotage; helped POWs and escapees; distributed illegal information and money; forged documents; and published newspapers and proclamations. Individuals and illegal groups helped Jews to find the necessities of life in the ghettos, to escape and to find arms.

Many people carried out sabotage and even executions. None are quite as compelling as Niuta Teitelbaum, a Communist. With blond hair done up in braids, she looked like an innocent teenager. But she was an assassin, a "self appointed executioner". Dressed as a Polish farm girl, "Little Wanda with the braids" as the Gestapo called her, walked calmly into the offices and homes of Gestapo agents and shot them in cold blood.[78]

"Let us not go as sheep to slaughter!"[79]

The underground in Bialystok (Poland) began in late 1941 with the establishment of groups to help Russian POWs, who received appalling treatment from the Nazis. The activists, the majority of whom were young, established contacts with Polish supporters and were able to smuggle in some weapons.

In late 1942, the Warsaw ZOB decided to organise armed resistance in the other key ghettos and sent Tenenbaum to Bialystok. Under his leadership all political factions including the Communists, Bundists, Labour Zionists and other Zionists united and started to prepare for an uprising.[80]

The Bialystok Judenrat, on the other hand, was dominated by older people. Although the Zionist chairman Efraim Barasz was aware of the mass murders and destruction of communities, he refused to cooperate with the underground, arguing that because the ghetto was "productive" the Germans would leave it alone.[81] When the Judenrat handed over 6,000 Jews to the Nazis in February 1943, some underground groups put up armed resistance, including 20 young men led by Edek Borak. Others resisted with acid, axes, knives and boiling water.[82] Afterwards people searched for informers who had led Nazis to hideouts. "When a cry of 'traitor' was heard, crowds rushed to the scene. They would tear and claw at the suspect, and lynch him on the spot".[83] May Day 1943 saw a strike among the forced labourers in the factories. Protest demonstrations or absence from work were not possible. But the workers stood idle near their inactive machines, turning them on when they saw a German approaching and off the moment the German left.[84]

Strategically the underground activists in the ghettos faced a terrible dilemma. An armed uprising could not hope to achieve anything if it was isolated; it would require the support of a significant section of ghetto inhabitants. But the ghettos were full of children, old people and other non-combatants and arms were difficult to come by. The other option was escape, usually with an intention of joining the partisans. While this had a better chance of success for individuals or small groups, it meant leaving the rest of the population to its fate.

The situation in Bialystok illustrates the predicament. The underground met on the evening of 27 February 1943, believing the Germans planned to attempt liquidation of the ghetto the next day. Minutes of this meeting have survived. The leader Mordecai Tenenbaum commented, "It's a good thing that at least the mood is good. Unfortunately, the meeting won't be very cheerful... We must decide today what to do tomorrow". He went on:

> We can do two things: decide that when the first Jew is taken away from
> Bialystok now, we start our counter-*Aktion*... It is not impossible that
> after we have completed our task someone may by chance still be alive...
> We can also decide to get out into the forest... We must decide for our-
> selves now. Our daddies will not take care of us. This is an orphanage.[85]

In fact liquidation did not occur until later in the year. The planned attack and mass escape into the forest failed. The underground staged a heroic ten-day uprising from 16 August 1943, but having failed to previously win the support of the ghetto population, it was isolated.

Vilna (Lithuania) was an important Jewish cultural centre. When the Nazis occupied the city in June 1941, they immediately attacked the Jewish population ferociously. They murdered 20,000 young men during the first week and by the end of October had massacred nearly half of the remaining population. Their next step was to murder all "non-productive" people. By the end of the year, only 15,000 of the original 80,000 Jews were left alive in Vilna.

It is not surprising that elements of resistance also developed early and that they developed the earliest demand for armed resistance. Hashomer Hatzair member Abba Kovner wrote an appeal:

> Don't allow them to drive you like sheep to the slaughter!... Our only dignified response to the enemy must be: Resistance!... Better to die as free fighters than survive on the clemency of the murderers. Resist until the last breath you breathe.[86]

Several different underground groups were set up, but as early as June 1942 they came together and formed the United Partisan Organisation (Fareynikte Partizaner Organizatsye, FPO), uniting Communists and Bund members and left and (unusually) right-wing Zionists. Their first action was a wave of sabotage in the arms industry: forced labourers destroyed whole ghettos of machinery or produced substandard and defective equipment.[87] In their first military action, Hashomer Hatzair member Vitka Kempner and two companions blew up a Nazi military transport carrying 200 soldiers on the outskirts of the town.[88] Abba Kovner recorded:

> Lithuanians did not do it, nor Poles, nor Russians. A Jewish woman did it, a woman who, after she did this, had no base to return to. She had to walk three days and nights with wounded legs and feet. She had to go back to the ghetto. Were she to have been captured, the whole ghetto might have been held responsible.[89]

The action was memorialised in a famous song by Hirsh Glik, "Still the night was full of starlight".[90] Vitka became one of Kovner's chief lieutenants and was later involved in many acts of resistance. She died in February 2012.

The FPO hoped to lead a ghetto uprising, to be followed by a mass breakout and escape to the forest to form partisan units. But they were thwarted in their efforts to gain support for armed resistance. This was at least partly due to the Judenrat, led by Jewish collaborator Jacob Gens, who opposed the call and refused cooperation, arguing that armed resistance would lead to destruction of the ghetto population.[91] When the Nazis liquidated the ghetto, virtually all of its inhabitants went to their deaths in forced labour camps, Sobibor death camp or were murdered directly. A few hundred members of the underground organisation including Kovner escaped to become partisans in the forest.[92]

In Kovno (Kaunus, central Lithuania), a large underground of 600 members was led by Chaim Yelin, a Jewish Communist who was able to unite the Communists and Zionist youth groups.[93] The Judenrat actively supported the underground as did a number of the ghetto's Jewish police. Among the Poles who helped the Jewish underground in Kovno was Dr Kutorghene. She explained why she risked her life in this way:

> You gave me courage, you gave a new lease of life, encouraged me. I feel I am stronger when I am with you and do not want you to go even though we both risk our lives and lives of our family members.[94]

Ultimately there was no uprising, but some 500 ghetto fighters escaped to join Jewish partisan groups. When the ghetto was liquidated the population refused to present themselves for deportation following an appeal from the underground. Many people went into hiding and hid as long as possible although the Nazis set the ghetto on fire.

Of the smaller ghettos, Lachva (Belarus) was among the first to show resistance as a united community in August 1942, possibly because the Judenrat supported the underground.[95] The uprising started during the liquidation of the ghetto. People had no guns so they set fires and attacked the Nazis with axes, knives, iron bars, pitchforks and clubs:

> The fire and smoke, along with the spontaneous Jewish attack, created panic among the Germans. The Jews took the opportunity to break through the ghetto fences. Under heavy fire, hundreds of Jews ran towards the swamps in the forest. 600 people escaped...including elderly people, women and children.[96]

Approximately 150 people made it to the swamps and later joined the partisans.

"Culture of solidarity between Jews and non-Jews"
Minsk deserves attention as the location of one of the most successful of the underground organisations.[97] In present day Belarus, Minsk had

been part of the Soviet Union before the war. Their experience during the war was perhaps unique in that Jews and non-Jews were united in one Communist-led underground organisation across the ghetto and the main city. Historian Barbara Epstein emphasises the "culture of solidarity between Jews and non-Jews" within the underground organisation but also points to personally based support and interaction outside the formal underground organisation.[98]

Formed in late 1941, the underground ran a clandestine press and smuggled Jewish children out of the ghetto to hide them in other parts of the city. Jews and non-Jews both engaged in sabotage within Nazi factories. For instance, shoemakers put nails into shoes to make them unwearable and tailors sewed left arms into right armholes of coats and vice versa.

Participation in the underground was very dangerous. One well known example is the case of Masha Bruskina, a 17-year-old Jewish member of a Communist underground group located outside the ghetto who helped wounded Soviet POWs. Captured in October 1941, she was hanged with two other non-Jewish members of the underground, Krill Trus and Volodya Sherbateyvich, the first public execution of resisters.

Rather than armed uprising, the Minsk underground focused on flight, which their circumstances particularly favoured. A barbed wire fence, rather than the high wall found in other ghettos, and relatively lenient guards made access to the nearby dense and impenetrable forest dangerous but possible. A major factor was also the support from the first two Judenräte, which were more closely intertwined with the underground than elsewhere. The courageous stand of the Judenrat members no doubt contributed very significantly to the high number of escapes, but they paid a high price once exposed.

Led by child guides and helped by non-Jewish contacts, roughly 10,000 Jews made their way into the forests; most of them survived the war. This was the most successful ghetto resistance in terms of numbers saved and deserves to be as widely recognised as the Warsaw Ghetto Uprising.

The Minsk underground supported and sent supplies to the partisans and also carried out successful sabotage within the town. A letter in a German newspaper in June 1943 describes the situation:

Partisans are everywhere, even in the city of Minsk. In the last months many Germans have been killed in the streets. You can't travel along the Vilna-Minsk highway. You can move in the direction of Baranovichi only escorted by tanks…a mine was planted in the city theatre…as a result more than 30 people were killed and about 100 were wounded. Then they blew up an electric power station and the steam tank at the dairy plant.[99]

The soldiers' cinema and hostel, a bakery and many vehicles were also targeted, many successfully.

The story of the fate of the surviving underground members after the war is a sorry one. Not only were they not treated as heroes by the Russian regime, they were arrested and many spent years in prison or keeping their heads down.[100]

"Ghetto girls"

The underground organisations in the ghettos could not have functioned without the thousands of couriers who worked to overcome the isolation of the ghettos at great risk to themselves. The vast majority were women. They could pass as non-Jews more easily: women often spoke Polish better than the men and, since virtually all Jewish men were circumcised within a few days of birth, the women did not need to fear the "pants-drop test".[101]

The word courier suggests perhaps someone who delivered messages, but these women did so much more. They smuggled people, cash, fake IDs, underground publications, information and weapons. They hid items in their clothes, their bras, in sanitary towels, in their shoes, in sacks of potatoes. They pretended to be carefree and even acted flirtatiously with soldiers and SS members all the time risking detection, torture, imprisonment and death. "The poise and composure required for this kind of work was superhuman".[102]

Judy Batalion has given us an extraordinarily compelling and passionate account of these women couriers in her book *The Light of Days*.[103] Most were members of Jewish socialist youth groups such as the Bund or socialist Zionist organisations. Their stories are full of the kind of material that usually makes it into film and notoriety. Yet they are virtually unknown. The "ghetto girls" smuggled guns in loaves of bread and coded intelligence messages in their plaited hair. They bribed

Gestapo guards with alcohol and assassinated Nazis. They endured prison, rape, humiliation and beatings and kept on fighting.

> Often courier girls appealed to Nazis with their displays of womanly elegance or "little girl" looks and faux naivete, even asking them for help carrying their bags—the very bags filled with contraband.[104]

Tema Schneiderman, a courier for the Jewish underground in Bialystok, Vilna and Warsaw, secretly delivered news and ammunition. Ania Rud, a former member of the Bialystok Ghetto underground, lived outside the ghetto as a White Russian and acted as a contact between couriers, the local underground and forest partisans. Marylka Rozycka, a member of the Communist Party in Łódź, was Jewish but looked like a Polish peasant. She maintained contacts between the Communist Party and the ghetto underground and later joined the partisans in the forest.[105]

Major efforts went into collecting information and recording events. Krakow activist Gusta Draenger was arrested after a grenade attack on a Nazi coffee shop. She recorded the history of the Krakow underground on toilet paper while in prison. This document still exists. Bund member Zalmen Frydrych met escapees near Treblinka and obtained information about the death camps.[106]

The astonishing bravery, intelligence, resourcefulness, drive, determination and self-sacrifice of these women fully destroys the myth that Jews "went as sheep to the slaughter".

"Today partisans are going to beat the enemy"[107]

Partisan units were a feature of the northern forest area. The partisan groups were very disparate but Soviet POWs who had escaped from the horrendous Nazi POW camps figured large. We should not romanticise the partisan movement. As Tec says, "Few forest dwellers resembled the idealised image of the fearless, heroic fighter".[108] The life of a partisan was extremely difficult and conditions so bad that one participant called them "inhuman".[109] Life in the forest where dirt, hunger, exhaustion, danger and fear were the daily experience naturally bred suspicion, hierarchy, internal conflict—and antisemitism. "In these jungle-like forests, a jungle-like culture emerged".[110]

In the early days the units tended to be anarchic, loose and disorganised. Many partisans in Belarus were Communists and later the units became more organised as Stalin implemented a programme of control over them with an eye on post-war Poland.[111] The partisan groups would very often only accept young men with arms whereas fleeing Jews often arrived without weapons or skills. Nonetheless approximately 20,000-30,000 Jews fought in about 30 Jewish partisan groups and 21 mixed groups; an estimated 80 percent died.[112]

In 1944 more than 159 Jewish partisans were active in the Parczew forest north of Lublin (Poland). They cooperated with the Soviet partisans in a number of engagements against the Nazis including the takeover of the city of Parczew in April 1944.[113]

Not all the partisans were Soviet controlled. When the Jewish partisan group "The Avengers" from Vilna moved into the forest after the liquidation of the ghetto, they destroyed the town power plant and the waterworks. In their time in the forest and acting independently they destroyed over 180 miles of train tracks, five bridges, 40 enemy train cars, killed 212 enemy soldiers, and rescued at least 71 Jews.[114] This group included a number of women, including Gertie Boyarski who, with a friend, marked International Women's Day by demolishing a wooden bridge used by the Nazis. They were both still in their teens.[115]

The dilemma of the ghettos also applied in the partisan setting. What were the many people who fled the ghettos but unarmed and unable to be fighters to do?

About 10,000 Jews survived in family camps which provided shelter and support for non-fighting people as well as armed partisans. The most famous, Bielski Otriad, focused on rescuing Jews and accepted anyone of any sex or age who could reach them.[116] Another non-military group was, astonishingly, a musical troupe based near the village of Sloboda in Belarus. The group of 25 included three Jews— Chana Pozner, her father Mordechai Pozner and Yehiel Borgin—and provided entertainment for the partisan units.[117]

"The crematorium was burning against a dark sky"

The horrors of life in camps are notorious and the degradation and misery led to bitter and corrupt behaviour. In her diary, Hanna

Levy-Hass, a Communist and inmate of Bergen-Belsen, describes her pain at the collaboration and servitude. But there were also many local and individual instances of resistance. For example, Levy-Hass describes how she represented 120 women who organised to demand more equitable food distribution.[118] Structured underground organisations arose in many camps and there were armed uprisings in three of the six extermination camps and 18 work camps.

The name of Auschwitz is virtually synonymous with death camp. It was in fact much more than that. Auschwitz-Birkenau, situated near the Polish town of Oświęcim in southwest Poland, consisted of three main sections including transit camps, labour camps, extermination ovens and 45 satellite camps.[119] Resistance occurred in many areas at Auschwitz. The Union Factory (Weichsel-Union-Metallwerke), which was owned by the leading German industrial company Krupp, employed forced labourers who manufactured a range of explosives and armaments. Krupp had complete control over production while punishment was "inflicted by the SS at Krupp's request". Workers, many of whom were Jews, carried out sabotage and participated in the uprising.[120]

The underground organisation at Auschwitz included Polish political prisoners, forced labourers and Jews from the Sonderkommando, the group responsible for dealing with the remains from the crematorium. The Auschwitz underground astonishingly published a newspaper and even transmitted by radio direct to London.[121] The group planned a revolt and prepared weapons using gunpowder smuggled out of the Union Factory by women forced labourers such as Rosa Robota.[122] Having heard that the Sonderkommando was about to be liquidated, on 7 October 1944 camp inmates attacked the guards with axes and knives while the SS responded with machine guns. The Sonderkommando members then blew up crematorium IV with grenades made from smuggled dynamite.[123]

> In no time the entire guard force of the camp was mobilised against the rebels. Bullets were flying all over the place. SS with dogs were chasing the...rebels, many of whom fell while trying to escape... When they realised that they had no chance of survival, they set the forest on fire... As the day was coming to an end Auschwitz was surrounded by guards

and fires. The crematorium was burning against a dark sky, as were small forests on opposite sides of the camp. The ground was covered with dead bodies of the members of the Sonderkommando.[124]

A total of 250 prisoners died during the uprising and 200 were later shot. None escaped. Perhaps two or three Nazis died with approximately 12 wounded. Robota and three other women were hanged in Auschwitz the following January, only three weeks before the camp was liberated by the Soviets. After the war the Krupp-owned Union Factory received 2.5 million marks as reparation for the factory they lost at Auschwitz. The forced labourers received nothing: the Allies agreed to postpone claims. The German Supreme Court barred claims from forced labourers. Finally in 1993, a group of 22 survivors sued the former factory, with back pay being awarded in 1997 to one of them only. The court determined that the others were sufficiently compensated by governmental reparations.[125]

The uprising in Sobibor concentration camp in eastern Poland was more successful. The underground leadership consisted of a Jew, Leon Feldhandler, and a Soviet POW, Sasha Pechersky. Having learned about the Warsaw Ghetto Uprising from deportees from that city, they made their own plans. On 14 October 1943, the group lured SS officers into the storehouses and attacked them with axes and knives, killing 11, including the camp commander. The rebels then seized weapons and ammunition and set fire to the camp. Tomasz Blatt describes what followed:

> During the revolt prisoners streamed to one of the holes cut in the barbed-wire fence. They weren't about to wait in line; there were machine guns shooting at us. They climbed on the fence and just as I was half way through, it collapsed, trapping me underneath. This saved me…[as the] first ones through hit mines. When most were through, I slid out of my coat, which was hooked on the fence, and ran till I reached the forest.[126]

Ultimately, 300 of the 600 prisoners escaped, of whom nearly 200 avoided recapture; some were hidden from the Nazis by Poles.[127]

The underground at Treblinka (northeast Poland) was organised by a former Jewish captain of the Polish Army, Dr Julian Chorążycki. After months of preparations on 2 August 1943, they stole arms from a warehouse, killed the guards, set the camp on fire and destroyed the extermination area. They then helped prisoners to escape into the forest. All resistance leaders were killed as the Germans retaliated. Out of 1,500 prisoners in the camp, approximately 600 escaped, the majority of whom were recaptured. Some of the escapees were helped by the Polish Home Army or by Polish villagers.[128]

Despite the losses, these two uprisings resulted in the closure of the camps, which must be regarded an achievement.[129]

"None of us would have survived [without] help"[130]

Much is made of Polish collusion with the Nazi extermination of Jews. Yet even the post-war Israeli War Crimes Commission could only identify 7,000 collaborators out of a population of over 20 million ethnic Poles.[131]

Poland had the most draconian penalties in occupied Europe for helping Jews in any way. In places like France and Germany people attempting to help Jews certainly faced severe consequences. But in Poland not only the person but their whole family would be executed. Up to 50,000 Poles were executed for aiding Jews and thousands more were arrested and sent to labour or concentration camps.[132]

At the same time Poles were themselves subject to genocidal attacks from the Nazis. For Hitler all Poles were "more like animals than human beings" and ethnic cleansing known as "housecleaning" displaced 900,000 people. Over 3 million non-Jewish Poles died. The Nazi food rationing allowed 2,613 calories for Germans but 669 for Poles—barely above that allowed for Jews.[133]

Yet even in these conditions, people did help Jews. It came in many forms and from both individuals and groups. Poland was the only country in occupied Europe with a secret organisation dedicated to helping Jews: the Council to Aid Jews (Rada Pomocy Żydom) known as Zegota, which helped approximately half of the Polish Jews who survived the war (thus over 50,000).[134]

Zegota was founded in September 1942 by Zofia Kossak-Szczucka, a Catholic activist, and Wanda Krahelska-Filipowicz ("Alinka"), who was a socialist. Members came from many of the left-wing organisations which had opposed antisemitism in the 1930s, including the Polish Socialist Party, the Peasant Party and the Bund. But there were also Catholic activists and Polish nationalists, students, the scout association, the writers' union, medical and social workers and activists in the Polish underground.

The first chairman, Julian Grobelny, had actively helped Jews before he joined Zegota and headed an underground cell composed mainly of socialist friends of the Bund. Because of his links to doctors and medical workers, he was able to hide people in quarantine. And due to his long involvement in trade unions, in particular his contacts with railway workers, he was able to arrange transport for Jews out of Warsaw.

Zegota's headquarters was the home of a Polish socialist (Eugenia Wasowska), who had worked closely with the Bund. The organisation held "office hours" twice each week at which time couriers went in and out. Despite the enormous number of people who knew its location, the headquarters were never raided by the Germans. One "branch office" was a fruit and vegetable kiosk operated by Ewa Brzuska, an old woman known to everybody as "Babcia" (Granny). Babcia hid papers and money under the sauerkraut and pickle barrels and always had sacks of potatoes ready to hide Jewish children.

The best known Zegota activist is Irene Sendler, head of the children's division. A social worker and a socialist, she grew up with close links to the Jewish community and could speak Yiddish. Sendler had protested against antisemitism in the 1930s: she deliberately sat with Jews in segregated university lecture halls and nearly got expelled. Sendler saved a total of 2,500 Jewish children by smuggling them out of the Warsaw Ghetto, providing them with false documents and sheltering them in individual and group children's homes outside the ghetto. [135]

Zegota was not the only support group. What Gunnar Paulsson called a "secret city" operated in Warsaw; between 70,000 and 90,000 people helped an estimated 28,000 Jews to live outside the ghetto. [136]

The divided stand on antisemitism taken by pre-war political currents continued during the war. So while the right-wing press contained antisemitic diatribes, the Polish Socialist Party and other left-wing newspapers published information about atrocities and death camps, as did the organ of the peasant movement and those of the Catholic underground groups. [137] Attitudes within the Polish Underground State, the clandestine resistance organisation in occupied Poland, varied considerably. The poor, rural north-eastern provinces such as Bialystok had significantly high levels of antisemitism before the war. Not surprisingly the most antisemitic components of the underground were in these provinces. In other areas there was active support despite the dangers. For example in Lwów the local Polish underground protected 250 Jews in one village.[138] One major contribution of the Polish underground was its pivotal role in conveying news of Nazi extermination policy to the west.[139]

Should the Poles have done more?

We often hear people say that the Poles or other non-Jewish nationalities should have or could have done more to help the Jews. For instance, historian Epstein states:

> If non-Jewish organisations with substantial influence and resources had done what they could to help the Jews, more Jews would have escaped and survived.[140]

But Epstein herself points out that most Jews in Eastern Europe died when "the Germans were at the height of their power and when they were engaged in killing not only Jews but also Poles, Belarusians, Ukrainians, and others".[141]

On this topic, Stewart Steven concludes, "Maybe Poland could have done more for its Jewish population, but then so could every country of occupied Europe. The record shows that the Poles did more than most".[142]

Paulsson reviewed a large range of available material and concluded that despite the much harsher conditions, Warsaw's Polish residents managed to support and conceal a similar percentage of Jews as residents of cities in safer, supposedly less antisemitic countries of western Europe.[143] The official count of Polish Righteous (people recorded at the Yad Vashem Holocaust Centre in Israel as having helped Jews) is 6,266. This is the highest count for any country. Everyone acknowledges that the list is incomplete and no one doubts more should be officially recognised. Any estimate is fraught with difficulties.[144] But as Martin Gilbert says, "Poles who risked their own lives to save the Jews were indeed the exception. But they could be found throughout Poland, in every town and village".[145]

Paulsson suggests the following:

> How many people in Poland rescued Jews? Of those that meet Yad Vashem's criteria—perhaps 100,000. Of those that offered minor forms of help—perhaps two or three times as many. Of those who were passively protective—undoubtedly the majority of the population.[146]

The Jews who created underground organisations, who carried out uprisings, who escaped from the ghettos and concentration camps or who survived the war in hiding did so overwhelmingly with the help of non-Jews. Jewish survival and resistance went hand in glove with resistance and help from non-Jews.

Polish antisemitism and the Holocaust

This support is even more significant in the light of the fact that the Polish antisemitism of the 1930s continued and intensified in the war period. Much has been written about the non-Jews who did not help Jews: from individuals who denounced hidden Jews to those who stood by and watched massacres through to those who actively participated. The last includes Poles who joined German established units where they fought partisans, guarded and cleared ghettos, hunted escaped Jews and assisted at mass killings.[147]

The wave of atrocities and pogroms in at least 23 localities of Eastern Poland shortly after the Nazis invaded territory previously held by the Russians in June 1941 has drawn significant attention in recent decades.

In early July 1941, Poles rounded up the Jews of the town of Radziłów, forced them into a barn and set it on fire. Mobs then hunted down and shot Jews in the surrounding area. Perhaps 1,000 people were murdered.[148]

Two days later, on 10 July 1941, a Polish mob in the nearby town of Jedwabne humiliated a group of about 40 men in various ways, following which they murdered them and threw them into a pit. They then locked most of the remaining Jews, around 300 men, women and children, into a barn and set it on fire. This event only became widely known with the 1990 screening of documentaries by film maker Agnieszka Arnold[149] and the publication of a book by author Jan Gross in 2001 with a subsequent official government forensic investigation.[150]

The "rediscovery" of these events caused major debates in Poland and elsewhere. This is not the place to evaluate them fully. However, some aspects are important to note here.

Crucial is the point that the similarity of pogroms in Jedwabne and elsewhere in the summer of 1941 cannot just be a coincidence. According to academic John Connelly, "they were orchestrated by the invader…the crime in Jedwabne cannot be comprehended outside the larger East European context".[151]

> Immediately after overrunning Soviet-held territory in 1941, in a band stretching from the Baltic states, through Eastern Poland and western Ukraine, and southward to Bessarabia, the Germans systematically fomented pogroms, and took measures to conceal their own role in these supposedly "spontaneous" acts of violence. In Lithuania, for example, SS General Walter Stahlecker gave orders "to initiate self-cleansing actions (*Selbstreinigungsaktionen*) and direct them to the proper channels, so that the goal of cleansing be achieved as quickly as possible. No less essential is that solid, irrefutable facts be created for posterity, showing that the liberated population embraced the harshest measures against Bolsheviks and Jewish enemies, and did so of its own initiative, without any German orders becoming visible".[152]

This action can be traced back to Himmler, who shortly after the Nazi takeover complained about the lack of pogroms in the newly conquered territory. The SS followed this with orders to its constituents.[153]

In Radziłów, the "leading role of the Gestapo and SS are beyond question".[154] And it is known that the Polish component was organised by the Camp of Greater Poland (Obóz Wielkiej Polski, OWP) a far-right group founded in 1926 by the Endecja, who we have already met. That such fascists would continue their activities under the Nazis should surprise no one.

Another factor may have been disproportionate Jewish support for the Soviet regime in Eastern Poland before June 1941 or at least a perception that such was the case.[155]

Beyond the immediate factors, it is important to situate the discussion of Polish atrocities in the context of the continuation of pre-war antisemitism into the war period, exacerbated by the licence and opportunities given by the presence of the Nazis, with their determination to divide and rule, carry out genocide on Jews and turn Poles themselves into a nation of slave labourers.

It is also essential to not just consider the Polish people as an undifferentiated mass. Much of the writing about the topic of Polish-Jewish relations in the war does precisely this. Undifferentiated phrases such as "a country pervaded by antisemitism"[156] gives the reader the impression that virtually the entire population was infected. According to Ezra Mendelsohn, "The attitude of most Jewish scholars has been, and continues to be, that interwar Poland was an extremely antisemitic country, perhaps even uniquely antisemitic".[157]

Such generalisations, and a failure to consider class and context, do not illuminate the issue very far. As we have seen, socialists and communists were not "pervaded by antisemitism" but were rather distinguished by their efforts to help Jews. More broadly, Connelly notes the remarkable fact of "how little Polish society aided Germany's war effort". Other Eastern European states became Germany's allies, passed their own racial laws, had collaborationist governments, delivered Jews to Germany and provided supportive military units, both for the war and to commit atrocities against Jews.

As always, reading academics on the subject of Polish antisemitism and how more could have helped Jews leaves one very aware of what is often not said. This is what Connelly refers to as the "major sin of omission in the Holocaust: Western passivity":

> Had more Poles and other east Europeans been willing to assist Jews, perhaps some thousands, or tens of thousands more would have been saved; but the fate of millions of east European Jews could only have been altered by the Allies... What is known is that the powerful West, unlike thousands of destitute Poles and other Europeans in Nazi-occupied Europe, failed to lift a finger.[158]

"This song shall be a signal through the years"[159]

We have seen that before and during the war the Allies showed little concern about the fate of the Jews. This continued in the aftermath. At the Nuremberg Trials Jews were not even accorded the status of a distinct category.[160]

Arnold Paucker, historian of Jewish resistance in Germany, comments on the fact that the historiography of the resistance in general, and Jews in particular, was a neglected subject prior to 1970.[161] He traces this to the influence of the Cold War environment:

> The communist influence on the resistance was simply hard for many to stomach. Indeed, on this point we encounter a whole range of taboos and considerable self-censorship on the part of historians.[162]

In the Eastern Bloc, on the other hand, Soviet policy—and subsequently the policy of the post-war Polish regime—was to emphasise the role of their own citizens without mentioning the specific experiences of Jews. In the immediate post war period, the Stalinist regime deliberately hindered the spreading of awareness of the concentration camps. They emphasised instead "Soviet heroism and glory in defending the Motherland" and at sites where massacres of Jews had taken place, such as Varvarivka in Ukraine, commemorative tablets referred only to the killing of "peaceful citizens". This was at least partly because Stalin did not want to lay himself open to comparisons between his own antisemitism and that of the Nazis.[163]

Jewish historians also participated in the neglect of the subject of resistance and perpetuated the myth of "going as sheep to the slaughter". According to Arnold Paucker, Bruno Bettelheim "wrote on a number of occasions that German Jews had no backbone and persisted in a passive ghetto mentality". And Raul Hilberg, a major historian of the Holocaust, "constantly emphasised that, in the face of mass extermination, resistance [was] so minimal as to be practically insignificant".[164]

This type of argument serves Zionism very well. Zionism argues that Jews are always outsiders and antisemitism can never be defeated. Herzl, the founder of Zionism, wrote in 1895 that he "recognised the emptiness and futility of efforts to 'combat anti-Semitism.'"[165] In 1925, Jacob Klatzkin, the co-editor of *Encyclopedia Judaica*, wrote:

> If we do not admit the rightfulness of anti-Semitism, we deny the rightfulness of our own nationalism... Instead of establishing societies for defense against the anti-Semites, who want to reduce our rights, we should establish societies for defense against our friends who desire to defend our rights.[166]

It was this kind of attitude that underlay the failure of mainstream Zionists to play any significant role in the fight against antisemitism in Poland in the 1930s, as we have seen.

But there is no way that Palestine could ever have been a solution for the poverty, oppression and antisemitism faced by the millions of European Jews. The Zionists themselves knew this and knew that their focus on Palestine meant leaving the bulk of the population to their fate. In fact, many of them deemed the bulk of the European Jewish population as too tainted and not worth saving. For example, Chaim Weizmann, leader of the WZO in the interwar years and a not insignificant figure, said in 1937:

> The old ones will pass; they will bear their fate, or they will not. They were dust, economic and moral dust, in a cruel world… Two million, and perhaps less…only a remnant shall survive. We have to accept it.[167]

Many Zionist functionaries who survived persisted in later years in their stand against the underground activities against the Nazis, condemning it as "a series of childish and irresponsible antics that had achieved nothing other than to harm and further imperil the lives of…a community of hostages".[168] However, one leading Zionist, Nahum Goldman, did change his mind after the war:

> But in this context success was irrelevant. What matters in a situation of this sort is a people's moral stance, its readiness to fight back instead of helplessly allowing itself to be massacred. We did not stand the test.[169]

In Bialystok and many other ghettos, Zionist youth did join and even provided leadership in the underground. Their actions are to be praised. But their actions were undertaken in spite of Zionist ideology and their underground struggle had to be conducted mostly in opposition to the position taken by leading Zionists and the Judenräte. The Zionist youth groups in the ghettos separated themselves from adult organisations because of their unwillingness to follow their "cautious and conciliatory approach".[170]

It suits mainstream Zionist ideology to emphasise that the Jews were on their own. Many historians, Jews and others, place great weight on how isolated and without help the Jews were. And no doubt this is how it must have felt to many. But the fact is that, aside from the small number who were able to pass themselves off as non-Jewish, almost all who did survive in Eastern Europe did so because they received help.

Epstein suggests the reason the Minsk experience has received little recognition may be due to the fact that the Warsaw Ghetto story, which emphasises Jews fighting virtually alone, suits Zionist myth making. The cooperation between Jews and non-Jews in Minsk is less suited to this:

> The forest/partisan model of resistance was predicated on the view that Jews and non-Jews had a common interest in fighting the Nazis, and it involved fostering such alliances…[171]
>
> The problem is not that this form of resistance [military uprisings] has been so extensively examined, but that a memory of the Holocaust has been constructed in which other forms of resistance barely exist.[172]

Epstein comments that, "Every political current…regarded armed struggle…as more important than saving lives" and concludes that had more underground organisation placed a higher value on escape, more Jews would have been saved.[173] Saving lives depended more on external help than did a heroic but doomed uprising.

Zionists in general and Israel in particular have sought to appropriate the Warsaw Ghetto Uprising to their own political purposes to the extent of casting the establishment of the Jewish state as an extension of the uprising.[174]

Not only were the Jews supposedly completely alone—they were also supposedly surrounded by an immense sea of anti-Jewish hostility. There is no dispute that antisemitism was a significant and major trend in Poland and the region already before the war and that groups from the local populations joined with the Nazis in committing atrocities. We have seen, however, the class nature of pre-war antisemitism. Furthermore, in the conditions of war, personal antisemitism was not necessarily determinant. Zofia Kossak-Szczucka, who was one of the instigators of Zegota, had antisemitic views which she never repudiated. She nonetheless worked untiringly to assist Jews. The leader of the Warsaw Uprising in 1944, General Bor-Komorowski, also had antisemitic tendencies. Nonetheless, the Uprising released Jewish prisoners from Gesiowska concentration camp. The Polish Home Army and Underground State included people of all political persuasions including antisemites.[175] But their formal position leaves no doubt. Operating underground, they enacted laws against antisemitism and executed perpetrators.

Finally, there is the question of why the Warsaw Ghetto was the only large ghetto in which not only unity of the political factions was achieved but also the support of the bulk of the population. This may be partly due to the fact that the ZOB ran the ghetto for three months before the uprising and therefore had a little time in which to win over the population. Furthermore, by this time, most of the children and older people had gone from the ghetto. Another pointer comes from Vladka Meed, a participant in the uprising:

> Jewish armed resistance…when it came, did not spring from a sudden impulse; it was not an act of personal courage on the part of a few individuals or organised groups: it was the culmination of Jewish defiance, defiance that had existed from the advent of the ghetto.[176]

In fact, defiance pre-dated the advent of the ghetto. We saw how, during the 1930s, the fight against the rising tide of antisemitism had involved Jews and non-Jews in mass struggle. This occurred in many cities and towns throughout Poland but was centred in Warsaw. The alliances that were forged at that time continued through the Nazi occupation and underlay much of the network of help and support that the ghetto inhabitants received. The population who rose up in April 1943 had been mobilising on the streets only a few years earlier in 1938. The memory must still have been there.

Jews did not go simply like lambs to the slaughter. They fought back against overwhelming odds and in the face of mass extermination. And they did not do this alone.

Let Hirsh Glik's song, with which this chapter began, continue to be an inspiration to all of us.

> *The morning sun shall set our day aglow,*
> *Our yesterdays shall vanish with the foe,*
> *And if time drags before the sun appears,*
> *This song shall be a signal through the years.*[177]

Section 4

Palestine and today

13

The impact of Palestine on the radical Jewish tradition

After the hopes raised in 1917 were dashed by Stalin's repression and the cold indifference of governments worldwide to refugees, mass murder in the Holocaust shifted the focus of the Jewish question to Palestine. Here the reformist strategy of combining national patriotism and socialism would be tested in its left Zionist form. That these did not hold together was illustrated when radical Jews who shared a common outlook beforehand took dramatically divergent paths after arrival. Two biographies give the picture.

Menachem Urman's autobiography recounts growing up in interwar Poland in an atmosphere of unrelenting antisemitism. When the Red Army took over the east of the country at the start of the Second World War, persecution stopped so he joined the Young Communists. In 1941 the Germans invaded and Urman became a forest partisan, eventually finding his way to Soviet Central Asia where he worked as an engineer in the munitions industry. He describes hearing Stalin on the radio declaring victory in 1945:

> I was Bolshevik with all my soul, I identified with the workers' struggle and with the slogan "Workers of the world unite," but…Stalin spoke of the Russian nation and its bravery, he didn't mention other nations that fought alongside Russia, spilled their blood, and said not a single word about the Jews… After hearing the speech I made up my mind that I was leaving the USSR.[1]

Arriving back in Poland, Urman learned of the 1946 pogrom in Kielce that killed 42 Holocaust survivors and was warned, "We incinerated a lot of Jews and apparently it was not enough, because now they are trickling back".[2]

So he emigrated to Palestine and joined a Zionist socialist Hashomer

Hatzair kibbutz (a communal agricultural settlement). A year later he was serving in the paramilitary Palmach forces fighting Arabs in the 1948 war that created the Israeli state. Afterwards, building on his Soviet armaments background, he established a factory producing tanks for the Israeli Defence Force. Then we read:

> In my search for additional work and income, I learned that in South Africa one can succeed... The white minority ruled and because of its policy of racist separation it was boycotted almost entirely by the international community. Israel, which also suffered from hostile attitudes...looked for markets and opportunities for cooperation in the field of defense.[3]

Off he went to produce tanks in apartheid South Africa too! It was at this time that, at the request of a Jewish colonel in the South African Police, the WZO closed Hashomer Hatzair's South African branch because so many of its members supported Black struggles.[4]

Chanie Rosenberg (mother of one of the authors of this book) was born in Cape Town and at the age of 17 witnessed the all-white government turn away one of the last refugee boats from Nazi Germany. In her memoir she wrote, "Being myself white and Jewish, I was simultaneously a beneficiary and victim of racism".[5] Some Jews tried to hide their ethnicity to fit in, but she felt that to deny "one's own identity was quite ridiculous", adding, "this sensitivity to anti-Jewish racism helped me to understand Black people's feelings".[6] She became a fervent Zionist (and Trotskyist), enrolled in South Africa's Hashomer Hatzair, learned Hebrew, and emigrated to Palestine. Like Urman she joined one of its kibbutzim.

Unlike Urman, however, the experience did not cement belief in Zionism but repulsion. Her kibbutz had bought the land of four adjacent Arab villages but:

> the Palestinian farmers refused to leave—naturally, as the payment had been pocketed by the head men and the farmers received nothing. The kibbutz members thereupon decided to climb the hill, picking up stones as they went, and threw them at the Palestinians... [I]t was not only the Jewish National Fund [JNF], government, and businessmen who stole Palestinian lands and evicted their inhabitants, but also the "socialist" kibbutzim... It was a cruel fraud.[7]

Quitting Palestine in 1947 as a confirmed Jewish anti-Zionist, she went to Britain and helped build the Socialist Workers Party with her Palestinian Jewish partner, Tony Cliff. Opposition to the policies of the South African and Israeli governments formed a fundamental part of her world view for the rest of her life.

Though the starting point for Urman and Rosenberg was the same, they ended up in opposite camps. Why had this happened? The explanation lay in the clash between left Zionist theory and the reality of Palestine.

Meeting a "rather tangible truth"

Migrants came in several waves, or Aliyah ("ascent"), between 1881 and 1948.[8] Each was shaped by the politics of the time. The First Aliyah (1881–1903) was mainly religious in character. The Second (1904–14) included leftists whose politics were not yet shaped by the reform/revolution split of 1917, while the Third (1919–1923) brought socialists and communists as separate contingents.[9] Later Aliyahs, coming at a time when worldwide restriction of Jewish movement made Palestine a last resort, were less homogeneous in character.

The impression given today is that the Zionist state founded in 1948 is a natural consequence of Jewish national destiny. Nothing could be farther from the truth. Not only did Zionism initially lack mass support among Jews, the country was not a blank sheet upon which immigrants could write whatever they wished. It was home to an overwhelmingly Arab population under Ottoman rule. In 1881 they formed over 90 percent of the inhabitants and in 1945, after over half a century of Jewish inflow and land settlement, were still 70 percent of the people, holding all but 6 percent of the land.[10] Ahad Ha'am, lauded as a forerunner of Zionist thought, wrote a remarkably prescient article on this subject as early as 1891. Unlike Borochov, who never visited, and Syrkin, who had only a passing acquaintance,[11] Ha'am made an extended trip and warned potential migrants that there was a sharp contrast between the "pleasant dream" and the "rather tangible truth".[12]

It is often claimed that Palestine was "A land without a people for a people without a land".[13] Ha'am disagreed:

From abroad we are accustomed to believe that Eretz Israel [the Holy Land] is presently almost totally desolate, an uncultivated desert… But in truth it is not so. In the entire land, it is hard to find tillable land that is not already tilled…[14]

From abroad we are accustomed to believing that the Arabs are all desert savages… But this is a big mistake.[15]

Being an overwhelmingly rural country, immigrants to Palestine would aspire to work in agriculture but he wrote that Jews were "ignoramuses in all the questions related to settling the land, even in the basic matters where knowledge is essential".[16] So "even though many swear to themselves that they are ready to sacrifice all their being and their happiness on its altar",[17] Jewish workers would despair of a life "which brings neither riches nor respect".[18] These problems were already affecting the relationship of newcomers to the local population:

> They were slaves in their land of exile… This sudden change has engendered in them an impulse to despotism, as always happens when "a slave becomes a king", and behold they walk with the Arabs in hostility and cruelty, unjustly encroaching on them, shamefully beating them for no good reason, and even bragging about what they do.[19]

Ha'am had anticipated a risk that would face Zionists of all political persuasions—that the victims of oppression turn into oppressors themselves.

The Zionist project had the goal enunciated in the title of Herzl's pamphlet—a *Jewish State*, but ideas differed about how it could be achieved. "Political Zionism" vainly sought a government willing to impose a ready-made state on its behalf, though hopes were maintained by the Balfour Declaration. However, when British imperialism acquired Palestine under League of Nations mandate, it would play off Jews against Arabs for its own ends, using the divide and rule tactic perfected in Ireland and India.

"Practical Zionism" took a different route. Its strategy was to promote large-scale Jewish immigration and land settlement. In 1908 the Zionist Organisation opened an office in Palestine to facilitate incomers, appointing Ruppin to oversee it.[20] But numbers fell far short of ambitions. Few of the millions on the move went to Palestine[21] and even fewer stayed. Fully 70 percent of the First Aliyah and two thirds of the Second departed,[22] reducing the pre-First World War Jewish population of 85,000 to 65,000 in 1918.[23] International restrictions on immigration in the mid-1920s boosted arrivals, but when a short economic crisis occurred, twice as many left as entered.[24] That ascent could so easily become descent jeopardised the notion of Palestine as a homeland.

The purpose of mass immigration was to settle Jews throughout the territory whatever the local population wished. As Ussishkin, leader of the Russian movement and inventor of practical Zionism put it, "Without property rights to the soil, Palestine will *never* be Jewish, no matter how many Jews there may be".[25] Indeed, the opening clause of the Zionist programme had called for "The promotion of the settlement of Jewish agriculturalists". Despite political differences with the right wing, socialist Zionists shared the same goal. For example, Berl Katznelson wrote, "All available land in this country will be placed under the auspices of the Jewish people for perpetuity".[26] An additional motive was to "normalise the Jewish existence"[27] after the urban lifestyle imposed in the diaspora.

Yet the prospects were dismal. Ha'am turned out to be right. The Palestinian economy was heavily dependent on Arab agricultural production;[28] recently established Arab landowners controlled most of the land,[29] and it was worked by Arab fellaheen (peasants),[30] three quarters of whom were for hire as paid labourers for some or all the time[31] on "the very lowest standard of living".[32] Little space remained for Jewish agriculturalists to implant themselves.

With no imperialist army to undertake a colonial land grab and supply farms for free, they had to be acquired piecemeal through purchase. That was a problem because financial assistance from the Jewish community abroad was limited. Baron Rothschild provided a dozen *moshavim* (cooperative farms) but he lost interest and passed them on to the Jewish Colonisation Association to administer. A small amount of additional land came through Zionist fund-raising.[33] Even when farms were established, they struggled. The First Aliyah settlers from Hoveve Zion (Lovers of Zion) ran the moshavim but planned grape production failed and they depended on subsidies to keep going. During the first decade of the 20th century Jewish landholdings amounted to just 1.5 percent of the total[34] and nine out of ten Jews ended up in towns despite the Zionist credo that in Palestine Jews should be less urban-based than they had been in Europe.[35]

If these obstacles were not enough, the small number of would-be Jewish agricultural labourers who arrived with the Second Aliyah found it hard to survive. Being Zionists, they expected the few Jewish farmers there would offer employment. Market considerations were applied instead, and this put the immigrants at a disadvantage. They were untutored in agricultural work[36] and bore subversive attitudes moulded by "the most revolutionary society of Europe at the time".[37] By comparison Arab farmhands were often experienced smallholders toiling for additional, but much needed, income.[38] They could flexibly adapt to the seasonal demands of agriculture whereas Jewish immigrants needed paid employment all year round and were accustomed to European living standards.

This produced an anomalous situation whereby even at subsistence level Jewish labourers' wages were considerably higher than Arabs', and this priced them out of work. In the first decade of the century, daily rates for Arab labourers ranged from 5 to 8 piastres while East European immigrants worked for between 7 to 12 piastres.[39] The latter were often jobless and endured almost slave market conditions. Ben Gurion was one such and wrote that, "The Jewish workers had to stand by the synagogue until the Jewish farmers came to look for a laborer; they'd feel the workers' muscles and take them for work or, mostly, leave them standing there".[40] Whether Arab or Jew, in class terms, agricultural workers faced poverty or unemployment at the hands of landowners, whether Arab or Jew.

The leading mainstream Zionists of the time cared little about the living standards of the radical immigrants and disliked their politics. All that mattered was that they came in numbers. Ussishkin, an avowed non-socialist Zionist,[41] came up with a right-wing tactic to solve the problem: "military duty" for Jewish immigrants. They should be compelled to offer "their services as laborers at the same wages as the Arabs receive. They will be obliged to live under the most trying conditions, exactly as a soldier does in the barracks".[42]

Subjective responses

How would left Zionists respond? They saw themselves as working class and socialist. Ussishkin's policy of lower wages under military conditions was unacceptable. One alternative might have been to follow the Jewish radical tradition of the diaspora. The curse of exploitation was felt by workers everywhere, and on innumerable occasions Jews united with non-Jews in joint struggle to combat it. Taking that approach in Palestine would have meant making common cause with the Arabs. Jewish employment and Arab incomes could both be boosted by demanding equal pay for all at the higher level. Such a strategy was indeed proposed at a Congress of Poale Zion in Palestine but was rejected.[43]

The Achilles heel was the nationalist element in left Zionism, as Ben Gurion's comment to an Arab worker showed. Instead of making the plight of exploited Jews and Arabs his starting point, he talked of a hierarchy of suffering:

> You say that the Arab workers are oppressed and his situation is downgraded. But our situation is even worse. If the Arab worker works in difficult conditions, the Jewish workers don't even have the opportunity to work.[44]

He felt the pain of his own community, but lacked empathy beyond that. So Ben Gurion called on Jewish farmers to sack the Arabs in favour of Jews, though this was given a leftish gloss: "Zionism aspires to bring the Jewish masses to Eretz Yis'rael [Land of Israel] and to labor, to transform here the Jewish masses into workers".[45]

Removal of Arabs from agricultural labour in Jewish enterprises was misleadingly called the "conquest of labour". The practice would later spread into the wider economy. The British mandate authorities defined it as "the penetration of Jewish Labour into all spheres of work, industry, trade, the public services and most of all into agricultural work".[46] This was a seminal moment for left Zionism. It was when the nick of separatism turned into gangrene.

The campaign began around 1908 and was pioneered by individuals of the Second Aliyah who became agricultural workers. Small in number and headed by Ben Gurion, they would dominate the left

Zionist movement for several decades.[47] Socialism remained their formal goal but only its outer appearance, the husk, was retained. "Conquest of labour" was presented as radical because the fight seemed to be with landowners resisting the right to work. The slogan was the opposite of progressive, nonetheless. In class terms the sectional interest of one group was being placed over wider working-class interest, Arab and Jew together, and ethnic enmities were being fostered. Although the well of radicalism was continuously replenished by idealistic new arrivals in flight from oppression in Europe, the process that began in 1908 tainted everything.

Plausible explanations for the adoption of "conquest of labour" come from various angles. Like Ha'am, Shafir notes there was a "hiatus between 'ideology' and 'reality'" and concludes that the latter had decisive influence. Left Zionist leaders acted "not so much from the grand cloth of general ideologies as from the simpler materials of concrete methods of settlement".[48] Sternhall says the opposite. He believes the left Zionists' approach "was not due to any objective conditions or circumstances beyond its control. These developments were the result of a conscious ideological choice".[49]

Subjective beliefs and the response to objective circumstances can usefully be combined to understand what happened. The decision to reject class solidarity as a strategy was not made in an ideological or material void. Ilan Pappé says that faced with conditions in Palestine socialist Zionists were ready to "quickly substitute their more universal dreams with the powerful allure of nationalism".[50] Because socialist Zionists already considered Palestine to be a special Jewish "homeland", when they were compelled to confront the realities of land settlement the result was the "conquest of labour".

The kibbutz

The campaign did not work out as planned. No small group who cuts themselves off from the majority of their fellow working-class comrades and then demands that the boss takes them seriously is likely to succeed. Appeals to the Jewish farmers' community spirit were ignored. Shafir gives the classic example of the Jewish-owned Hulda farm. Arabs were paid to plant trees in memory of Herzl, no less. Jewish labourers then uprooted them in protest.[51] However, in the long-term the effort to expel all Arab labourers from Jewish-owned plantations failed. Thousands remained in employment.[52]

This setback led to an unexpected outcome—the kibbutz. Although that institution never encompassed large numbers, it was pivotal in the ideology of left Zionism and so requires investigation. In 1910, after various experiments in land tenure, a group of enthusiasts set up an exclusively Jewish self-governing farm, with neither employers nor employees. Out of this small beginning various federations of kibbutzim would develop.

The most politically ambitious was launched by militants of the Third Aliyah arriving from revolutionary Russia. Gedud haAvoda's full name translates as the Yosef Trumpeldor Labour and Defence Battalion. Trumpeldor was an activist killed in fighting with Arabs. They wished to organise "a communist society in Palestine, while at the same time fulfilling the national task". This would be accomplished by building communes in which "the economic basis of the main cell of capitalist society—the bourgeois family" was abolished. Backed up by "a class-oriented armed force" Gedud haAvoda kibbutzim were to be formed in towns as well as the countryside to lead "the class struggle against the capitalist order".[53] Gedud haAvoda's plans failed and in 1927 disappointment at insufficient progress led key leaders to return to Soviet Russia to continue their work. They perished in Stalin's purges.

One of the larger and long-lasting federations was run by Hashomer Hatzair. Its adherents arrived in Palestine committed to a socialist system "placing the interests of the whole society before the interests of the individual". Through the kibbutz they felt themselves to be pioneers committed to "the personal realisation and implementation of principles".[54] Dan Leon summarised what the Hashomer Haztair kibbutz stood for as:

settlement, colonisation and physical security;…democratically self-governed, and completely equalitarian…in everything [including] between men and women…regardless of the work performed;…based exclusively on self-labour by Jewish workers;…a new socialistic society [through] collective ownership of all the means of production.[55]

The numbers involved in the kibbutzim were small. One hundred and eighty individuals in 1914 and 735 in 1922. In 1948 they encompassed just 8 percent of Palestinian Jews[56] and 2.6 percent of the overall population. Yet a spell was cast by this institution. It was exemplified in the words of Tony Benn, leader of Britain's Labour left. His 1961 introduction to Dan Leon's book says that this was "no land élite living off the labour of native workers like the settlers of South Africa". It stood instead for "the elimination of class-exploitation" and "grass roots socialist democracy at work".[57] Another commentator saw it as the culmination of the Jewish radical tradition: "the biggest and most successful...revolutionary experiment that has been attempted and the closest approach to the way of living at which Communism aims".[58]

The real function of the kibbutz was far more prosaic than these high-flown claims would have us believe. That would be most clearly seen in the 1948 war when the "colonisation and physical security" role was paramount.

Then there was the phrase "land settlement". The pioneers were penniless, so how were kibbutz fields acquired? They were donated by the non-socialist Jewish National Fund, which used contributions from abroad to purchase land for exclusive Jewish use. The JNF's Land Agent was Ruppin, of whom Katznelson said, "Do not make a mistake and think Arthur Ruppin was a socialist dreamer".[59] The JNF's President was Ussishkin, the openly anti-socialist hard-nosed leader who got what he wanted all along—Zionist colonisation under "military duty". [60]

Nonetheless, the rhetoric served as an essential emblem for left Zionism as a whole. Recruitment to land working depended on "Halutzim" (pioneers)[61]—young enthusiasts such as Urman and Rosenberg brought by left-wing Zionist youth movements.[62] Since most Jews in the diaspora lived in urbanised communities it required the idealism of the kibbutz to win volunteers for the spartan rigours of agricultural labour under Palestinian conditions.

Overall, the kibbutz skilfully blended four factors—an image of radical communism, retention of immigrants, Jewish exclusivity, and colonial land settlement. In 1948 military recruits from the kibbutzim would take centre stage.

Class and nation in the urban environment

In agriculture Arab exclusion was portrayed as left wing, but exactly the same was happening in the towns, led at this stage by what was called General (and non-socialist) Zionism. The story of urbanisation demonstrates this. The Jewish community in Palestine took the name *Yishuv*. The old Yishuv, pre-dating the rise of nationalism, was religious and two thirds lived in Jerusalem, a mixed ethnicity city.[63] The new Yishuv was nationalist. Under bourgeois Zionist leadership, Tel Aviv, near majority-Arab Jaffa, was founded in 1909 as "a Hebrew urban center... Because of this, the Tel Aviv municipal and Zionist leadership needed (from the start) to use every method at their disposal for creating and enforcing separation between Jews and Arabs".[64] Right-wing Zionists felt no compulsion to present their actions in radical clothing. By the Second World War one in three Jews lived in Tel Aviv,[65] and the proportion living in Jewish-only towns had doubled in two decades to 52 percent.[66]

As Chapter 2 shows, at this time Jews in the rest of the world were keen to escape the ghetto and mingle with others in society at a multitude of levels. Palestine's Zionists were doing the very opposite of the majority, the paltry number of immigrants arriving there being proof.

The dichotomy between Jews in Palestine and the 97 percent of the community in the diaspora[67] was particularly evident when it came to language. Hebrew had died out as a medium for daily communication around 200 AD, continuing as the language of prayer and later on as a literary vehicle. Revived as vernacular at the end of the 19th century, the first native speaker was born in 1882 in Palestine. His father, Eliezer Ben Yehuda, had to invent vocabulary to cope with modern times, and he brought his son up in strict isolation to avoid linguistic pollution.[68] Ben Yehuda's aim was "to revive the Hebrew tongue...in a country in which the number of Hebrew inhabitants exceeds the number of gentiles".[69] Ben Gurion agreed. In 1910 he declared, "We may not use any language except Hebrew in our cultural work".[70]

This made Jews as well as Arabs the problem because at the time just one in 400 overall routinely employed Hebrew.[71] By comparison 1,000-year-old Yiddish was still the mother tongue for two thirds of Jews in Palestine and 10 million out of 16 million Jews worldwide.[72] A "Language War" ensued during which "Yiddishland" culture was suppressed in Palestine along with its equivalent for Jews arriving from Arab countries.[73] By 1948, 70 percent of adult Palestinian Jews and 93 percent of their children conversed regularly in Hebrew.[74] Zionism claimed to be preserving Jewish cultural identity, but voluntary or not, existing patterns were replaced with what was called the "New Jew" or super-masculine "muscle Jewry". This was a major rupture from contemporary Jewish diaspora cultures.[75] If the Zionist rule for cultural identity were applied, the Jews in Palestine would "not be Jews at all" or "self-hating", but as Marxists we note simply that the social construction of the Jewish community in Palestine was recently invented, distinct, and a tiny minority.

The economy was also subject to social engineering. By 1935 an incredible 97 percent of the 130,000 Jewish labour force operated in a Jewish-only environment despite being in a mostly Arab country. The British Mandate authorities (who took on Arabs and Jews) employed most of the remaining three percent. Only 0.5 percent of Jews worked for or provided services to Arabs.[76] This separate economy was fuelled by an influx of private capital, three quarters of which was brought by the members of the Fourth and Fifth Aliyahs (1924–1929, 1929–1939).[77] The rest came in through growing Zionist contributions. As a result, between the wars, Jewish landholdings multiplied four times over from their very low base[78] and capital formation rates were the highest in the world.[79] This pre-state colonisation process was tolerated by the British authorities and undersigned by the Balfour Declaration.

Jewish workers in Palestine responded to burgeoning capitalism and its class antagonisms through Labour Zionism. It consisted of a political wing led by Mapai (Workers' Party of the Land of Israel) and a union wing, the Histadrut (the General Federation of Labour in Israel). From small beginnings Labour Zionism came to dominate both at home and abroad. By 1933 Mapai's leaders controlled world Zionism and would rule Israel for decades.[80]

In some respects the Histadrut was even more important than the political party. Formed in 1920 it was formally a trade union and within three years organised 55 percent of the Jewish workforce, rising to 75 percent from 1931 onwards.[81] No other free trade union federation in the world could claim such density. It also had an extraordinarily ambitious constitution:

Establishing and developing agricultural enterprises and factories in all branches of industry, both in towns and in the country, creating credit institutions and funds for settlement and other branches of economic activity; acting as a contractor, organising work and increasing productivity; organising supply on a cooperative basis and enabling workers to meet their own needs by creating diverse branches of production.[82]

The Histadrut ran banks, insurance, and the largest shipping company. It provided housing, kitchens and medical help. Conventional trade union functions were not overlooked. Pay was fought for, dismissals resisted, and work accident cases taken up.[83] However, at one point most of the Histadrut's members were employed by subsidiaries of the Histadrut itself.[84] A strange "trade union" indeed. Others found placements through its labour exchanges and where necessary, the union rationed work by allotting a number of days per worker to achieve "equity of job opportunities".[85] In return workers voted for the left in elections.[86]

Labour Zionism's institutions and growth appeared to be a striking vindication of the predictions of Syrkin and Borochov. Only in Palestine could working-class Jews develop "powers for the class struggle" (Syrkin)[87] and "wield the necessary social, economic and political influence" (Borochov).[88] An article by Ben Gurion in 1925 announced nothing less than a "Hebrew revolution" that:

conquers positions in the workplace, the economy and the community. [The worker] in his every action and his every activity, small or large, in his work in the countryside and the city, in the building of agriculture and of industry, in the conquest of the language and of the culture, in guard duty and national defense in the war against his interests and his rights to work, in the satisfaction of his national and personal needs, in the establishment of institutions and unions—in all these things, floating before him is the historic mission of the class to which he belongs and to which the building of a country opens the path: the historic mission of the working class in preparation for the revolution that will establish the rule of labor upon the nation and the land.

Labour Zionism, he said, was at war with "all the remaining classes", the "private enterprise parasites, who do not bring to the Land wealth or property, but rather greed".[89]

As with the kibbutz, appearance and reality were at loggerheads. In form the programme appeared to be directed against capitalism. Yet the illusion could only be sustained if Labour Zionism was abstracted from its material underpinnings. It was noted earlier that the kibbutzim were on land purchased for them by non-socialist Zionists. The same dependency was true of the urban edifice built by Labour Zionism and the Histadrut. Overall, the operation was loss-making and could only exist because it was under-written from outside. But why should non-socialists not only tolerate but bankroll a movement that called for their revolutionary overthrow and described them as greedy parasites?

A telling discussion took place in 1921 between the American Zionist leader, US Supreme Court Justice Louis Brandeis, and Weizmann, who led European Zionism. Brandeis believed "the Jewish spirit [is] essentially American".[90] He was a supporter of private enterprise and suspicious of Labour Zionist activities. Weizmann, no socialist himself, feared Brandeis would therefore put a "premature emphasis on private enterprise and profits" in Palestine. Weizmann need not have worried.

Brandeis formulated the common WZO approach as follows: "The cooperative principle should be applied as far as feasible in the organisation of all agricultural, industrial, commercial, and financial undertakings".[91] Notwithstanding "the present unremunerative character of these needed investments", he explicitly backed "the ownership and control by the whole people of the land, of all natural resources, and of all public utilities".[92] How could this stark departure from sound entrepreneurial principles and the American way be justified? The answer was "expenditure must be made immediately like a war expenditure regardless of cost".[93]

The last phrase is key. Brandeis, Weizmann and the other non-socialists stomached the insults and flowery rhetoric about proletarian mission and the rule of labour because they knew colonisation could not succeed on a profit-or-loss basis. It was just "like a war" even if dressed up in socialist clothing.[94]

They also realised that, a few Halutzim aside, an economically backward country like Palestine was unattractive to both capital and labour. Workers had to be enticed to stay. The importance of this monetary element should not be under-estimated. At the Nesher cement factory, for example, Jews were paid 20 piastres for an eight-hour day while

Arabs received just 10 piastres for up to ten hours per day. These rates were typical.[95] The Histadrut might clash with local private capitalist entrepreneurs on occasion, but the non-socialists had Histadrut's back. There was a material basis for cross-class collaboration in Palestine's Jewish economy, even though an illusion of class struggle was required to placate radical Jewish immigrants until they had adjusted their principles appropriately.

Despite the scale of the Histadrut and its undertakings, the Jewish mixed economy was no more socialist than the mixed economy of Britain and other post-Second World War social democracies. Left Zionist class struggle front-of-house was belied by real social relations behind the scenes. Thus, when Labour Zionism took over the WZO, the economic policy did not change in any essentials. Idealistic socialist Zionists believed they had conquered, but it was they who had been conquered. The tragedy was that a movement arising originally from oppression resulted in providing left cover for a non-socialist programme of new oppression.

Arab-Jewish relations and the slide to war

Shapira writes that, "The separation of the two economies (despite points of contact, cooperation, and even common interests, such as among citrus growers) reflected the aspirations of both sides to preserve their uniqueness, tradition, and culture".[96] The notion of "separate development" has echoes of the justification given to the apartheid system. It is doubtful Arabs saw what was happening as a contribution to preserving their cultural aspirations and traditions. It looked more like a hostile takeover.

Referring to earlier times one Arab newspaper wrote about how "Jews were living as Ottoman brothers loved by all".[97] But now "we see the Jews excluding themselves completely from the Arabs in language, school, commerce, customs, in their entire economic life... This is the reason for the grievance of the Arabs".[98] Later still the Arab Palestinian trade unionist George Mansour bitterly commented that, "The Jews had by now bought a great part of the most fertile land in the country, and the Histadrut was concerned in expelling Arab labour from all those areas".[99]

Before the "conquest of labour" inter-ethnic tension had been low, but by the First World War clashes and even deaths were becoming regular.[100] Such an outcome had been factored in when the strategy was elaborated. In 1910 Ben Gurion predicted that Arab hostility would "force, and bit by bit is already forcing Jewish farmers to take on Jewish workers, whom they hate so much".[101] The kibbutz also played its part in settler colonisation. As the prominent Israeli General Yigal Allon stated:

> The planning and development of pioneering Zionist settlements were from the start at least partly determined by politico-strategic needs. The choice of the location of the settlements, for instance, was influenced not only by considerations of economic viability but also and even chiefly by the needs of local defence, overall settlement strategy (which aimed at ensuring a Jewish political presence in all parts of the country), and by the role such blocks of settlements might place in some future, perhaps decisive all-out struggle.[102]

The transformation from resistance to inflicting oppression was seen in the emergence of a Jewish militia. It began as an extension of the self-defence methods used against pogroms in Russia. The story of Manya Wilbushewitz-Shohat demonstrates this well. As a Russian Populist, in 1903 she was involved in plotting to assassinate Plehve, the architect of pogroms.[103] After emigrating to Palestine she established the breakaway Sejera collective farm (1907–8), the prototype for the kibbutz.[104] Simultaneously, she set up Bar Giora, the first Jewish militia, with Ben-Zvi (a future Israeli PM), her future husband, Israel Shohat, and other left Zionists who had also been involved in pogrom self-defence back in the Pale.[105] Bar Giora expanded into the Guard or Watchman organisation.[106] Eventually it morphed into the Haganah ("Defence")[107]—kernel of the Israeli army.

During the 1948 war that led to the mass expulsion of Arab Palestinians, the Haganah played a far greater role than any other Zionist formation. It was up to 20 times the combined size of its far-right revisionist competitors, the Irgun and Stern gang forces.[108]

The Haganah's elite section, the Palmach, was recruited directly from the kibbutzim. Gestures towards the past remained. We are told that "in the knapsack of every Palmach soldier was a copy of Alexander Bek's *Panfilov's Men*, which described the heroism of a Red Army unit in defending Moscow".[109] Yet once transplanted into Palestinian soil, self-defence became the very opposite, and the kibbutzim played their allotted military role in the 1948 expulsion of Palestinians[110] and beyond. Even in the 1960s when only 4 percent of Israelis lived in kibbutzim, 22 percent of Israeli army officers came from there.[111] Half of Israel's Chiefs of Staff came from a kibbutz background, including the veterans of Israel's war: Moshe Dayan, Yitzhak Rabin (1967 war); David Elazar (1973 Arab-Israeli war); Rafael Eltan (1982 Lebanon war), plus many generals such as Ariel Sharon.

Was there a middle road?

Could the former victims of racism and capitalist exploitation in the diaspora have avoided this transmutation? Could solidarity and separatism be reconciled? Gedud haAvoda, for example, called for "a unified Jewish-Arab front against English imperialism in place of the Arab-Jewish antagonism".[112] Writing about Hashomer Hatzair in the 1960s Benn wrote that "Jew and Arab can find their common destiny within a united and peaceful Middle East" because there one met more of "the non-racial socialist ideology…than with any other group of Zionists".[113] However, whether the offer of friendship was sincere or not, Zionists of all stripes upheld the notion that Jews and Arabs should be separately organised economically and socially, and this negated peace.

The impossibility of squaring the circle was revealed in discussions over Jewish-Arab working-class collaboration. Though rare, there were a few industries and institutions which lay outside the split economies. These included the railway system and emanations of the British Mandate. Where Jewish and Arab workers had the same employer the possibility of unity on a class basis existed.

Indeed, Labour Zionism claimed to be for cooperation. In 1922 Ben Gurion told the Histadrut that now security of Jewish employment had been achieved both communities could work together to address the common wage question. He suggested the income levels of Jewish workers were depressed because of "easily exploitable cheap labour", by which he meant Arabs. So the Histadrut should unionise them. This would be "an organised class force of Jewish and Arab workers" and a "single common front for all the country's workers to deal with their common affairs". That was an "obligation" and "the mission of Jewish workers".[114]

Given what we know of Ben Gurion's other statements, the reader could be justifiably cynical. His desire to outflank the communist trend from the Third Aliyah and to control Arabs to prevent them organising themselves independently were probably the real reasons for his initiative. Fitful efforts at creating a joint Jewish-Arab Labour Union were indeed undertaken by the Histadrut. These are ably recounted in Zachary Lockman's *Comrades and Enemies*. Writing at the time, Cliff noted the joint union was:

> mainly a weapon for Zionist propaganda abroad. The Histadrut…does not allow the organisation to have one elected committee, all being appointed by the Histradrut. The leadership of the organisation is the Arab department of the Histradrut, in which there is no single Arab. The local branches are administered by Jewish secretaries appointed by the above-mentioned department… There are no democratically elected branch committees and conferences have never been convened.[115]

Even if those involved in the project had been sincere, three decades of effort brought in just 1,000 out of Palestine's 70,000 Arab industrial workers. They were probably attracted by the prospect of finding work through Histadrut's labour exchanges.[116]

Class solidarity could occasionally break through and express itself in joint action. The most important episode was an Arab-Jewish general strike in 1946 that drew in tens of thousands of workers in the post, telephone, telegraph, railways, ports and civil service.[117] What happened at the Haifa railway workshops two years before gives a flavour of the difficulties such disputes faced. A strike was sparked by an industrial accident to an Arab worker. Very quickly the entire workforce of 1,400, including 200 Jews, began an occupation to demand improvements in safety, wages, and pensions. The Arab workers' organisations provided food that was shared with the Jewish workers, and they reciprocated. However, as Lockman writes, the Histadrut feared "the Arab railwaymen would learn to organise and use the strike weapon effectively". The Arab trade union body "was not interested in a long, militant, and politically risky strike", and together Jewish and Arab leaders conspired to kill off the action.[118] Lockman provides many grim examples of even worse cases where the respective union organisations had their members scab on workers from the other community. The policy of settler separatism, which the Zionists of all persuasions pursued, poisoned joint class action. There was no basis for such a movement, even though both Jewish and Arab workers had much to gain.

Beyond the workplace, at the level of political relations between the communities, the situation was no better. There was a compromise position which claimed to simultaneously recognise Jewish and Arab national rights. This was the policy of Hashomer Hatzair that became the second strongest force in Labour Zionism during the Second World War and the main left opposition to Mapai.[119] It proposed "a regime based on the political equality of both peoples; which will enable Zionism to realise its aims undisturbed and will advance Palestine towards political independence in the frame of bi-nationalism".[120]

The leader of Hashomer Hatzair's efforts was Aharon Cohen (1910–1980). Lockman says he had "passionate commitment to the cause of Arab-Jewish cooperation and compromise", but "went to his grave unable to fully acknowledge…there were no significant left-wing forces within the Arab community ready to compromise with Zionism, of whatever variant".[121] This should not have been a surprise. Hashomer Hatzair had been enthusiastically participating in the kibbutz movement and in towns to exclude Arabs from the land and create a separate Jewish economy. It mattered little to Arabs whether this happened at the hands of left Zionists or not. The exclusive Jewish presence was a direct threat to their very presence in Palestine.[122] The gap between radical appearance and reactionary content, already wide for mainstream Labour Zionism, turned out to be a chasm for Hashomer Hatzair. In practice its supporters played an important military role in expelling Arabs from Palestine.

The Palestine Communist Party was the one major force inside Palestine's Arab and Jewish communities that rejected Zionism. However, it too was broken on the reefs. Formed in 1923 it was caught between diametrically opposed positions from the start. One faction, looking to class unity, regarded Jewish immigrants as contributors to a joint Arab-Jewish workers' revolution. The other stressed anti-imperialist struggle and saw the Balfour Declaration and Zionism's colonial settlement policy as the enemy.[123] Unable to resolve its differences, in 1943 the party divided into a Jewish Palestine Communist Party and an Arab one.[124] Five years later, the former facilitated arms shipments from Eastern Europe used in ethnic cleansing and joined the Israeli government.[125] The other half was driven into exile with the Nakba (catastrophe) and was absorbed into Arab nationalism.

Retaining radical phraseology meant left Zionism spread ideological confusion. It carried out a kind of reverse alchemy that turned gold into lead. The conversion of radical proletarian into settler was encapsulated in the title of Ben Gurion's article quoted above, "On the National Mission of the Working Class". Ominously, it began with the words, "The Hebrew worker did not come here as a refugee, seeking sanctuary [but] as an emissary of the nation".[126] Sanctuary from oppression should not have been turned into a "national mission" to drive out the inhabitants of the sanctuary. Capitalist divide and rule oppression bore original responsibility for the situation, but when working-class Jews forsook their fellow workers, they became accomplices to the very system they had once opposed.

It was a tragedy that those once inspired by the ideas of the left could become party to the forcible displacement of the Palestinian majority from their homes and country. This was the final nail in the coffin of the remarkable phenomenon of mass Jewish radicalism.

A balance sheet

For six decades after 1881 Jews around the world engaged in struggles against antisemitism and their exploitation and did so as conscious fighters and agitators, as socialists and radicals. Alas, the counter was crushing. The social system that lay behind pogroms, Stalinist counter-revolution, the appointment of Hitler, doors slammed shut to refugees, and imperialist war devastated the global Jewish community. Many in the diaspora accepted the violent foundation of Israel as the answer and Zionism replaced radicalism as the predominant current in the Jewish community.[1] Since then, alongside countries such as Saudi Arabia and Egypt, Israel has become a willing tool of the very imperialist system that previously had produced the Jewish agony. Until the Russia-Ukraine war, it was the largest recipient of US military aid. The decline of radicalism was compounded by post-war demographic shifts which restructured what were once working-class Jewish communities.[2]

Nonetheless, the significance of the left Jewish tradition remains undiminished for the current era. For Jews, perhaps more than any other group, our history is not a matter of academics discussing arcane footnotes but part of contemporary politics. Take the example of Poland, which played such a central part in the Jewish drama. Chapter 12 focussed on the support that Jews received from Poles. That did not derive from nationalist and right-wing currents but from socialists. Today antisemitic and right-wing forces want to wipe out awareness of this tradition of solidarity and radical alternatives. The battle for memory is also a battle for the present.

A new era of historiographical research after 2000 began with the exposure of the Jedwabne massacre. The work of Polish-Canadian historian Jan Grabowski raised serious issues about the role of non-Jewish Poles in the Holocaust.[3] Right-wing post-war governments and reactionary historians have consistently denied any culpability by Poles during the Holocaust and continue to attempt to explain away collaboration, betrayals and the killing of Jews. The subject has been weaponised into a significant part of the arsenal of the right in Poland today.[4]

The trend is not just confined to Poland. Nationalist regimes in Hungary, Ukraine and other countries and the far right across the continent are engaged in a systematic attempt to legitimise the pre-war and wartime regimes, to deny collaboration and any role in the Holocaust, while simultaneously relativising the latter. This can be seen in legislation against Holocaust researchers in Poland; in Hungary, the imposition of school curricula expunging Jewish poets and replacing them with collaborators and Nazis (sparking teacher and pupil protests); the distorted memoralisation of "genocide" that diminishes the fate of Jewry.

It is not just in the realm of ideas that the past flows into the present. In the midst of a new economic crisis reminiscent of the 1930s, extreme right-wing parties like the French Rassemblement National and Italian Brothers of Italy with links to the Axis and the Holocaust have been gaining ground. Prominent individuals like Donald Trump, Kanye West and Elon Musk vilify Jews,[5] and there have been racist killings at synagogues in Pittsburgh in the US and Halle in Germany. Right-wing politicos single out George Soros while ignoring non-Jewish financiers and billionaires. For instance, Hungary's Viktor Orbán writes, "Today the Soros network…is the greatest threat faced by the states of the European Union".[6]

This conjuncture is a reminder that racism, against Jews or anyone else, is not the result of human nature or irreconcilable hostility between ethnic groups. It is the product of a social system which periodically needs scapegoats and which Jewish radicals fought, often to the death.

Awareness of real Jewish history is also essential because, in a perverse twist, the establishment has recently invented yet one more divide and rule strategy to deploy. In the past it victimised Jews to weaken the left. Now it draws on the disgust its very actions evoke to discredit the left once more. Here is an example of how the blame is shifted from the originators to its opponents:

Whereas in the past antisemitism was generally a bulwark of the Right, today a significant number of people identifying with the Left have adopted the language and imagery of antisemitism in order to delegitimise Israel. And the antisemitism of the New Left has escalated frighteningly in recent years.[7]

When capitalist politicians defend obscene wealth by reducing working-class living standards or pursue imperialist foreign policies abroad, their motives are relatively easy to spot. It is more difficult when they hide behind spokespeople from a community which suffered genocide and is still exposed to prejudice and violence. The trick is to make Israel, which repudiated Jewish diaspora culture, the touchstone for all things Jewish. Anyone on the left (Jewish or not) who dares to criticise Israel is liable to denunciation as a racist antisemite.

The definition of what is racism or who in the community is entitled to speak as a Jew is not the prerogative of Western politicians and the media or the mouthpieces of a Jewish state in Palestine. As we have seen, who was a "real Jew" emerged from an interaction between individuals and their circumstances. There were many different Jewish self-images between 1881 and 1948. The orthodox had little in common with assimilationists, the working class little in common with the upper class, and so on. Zionist socialists claimed allegiance to the left (however confusingly it was mixed with nationalism). Others supported the wider left or Bundism. They were all Jews and a calamitous proportion died as such in the Holocaust.

If the past teaches us anything it should be to reject stereotyping of whole communities, and the Jewish community in particular. However, this is what happens if ahistorical priority is afforded to the trickle of settlers who went to Palestine while the vastly greater number who deliberately chose to go elsewhere are seen as illegitimate. That substitutes the tawdry political needs of the present[8] (such as Western imperialist interests in the Middle East) for a richer and more interesting past of which the left tradition was an important element. We have seen that in Russia, Poland, Germany, Britain, South Africa and the US, it was valid, authentic, popular and grounded in daily life. Many more countries could be added to that list.[9] The radical tradition embodied the desire of the working-class segment of the community for equality, freedom and dignity, a sentiment that had been developing since formal emancipation.

The problem goes further than the bulldozing of history to colonise the mind. Indiscriminately scattering false allegations of antisemitism is dangerous. In 2022 the Israeli PM slammed the entire United Nations as antisemitic for reporting human rights violations against Palestinians.[10] If the UN had only looked at Israel, accusations of bias could perhaps be made. But it has recently reviewed the human rights records of its 193 member states three times and found many wanting. Obscuring a meaningful definition of antisemitism makes the fight against the real antisemites harder.

We have shown who historically has engaged in the fight against antisemitism. Based in the working class it was left-wing Jews and their non-Jewish comrades who defended the Jewish community against pogroms and won emancipation in Russia. The Revolution created the opportunity on an international scale to end capitalism and its divide and rule policies which bring misery to the oppressed everywhere. It was that same combination that stopped Mosley's Blackshirts in London in the 1930s and the fascist German American Bund in the US. In Germany they battled Hitler's stormtroopers and continued to resist his regime after 1933. It was left-organised working-class action that helped Jews to escape grinding poverty and live lives of dignity; and it fought to win the same for Black people in South Africa and the US too.

Despite attempts to ignore or deny, the progressive role of the left, and the working-class basis for it, endures.

Because contemporary Zionists espouse a hierarchy of oppression, they cannot see that anti-racism necessarily includes opposing oppression of Jews alongside others. Letting the real antisemites off the hook, they target anti-racists such as Jeremy Corbyn and Bernie Sanders with false accusations of antisemitism. In the case of Corbyn, the right wing of the British Labour Party, smarting from the ignominy of PM Tony Blair's imperialist adventures alongside President George Bush in Iraq, found the theory particularly useful as a weapon to destroy the reputation of a newly elected left-wing leader. The Labour right's actions contributed to losing general elections but was seen as worthwhile collateral damage as long as left-wing policies were blocked.

If Corbyn and Sanders only criticised the Israeli government and ignored injustice elsewhere perhaps that would amount to bias, although even then it wouldn't necessarily be antisemitic—that would depend on the validity of the criticisms. But these are two leaders who have consistently stood up for human rights across the board.[11] To argue as they do that Palestinians deserve the same human rights everyone should have is not racism but a rejection of it. And note that it was not Corbyn or Sanders but Benjamin Netanyahu who visited Orbán in 2017 in what was described in the press as "a meeting of minds".[12]

The six decades we cover in this book were a laboratory for experiments to fight oppression, poverty, and exploitation. Non-Jewish workers had the choice of lining up with their exploiters against scapegoats or uniting with the oppressed to beat the real enemy. From their side Jews could dream of Palestine or engage in radical activity. Socialist Zionists tried to do both at the same time. We can learn much from the way policies of separatism and solidarity were played out on a vast canvas and led to both successes and failures (the Bund being an outstanding example). The key lesson was that the antidote to divide and rule lay in unity and revolt.

The dilemma for activists has not gone away. When divisions are fostered, this can lead the oppressed towards self-defeating isolationism as a way to survive, but that scenario is not inevitable. There are multiple oppressions today—racism and sexism, Islamophobia, antisemitism, transphobia and homophobia and more. The radical Jewish experience shows that a Marxist analysis, which emphasises the class nature of society, the role of oppression in maintaining that society and strength gained through the unity of the oppressed and exploited, offers the best explanation of how oppression fits into society and how it can be fought.

The radical Jewish tradition also shows the explosive power of a movement combining resistance with oppression and exploitation. Jewish workers developed a whole arsenal of modern class weaponry, struggling in many different, innovative and inspiring ways. Defying imprisonment and death, going far beyond the narrow confines of the community, often alongside their non-Jewish comrades, the radicals launched mass demonstrations, strike action, self-defence, revolutionary uprisings, left parties, revolutionary newspapers, and more. At the heart of all was irrepressible activism and optimism for the human race—the belief that no matter how difficult and desperate the situation, action can and must be taken.

Consider the trajectory of Marek Edelman, a Bundist and one of the leaders of the Jewish Fighting Organisation (ZOB) during the Warsaw Ghetto Uprising. He participated in the general Warsaw Uprising of 1944. Then after the war Edelman refused to emigrate to the US or Israel, but instead returned to Poland where he became a heart surgeon. Edelman remained committed to a radical political vision for the remainder of his life.

In 1981 Edelman supported the formation of the Polish trade union movement Solidarity, which stood up for workers against the Stalinist government.

Twenty years later, during the second Palestinian Intifada (uprising), Edelman wrote a letter of solidarity to the Palestinian movement. Having always resented Israel's attempts to hijack the Warsaw Ghetto Uprising for themselves, Edelman now said this historic event belonged to the Palestinians. He addressed his letter to what he called the Palestinian ZOB, "commanders of the Palestinian military, paramilitary and partisan operations—to all the soldiers of the Palestinian fighting organisations".[13]

This bears repeating: Marek Edelman, a member of the ZOB, which led the Warsaw Ghetto Uprising, declared that the uprising belongs to the Palestinians.

We agree but we would add—the Warsaw Ghetto Uprising also belongs to all of us; and not just the Ghetto Uprising but the whole history presented in this book. This is not a sectional history; it belongs not just to Jews or Jewish socialists but to all people who fight back against the horrors of capitalism, who engage in the struggle to transform the world. It is a core part of the history of all of us and a guide to uniting to resist the threat of annihilation that has returned today.

The fighters at the Warsaw Ghetto Uprising saw themselves as part of a broader struggle. They pasted a placard with this appeal to the Polish people on the wall of the ghetto on 23 April 1943.[14] The words still resound today:

Poles, Citizens, Soldiers of Freedom,

Amid the noise of cannons which the German army is using to storm our homes…

Amid the rattle of machine-gunfire …

Amid the smoke of fires and dust, of the blood of the murdered Warsaw Ghetto, we send you brotherly, sincere greetings.

Perhaps we will all perish in this fight but we will not give in. [You know] that we, like you, long for revenge and punishment for all the crimes of our common enemy.

A battle is raging for your Freedom and ours.

For your and our human, social, national honour and dignity.

We will avenge the crimes of Auschwitz, Treblinka, and Majdanek.

Long live Freedom!

Death to the butchers and henchmen!

Abbreviations and acronyms

ACW: Amalgamated Clothing Workers of America
AFL: American Federation of Labor
BBL: British Brothers' League
BUF: British Union of Fascists
CIO: Congress of Industrial Organizations
CPGB: Communist Party of Great Britain
CPUSA: Communist Party of the United States of America
CSP: Christian Social Party
Evkom: Commissariat for Jewish National Affairs (Evreiskii Komissariat)
FPO: United Partisan Organisation (Fareynikte Partizaner Organizatsye)
IFLWU: International Fur and Leather Workers Union
ILGWU: International Ladies' Garment Workers' Union
ILP: Independent Labour Party
KPD: Communist Party of Germany (Kommunistische Partei Deutschlands)
KPP: Communist Party of Poland (Komunistyczna Partia Polski)
NKVD: People's Commissariat for Internal Affairs (Soviet police and secret police)
NSDAP: National Socialist German Workers' Party = Nazi party
OWP: Camp of Greater Poland (Obóz Wielkiej Polski)
POW: prisoner of war
PPS: Polish Socialist Party (Polska Partia Socjalistyczna)
RSDLP: Russian Social Democratic Labour Party
SDKPiL: Social Democracy of the Kingdom of Poland and Lithuania (Socjaldemokracja Królestwa Polskiego i Litwy)
SPD: Social Democratic Party of Germany (Sozialdemokratische Partei Deutschlands)
SR: Social Revolutionary Party
SS: Schutzstaffel
STDL: Stepney Tenants' Defence League
SWP: Socialist Workers Party (USA)
UHT: United Hebrew Trades
WZO: World Zionist Organisation
Żegota: Council to Aid Jews (Rada Pomocy Żydom)
ŻOB: Jewish Fighting Organisation (Żydowska Organizacja Bojowa)
ŻZW: Jewish Military Union (Żydowski Związek Wojskowy)

Glossary

Aktion (German), "campaign, action": used to describe Nazi attacks or military actions against Jews such as liquidation of the ghettos.

Aliyah (Hebrew), "ascent": used to describe waves of Jewish immigration to Palestine.

Ashkenazi Jews: Jews of Eastern Europe, main language Yiddish.

Assimilationism: political current that believes that Jews should or will fully blend into the local society.

Balfour Declaration: statement in support of a "Jewish homeland" in Palestine issued by the British government in 1917.

Baudienst (German), Construction Service. Full name: Baudienst im Generalgouvernement (Construction Service in the General Government). Nazi established forced labour organisation in occupied Poland.

Betar: Youth group of the Revisionist Zionists.

"Blue Police": Polish Police, established by the Nazis in occupied Poland, based on the forced draft of previous Polish police officers.

British Mandate: British rule over Palestine formally signed off by the League of Nations in 1922.

Camp of Greater Poland: far right nationalist political organisation in interwar Poland.

Congress Poland: following the partitions of Poland, 1772, 1793 and 1795, the area that in theory retained some autonomy but that in practice was a puppet state of the Tsarist Empire.

Cultural autonomy: the concept whereby different ethnic groups are allowed to freely develop within a multinational state.

Diaspora: a concept covering people who have left an ancestral homeland but in theory retain some kind of relationship with each other. Commonly used to refer to Jews not living in Israel/Palestine.

Diaspora nationalism: belief that Jews can achieve nationalist aims without physically congregating in one place or under one state through maintaining and developing a common culture and "spirit".

Dror, "Freedom": a socialist Zionist youth group in Eastern Europe, mainly Poland, in the 1930s and during the Second World War.

Duma (Russian): Russian assembly with advisory or legislative functions. In this work, the word is used to refer to the assembly created in the 1905 Revolution in Russia.

Emancipation: legal equality of Jews and non-Jews.

Endecja (Polish): National Democracy (Narodowa Demokracja). Leading Polish right-wing political party in the 1930s.

Endeks: members of Endecja.

Eretz Israel (Hebrew), "Land of Israel" (not to be confused with the present State of Israel): this term is used by some Zionists to refer to a Jewish state matching the largest expanse of biblical Israel.

Evkom: the Commissariat for Jewish National Affairs was affiliated with the People's Commissariat for Nationality Affairs in the USSR. Its main purpose was to win Jewish support for the Bolshevik regime.

Gedud haAvoda (Hebrew): Zionist work squads, the main branch being Communist-influenced.

General Zionism: mainstream Zionist current led by Chaim Weizmann that belonged neither to the left nor the religious wings.

German American Bund: American Nazi organisation established in 1936. Not to be confused with the Jewish Labour Bund.

Gleichschaltung (German), Nazi "coordination" of society: Nazification.

Halutzim (Hebrew): Zionist immigrants in early agricultural settlements in Israel, usually understood by Zionists to be "pioneers".

Hashomer Hatzair, "Young Guard": Left-wing Jewish youth movement founded in 1913.

Haskalah (Hebrew): Often called the Jewish Enlightenment, this was an intellectual movement among Jews in Europe in the eighteenth century.

Histadrut (Hebrew): General Federation of Labour in Israel. A corporatist trade union body.

Holocaust: systematic extermination of millions of human beings by the Nazis during the Second World War, Jews being the primary target.

Jewish Board of Deputies: with slightly varying names, the Board of Deputies is a communal organisation existing in most countries where there is a significant Jewish community. As an umbrella organisation it usually claims to represent all Jews, but it is not elected by any democratic constituency. In this work we refer to the British and the South African bodies.

Jewish Labour Bund ("the Bund"): General Jewish Workers' League of Lithuania, Poland and Russia (Algemeyner Yidisher Arbeter-bund in Lite, Poyln un Rusland), established in 1897, was a Marxist revolutionary organisation which aimed to unite all Jewish workers in the Tsarist Empire into one body. Subsequently, related parties were established in Poland and many other countries including the UK and the US. Not to be confused with the German American Bund.

Judenrat (plural Judenräte) (German), Jewish Council: administrative bodies set up by Nazis as intermediaries between themselves and the local Jewish community, most commonly in the ghettos.

Kehillah (Hebrew), "community": in the present study it refers to the local Jewish communal structure that managed matters such as welfare, education and community services.

Kibbutz: Communally run Jewish agricultural settlement in Israel.

Luftmenshen (Yiddish), "air people": people who live on air, have no visible means of support.

Labour Zionism: "Left-wing" Zionist current which was counterposed to Herzl's Political Zionism. Labour Zionism was the major current at the time of the establishment of the State of Israel.

Mapai: Workers' Party of the Land of Israel founded in 1930 and led by David Ben Gurion.

Mizrachi Zionism: Religious Zionist current.

Moshavim: settlement movement in Israel/Palestine based on cooperative farmers' villages, less communal than kibbutzim.

Naqba (Arabic), literally "catastrophe": forced expulsion of the Palestinians in 1948.

Nara: National Radical Camp: Fascist organisation in Poland in 1930s.

numerus clausus (Latin), "closed number": in this study, the term used in Poland to limit the number of Jewish students allowed to attend university.

Ordenergrupe (Yiddish), Marshals Group: Bund led self-defence militia in interwar Poland.

Pale of Settlement: the territories of the Russian Empire in which Jews were permitted permanent settlement.

Poale Zion, literally "Workers of Zion", also known as the Jewish Social Democratic Workers' Party: established in the Tsarist Empire in 1906.

Polish Bund: the Jewish Labour Bund ceased to exist in Russia after 1917. It was refounded on an independent basis in Poland in the interwar period.

Political Zionism: led by Theodor Herzl, the goal of this current was to establish a Jewish state in Palestine. Its strategy was to achieve this by reaching an agreement with a powerful government.

Practical Zionism: movement to build Jewish control of Palestine through immigration and land settlement.

The Protocols of the Elders of Zion: fabricated antisemitic text initially published in the Tsarist Empire in 1905 and subsequently widely disseminated by extreme right-wing groups.

Revisionist Zionism: politically far-right movement founded by Ze'ev Jabotinsky and calling for exclusive focus on an expanded Israeli state.

Sejm (Polish): Polish parliament.

Sephardic Jews: Jews who left Spain following the mass expulsion of 1492, who settled in the Ottoman Empire and the Middle East.

Socialist Zionism: organisations such as Poale Zion that tried to combine socialist activism locally with a nationalist concept of the need for Jews to establish a state in Palestine.

Sonderkommando (German), Special Command Unit: work units usually consisting of the Jewish prisoners in concentration camps forced to work in the gas chambers removing dead bodies.

Sonderweg (German), "special path": the combination of Prussian aristocrat (Junker) rule and big business that characterised German history in the nineteenth century.

Soviets: Workers' councils. Russian mass direct democracy organs mainly organised through workplaces instead of geographical constituencies.

SS: originally Hitler's personal body guards, the black uniformed elite corps became the major Nazi paramilitary organisation throughout German occupied Europe.

Territorialist Zionism: movement to find a Jewish homeland not necessarily in Palestine.

Torah: the first five books of the Hebrew Bible.

Tsukunft: youth organisation of the Jewish Labour Bund in Poland in the 1930s.

Wehrmacht (German): German army.

Yishuv (Hebrew), "settlement": Jewish communities settled in Palestine in two phases: prior to 1882 (old Yishuv) and post 1882 (new Yishuv).

Notes

Introduction

1   An earlier version of chapters 6, 7, 8 and 10 and part of chapter 4 of this book were published in Stone, Janey, 2022, "Revolutionaries, resistance fighters and firebrands: the radical Jewish tradition", *Marxist Left Review*, no 23, supplement. An earlier version of chapter 12 was published in Gluckstein, Donny (ed), *Fighting on all Fronts*, Bookmarks, London 2015.

2   Zable, Arnold, 1991, p23.

3   Cited in Brossat, Alain and Klingberg, Sylvia, 2017, p15.

4   Cohen, Rachel, 2014.

5   Cohen, Rachel, 2014.

6   There is some debate about what name to use for this country after the First World War. As Russia was only one component, we prefer not to call it that. Some people argue against the use of the word USSR or Soviet Union as there were no actual soviets in its makeup. We have, however, reluctantly settled on the name USSR.

7   See for example Kuhn, Rick, 2002.

Chapter 1
Antisemitism and its adversaries

1   Mendelsohn, Ezra, 1993, p95.

2   Fischer, Lars, 2017, p67. See also Fischer, Lars, 2007.

3   Carlebach, Julius, quoted in Perry, Marvin and Schweitzer, Frederick, 2002, p157.

4   Cesarini, David, 2004, p23.

5   Cesarini, David, 2004, p32.

6   McGeever, Brendan, 2019, p2.

7   Advocates of the "antisemitism of the

left" thesis get round this by a tortuous detour. They treat left-wing Jews as "self-haters" who delight in attacking other Jews and push themselves to the front of antisemitic left-wing parties in an act of self-flagellation. For example, Robert Wistrich writes of "The most paradoxical element in the relationship between the Jews and socialism— namely, the role that Jewish self-hatred played in activating latent prejudices in the socialist movement". To make this bizarre argument more palatable, it is suggested "that self-hatred is frequently "hidden from the self-hater, and not visible to his closest colleagues" (Wistrich, Robert, 1976, p6). Nice try, but even with such a wonderfully invisible potion, this theory cannot explain how non-Jewish leftists (who are apparently irredeemably antisemitic) would welcome as leaders people identifiable as Jews (self-hating or not, conscious of it or not). A more nuanced, though still inaccurate, exposition of the "antisemitism of the left" charge is given in Fine, Robert and Spencer, Philip, 2017.

8   Herzl, Theodor, 1896, pp2-3.

9   Herzl, Theodor, 1896, p15.

10 Herzl, Theodor, 1896, p14.

11 Prager, Dennis and Telushkin, Joseph, 1983, p20.

12 Prager, Dennis and Telushkin, Joseph, 1983, p21. A satirical version of this explanation is given in *Beyond Tribal Loyalties*: "We're proud to be Jews, members of this ancient group that everybody hates for no reason. We love Israel, our Jewish country that we need

as our refuge in case another Hitler comes to power. Everybody hates Israel for no reason, just like everybody hates Jews for no reason" (Abarbanel, Avigail, 2018, p256).

13 Prager, Dennis and Telushkin, Joseph, 1983, p22. The Torah is the compilation of the first five books of the Hebrew Bible.

14 Quoted in Aly, Götz, 2014, p227.

15 Aly, Götz, 2014, p232.

16 Postone, Moishe, 2017, pp48-49.

17 Marx, Karl and Engels, Friedrich, 1846.

18 "The ideas of the ruling class are in every epoch the ruling ideas" (Marx, Karl and Engels, Friedrich, 1846).

19 The fiction can be turned on or turned off, and target groups switched around. For example, during Europe's post-Second World War economic boom, labour was scarce and governments encouraged immigration. Today, in different economic circumstances, and when there is a political advantage to demonising some migrants but not others, certain groups are suddenly portrayed as dangerous "illegals" while others are welcomed as "foreign investors" or, like Ukrainians, tragic victims of evil states in the rival imperialist camp.

20 Marx, Karl, 1870.

21 Rabinovitch, Simon, 2012, loc 195.

22 Borochov, Ber, 2020, p78.

23 Leon, Abram, 1970, ch 1.

24 In late 1843, he wrote to a friend "Our whole object can only be—as is also the case in Feuerbach's criticism of religion—to give religious and philosophical questions the form corresponding to man who has become conscious of himself". This focus included both Jews and Christians (Marx, Karl, 1843b).

25 Traverso, Enzo, 2019, p16.

26 For a full discussion of Marx's work see Traverso, Enzo, 2019, pp11-23.

27 See Baron, Salo, 1949, p224: "Active participation of Jews in the revolutionary movements gradually changed the attitude of radical groups… In the 1840s most socialists had identified Jews with the spirit of capitalism."

28 Marx, Karl, 1844(1).

29 Quoted in Hernon, Ian, 2020, p13. See also his discussion, pp11-22.

30 Herzl, Theodor, 1920, p15, p64. Other examples show how selective quotation without proper context can be misused. All the quotes are from Herzl, Theodor, 1920, *The Jewish State*: "the Jews being a bourgeois people…the power they now possess creates rage and indignation" (p5). "The infiltration of immigrating Jews" (p5). "We have attained pre-eminence in finance…now it is the stock exchange" (p12). "The world is provoked somehow by our prosperity" (p16). "Benefits of the Emigration of the Jews… A great period of prosperity would commence in countries which are now Anti-Semitic… Another, and perhaps one of the greatest advantages, would be the ensuing social relief" (pp62-3). "[A]ny official acts of injustice against the Jews invariably brings about economic crises" (p66).

31 Marx, Karl, and Engels, Friedrich, 1844, p149.

32 Marx, Karl, and Engels, Friedrich, 1844.

33 Marx, Karl, 1835.

34 This position is very different to that of Louis Althusser, who argued that there was an "epistemological break" between the earlier "humanist" Marx and a later "scientific" Marx. In our view no such distinction between early and later Marx should be drawn, and the Jewish radical tradition was a manifestation in the real world of the case.

35 Eckhardt, Alice, 1989, p26.

36 Halpern Amaru, Betsy, 1984, p97.

37 Quoted in Bainton, Roland, 1950, pp393-394.

38 One account of the peasant revolt has this passage: "The feuds of their masters mostly served them to ruin; not enough that they had to put their sons under the banners; the attacking enemy burned their villages, destroyed their crops, and the revenge of the injured knight always hit the enemy's peasants first according to the well-known principle: If you slay my Jew, I'll slay your Jew!" (Köhler, Ludwig, 1845,

loc 143). See also Eckhardt, Alice, 1989, pp39-41.

39 Bainton, Roland, 1950, pp283-287.

40 Luther, Martin, 1543. See also Kaufmann, Thomas, 2019.

41 Halpern Amaru, Betsy, 1984, p99.

42 See discussion in Arkush, Alan, 2009.

43 Walsh, Nick, 2006.

44 Neserius, Philip, 1926, p35. See Levy, Richard, 1991, pp37-46, and de Dijn, Annelien, 2012, pp785-805. For a discussion of Diderot, who has been unjustifiably bracketed with Voltaire, see Gendzier, Stephen, 1973, pp35-54.

45 Levy, Richard, 1991, p40.

46 Lessing, Gotthold, 1894, p248.

47 Marks, Jonathan, 2010, p464.

48 See Marks, Jonathan, 2010, pp463, 465.

49 Ages, Arnold, 1969, p218.

50 Montefiore, Dora, 1902.

51 Montefiore, Dora, 1902 and Wagner, Richard, 2002, pp9, 14.

52 Katz, Jacob, 1986, p21.

53 Goldman, Albert and Sprinchorn, Evert, 1964, p53.

54 Levi, Richard, 1991, pp52-3.

55 Traverso, Enzo, 2016, p32. Rather than burden the text with additional statistics, here is the account from Jacobs, Jack, 2017, pp9-10:
"An analysis of the family backgrounds of those who participated in the Russian Social Democratic Workers' Party congress in 1907 reveals that 23 percent of the Menshevik delegates were Jewish, and that 11 percent of the Bolsheviks at this congress were Jews. Robert Michels noted in 1911 that 'among the eighty-one socialist deputies sent to the [German] Reichstag in the penultimate general election, there were nine Jews, and this figure is an extremely high one when compared with the percentage of Jews among the population of Germany, and also with the total number of Jewish workers [in Germany] and with the number of Jewish members of the socialist party.' Eighteen of the twenty-nine people's commissars in the government of the Hungarian Soviet Republic of 1919 were Jewish. Eduard

Bernstein suggested in 1921 that there were roughly five hundred journalists employed by social democratic newspapers in Germany, and that it would not be unreasonable to estimate that fifty of those journalists were of Jewish descent. By the end of 1923, roughly 20 percent of the membership of the Communist Party of Poland (KPP) was Jewish. Official Communist sources (not inclined to exaggerate on this subject) estimated that 35 percent of the KPP membership was Jewish in 1930. In 1949, it has been alleged, approximately half of those in the American Communist Party were Jews."

56 Mendes, Philip, 2014, p131.

57 Mendes, Philip, 2014, p131.

58 Mendes, Philip, 2014, p131. The figure for 1922 refers to the Bolshevik Party. See also Jacobs, Jack, 2017, p153.

59 Mendes, Philip, 2014, p35. See also Frankel, Jonathan, 2009, p60. The figure for Social Democracy covers the period between 1905 and 1922. Gitelman gives the figure of 4 percent for Jewish Bolsheviks in 1917 (Gitelman, Zvi, 1988, p120).

60 Frankel, Jonathan, 2009, p60.

61 The figure is for the 1870s. Jacobs, Jack, 2017, p184.

62 The figure is for 1905. Jacobs, Jack, 2017, p207.

63 Mullaney, Marie, 1984.

64 Jacobs, Jack, 2017, p2.

65 See Mendes-Flohr, Paul and Reiharz, Jehuda, 1995, p260.

66 In 1924, for example, the figure came to 60 percent (Hersh, Liebman, 1931, p511).

67 Stevens, Richard, 1971, p123.

68 Shimoni, Gideon, 1988, p4.

69 Stevens, Richard, 1971, p125.

70 Hirson, Baruch, 2005, p1.

71 Quoted in Hirson, Baruch, 2005, p11.

72 Johns, Sheridan, 1976, p378. The same was true of the syndicalist movement. See Cole, Peter and van der Walt, Lucien, 2011, pp87-8.

73 Shimoni, Gideon, 1988, p9.

74 Shur, Chaim, 1998, p13.

75 Shimoni, Gideon, 1988, p11.

76 Shindler, Colin, 2018a.

77 Adler, Franklin, 2000, p186.
78 See Shimoni, Gideon, 1988, p30.
79 See Shimoni, Gideon, 1988, p35.
80 Shimoni, Gideon, 1988, p33.
81 Mendes, Philip, 2014, p129.
82 For a discussion of this see Corrs, in Stephen, 1998, pp131-160 and Perlmann, Joel, 1993, pp23-30.
83 Jacobs, Jack, 2017, p342.
84 Tobias notes this feature in the formation of the Vilna Group, which established and dominated the early Bund in Russia, in Tobias, Henry, 1972, pp11-13. See also Harman, Chris, 1987.
85 Shapira, Anita, 2016, loc 460.
86 Shapira, Anita, 2016, loc 442.
87 Quoted in Baron, Salo, 1987, p56.
88 *Times of Israel*, 2013.
89 *Vedomosti*, 2013.
90 Churchill, Winston, 1920.
91 Churchill, Winston, 1920.
92 Hitler's *Mein Kampf* quoted in Gluckstein, Donny, 1999, p25.
93 Polonsky, Antony, 2001, p168.

Chapter 2
The shaping of modern Jewry

1   Leon, Abram, 1970, ch 1.
2   Rennap, Ike, 1942, pp13-14.
3   Leon, Abram, 1970, ch 2 and Ali, Tariq, 2022, p397.
4   Goitein, Schlomo, 1974, p106.
5   Ephesians, 6.5.
6   See for example, Baron, Salo, 1987, pp67-9.
7   Mendes-Flohr, Paul and Reiharz, Jehuda, 1995, p708; Gross, Nachum, 1976, pp35-47.
8   Gross, Nachum, 1976, pp35-47.
9   The village was Talavera de la Reina, discussed in Gross, Nachum, 1976, p39.
10 Prince Vorontsov quoted in Tobias, Henry, 1972, p4.
11 *Papal Encyclicals Online*, 2020.
12 Leon, Abram, 1970.
13 Gross, Nachum, 1976, p36.
14 Rennap, Ike, 1942, pp21-22.
15 Borochov, Ber, 2020, p45. Dubnov, a historian much quoted by Zionists, wrote of mediaeval Poland, for example, in these terms:
    "In a land which had not yet emerged from the primitive stage of agricultural economy, and possessed only two fixed classes, owners of the soil and tillers of the soil, the Jews naturally represented the 'third estate,' acting as the pioneers of trade and finance. They put their capital in circulation, by launching industrial undertakings, by leasing estates, and farming various articles of revenue (salt mines, customs duties), and by engaging in money-lending" (Dubnow, Simon, 2020, p29).
16 Schöffer, I, 1981, p87.
17 Molyneux notes that one fifth of sitters for Rembrandt's male portraits were Jewish in a population that was 1 percent Jewish (Molyneux, John, 2020, p114).
18 Israel, Jonathan, 2021, p43.
19 Quoted in Curley, Edwin, 1994, p8.
20 Osterman, Nathan, 1941.
21 See Mahler, Raphael, 1971, pxviii.
22 Gross, Nachum, 1976, p76.
23 Marx, Karl, 1843a.
24 Mahler, Raphael, 1971, p431.
25 See Mahler, Raphael, 1971, pp430-535.
26 Medem, Vladimir, 2011, p115.
27 Baron, Salo, 1987, p23.
28 Mendelssohn, Moses, 1782, p34, 63.
29 Yale Law School, nd.
30 Mahler, Raphael, 1971, pp40-41.
31 Thus, the National Assembly decree of 14 December 1789 stated that "non-Catholics" should have equal rights but explicitly excluded Jews, whose fate would be discussed at a later date (Roberts, John Morris, 1966, p222).
32 James, C L R, 1938, pp54-66.
33 Necheles, Ruth 1971, p128 and Mendes-Flohr, Paul and Reiharz, Jehuda, 1995, pp49-53.
34 James, C L R, 1938, p44.
35 Count of Clermont-Tonnerre, quoted in Mahler, Raphael, 1971, p32.
36 Mendes-Flohr, Paul and Reiharz, Jehuda, 1995, p114.
37 Vital, David, 1999, p558.
38 Cohen, Mitchell, 2017, p123.
39 Quoted in Mahler, Raphael, 1971, p427.
40 Baron, Salo, 1949, p213.
41 Baron, Salo, 1949, p216.
42 Baron, Salo, 1949, p219.
43 Mendes-Flohr, Paul and Reiharz, Jehuda, 1995, pp150-1.

Notes

44 Vital, David, 1999, p561.

45 Polonsky, Antony, 2017, p165.

46 Quoted in Rabinovitch, Simon, 2012, pp25-26. Dubnov was a diaspora nationalist rather than a Zionist, but his overall view was shared by Jewish nationalists in general. It is notable that in the original German of Herzl's *The Jewish State* he writes: "Wir sind ein Volk, *ein* Volk" (Herzl, Theodor, 1920, p11. His emphasis) ('We are a people. *One* people'). The italicised ein stresses the sense of a single entity and he employs the term Volk forty-one times compared to eight occurrences of the alternative—Nation—to define it (see Herzl, Theodor, 1920). The word Volk is ambiguous and can mean common folk, a people, or a nation. But it can also be used in an overtly racist manner as in *Völkisch*. Herzl used the term at a time of transition towards that latter sense. Before German unification a variety of local Volk were recognised as in Bavarian Volk or Swabian Volk etc, but in Germany after 1871 the term was applied to the unified Empire and given an overarching and potentially racist complexion.

Herzl's ambiguity on this score is brought out in the following passage. He "wrote about Jewishness deriving from religion, a month later he claimed that Jewishness had 'nothing to do with religion' and that all Jews 'are of the same race.' Four months after that, he appeared to contradict himself yet again… 'We are an historical unit, a nation… No nation has uniformity of race'" (Penslar, Derek, 2020, p81).

Incidentally, neither the word Volk nor Nation appears in Karl Marx's *On the Jewish Question*.

47 Ruppin, Arthur, 1934, pp26-7.

48 Ruppin, Arthur, 1934, p271.

49 Ruppin, Arthur, 1934, p271.

50 Hertz, Deborah, 2017, p201.

51 See Zuckerman, Martin, 2020, p4.

52 Blobaum, Robert, nd, loc 568.

53 Ruppin, Arthur, 1934, p287.

54 Ruppin, Arthur, 1934, p287.

55 Vital, David, 1999, p306.

56 Polonsky, Antony, 2017, p152.

57 Ruppin, Arthur, 1934, p290.

58 Mendelsohn, Ezra, 1993, p67.

59 See *YIVO Institute for Jewish Research*, 1946.

60 Ruppin, Arthur, 1934, pp300-301.

61 See Ruppin, Arthur, 1934, pp299-315.

62 Smolenskin, Perets, 1872, p5.

63 Cohen, Rachel, 2014.

64 Sharot, Stephen, 1973, p153. It is interesting to note that attendances dramatically *increased* after the Second World War. The post-war increase in synagogue attendance in the US was perhaps provoked by the horrors of Auschwitz. This suggests that breaking from a predetermined identity nailed on by oppression had not led to a loss of identity as such. Emancipation did not have to be a one-way street to disappearance. It gave people a choice of identity, how they built their lives, and who they wanted to be and so events like the Holocaust could lead to re-adopting earlier identities.

65 Ruppin, Arthur, 1934, p317.

66 Ruppin, Arthur, 1934, pp319-320.

67 Polonsky, Antony, 2017, p152.

68 Quoted in Birchall, Ian, 2011, p8.

69 It is notable how many Jews chose to reject the nationalists' racial/separatist version of who they were. One example is the family of the composers Felix and Fanny Mendelssohn, grandchildren of Moses Mendelssohn (founder of the Haskalah enlightenment trend in Jewry). We have quoted Vital's criticism of his descendants for "abandoning their own social structures and accepting the culture and values of the host nation" (Vital, David, 1999, p558). The complexity of the situation is illustrated by the composers' surname which was amended for the following reason:

"Felix, along with his siblings, were baptized into the Protestant faith. At about this time, the family added the surname 'Bartholdy' to their existing name (to become Mendelssohn-Bartholdy). The addition of this surname…the name of a family dairy farm indicates the lengths to which even cultured, protected, monied, educated

327

Jews felt constrained to conceal their heritage within an intolerant society" (Library of Congress, nd(1)).

Though carrying a price this situation was not simple "abandonment" or "accepting the culture…of the host nation". It included self-actualisation and the creative shaping of that wider culture.

70 An example of how oppression led to solidarity with other oppressed groups is Gershwin's 1935 opera, *Porgy and Bess*. Porgy is a disabled Black street beggar and Bess a drug-addicted victim of domestic violence. In an unprecedented move, Gershwin stipulated that only African-Americans could perform the roles. Gershwin grew up in Lower East Side Manhattan, the geographical focus of much of Chapter 8, while the inter-war "Negro-Jewish Alliance" is discussed in Chapter 9. Jazz, a genre developed by the African-American community in the US, was shunned by "high-brow" society but influenced Gershwin's music and this was paralleled by many other Jewish composers such as Irving Berlin and Kurt Weill, as well as performers like Benny Goodman and Artie Shaw.

71 Ruppin, Arthur, 1934, p399.

72 Taking 1900 as the baseline, some 36 percent of world Jewry and 44 percent of its European contingent chose to migrate. Ruppin gives 46 percent of the East European heartland for the 1881-1914 period, p45. Total Jewry stood at 11 million in 1900 (Vital, David, 1999, p298) and 16 million in 1933 (Ruppin, Arthur, 1934, p21).

73 Ruppin, Arthur, 1934, p24.

74 Hersh, Liebman, 1931, p479. Figures are for between 1899 and 1924.

75 Hersh, Liebman, 1931, p481.

76 McKeown, Adam, 2007, pp7-8.

77 Hersh, Liebman, 1931, p473. 1.8 million Jews, 1899-1924 compared to 1.5 million Poles.

78 Hersh, Liebman, 1931, p512.

79 *CJPME*, 2022. Ian Black gives an even lower figure for Jews in Palestine in 1914 of 59,000 (Black, Ian, 2018, p17).

80 1.5 million in 1900 to which another 1.5 million were added between 1900

and 1914 (Hersh, Liebman, 1931, p475).

81 Alroey, Gur, 2003, p38.

82 Segev, Tom, 2019a, pp69-70.

83 The figure is for the mid-1920s when US immigration restrictions began. Seventeen percent of the population in Palestine was Jewish compared to 3 percent in the US (Hersh, Liebman, 1931, p473).

84 Herzl, Theodor, 1896, p17.

85 Lestchinsky, Jacob, 1944, p9.

86 Lestchinsky, Jacob, 1944, p9.

87 Lestchinsky, Jacob, 1944, p19.

88 Ruppin, Arthur, 1934, p48.

89 Ruppin, Arthur, 1934, p47. Halamish, Aviva, 2010, loc 3100. This exceeded the US in total Jewish immigration. Lestchinsky, Jacob, 1944, p7 gives the figures for 1925-1942 as 33 percent of total Jewish migration to Palestine and 27.5 percent for the US.

90 Hersh, Liebman, 1931, p515.

91 In the first quarter of the twentieth century Jews were just one tenth of all immigrants. Others included 3.8 million Italians, 1.5 million Poles, 1.3 million Germans, 1 million Britons, and so on (Hersh, Liebman, 1931, p473).

92 The figures are for the years 1908–1924 (Hersh, Liebman, 1931, p477).

93 Jewish children under fourteen were twice the average percentage for immigrants. See Hersh, Liebman, 1931, p483, 485.

94 See for example Frankel, Jonathan, 2009, pp94-8.

95 Lestchinsky, Jacob, 2012, pp127-8. See also Zhitlovsky, Chaim, 2012, pp83-104 and Brossat, Alain and Klingberg, Sylvia, 2016, p31.

96 Baron's analysis of economic patterns in Russia alone suggests equal proportions of commerce and industry in 1897 (Baron, Salo, 1987, p81).

97 Ruppin, Arthur, 1934, p146.

98 Vallois, Nicolas and Imhoff, Sarah, 2020, p95.

99 Ruppin, Arthur, 1934, p113.

100 Hersh, Liebman, 1931, p488. The period is 1899-1924.

101 Hersh, Liebman, 1931, p503.

102 See also Ruppin, Arthur, 1934, p124.

Chapter 3
Jewish political currents

1 Vital, David, 1999, pp298-9.

2 The pattern is illustrated by the dates when Social Democratic (Marxist) parties were founded. The German party was established in 1875. Then came Spain (1879), France (1880), Britain (1881), and Belgium (1885). The Second International first met in 1889 and subsequently took in new members including Italy (1892), Poland (1892), Russia (1898), US (1901).

3 Greece gained independence in 1829. Italy unified in 1860, Germany in 1871, and the Japanese equivalent—the Meiji Restoration—occurred in 1867. Romania became independent in 1877 with Bulgaria and Serbia a year later. There were uprisings for Polish independence in 1830 and 1864. The Czech national revival began in 1848 and Ireland's Fenian Rising was in 1867.

4 Mendelsohn, Ezra, 1987, p48.

5 Quoted in Vital, David, 1999, p108. See also Mendes-Flohr, Paul and Reiharz, Jehuda, 1995, p137.

6 See Brossat, Alain and Klingberg, Sylvia, 2017, pp37-46.

7 Vital, David, 1999, p625.

8 Isaac Breuer, quoted in Vital, David, 1999, p623. See also Shapira, Anita, 2016, loc 182.

9 Volkov, Shulamit, 2006, p202.

10 Sternhell, Zeev, 1999, locs 1014-1015.

11 "The national religious movement and the three movements of secular Zionism (General, Revisionist, and Labor) showed the same determination in combating assimilation and the loss of traditional Jewish identity. At that time all branches wanted as large a country as possible, and they differed only in their views of how it should be attained. For all of them, Zionism was defined in terms of culture, history, religion, and even mysticism." (Sternhell, Zeev, 1999, locs 5653-5655).

12 Shapira, Anita, 2016, loc 238.

13 Davis, R W, 1996, pp9-19.

14 Lockman, Zachary, 1996, p25.

15 Sternhell, Zeev, 1999, locs 348-9.

16 Deutscher, Isaac, 1968, p86. For an interesting discussion of the practical issues this question raised in Russia, see Tobias, Henry, 1972, pp17-19.

17 Quoted in Nedava, Joseph, 1971, p225.

18 Pappé, Ilan, 2017, pp34-5.

19 Penslar, Derek, 2020, pp61-2.

20 Penslar, Derek, 2020, pp61-9. See also Kornberg, Jacques, 1993.

21 For example, he writes: "if all or any of the French Jews protest against [my] scheme on account of their own 'assimilation,' my answer is simple: The whole thing does not concern them at all. They are Jewish Frenchmen, well and good! This is a private affair for the Jews alone. The movement towards the organisation of the State I am proposing would, of course, harm Jewish Frenchmen no more than it would harm the 'assimilated' of other countries. It would, on the contrary, be distinctly to their advantage" (Herzl, Theodor, 1896, p6).

22 Herzl, Theodor, 1896, p12.

23 Herzl, Theodor, 1896, p15.

24 Herzl, Theodor, 1896, p65.

25 Quoted in Avineri, Schlomo, 1981, p83.

26 Sternhell, Zeev, 1999, loc 325: "the Jewish national movement was no worse than other national movements, no more aggressive or intolerant but also not much better".

27 Dubnow, Simon, 2012, p19.

28 A good example of this is the 1935 Nuremburg Laws, which pretended to give a scientific (eugenic) gloss to race, with half, quarter and other fractions of how Jewish a person might be. You were Jewish if you had three or four grandparents who belonged to the Jewish religious community.

29 Dubnow, Simon, 2012, p5.

30 Dubnow, Simon, 2012, p19.

31 *Jewish Virtual Library*, 2023.

32 Shapira, Anita, 2016, loc 404.

33 Segev, Tom, 2019a, p56.

34 Laqueur, Walter, 1972, p414; Wiggins, Nick and Arnold, Ann, 2020. For an amusing take on this aspect, see Michael Chabon's crime novel, *The Yiddish Policeman's Union*, which has the

premise that the Zionists lost the war in 1948 and set up a state in Alaska instead.

35 Herzl, Theodor, 1896, p1.

36 Herzl, Theodor, 1896, p58.

37 This phenomenon was not unique. An increasing absence of capitalist backing for nationalism was identified by Trotsky (using Marx's earlier insights from 1848) in his theory of permanent revolution. In the twentieth century, there have been many occasions where the fight for national independence has been led by other social forces. In Russia 1917 and China 1927 it was the working class. In China in 1949 and Cuba it was the intelligentsia. See Cliff, Tony, 1963. In terms of agency the argument can be applied to Israel in 1948. The role of the intelligentsia using the language of socialism in state construction looks like deflected permanent revolution. However, other parts of the theory do not apply. Above all, the result was not a break from imperialist control since the process was thoroughly dependent on the imperialists.

38 Penslar, Derek, 2020, p7.

39 Herzl, Theodor, 1896, p8.

40 Penslar, Derek, 2020, p7.

41 Portnoy, Samuel, 1979, p267. Zionist sympathisers even planned to assassinate Plehve for his actions. Herzl reported his meeting in these terms: "I have his positive, binding promise that in fifteen years, at the maximum, he will effectuate for us a charter for Palestine. But this is tied to one condition: the Jewish revolutionists shall cease their struggle against the Russian government." Quoted in Katz, Daniel, 2011, p19.

42 Laqueur, Walter, 1972, p155.

43 Ussishkin, Abraham, 1905, pp5-6.

44 Koestler, Arthur, 1949, p6.

45 See Shapira, Anita, 2016, locs 1617, 1636 and Jacobs, Jack, 2017, p117.

46 Weizmann, Chaim, 2013, loc 4879.

47 Storrs, Ronald, 1943.

48 Lloyd George quoted in Koestler, Arthur, 1949, p6. One mistake that is sometimes made when discussing contemporary relations between Zionism and US imperialism is to imagine the Zionist tail wags the imperialist dog. This is back to front. Imperialism only has loyalty to its own self-interest, and the same applied to the Balfour Declaration.

49 Laqueur, Walter, 1972, p503.

50 Laqueur, Walter, 1972, p156.

51 Laqueur, Walter, 1972, p157.

52 Shapira, Anita, 2016, loc 460.

53 Herzl, Theodor, 1896, p15.

54 Herzl, Theodor, 1896, p46.

55 Horowitz, Brian, 2017, p112.

56 Medem, Vladimir, 2011, p119.

57 Medem, Vladimir, 2011, p124.

58 Zionist Congress, no 2, 1898, p4.

59 Syrkin, Marie, 2018, p234.

60 Syrkin, Marie, 2018, p287.

61 Syrkin, Marie, 2018, p287.

62 Syrkin, Marie, 2018, p291.

63 Syrkin, Marie, 2018, pp291-2.

64 Though it should be noted that unlike political Zionism, the socialist Zionist approach did not preclude planning revenge on perpetrators of pogroms. See Hertz, Deborah, 2017, pp210-2.

65 Syrkin, Marie, 2018, p292.

66 He was part of the Territorialist faction for a number of years and only came to see Palestine as the goal later on.

67 Syrkin, Marie, 2018, p34.

68 Quoted in Portnoy, Samuel, 1979, pxxv.

69 Syrkin, Marie, 2018, p262.

70 Syrkin, Marie, 2018, p319.

71 Borochov, Ber, 1905.

72 Borochov's approach is reminiscent of the argument sometimes made by reformist political and trade union leaders today in relation to globalisation. Rather than confronting the common enemy by calling for solidarity between working people wherever they are from, it leads to reactionary slogans such as "British jobs for British workers", which makes concessions to divide and rule. Nonetheless, Borochov's position was different from that given by Shapira who recruits him to the "antisemitism of the left" argument: "Ber Borochov created a synthesis between Marxism, then considered the dominant ideology,

and Zionism. He explained that the Jews in their respective countries were unable to become part of the proletariat, the class of the future, because they were not allowed to work in industry. Instead they were being pauperised and turning into a proletariat of tatters, a lumpenproletariat. Consequently the Jews were doomed to be ground down in the imminent great battle between capitalism and socialism" (Shapira, Anita, 2016, loc 1023). See the quote from Borochov in the text, where he talks about Jewish workers finding employment. He did not see socialism as a threat to Jews, though he did think Jews could only fight for socialism in Palestine.

73 Borochov, Ber, 1905.
74 Borochov, Ber, 2020, p92.
75 Borochov, Ber, 2020, p91.
76 Meyers, Joshua, 2020.
77 Mendelsohn, Ezra, 1993, p3. Elsewhere his list is as follows: "religious Zionism and secular Zionism, cultural Zionism and political Zionism, socialist Zionism, general Zionism and right-wing revisionist Zionism" (Mendelsohn, Ezra, 1993, p57).
78 Mendelsohn, Ezra, 1987, p65.
79 Herzl, Theodor, 1920, p11.
80 Jabotinsky, Vladimir, 1923.
81 Sternhell, Zeev, 1999, locs 149-150.
82 Portnoy, Samuel, 1979, p263.
83 Portnoy, Samuel, 1979, p234.
84 Jacobs, Jack (ed), 2001, p31.
85 Jacobs, Jack (ed), 2001, p32.
86 Jacobs, Jack (ed), 2001, p41.
87 Jacobs, Jack (ed), 2001, p205.
88 Samuel Gozhansky, quoted in Tobias, Henry, 1972, pp31-2.
89 Calculated from figures for "Jewish" at *Demoscope Weekly*, 2023. Across the Kingdom of Poland, Jews were 38.6 percent of all urban dwellers in 1897, compared with a 13.7 percent share of the Kingdom's total population (Blobaum, Robert, nd, loc 578).
90 Rowland, Richard, 1986, p212. Vilna had one of the highest concentrations of Jews. Across the Pale, Tobias notes that Jews formed "57.9 percent of the urban population in the northwest region, 38.1 percent in the southwestern provinces and only 26.3 percent in the southernmost areas. The differences between areas were even greater when it came to the respective labor forces. In the northwest Jews made up 43 percent of the labor force, whereas in the southwest they formed only 8.8 percent and in the south only 2.7 percent" (Tobias, Henry, 1972, p116).
91 Greene, Doug, 2017.
92 Woodhouse, Charles and Tobias, Henry, 1966, p338.
93 Tobias referring to the memoirs of Kremer. Tobias, Henry, 1972, p95.
94 Jacobs, Jack (ed), 2001, p13.
95 Shmuel Gozhanski, quoted in Jacobs, Jack (ed), 2001, p14. It is interesting to note the distinction between leadership and grass roots continued in some form: "Up until World War One, Russian and not Yiddish was the primary language used at the Bund conferences, because so many activists spoke Russian better than they did Yiddish" (Hertz, Deborah, 2017, p205).
96 Blobaum, Robert, nd, loc 589.
97 Jews were 29 percent of the town population while Poles came to 46 percent and Germans 21 percent. As elsewhere, the Jewish portion of the working class was much smaller—at around 12 percent. Here Poles stood at 57 percent and Germans at 25 percent (Jacobs, Jack (ed), 2001, p91).
98 Blatman, Daniel, 2010.
99 Jacobs, Jack (ed), 2001, p93.
100 Getzler, I, quoted in Brumberg, Abraham, 1999, p208.
101 Rogger, Hans, 1983, p109.
102 See the general point made in Rozenblit, Marsha and Karp, Jonathan, 2017, p45.
103 Quoted in Brumberg, Abraham, 1999, p202.
104 Englert, Sai, 2012.
105 Frankel, Jonathan, 2009, p165.
106 Summary of the position by Charnock Smith, Jeremy, nd, p31.
107 Kuhn, Rick, 2001, p148.
108 Quoted in Avineri, Schlomo, 1981, p123.

Ha'am is counted a Zionist because alongside the diaspora he believed in a Jewish community living in Palestine but did not expect it to form a state or attract a substantial number of Jews.

109 Zimmerman, Joshua, 2003, p34.

110 Marx, Karl and Engels, Friedrich, 1848.

111 Proudhon, Pierre, 1847.

112 Bakunin, Mikhail, 1872. See also Baker, Zoe, nd.

113 Meyers, Joshua, 2020 and Tobias, Henry, 1972, p140. The figure is for 1903–4.

114 Crabapple, Molly, 2018.

115 Quoted in Tobias, Henry, 1972, p61.

116 Jacobs, Jack (ed), 2001, p30.

117 Quoted in Mullen, Richard, 2010, p166.

118 Portnoy, Samuel, 1979, p176.

119 Portnoy, Samuel, 1979, p227.

120 Lenin, Vladimir, 1901.

121 Quoted in Mullen, Richard, 2010, p168.

122 Jacobs, Jack (ed), 2001, p36.

123 Englert, Sai, 2012.

124 Portnoy, Samuel, 1979, p234.

125 Mendes-Flohr, Paul and Reiharz, Jehuda, 1995, p428.

126 Lenin, Vladimir, 1902.

127 Lenin, Vladimir, 1903.

128 McGeever, Brendan, 2019, p13.

129 Shlomo Szlein quoted in Brossat, Alain and Klingberg, Sylvia, 2017, p61.

130 Rabbi Lerner quoted in Mendes, Phillip, 2013, p283.

131 Grace Paley, quoted in Mendelsohn, Ezra, 1987, p94.

132 Adler, Franklin, 2000, p186.

Chapter 4
Tsars, pogroms and revolutionaries: Tsarist Empire 1880s–1906

1 Grinberg, Daniel, nd.

2 *YIVO Institute for Jewish Research*, 1946.

3 Jewish Virtual Library, nd(1).

4 Baron, Salo, 1987. See for example pp13-17.

5 Dubnow, Simon, 2020, p528.

6 Pritsak, Omeljan, 1987, pp12-13.

7 Quoted in Nedava, Joseph, 1971, pp55-6.

8 See for example Wiese, Stefan, 2012.

9 Vital, David, 1999, p288.

10 Vital, David, 1999, p289.

11 Quoted in Baron, Salo, 1987, pp45-6.

12 Baron, Salo, 1987, p50.

13 "A horde of tramps arrived at the railway station of Berdychev. But in this populous Jewish center they were met at the station by a large Jewish guard who, armed with clubs, did not allow the visiting 'performers' to leave the railway cars, with the result that they had to turn back" (Dubnow, Simon 2020, p539n).

14 Fishman, William, 2004, pp28-29.

15 Shapira, Anita, 2016, loc 347.

16 Count Ignatev, quoted in Baron, Salo, 1987, p46.

17 McGeever, Brendan, 2019, p19.

18 Vital, David, 1999, p294.

19 Vital, David, 1999, p295.

20 Baron, Salo, 1987, p26.

21 Rogger, Hans, 1983, pp314-5. A particular example of this was textiles in Łódź. See Nykänen, Nooa, 2015. Brossart refers to the cigarette industry in Belarus as the first concentration of Jewish proletariat (Brossat, Alain and Klingberg, Sylvia, 2017, p30).

22 Blobaum, Robert, nd.

23 Brossat, Alain and Klingberg, Sylvia, 2017, pp30-1.

24 Englert, Sai, 2012.

25 Brossat, Alain and Klingberg, Sylvia, 2017, p32.

26 Fishman, William, 2004, p20.

27 Mendelsohn, Ezra, 1968, p1.

28 Mendelsohn, Ezra, 1968, p156.

29 Borochov, Ber, 1916, pp2, 4.

30 Kaplan, Peisach, 1982, p21.

31 Mendelsohn, Ezra, 1970, p28.

32 Borochov, Ber, 1916, p177.

33 Shmulewitz, I (ed), 1982.

34 Mendelsohn, Ezra, 1970, p28.

35 *Encyclopedia.com*, nd. These Łódź socialists helped to form the Polish Socialist Party in the following year.

36 Borochov, Ber, 1916, p4.

37 Mendelsohn, Ezra, 1970, p40.

38 Mendelsohn, Ezra, 1970, pp52, 86.

39 Pogorelski, Mordechai, 1982, p12.

40 Borochov, Ber, 1916, p175.

41 Mendelsohn, Ezra, 1970, p92.

42 Pogorelski, Mordechai, 1982, p12.

43 Mendelsohn, Ezra, 1970, p83.

44 Mendelsohn, Ezra, 1970, p53.

45 Mendelsohn, Ezra, 1970, p47.

46 Englert, Sai, 2012.

47 Mendelsohn, Ezra, 1970, p68.
48 Brossat, Alain and Klingberg, Sylvia, 2017, p32.
49 *YIVO Institute for Jewish Research*, 1999, "In ale gasn" (In every street).
50 Cited in Mendelsohn, Ezra, 1970, p85.
51 Mendelsohn, Ezra, 1970, p87.
52 Mendelsohn, Ezra, 1970, p77.
53 Mendelsohn, Ezra, 1970, p90.
54 Mendelsohn, Ezra, 1968, p245.
55 Englert, Sai, 2012.
56 Mendelsohn, Ezra, 1968, p245.
57 Mendelsohn, Ezra, 1968, p246.
58 Mendelsohn, Ezra, 1968, p246.
59 Mendelsohn, Ezra, 1970, pp90-1.
60 Mendelsohn, Ezra, 1968, p244. Parentheses in the original.
61 Mendelsohn, Ezra, 1968, p250.
62 Mendelsohn, Ezra, 1970, p100.
63 Wrobe, Piotr, 2001, p155.
64 *ANU Museum*, nd.
65 Crabapple, Molly, 2018.
66 *Jewish Heritage*, 2001.
67 Crabapple, Molly, 2018.
68 Bittelman, Alexander, 2012, pp49-56. The following quotes are all from this source.
69 Bittelman, Alexander, 2012, p56.
70 *Jewish Virtual Library*, nd(2).
71 Cited in Brossat, Alain and Klingberg, Sylvia, 2017, pp42-3.
72 *Jewish Virtual Library*, nd(2). See also Meyers, Joshua, 2020 and Tobias, Henry, 1972, p140. Sources vary as to the exact figures but the dramatic decrease is unquestionable.
73 Blobaum, Robert, nd, loc 1680.
74 Ascher, Abraham, nd.
75 Ascher, Abraham, nd.
76 Wrobel, Piotr, 2001, p158.
77 Englert, Sai, 2012.
78 *YIVO Institute for Jewish Research*, 1999. "Hey, hey daloy politsey" (Hey, hey, down with the police).
79 Blobaum, Robert, nd, loc 2018. Jacobs, Jack (ed), 2001, p96.
80 Blobaum, Robert, nd, loc 2232.
81 Meyers, Joshua, 2020.
82 Blobaum, Robert, nd.
83 *New York Times*, 2023.
84 Quoted in Halkin, Hillel, 2014, p46.
85 Baron, Salo, 1987, pp55-6.
86 Lambroza, Shlomo, 1981, pp124, 125.
87 Lambroza, Shlomo, 1981, p125.
88 Lambroza, Shlomo, 1981, p125.
89 Lambroza, Shlomo, 1981, p126.
90 Lambroza, Shlomo, 1981, p126.
91 Lambroza, Shlomo, 1981, p131. It is not permitted to travel on the Sabbath (Saturday)—Shabbos in Yiddish.
92 Blobaum, Robert, nd.
93 Ascher, Abraham, nd.
94 Lambroza, Shlomo, 1981, p128.
95 Lambroza, Shlomo, 1981, p128.
96 Lambroza, Shlomo, 1981, p128; quotes from Ascher, Abraham, nd.
97 Weinberg, Robert, 1992.
98 Weinberg, Robert, 1993, p171.
99 Lambroza, Shlomo, 1981, p131.
100 Ascher, Abraham, nd.
101 Quoted in Baron, Salo, 1987, p60.
102 Sohn, David, 1982, p16.
103 Schear, Stuart, nd.
104 Lambroza, Shlomo, 1981, p125.
105 Serge, Victor, 1930, ch 1, n24. Serge gives the figure of 4,000 Jews killed and 10,000 injured, while Baron says 1,000 dead and 8,000 injured (Baron, Salo, 1987, p57).
106 Quoted in Frankel, Jonathan, 2009, p64.
107 Dubnow, Simon, 2020, p795.
108 Trotsky, Leon, 1907, ch 21, "December".
109 Meyers, Joshua, 2020.
110 Mendelsohn, Ezra, 1970, p153.
111 Mendelsohn, Ezra 1970, p155.

Chapter 5
Russia: 1917 and beyond

1 Frankel, Jonathan, 2009, p133.
2 Rozenblit, Marsha and Karp, Jonathan, 2017, p37.
3 Hickey, Michael, 1898, p826.
4 Sachar, Howard, 2005, p318.
5 Frankel, Jonathan, 2009, p135.
6 Rozenblit, Marsha and Karp, Jonathan, 2017, pp92-3.
7 Rozenblit, Marsha and Karp, Jonathan, 2017, p219; Barnavi, Eli, nd; Sachar, Howard, 2005, p318.
8 *Jewish Chronicle*, 2014.
9 *Jewish Chronicle*, 2014.
10 Rozenblit, Marsha and Karp, Jonathan, 2017, p63.
11 Rozenblit, Marsha and Karp, Jonathan, 2017, p64.

12 Weizmann, Chaim, 2013, loc 3994-4025. See also Rozenblit, Marsha and Karp, Jonathan, 2017, p69.

13 Quoted in Laqueur, Walter, 1972, p172.

14 Weizmann, Chaim, 2013.

15 Segev, Tom, 2019a, pp117-8.

16 Halkin, Hillel, 2014, p106.

17 Luxemburg, Rosa, 1915.

18 Lenin, Vladimir, 1915.

19 Luxemburg, Rosa, 1915.

20 Luxemburg, Rosa, 1915. The Herero were an African people incarcerated by Germany in Windhoek, Namibia between 1904-8, in what can be considered to be a forerunner of Hitler's concentration camp system, and were victims of what has been described as the first genocide of the twentieth century.

21 Vital, David, 1999, p277.

22 Vital, David, 1999, p277.

23 Cesarini, David, 2004, p32.

24 Mendes-Flohr, Paul and Reiharz, Jehuda, 1995, pp261-2.

25 Farber, Samuel, 2017b, p347.

26 Blobaum, Robert, nd, loc 4318.

27 Wynot, Edward, 1971, p1036.

28 Luxemburg, Rosa, 1976, p182.

29 Quoted in Leuschen-Seppel, Rosemarie, 1978, p71.

30 Luxemburg, Rosa, 1976, p175.

31 See Tobias, Henry, 1972, pp290-294.

32 For full text see Castle Jones, Rory, 2016.

33 In his autobiography, *My Life*, Trotsky also steers clear of any hierarchy of oppression, something for which he is much criticised and is seen as unforgivable proof of antisemitism: "The national inequality [of Jews] probably was one of the underlying causes of my dissatisfaction with the existing order, but it was lost among all the other phases of social injustice. It never played a leading part" (Trotsky, Leon, 1930b, p65). Critics conveniently choose to ignore that, as with Luxemburg, Trotsky's failing to privilege Jews over others did not mean ignoring antisemitism. He denounced the 1905 pogroms in these terms: "the cries of slaughtered infants, the frenzied curses of mothers, the dying gasps of old people, and savage howls of despair rose to the heavens from every corner of the country. A hundred of Russia's towns and townlets were transformed into hells. A veil of smoke was drawn across the sun. Fires devoured entire streets with their houses and inhabitants" (Trotsky, Leon, 1907, ch 12, "The Tsar's Men at Work"). In 1913 he wrote at length about the Beilis trial in which a Jew was accused of murdering a Christian child for ritual purposes, saying this proved the "depravity of the court-monarchy" (Nedava, Joseph, 1971, p77). Of the Romanian Jews he wrote: "the Jew, deprived of his rights, has to serve at the same time as lightning rod for the indignation of the exploited" (Nedava, Joseph, 1971, p79).

34 In "Does the Left have a Zionist problem?" Mitchell Cohen puts it crudely. He attacks the left because "It assumes that all oppressions are Oppression" (Cohen, Mitchell, 2017, in Jacobs, Jack, 2017, p125). It would be good to know whose oppression does not merit a capital "O". One wonders if this writer has Palestinians in mind. A recent version of the approach can be seen in relation to Ukraine. Western governments have, quite rightly, welcomed refugees from there but Afghans, Syrians and other non-white refugees are not entitled to the same consideration. By Cohen's logic, is it antisemitic to stand for the equality of their rights?

35 Trotsky, Leon, 1930b, ch 7.

36 Levine, Aaron, 2014, p13.

37 Smith, Stephen, 1983, p23.

38 See Gluckstein, Donny, 1985.

39 Trotsky, Leon, 1907, ch 12.

40 McGeever, Brendan, 2019, pp22-8.

41 *Presidential Library*, nd.

42 McGeever, Brendan, 2019, p26.

43 "Milyukov's note to the Allies", nd.

44 Pavel Miliukov, quoted in Siegelbaum, Lewis, 2014.

45 McGeever, Brendan, 2019, p20.

46 Levine, Aaron, 2014, p16.

47 McGeever, Brendan, 2019, p28.

48 Seventeen Moments in Soviet History, 2015.

Notes

49 Block, A, quoted in Tsvetkov, V Zh, nd.

50 Trotsky, Leon, 1930b, ch 33.

51 Quoted in McGeever, Brendan, 2019, p29.

52 Frankel, Jonathan, 2009, pp148-9.

53 Baron, Salo, 1987, p231.

54 McGeever, Brendan, 2019, p29.

55 McGeever, Brendan, 2019, p2.

56 McGeever, Brendan, 2019, p34.

57 McGeever, Brendan, 2019, p16.

58 McGeever, Brendan, 2019, p78.

59 McGeever, Brendan, 2019, p79.

60 Though there is no space to offer a full discussion of his book here, it should be noted McGeever believes that the language of class war and revolution shares common ground with antisemitism, leading him to write an article (with David Feldman) that states: "the political culture of the left has long been a source of antisemitism" (Feldman, David and McGeever, Brendan, 2018). The logic of the left position leads it to oppose antisemitism, even if not all its adherents prove up to the task, because divide and rule tactics weaken the working class. The political culture of the left also leads to opposing the oppression of Palestinians. The left must be anti-racist whoever is the target of racism.

61 Vital, David, 1999, p704.

62 Gluckstein, Donny, 1999, p165.

63 Vital, David, 1999, p706.

64 See Vital, David, 1999, Table 8.1, p706.

65 See Dando, William, 1966.

66 Frankel, Jonathan, 2009, pp149-50.

67 McGeever, Brendan, 2019, p79.

68 Jacobs, Jack (ed), 2001, p81; Meyers, Joshua, 2020.

69 Rose, John, 2020; McGeever, Brendan, 2019, pp57-8.

70 Quoted in Faigan, Suzanne, 2018.

71 Rose, John, 2020; McGeever, Brendan, 2019, pp57-8.

72 Quoted in Shapira, Anita, 1989, p627.

73 The date was 1920. Quoted in Shapira, Anita, 1989, p634.

74 Shapira, Anita, 2016, loc 3035.

75 Quoted in Gluckstein, Donny, 1994, p20.

76 Quoted in Gluckstein, Donny, 1994, p20.

77 Gluckstein, Donny, 1994, pp33-4.

78 See Gitelman, Zvi, 1988, pp136-140.

79 Luxemburg, Rosa, 1918, ch 1.

80 Baron, Salo, 1987, p183.

81 Quoted in Baron, Salo, 1987, p183.

82 Quoted in Frankel, Jonathan, 2009, p148 n6.

83 Baron, Salo, 1987, p184 and Tenorio, Rich, 2021.

84 Rennap, Ike, 1942, p39.

85 McGeever, Brendan, 2019, pp45-6.

86 McGeever, Brendan, 2019, p51.

87 McGeever, Brendan, 2019, p4.

88 Gitelman, Zvi, 1988, p152.

89 Gitelman, Zvi, 1988, p133.

90 Gluckstein, Donny (ed), 2015, p183.

91 Trotsky, Leon, 1969, p243.

92 Gluckstein, Donny, 1994, p38.

93 Gluckstein, Donny, 1994, p113.

94 Polonsky, Antony, 2017, p155. See also Stalin, 1954, p332.

95 Korey, William, 1972, p114.

96 Krushchev, Nikita, 1956.

97 See Gitelman, Zvi, 1988, pp135-142.

98 Weinryb, Bernard, 1980, p561.

99 Ward, Chris, 1993, p205.

100 Polonsky, Antony, 2017, p156.

101 Gluckstein, Donny, 2015, pp165-188.

102 Frankel, Jonathan, 2009, pp178-9.

103 Gluckstein, Donny, 2015, pp181-2.

104 Redlich, Shimon, 1969, pp25-36.

105 Szaynok, Bozen, 2002, p302.

106 See Brent, Jonathan and Naumov, Vladimir, 2003.

Chapter 6
A Jewish ghetto in London's East End: 1880s–1912

1 *Museum of London*, 2023.

2 Fishman, William, 2004, p90.

3 Note that sweating is not just poor working conditions. It was a specific form of sub-contracting whereby middlemen contracted out work from large manufacturers to small workshops, resulting in super-exploitation. The middlemen were said to "sweat out a profit" and the small workshops were called "sweatshops". Thus, campaigns against sweating were not directly about working conditions but about employer/employee relationships.

4 Fishman, William, 2004, p103.

5 Rosenberg, David, 2019, p165.

6   Fishman, William, 2004, p115.
7   Fishman, William, 2004, p117.
8   Fishman, William, 2004, p118. *Cupal* is an alternative spelling for a *kippe*, the brimless cap worn by observant Jewish men.
9   Fishman, William, 2004, p106.
10 Fishman, William, 2004, p165.
11 Fishman, William, 2004, p166.
12 Fishman, William, 2004, p166.
13 Fishman, William, 2004, p168.
14 Fishman, William, 2004, p205.
15 Fishman, William, 2004, p240.
16 Fishman, William, 2004, p97.
17 Brecht, Bertolt, 1964.
18 Fishman, William, 2004, p154.
19 Rosenberg, David, 2016.
20 Fishman, William, 2004, pp154, 261.
21 Fishman, William, 2004, p244; Rosenberg, David, 2019, p123.
22 Rosenberg, David, 2019, p87.
23 Rosenberg, David, 2019, p111.
24 Fishman, William, 2004, p171.
25 Rosenberg, David, 2015.
26 Rosenberg, David, 2019; Fishman, William, 2004, p176.
27 Fishman, William, 2004, Appendix 2.
28 Rosenberg, David, 2019, p115.
29 Rosenberg, David, 2019, p115.
30 Rosenthal, Henry, 1987.
31 All information on Eleanor Marx from Kapp, Yvonne, 1976, pp519, 523-4 unless otherwise indicated.
32 Rosenthal, Henry, 1987.
33 Fishman, William, 2004, p256.
34 *Past Tense*, 2016.
35 Cited in *Past Tense*, 2016.
36 "In Kamf" (In Struggle), *YIVO Institute for Jewish Research*, 1999.
37 Rosenberg, David, 2019, p123; Nadel, Benjamin, 1986.
38 Fishman, William, 2004, p253.
39 Fishman, William, 2004, pp253, 278, 279fn.
40 Fishman, William, 2004, pp279-81.
41 Fishman, William, 2004, p281. Strange punctuation in the original.
42 Fishman, William, 2004, pp281-3.
43 Fishman, William, 2004, pp283, 286.
44 Rosenberg, David, 2019, p132.
45 Rosenberg, David, 2019, p132.
46 Fishman, William, 2004, p299.
47 Fishman, William, 2004, p300.

48 Fishman, William, 2004, p300.
49 Fishman, William, 2004, p158.
50 Fishman, William, 2004, p267.
51 Fishman, William, 2004, p267.
52 Fishman, William, 2004, p264.
53 Fishman, William, 2004, pp264-5.
54 Fishman, William, 2004, pp121, 237.

Chapter 7
Fascists and the fight back: interwar London East End
1   Rosenberg, David, 1985, p7.
2   Rosenberg, David, 1985, p9.
3   Laski, Neville, 1934.
4   Rosenberg, David, 1985, p9.
5   Even then, Tory opponents waged an antisemitic campaign against the Act, complete with all the mediaeval superstitions such as Jewish responsibility for the crucifixion and the blood libel. See Dresser, Madge, nd(1), Dresser, Madge, nd(2).
6   Judd and Surridge, 2013.
7   Fishman, William, 2004, p216.
8   Rosenberg, David, 2019.
9   Dresser, Madge, nd(2).
10 Bush, Lawrence, 2017.
11 Rosenberg, David, 2019.
12 Rosenberg, David, 2019.
13 Fishman, William, 2004, p215; Rosenberg, David, 2011, p24.
14 Bloom, Cecil, 1994, p188.
15 Bloom, Cecil, 1994, p189.
16 Bloom, Cecil, 1994, p190.
17 Rosenberg, David, 2020.
18 Rosenberg, David, 2019.
19 Rosenberg, David, 2011, p114. Over 500 Jewish refugees were granted political asylum in 1906, twenty in 1908 and five in 1910. In the same period, 1,378 Jews were deported.
20 Report of the Royal Commission on Alien Immigration 1903, vol 1.
21 Rosenberg, David, 2011, pp3, 37-8.
22 Rosenberg, David, 2011, p68.
23 Rosenberg, David, 2011, pp69, 74.
24 Rosenberg, David, 2011, pp71-72.
25 Rosenberg, David, 2011, p77.
26 Rosenberg, David, 2011, pp143-4.
27 Rosenberg, David, 2011, p78.
28 Cited in Rosenberg, David, 2011, p130.
29 Rosenberg, David, 2011, p130.

30 Note that "Jew" did not always connote "communist"—it could also imply "financier" or "bloated capitalist".
31 Hodgson, Keith, 2010, p125.
32 Zukerman, William, 1936, p41.
33 Quotes cited in Rosenberg, Chanie, 1988.
34 Jacobs, Joe, 1978, p238.
35 Price, Richard and Sullivan, Martin, 1994.
36 Weston, Reg, 2005.
37 Weston, Reg, 2005.
38 Hitchen, Alice, 2010.
39 Cited in O'Shea, Joe, 2016.
40 *The Guardian*, 1936.
41 *East End Women's Museum*, 2016.
42 Cited in Doherty, Rosa, 2018.
43 Hitchen, Alice, 2010.
44 Cited in Silver, Steve, 2011.
45 Cited in Brooke, Mike, 2014.
46 Hodgson, Keith, 2010, pp140-1.
47 Hodgson, Keith, 2010, p135.
48 Crouch, Dave, 2006.
49 Hodgson, Keith, 2010, pp140, 145.
50 Crouch, Dave, 2006.
51 Simons, Mike, 2020.
52 Hodgson, Keith, 2010, p140.
53 Hodgson, Keith, 2010, p148.
54 Hodgson, Keith, 2010, p148.
55 Piratin, Phil, 1978.
56 Rosenberg, David, 2011, p163.
57 Freedland, Jonathan, 2005.
58 Srebrnic, Henry, 1995.
59 Mindel, Mick cited in *East End Women's Museum*, 2016.
60 Crouch, Dave, 2006; quote from Glynn, Sarah, 2005, p4. It is not clear what the response to BUF members at lectures was, but it seems likely they were tolerated here as long as they came as individuals to hear the lectures, in a similar way to the attempts to involve rank and file BUF members in the tenants' strikes. See the next section.
61 Simons, Mike, 2020.
62 Glynn, Sarah, 2005, p5.
63 Piratin, Phil, 1978, pp36-7. Emphasis in the original.
64 Piratin, Phil, 1978, p37.
65 Piratin, Phil, 1978, p29.
66 Piratin, Phil, 1978, p32.
67 Crouch, Dave, 2006.
68 Srebrnik, Henry, 1995, p288.
69 Srebrnik, Henry, 1995, p288.
70 Srebrnik, Henry, 1995, p289.
71 Srebrnik, Henry, 1995, p289.
72 Srebrnik, Henry, 1995, pp287-8.
73 Srebrnik, Henry, 1995, p289.
74 See Stone, Janey, 2022.
75 Srebrnik, Henry, 1995, p289.
76 Piratin, Phil, 1978, p46.
77 Piratin, Phil, 1978, p48.
78 Srebrnik, Henry, 1995, p292.
79 Srebrnik, Henry, 1995, p285.
80 Piratin, Phil, 1978, p47.
81 Piratin, Phil, 1978, p47.
82 Piratin, Phil, 1978, p48.
83 Piratin, Phil, 1978, p46.
84 Rosenberg, David, 2019, p345.
85 Rosenberg, David, 2019, p347.
86 Rosenberg, David, 2019, p347.
87 Rosenberg, David, 2019, p347.
88 Rosenberg, David, 2019, p348.

Chapter 8
Yearning to be free: United States 1880s-191

1 Library of Congress, nd(2), quote from Cavitch, Max, 2006.
2 Allen, Austin, 2017.
3 Michels, Tony, 2012, p7.
4 Foner, Philip, 1973, p11.
5 The main four robber barons were J P Morgan, Cornelius Vanderbilt, John D Rockefeller and Andrew Carnegie. A recent example of a television show is "The Gilded Age", which premiered in January 2022 on American pay television network HBO.
6 Foner, Philip, 1973, p257.
7 Foner, Philip, 1973, p13; quote from song "Eyder ikh leyg sikh shlofn" (No sooner do I lay down to sleep), *YIVO Institute for Jewish Research* 1999.
8 Weinstein, Bernard, 2018, p23.
9 Levine, Louis, 1976, pp100-103.
10 Meyer, Michael, 2010, p7.
11 Meyer, Michael, 2010, p10.
12 Jacobs, Paul, 2012, pp72-3.
13 August Spies was one of the martyrs following the Haymarket bombing in Chicago on 4 May 1886, a landmark event in US labour history. He was convicted despite evidence that he was still on stage when the blast occurred. Just before he was hanged, Spies

shouted, "The day will come when our silence will be more powerful than the voices you strangle today".

14 Bisno, Abraham, 1925, p34.

15 Schappes, Morris, 1954.

16 Foner, Philip, 1973, p257; Waldinger, Roger, 1985, p89.

17 Waldinger, Roger, 1985, pp90, 96.

18 Foner, Philip, 1973, p258.

19 Soyer, Daniel; Michels, Tony, 2012, p2; Schappes, Morris, 1955a, p20.

20 Founded in 1900, the ILGWU was initially dominated by male workers (Jewish and Italian) but grew massively among women workers during the strike wave around 1909/1910.

21 Foner, Philip, 1973, p261.

22 Vaynshteyn, Bernard, 2012, p88 (note: this is the same person elsewhere spelt Weinstein).

23 Vaynshteyn, Bernard, 2012, p88.

24 Foner, Philip, 1979, p296.

25 Foner, Philip, 1979, p296.

26 "Arbeter-Froyen" (Women Workers), *YIVO Institute for Jewish Research*, 1999.

27 Weinstein, Bernard, 2018, p140; Brune, Eva, 2020.

28 Weinstein, Bernard, 2018, p87.

29 Weinstein, Bernard, 2018, pp87-8.

30 "Wacht Oyf!" (Awake!), *YIVO Institute for Jewish Research*, 1999.

31 Joselit, Jenna, nd.

32 Sampson, Elissa, 2016.

33 Sampson, Elissa, 2016.

34 Cited in Feldberg, Michael, nd.

35 Cited in Feldberg, Michael, nd.

36 Cited in Feldberg, Michael, nd.

37 Foner, Philip, 1979, p125.

38 Cited in Foner, Philip, 1979, p125.

39 *New York Times*, 1976, pp186-7.

40 Hyman, Paula, 1980.

41 *New York Times*, 1902, cited in Baxandall, Rosalyn, Gordon, Linda and Reverby, Susan (eds), 1976, pp184-5.

42 Cited in Joselit, Jenna, nd.

43 Cited in Joselit, Jenna, nd.

44 Cited in Joselit, Jenna, nd.

45 Cited in Joselit, Jenna, nd.

46 "A teenager leads the great rent strike of 1907"; Joselit, Jenna, nd.

47 Joselit, Jenna, nd.

48 Cited in Joselit, Jenna, nd.

49 Cited in Joselit, Jenna, nd.

50 Robbins, Glyn, 2021.

51 Wertheimer, Barbara, 1977, p297.

52 Wertheimer, Barbara, 1977, p297; Foner, Philip 1979, p134 (quote from Foner).

53 *New World Encyclopedia*, nd; Foner, Philip, 1979, p154; *Yes! Solutions Journalism*, 2013.

54 Foner, Philip, 1979, p137.

55 Cited in Foner, Philip, 1979, p137. Lemlich became a Communist and remained a radical organiser until her death in the 1980s.

56 Foner, Philip, 1979, p137.

57 Cited in Marot, Helen, 1976, p189.

58 Katz, Daniel, 2011, p51.

59 Foner, Philip, 1979, p139.

60 Foner, Philip, 1979, p139.

61 Quoted in Foner, Philip, 1979, p139.

62 Wertheimer, Barbara, 1977, p303.

63 Wertheimer, Barbara, 1977, p303.

64 This feminist organisation of mostly wealthy and middle-class women supported a number of struggles of women workers in this period, the most famous being the 1912 Lawrence textile strike.

65 Katz, Daniel, 2011, p54.

66 Katz, Daniel, 2011, p52.

67 Katz, Daniel, 2011, p52.

68 Foner, Philip, 1979, p147; Wertheimer, 1977, p308. The Triangle Shirtwaist factory was the scene of the notorious tragic fire only a year later when 146 workers died in what was the deadliest industrial disaster in the history of New York. This is one of the clearest indicators that the success of the strike was only partial, and did not result in improved health and safety, most significantly it did not end the practice of locking fire doors, carried out to stop workers from taking breaks and to reduce theft. The fire itself did result in improved factory standards and contributed to the growth of the ILGWU (*Cornell University*, 2018a).

69 *Cornell University*, 2018b.

70 Foner, Philip, 1979, pp155-9.

71 Foner, Philip, 1979, p171.

72 Foner, Philip, 1979, p172.

73 Foner, Philip, 1979, p173.
74 Cited in Foner, Philip, 1979, p174.
75 Cited in Schappes, 1955a, p24.
76 Cited in Schappes, 1955a, p24.
77 Foner, Philip, 1979, p176.
78 Foner, Philip, 1979, p176.
79 Foner, Philip, 1979, p176.
80 Foner, Philip, 1979, p174.
81 Cited in Foner, Philip, 1979, p174.
82 Foner, Philip, 1979, p174.
83 Foner, Philip, 1979, p179.
84 Foner, Philip, 1979, p179.
85 Foner, Philip, 1979, p179.
86 Foner, Philip, 1979, p179.
87 Schappes, Morris, 1955a, p20.
88 *New York Times*, 1910.
89 *New York Times*, 1910.
90 Wisotsky, Isadore, 2012, pp99-101.
91 Waldman, Louis, 2012, p214.
92 Waldman, Louis, 2012, p214.
93 Michels, Tony (ed), 2012, "Introduction", p14; Ackerman, Kenneth, 2017.
94 Schappes, Morris, 1955a, p20; Soyer; Michels, Tony (ed), 2012, "Introduction", pp2-6.
95 "*Forward*", nd.
96 Soyer, Daniel, nd.
97 Soyer, Daniel, nd.
98 Michels, Tony (ed), 2012, "Introduction", p2.
99 Michels, Tony (ed), 2012, "Introduction", p5.
100 Soyer, Daniel, nd.
101 Michels, Tony (ed), 2012, "Introduction", pp4-5.
102 Mendes, Phillip, 2013.

Chapter 9
Roaring and battling: interwar United States

1 Brecher, Jeremy, 1972, p101.
2 Brecher, Jeremy, 1972, p101-103.
3 Brecher, Jeremy, 1972, p116.
4 Quoted in Brecher, Jeremy, 1972, p117.
5 Howe, Irving, 1976, p308.
6 US "New Unionism" of the 1930s is not to be confused with the same term used in the UK in the late nineteenth century to describe the surge of industrial unionism including the 1889 dockers' strike, and gasworkers' struggles.
7 Boyer, Richard and Morais, Herbert, 1980, p237.
8 Cunningham, John, 2023.
9 Cited in Boyer, Richard and Morais, Herbert, 1980, p237.
10 Boyer, Richard and Morais, Herbert, 1980, p222.
11 Foster, William Z, 1945.
12 Boyer, Richard and Morais, Herbert, 1980, p235.
13 Boyer, Richard and Morais, Herbert, 1980, p232.
14 According to the official report of the La Follette Committee of the US Senate. Boyer, Richard and Morais, Herbert, 1980, p211.
15 Spencer, Joseph, nd.
16 Tony Michels quoted in Cohen, Rachel, 2014.
17 Hochschild, Adam, 2019. As late as 1939, a bill proposing to admit 20,000 German child refugees never came to the vote, *United States Holocaust Memorial Museum*, nd(1).
18 Quoted in Diamond, Anna, 2020.
19 Howe, Irving, 1976, p323. Howe does not deny the genuine character of early Jewish socialism as Herberg does but he does also subscribe to the school that it was just a phase "to be stored in the attic of memory" (Cohen, Rachel, 2014).
20 Herberg, Will, 1952, pp7, 61.
21 Cohen, Rachel, 2014.
22 Quoted in Cohen, Rachel, 2014.
23 Quoted in Liebman, Arthur, 1979, p221.
24 Liebman, Arthur, 1979, p221.
25 Liebman, Arthur, 1979, p221.
26 Liebman, Arthur, 1979, pp322-357.
27 Wald, Alan 1987, p27.
28 Wald, Alan, 1987, p6.
29 Wald, Alan, 1987, p60.
30 Wald, Alan, 1987, p47.
31 Wald, Alan, 1987, pp44-5.
32 Wald, Alan, 1987, p45.
33 Geier, Joel, 2023.
34 Margolis, Peter, 1997.
35 *Jewish Virtual Library*, nd(3).
36 Margolis, Peter, 1997.
37 Quoted in Naison, Mark, 2012.
38 Naison, Mark, 2012.
39 Naison, Mark, 2012.
40 Klehr, Harvey, 1984, p32.

41 Boyer, Richard and Morais, Herbert, 1980, p261.
42 Klehr, Harvey, p53.
43 Naison, Mark, 2012.
44 Naison, Mark, 2012.
45 McBrearty, Michael, 2020.
46 McBrearty, Michael, 2020.
47 Boyer, Richard and Morais, Herbert, 1980, p261.
48 McBrearty, Michael, 2020.
49 Naison, Mark, 2012.
50 Naison, Mark, 2012.
51 Naison, Mark, 2012.
52 Naison, Mark, 2012.
53 Naison, Mark, 2012.
54 Naison, Mark, 2012.
55 Naison, Mark, 2012.
56 Naison, Mark, 2012.
57 Boyer, Richard and Morais, Herbert, 1980, p262.
58 Geier, Joel, 2023.
59 Boyer, Richard and Morais, Herbert, 1980, p259.
60 Liebman, Arthur, 1979, p211.
61 Quoted in Liebman, Arthur, 1979, p220.
62 Howe, Irving, 1976, p322.
63 Howe, Irving, 1976, p337.
64 Boyer, Richard and Morais, Herbert, 1980, p246.
65 Weinstein, Bernard, 2018, p233.
66 Howe, Irving, 1976, p333.
67 Howe, Irving, 1976, p335.
68 Boyer, Richard and Morais, Herbert, 1980, p246.
69 Boyer, Richard and Morais, Herbert, 1980, p247.
70 Quoted in Boyer, Richard and Morais, Herbert, 1980, p247.
71 Boyer, Richard and Morais, Herbert, 1980, p247.
72 Howe, Irwing, p339.
73 Quoted in Boyer, Richard and Morais, Herbert, 1980, p247.
74 Foner, Philip and Roediger, David, 1997.
75 Boyer, Richard and Morais, Herbert, 1980, p248.
76 Quoted in Liebman, Arthur, 1979, p228.
77 Katz, Daniel, 2011, p213.
78 Katz, Daniel, 2011, p219.
79 Liebman, Arthur, 1979, p250.
80 Howe, Irving, 1976, p325.
81 Klehr, Harvey, 1984, p5.
82 *Revolution's Newsstand*, nd.
83 Michels, Tony, nd, p1.
84 Michels, Tony, nd, p1.
85 Klehr, Harvey, 1984, p163.
86 Klehr, Harvey, 1984, p163.
87 Klehr, Harvey, 1984, p382.
88 Klehr, Harvey, 1984, p382.
89 Leibman, Arthur, 1979, pp367-8.
90 Srebrnik, Henry, 1995.
91 Furmanovsky, Michael, 2001.
92 Klehr, Harvey, 1984, p163.
93 Klehr, Harvey, 1984, p5.
94 Liebman, Arthur, 1979, p497.
95 Liebman, Arthur, 1979, p59. None of this is meant to imply that the Party had any significant proportion of the total Jewish population of the US.
96 Liebman, Arthur, 1979, p504.
97 Liebman, Arthur, 1979, p504.
98 Liebman, Arthur, 1979, p506.
99 Liebman, Arthur, 1979, p507.
100 Quoted in Liebman, Arthur, 1979, p372.
101 Naison, Mark, 2005, p47.
102 Naison, Mark, 2005, p322-23.
103 Quoted in Naison, Mark, 2005, p321.
104 Quoted in Naison, Mark, 2005, p325.
105 Harrington, John, 1935.
106 Naison, Mark, 2005, p149.
107 Quoted in Naison, Mark, 2005, p149.
108 McBrearty, Michael, 2020.
109 McBrearty, Michael, 2020.
110 Naison, Mark, 2005, p324.
111 James Ford addressing the National Council of Jewish Communists in 1938. Quoted in Naison, Mark, 2005, p324.
112 Naison, Mark, 2005, p326.
113 Open antisemitism only began to decline post-Second World War. Restrictive covenant clauses, which stated houses could not be sold to Jews or Black people, were legal until 1948, and continued informally after that. Job ads stated openly "No Jews need apply" or "Gentiles only" and many colleges would not hire Jewish faculty. Paul Samuelson, the leading economist of the period after the Second World War, was denied a job at Harvard. Even in the 1950s, hotels had signs denying entry to Jews, Negroes and dogs (Geier, Joel, 2023).
114 Schappes, Morris, 1955b, "The Jews and the post-war reaction after 1918", p24.

115 Schappes, Morris, 1955b, p24.

116 Smith, Jack, 2017. Ironically, square dancing was largely invented by Black slaves.

117 *ADL*, 2017.

118 Geier, Joel, 2023.

119 Schappes, Morris, 1955b, p25; *ADL*, 2017.

120 *United States Holocaust Memorial Museum*, nd(2).

121 Shappes, Morris, 1955c, p18.

122 Schappes, Morris, 1955c, p18.

123 *United States Holocaust Memorial Museum*, nd(2).

124 Schappes, 1955c, p19.

125 Howe, Irving, 1976, p409.

126 Burrow, Gerard, 2008, p107.

127 Caestecker, Frank and Moore, Bob (eds), 2010, loc 4069.

128 Jaher, Frederick, 2009; Welch, Susan, 2014.

129 Schrag, Peter, 2010.

130 Allen, Joe, 2021.

131 Haberman, Clyde, 2022.

132 Quoted in Allen, Joe, 2021.

133 Quoted in Allen, Joe, 2021.

134 Allen, Joe, 2021.

135 *Socialist Appeal*, 1939a.

136 Allen, Joe, 2021.

137 Not to be confused with the Socialist Workers Party (UK).

138 Allen, Joe, 2021.

139 Allen, Joe, 2021.

140 *Socialist Appeal*, 1939b.

141 Allen, Joe, 2021.

142 Allen, Joe, 2021.

143 Meeropol wrote the music under his pseudonym Lewis Allen. Later he and his wife adopted the sons of Ethel and Julius Rosenberg, executed for espionage in 1953 (*New York Times*, 1986).

144 Muraskin, Bennet, nd.

145 Muraskin, Bennet, nd.

146 According to writer Rachel Cohen, Jews comprised at least 30 percent of white Freedom Riders and a significant proportion of voter registration volunteers in the Civil Rights movement in the US in the 1960s. They also made up between one-third and one-half of all New Left activists on college campuses (Cohen, Rachel, 2014).

Chapter 10
Antisemitism intensifies:
interwar Poland

1 Jacobs, Jack, 2013.

2 Bacon, Gershon, nd.

3 Peled, Yoav, 2020.

4 Bacon, Gershon, nd.

5 Teller, Adam, 2010; Bacon, Gershon, nd.

6 Weinstock, Nathan, 1979, p13.

7 Peled, Yoav, 2020; Brossat, Alain and Klingberg, Sylvia, 2017, pp43, 80; Jacobs, Joe, 2013.

8 Brossat, Alain and Klingberg, Sylvia, 2017, p36.

9 Jewish Telegraphic Agency, 1933; Tomaszewski, Jerzy, nd.

10 Heller, Daniel, 2017, p2.

11 Quoted in Weibaum, Lawrence, 2008, p164.

12 Brenner, Lenni, 1983, ch 20.

13 *Jewish Weekly News*, 1933.

14 Zable, Arnold, 1991, p41.

15 Novershtern, Avraham, nd.

16 "Barikadn" (Barricades), *YIVO Institute for Jewish Research*, 1999.

17 Goldstein, Bernard, 2016, p4; Jacobs, Jack, 2013.

18 Brossat, Alain and Klingberg, Sylvia, 2017, p55.

19 Hanna Levy-Haas, cited in Brossat, Alain and Klingberg, Sylvia, 2017, p57.

20 Goldstein, Bernard, 2016.

21 Brossat, Alain and Klingberg, Sylvia, 2017, p37.

22 Brossat, Alain and Klingberg, Sylvia, 2017, pp78.

23 Brossat, Alain and Klingberg, Sylvia, 2017, p72.

24 Brossat, Alain and Klingberg, Sylvia, 2017, p74.

25 Brossat, Alain and Klingberg, Sylvia, 2017, p75.

26 Cited in Brossat, Alain and Klingberg, Sylvia, 2017, p73.

27 Brossat, Alain and Klingberg, Sylvia, 2017, pp51, 61.

28 Brossat, Alain and Klingberg, Sylvia, 2017, p71.

29 Goldstein, Bernard, 2016; Farber, Samuel, 2017b. There are a number of reasons why the Polish Communist Party was the only one to be actually

disbanded during the Stalinist purges. But, given the significant Jewish membership of the Party, one wonders whether antisemitism was a factor.

30 Cited in Brossat, Alain and Klingberg, Sylvia, 2017, p91.

31 Goldstein, Bernard, 2016, pp287-8.

32 Brossat, Alain and Klingberg, Sylvia, 2017, p74; Kassow, Samuel, 2010.

33 Brossat, Alain and Klingberg, Sylvia, 2017, p74.

34 Silber, Marcos, 2010.

35 Brossat, Alain and Klingberg, Sylvia, 2017, p23; Silber, Marcos, 2010.

36 Englert, Sai, 2012.

37 Goldstein, Bernard, 2016, pp277-8.

38 Farber, Samuel, 2017b.

39 Goldstein, Bernard, 2016, p146.

40 Goldstein, Bernard, 2016, p269.

41 Farber, Samuel, 2017b; Englert, Sai, 2012.

42 Goldstein, Bernard, 2016; Farber, Sam; Jacobs, Jack, 2013.

43 Wrobel, Piotr, 2001, p166; Farber, Samuel, 2017b.

44 See, for example, Brumberg, Abraham, 1999.

45 Englert, Sai, 2012.

46 Brossat, Alain and Klingberg, Sylvia, 2017, p80.

47 Heller, Celia, 1980, p290.

48 Rowe, Leonard, 1974, p121; Goldstein, Bernard, 2016, pp295-7.

49 Goldstein, Bernard, 2016, pp297-8.

50 Rowe, Leonard, 1974, p124.

51 Goldstein, Bernard, 2016, p363.

52 Stone, Janey, 2015; Pasternak, Velvel, 1998.

53 Translation modified by Rachel Sztanski and Janey Stone from "Our town is burning", 1936, *United States Holocaust Memorial Museum*, nd(3).

54 Brossat, Alain and Klingberg, Sylvia, 2017, p86.

55 *Palestine Post*, 1936.

56 Goldstein, Bernard, 2016, p305.

57 Zukerman, William, 1937.

58 *Palestine Post*, 1936.

59 Goldstein, Bernard, 2016, pxxi.

60 Cited in Heller, Celia, 1980, p286.

61 *Palestine Post*, 1936.

62 Lestchinsky, Jacob, 1936.

63 Erlich, Alexander, cited in Brenner, Lenni, 1983, ch 20.

64 Ringelblum, Emmanuel, 1992, p247.

Chapter 11
Germany: counter-revolution unleashed

1 Mahler, Raphael, 1971, p129.

2 Fischer, Klaus, 1998, p167.

3 Fischer, Klaus, 1998, p55.

4 Beider, Alexander, nd. A surname a literal form of identity and Jewish surnames are an interesting indication of how identity is a social product. Under feudalism, when most of the community was within the ghetto environment of the Kehillah, Jewish first names were chosen and were followed by "daughter of" or "son of". This was a common method of naming in small communities and persists, for example, in Iceland. The rise of the bourgeois state meant governments wanted more control of information about their subjects in order to tax and administer populations, and so wanted to identify people beyond the local level. In 1787 the Austrian government demanded Jews adopt fixed hereditary surnames to limit numbers in various regions, and the tsars adopted this in 1804 for similar purposes and the census. Some surnames were picked from Biblical sources (such as Cohen or Levi), some from places (eg Horowitz from Horowice in Bohemia), or occupations. But many came from Yiddish. Thus the names of the authors of the present work, Stone and Gluckstein, have the same origin though their difference shows the impact of oppression with the former anglicised to seem less Jewish. The interaction of external pressure (the demand to have a hereditary, traceable and taxable, name) and internal self-determination (the selection of that name) is well illustrated here. American slaves had the surname of their masters imposed, the difference with Jews being their social and economic role.

5 See Aschheim, Steven, 1989, pp77-87. Dubnov wrote: "the Jewish settlements

Notes

in Poland were founded by new-comers from Western Europe, from the lands of German culture and 'the Latin faith'" (Dubnow, Simon, 2020, pp26-8).

6 Reinharz, Jehuda, 1980, pp119-146.
7 Voigtländer, Nico and Voth, Hans-Joachim, 2012, p1348.
8 Dubnow, Simon, 2020, pp34-5.
9 See Aly, Götz, 2014, p42.
10 Fischer, Klaus, 1998, p56.
11 Volkov, Shulamit, 2006, p174.
12 Mahler, Raphael, 1971, p139.
13 See Aly, Götz, 2014, pp42-6.
14 Volkov, Shulamit, 2006, p172.
15 Mendes-Flohr, Paul and Reiharz, Jehuda, 1995, p141.
16 Haenisch, Horst, 2023, p69.
17 Quoted in Fischer, Klaus, 1998, p65.
18 There were in addition anti-Jewish riots close to the Polish border in Neustettin (1881), Xanten (1891), and Konitz (1900), which the authorities acted to curb, but their scale was limited. See Brinkmann, Tobias, 2003.
19 Mendes-Flohr, Paul and Reiharz, Jehuda, 1995, p143.
20 Holst, Ludolf, 1818, section 2-14-216.
21 Wolpe, Rebecca, 2020.
22 Grebing, Helga, 1985, p51.
23 Ruppin, Arthur, 1934, p287.
24 See Ruppin, Arthur, 1934, pp319-320.
25 Ruppin, Arthur, 1934, p322.
26 Volkov, Shulamit, 2006, p33.
27 Volkov, Shulamit, 2006, p176, and Aschheim, Steven, 1989.
28 Aly, Götz, 2014, p30.
29 The figure is for 1905-6. Leuschen-Seppel, Rosemarie, 1978, p62.
30 Haenisch, Horst, 2017, p49.
31 Sources are unanimous on this point. "The Jews played hardly any role in political life" (Herzig, Arno, 2016). "Administration and politics…it was precisely here that the discriminatory state and social practice in the Empire was most notable [and] prevented careers not only in the military or imperial politics" (Mangold-Will, Sabine, nd). "Until the early 20th century, Jews were generally denied a career in the civil service for both formal and informal reasons" (Jensen,

Uffa, nd).
32 Haenisch, Horst, 2017, p49.
33 Ruppin, Arthur, 1934, p63. See also Leuschen-Seppel, Rosemarie, 1978, p55.
34 Shafir, Gershon, 1996, p148.
35 Leuschen-Seppel, Rosemarie, 1978, p197.
36 Aschheim, Steven, 1989, pp81-2.
37 Herzl, Theodor, 1920, p11.
38 Quoted in Shapira, Anita, 2016, p244, n4.
39 Quoted in Levy, Richard, 1991, p70.
40 Quoted in Fischer, Klaus, 1998, p185.
41 Volkov, Shulamit, 2006, pp259-260. However, reflecting his class position as a wealthy industrialist he attributed "antisemitism to what he called the Jews' own boorish and unethical behaviour" (Penslar, Derek, 2020, p165).
42 Leuschen-Seppel, Rosemarie, 1978, p186.
43 Our emphasis. Quoted in Grebing, Helga, 1985, p58.
44 See Grebing, Helga, 1985, p60.
45 Gluckstein, Donny, 1999, p9.
46 Levy, Richard, 1991, pp2-3.
47 Marr, Wilhelm, 1879, p5 (ie after the introduction).
48 Prager, Dennis and Telushkin, Joseph, 1983, p21.
49 Shapira, Anita, 2016, loc 366.
50 Quoted in Leuschen-Seppel, Rosemarie, 1978, p94.
51 Leuschen-Seppel, Rosemarie, 1978, p60.
52 Marr is an interesting figure in this discussion. He may have been an example of opportunism. Like Wagner he was a revolutionary democrat in 1848 who switched to reactionary politics afterwards. His first three wives were of Jewish origin and his decision to foment racism came after he suffered "downward social mobility… and personal failures" (Zimmermann, Moshe, 1987, px) linked to being blocked as a journalist by Jewish-owned newspapers. When, in later life, his antisemitic campaigning did not produce the expected financial rewards he recanted.
53 Leuschen-Seppel, Rosemarie, 1978, p63.
54 Gluckstein, Donny, 1999, p11.
55 Previous to this time, according to Röhl, he showed little evidence of antisemitism. See Röhl, John, 1994, p195.

56 Wilhelm II was crowned in 1888.
    Quoted in Röhl, John, 1994, p200.

57 Quoted in Röhl, John, 1994, p204.
    The presence of these three groups
    (calculators, believers, and combiners)
    may stand for the current British Tory
    government with its large number of
    non-white and female ministers who
    wield the racist axe with such blatant
    enthusiasm.

58 See Leuschen-Seppel, Rosemarie, 1978,
    pp64-5.

59 See Volkov, Shulamit, 2006, p104.

60 Leuschen-Seppel, Rosemarie, 1978, p88.

61 Quoted in Leuschen-Seppel,
    Rosemarie, 1978, p90.

62 Levy, Richard, 1991, p59.

63 Volkov, Shulamit, 2006, p89.

64 Marr, Wilhelm, pp20-21. See also Levy,
    Richard, 1991, pp76-93.

65 Volkov, Shulamit, 2006, p97.

66 Quoted in Grebing, Helga, 1985, p54.
    See also Treitschke, Heinrich, 1914,
    p100.

67 Quoted in Engels, Friedrich, 1877, ch 9.

68 Engels, Friedrich, 1877. See, however,
    the point below.

69 Leuschen-Seppel, Rosemarie, 1978, p73.

70 Quoted in Leuschen-Seppel,
    Rosemarie, 1978, p98, n54. He was not
    alone in thinking this way. Engels
    also believed antisemitism was
    destined to fade away due to economic
    development, as he explained in his
    letter of 21 March 1890. See Fischer,
    Lars, 2007, p41.

71 The SPD's position was influenced by
    Engels's article "On Anti-Semitism" of
    1890, which is prescient in many ways
    but states:
    "[A]nti-Semitism betokens a
    retarded culture, which is why it is
    found only in Prussia and Austria,
    and in Russia too. Anyone dabbling in
    anti-Semitism, either in England or in
    America, would simply be ridiculed...
    In Prussia it is the lesser nobility, the
    Junkers with an income of 10,000
    marks and outgoings of 20,000, and
    hence subject to usury, who indulge in
    anti-Semitism, while both in Prussia
    and Austria a vociferous chorus is
    provided by those whom competition
    from big capital has ruined—the petty
    bourgeoisie, skilled craftsmen and small
    shop-keepers. But in as much as capital,
    whether Semitic or Aryan, circumcised
    or baptised, is destroying these classes
    of society which are reactionary through
    and through...it is helping to impel
    the retarded Prussians and Austrians
    forward until they eventually attain the
    present-day level at which all the old
    social distinctions resolve themselves in
    the one great antithesis—capitalists and
    wage-labourers" (quoted in Hernon,
    Ian, 2020, pp22-3).

72 The complications were evidenced
    by the position of Franz Mehring, a
    leading SPD figure on the left. Faced
    with antisemites claiming to be radical
    and liberal capitalists opposed to
    antisemitism Mehring wrote: "If the
    [antisemite] claims to fight capitalism
    by persecuting the Jews, the former
    claims to protect the Jews by defending
    capitalism through thick and thin"
    (quoted in Haenisch, Horst, 2023, p51).
    In the end, liberal capitalism proved
    far less politically important than
    antisemitic trends. Mehring is a favourite
    target for the "antisemitism of the left"
    brigade, but as usual, this is unjustified.

73 Leuschen-Seppel, Rosemarie, 1978, p79.

74 Quoted in Leuschen-Seppel,
    Rosemarie, 1978, p105.

75 Leuschen-Seppel, Rosemarie, 1978, p108.

76 Jacobs, Jack, 2017, pp9-10.

77 Fischer, Lars, 2007, pp227-8.

78 Volkov, Shulamit, 2006, pp124-6.

79 Leuschen-Seppel, Rosemarie, 1978, p131.

80 Leuschen-Seppel, Rosemarie, 1978, p189.

81 Goebel, Malte, 1999, p7.

82 Röhl, John, 1994, p207.

83 Blackbourn, David, 1997, p437.

84 Wheeler-Bennett, John, 1953, p4. Klaus-
    Jürgen Müller makes the identical
    point: "the old Prusso-German military
    monarchy...is a characteristic feature
    of the Prusso-German state. Its
    historical importance can scarcely be
    overestimated" (Müller, Klaus-Jürgen,
    1987, p39).

85 Crim, Brian, 2011, p628.

Notes

86 Crim, Brian, 2011, p629.

87 Fischer, Klaus, 1998, p92.

88 Hoyer, Katja, 2021, p197.

89 Haenisch, Horst, 2023, p70.

90 Crim, Brian, 2011, p637.

91 SPD and the recent breakaway USPD combined. The voter turnout in 1919 was 30 million, compared to 37 million in July 1932.

92 See also Kershaw, Ian, 1998, p98.

93 Quoted in Crim, Brian, 2011, p635.

94 Kershaw, Ian, 1998, p97.

95 Borochov, Ber, 2020, p83.

96 Wheeler-Bennett, John, 1953, p99.

97 Fischer, Klaus, 1998, p128.

98 Wheeler-Bennett, John, 1953, p77.

99 Müller, Klaus-Jürgen, 1987, p29.

100 Wheeler-Bennett, John, 1953, p159.

101 Quoted in Gluckstein, Donny, 1999, p25.

102 Gluckstein, Donny, 1999, p35.

103 Quoted in Gluckstein, Donny, 1999, p36.

104 Wheeler-Bennett, John, 1953, p157.

105 Gluckstein, Donny, 1999, p50.

106 See Gluckstein, Donny, 1999, p79.

107 Gluckstein, Donny, 1999, pp69-70.

108 See Noakes, Jeremy and Pridham, Geoffrey (eds), 1991, pp72-3.

109 Childers, Thomas, 1976, p26.

110 Childers, Thomas, 1976, p29.

111 Gluckstein, Donny, 1999, p76.

112 Wheeler-Bennett, John, 1953, p205.

113 See table in Gluckstein, Donny, 1999, p88. Fifty-seven percent of NSDAP joiners in 1933 were middle class and 5 out of 6 of these were from the old middle class. See also Noakes, Jeremy and Pridham, Geoffrey (eds), 1991, pp86-7.

114 Quoted in Gluckstein, Donny, 1999, p26.

115 Jacobs, Jack, 2017, pp11-12.

116 Gluckstein, Donny, 1999, pp24-5.

117 For a discussion see Gluckstein, Donny, 1999, ch 5. Driven by Stalin's "Third Period" line, a lurch to the ultra-left to cover his counter-revolution in Russia, the KPD accused the SPD of being "social fascists" and worse than the real fascists of Hitler. This led the KPD to try to de-stabilise the SPD Prussian government in tandem with the Nazis, allowing the government to depose the administration by fiat. For its part the SPD not only played a dangerous game through the Ebert-Groener deal, it accused the KPD of being as bad as the Nazis, and foolishly believed the constitution would keep democracy safe.

118 Siegfried Moses who would become head of the German Zionist Federation quoted in Brenner, Lenni, 1983, ch 3.

119 Quoted in Segev, Tom, 2019b, p25.

120 Trotsky, Leon, 1931.

121 Quoted in Gluckstein, Donny, 1999, p62.

122 Quoted in Gluckstein, Donny, 1999, p61.

123 General Kurt von Schleicher, quoted in Wheeler-Bennett, John, 1953, p235.

124 Quoted in Gluckstein, Donny, 1999, p66.

125 Quoted in Aly, Götz, 2014, p227.

126 Allen, William Sheridan, 1989, p84.

127 Allen, William Sheridan, 1989, p218.

128 See Gluckstein, Donny, 2012, pp128-9.

129 As previously quoted. Fischer, Lars, 2017, p67; Perry, Marvin and Schweitzer, Frederick, 2002, p157.

130 Haenisch, Horst, 2023, pp71-6.

131 Gluckstein, Donny, 1999, p56. Flechtheim writes that, in the month after 28 June and the lifting of the ban on stormtroopers, 99 died with 125 badly wounded in Prussia (Flechtheim, Ossip, 1969, p284).

132 Quoted in Gluckstein, Donny, 1999, p211.

133 Gluckstein, Donny, 1999, p211.

134 Gluckstein, Donny, 1999, pp212-3.

135 Weitz, Eric, 1997, p302.

136 Gluckstein, Donny, 1999, p211.

137 Chatzoudis, Georgios, 2015.

138 Gluckstein, Donny, 1999, p198.

139 Haenisch Horst, 2023, pp48-9.

140 Wachsmann, Nikolaus, 2015, loc 971.

141 Wachsmann, Nikolaus, 2015, loc 674.

142 Wachsmann, Nikolaus, 2015, loc 971.

143 Allen, William Sheridan, 1989, p290.

144 Haenisch, Horst, 2023, pp53-4.

145 Wachsmann, Nikolaus, 2015, loc 4075.

146 Callinicos, Alex, 2001.

147 Gluckstein, Donny, 1999, p179.

148 Gluckstein, Donny, 1999, p179.

149 See for example Gitelman, Zvi, 1988, pp217-8.

150 Dubnow, Simon, 2012, p9.

151 Quoted in Gluckstein, Donny, 1999, p184.

152 Quoted in Gluckstein, Donny, 1999, p184.

Chapter 12
Jewish resistance to the Nazis in Eastern Europe

1   Caestecker, Frank and Moore, Bob (eds), 2010, loc 1574.

2   Quoted in Gluckstein, Donny, 2012, p115.

3   Caestecker, Frank and Moore, Bob (eds), 2010, loc 1300.

4   Caestecker, Frank and Moore, Bob (eds), 2010, loc 2645.

5   Caestecker, Frank and Moore, Bob (eds), 2010, loc 2651.

6   Caestecker, Frank and Moore, Bob (eds), 2010, loc 2872.

7   Butler, R A, 1938.

8   London, Louise, 2000, p131.

9   Caestecker, Frank and Moore, Bob (eds), 2010, p266.

10 Rubenstein, Hilary, 1991, p171.

11 Wiggins, Nick and Arnold, Ann, 2020.

12 Wiggins, Nick and Arnold, Ann, 2020.

13 Gordon, Oliver, 2018.

14 Gordon, Oliver, 2018.

15 Dominique Reeves, lawyer for the Miriuwung Gajerrong Corporation [leading Indigenous organisation in the Kimberley region of North West Australia] quoted in Gordon, Oliver, 2018.

16 Blakeney, Michael, 1985, p161.

17 Blakeney, Michael, 1985, p161.

18 Auden, W H, 2022.

19 Jones, Nigel, 2011; Lanzmann, Claude, 2011.

20 Jan Karski, personal communication to Nechama Tec, December 1999, cited in Tec, Nechama, 2004, p262.

21 Cited in Novick, Peter, 2000, p578.

22 London, Louise, 2000, p1.

23 Gluckstein, Donny, 2012, p117.

24 Gluckstein, Donny (ed), 2015, p137.

25 Caestecker, Frank and Moore, Bob (eds), 2010, loc 2196.

26 Laqueur actually argues that not only was no action taken but the information was actively suppressed (Laqueur, Walter, 1982, p202).

27 Breitman, Richard, Goda, Norman, Naftali, Timothy and Wolfe, Robert, 2005, p37.

28 Neufeld, Michael, 2000, p9.

29 Quoted in Gluckstein, Donny, 2012, p116.

30 Hersh Glik, the Jewish folk poet and resistance fighter from Vilna, was a Labour Zionist. Inspired by a partisan battle and the Warsaw Ghetto Uprising, this song has been widely sung ever since. The phrase "We are here!" (*Mir zaynen do!*) also appears in the work of Shmerke Kaczerginski and stresses the idea of Jewish endurance often in a spirit of rebelliousness and defiance (Gilbert, Shirli, 2005, p73). See *Jewish Heritage Online Magazine*, nd, for the full lyrics.

31 A summary of this myth and its development can be found in Middleton-Kaplan, Richard, 2014, p3.

32 Henry, Patrick, 2014, p177.

33 Cited in Dwork, Deborah and van Pelt, Robert, 2002, p243.

34 Edelman, Marek, 1990, pp36-7.

35 A ghetto inhabitant commented that the police were "already known for their terrible corruption, but reached the apogee of depravity at the time of the deportation" (Antony Polonsky (ed), 1988, cited in John Rose's introduction to Edelman, Marek, 1990, p22).

36 Dwork, Deborah and van Pelt, Robert, 2002, p246.

37 Kaplan, Chaim, 1973, cited in Dwork, Deborah and van Pelt, Robert, 2002, p216.

38 The German term Judenrat (plural Judenräte) has been used throughout.

39 Klein, Bernard, 1960; Berenbaum, Michael, 2011.

40 Seidman, Hillel, 1997.

41 Weiss, Aharon, 1977.

42 *United States Holocaust Memorial Museum*, nd(4).

43 Bauer, Yehuda, 2001, p131.

44 Tec, Nechama, 2001, pp15-17.

45 Dobroszycki, Lucjan, 1993, cited in Tec, Nechama, 2001, p18.

46 For a 2003 listing of works relating to Jewish resistance see *Jewish Resistance: a Working Bibliography*, 1999.

47 Tzur, Eli, 1998, p40.

48 Tec, Nechama, 2001, p8; Schilde, Kurt, 2007.

49 Tec, Nechama, 2003, p261.

50 *Holocaust Education & Archive Research Team*, nd. One reason we have presented examples from Biala Podlaska, which was not a major centre,

is because that is the town of origin of the mother of author Janey Stone. Rose Stone reached safety in Australia in 1938 but her parents and younger siblings died in the Holocaust as did all members of her extended family who had remained in Poland.

51 Tec, Nechama, 2001, p20.

52 Batalion, Judy, 2020, p133.

53 We have used lines from songs as section headings to give an indication of their power.

54 Rosner, Hela, 1998.

55 *Sydney Jewish Museum*, 2018.

56 Non-military Jewish opposition activities are often labelled "spiritual resistance". My argument is that all resistance by Jews to the Nazis was political whether armed or not and whether ideologically based or not. In fact, the ideological basis of the Zionists did not assist them or provide guidance as to how to fight the Nazis.

57 Two major sources for the Warsaw Ghetto Uprising are Zuckerman, Yitzhak, 1993 and Edelman, Marek, 1990.

58 For instance, the Labour Zionist youth group newspaper called for armed self-defence in March 1942 (*Yad Vashem*, nd(1)).

59 Edelman, Marek, 1990, p71.

60 The right-wing Zionists, led by Ze'ev Jabotinsky, known as the Revisionists, were organisationally isolated from mainstream Zionism in the 1930s and 1940s.

61 *Stroop Report*, 1946. "Bandits" was the Nazi term for the non-Jewish Poles who fought alongside Jews in the Uprising.

62 Batalion, Judy, 2020, p201.

63 Edelman, Marek, 1990, p112.

64 Batalion, Judy, 2020, p200.

65 *The Telegraph*, 2009.

66 Cited in Tec, Nechama, 2013, p20.

67 Rose, John, 2009a.

68 Polonsky, Antony, 2019, p23.

69 Brenner, Lenni, 1983, ch 21.

70 Edelman, Marek, 1990, p55.

71 Brumberg, Abraham, 2003; Blatman, Daniel, 2003.

72 Blatman, Daniel, 2003; Edelman, Marek, 1990, p63.

73 Brumberg, Abraham, 2003; Minc, Matitiahu, 2023.

74 Ringelblum, Emmanuel, 1975, p102.

75 Zuckerman, Yitzhak cited in Brenner, Lenni, 1983, ch 21.

76 *Holocaust Education & Archive Research Team*, nd.

77 *United States Holocaust Memorial Museum*, nd(5); *United States Holocaust Memorial Museum*, nd(6); Tec, Nechama, 2013.

78 Batalion, Judy, 2020, p219.

79 *Facing History*, 2020.

80 *Aktion Reinhard Camps*, 2006a.

81 *Holocaust Research Project*, nd.

82 Zable, Arnold, 1991, p146.

83 Zable, Arnold, 1991, p151.

84 Datner, Szymon, 1945.

85 *Yad Vashem*, nd(2).

86 Strobl, Ingrid, 2008, p142.

87 Strobl, Ingrid, 2008, p195.

88 *Jewish Partisan Educational Foundation*, 2017a.

89 Cited in *Aktion Reinhard Camps*, 2006b.

90 *Milken Archive of Jewish Music*, nd.

91 Strobel, Ingrid, 2008, p191.

92 Tec, Nechama, 2013, p13.

93 Tec, Nechama, 2013, p17; *United States Holocaust Memorial Museum*, nd(7).

94 Yelin, Chaim and Ghelpernus, Dimitri, nd.

95 Pallavicini, Stephen and Patt, Avinoam, nd.

96 Lichtenstein, Izak, 1947.

97 All information on Minsk from Epstein, Barbara, 2008 unless otherwise indicated.

98 Epstein, Barbara, 2008, p18.

99 Cited in Epstein, Barbara, 2008, p252.

100 Epstein, Barbara, 2008, pp228-257. This was partly due to an assumption by the Soviets that anyone who came under Nazi rule and survived must have been a collaborator. The whole process was exacerbated by a local communist who invented an account of a massive evacuation from Minsk in order to conceal the fact that he and his friends had fled. Those arrested were not exonerated until 1962.

101 Virtually all Jewish men were circumcised within a few days of birth.

102 Batalion, Judy, 2020, p177.

103 Batalion, Judy, 2020.

104 Batalion, Judy, p177.

105 Tec, Nechama, 2001, p10.

106 Peled, Yael Margolin, 1999; Edelman, Marek, 1990, p57.

107 Shmerke Kaczerginski, nd.
Kaczerginski wrote "Partizaner-marsh" (Partisan march). He was a writer of revolutionary poems and songs who had worked with communist youth as a young man and participated in the formation of the FPO (United Underground) in the Vilna Ghetto. This song was written in August 1943 when many were going to the partisans (Gilbert, Shirli, 2005, p73).

> *Hey FPO!*
> *We are here!*
> *Boldly and with courage into battle.*
> *Today partisans*
> *Are going to beat the enemy,*
> *In the struggle for workers' power.*

108 Tec, Nechama, 2003, p284.

109 Comment by Eva Kracowski quoted in Tec, Nechama, 2003, p309. *Jewish Partisan Educational Foundation*, 2016.

110 Tec, Nechama, 2013, p11.

111 Tec, Nechama, 2003, p283.

112 Krakowski, Shmuel, 1984, cited in Tec, Nechama, 2013, p11.

113 Tec, Nechama, 2013, p32.

114 *Jewish Partisan Educational Foundation*, 2017b.

115 *Jewish Partisan Educational Foundation*, 2017c.

116 Tec, Nechama, 2013, p300. A fascinating account of the Bielski brothers' partisan group can be found in Tec, Nechama, 1993.

117 *United States Holocaust Memorial Museum*, nd(8).

118 Levy-Hass, Hanna and Hass, Amira, 2009. Amira Hass is well known today for her role as a Jewish Israeli journalist who exposes the treatment of Palestinians in the West Bank.

119 The experiences of Roma (Gypsies) in many ways parallel that of the Jews. They were imprisoned in dedicated camps or sometimes Jewish ghettos and some participated in partisan activities or assisted underground activities. Approximately 20,000 Roma were herded into a "family camp" in Auschwitz where they lived in conditions appalling even by Auschwitz standards. On 15 May 1944 SS guards armed with machine guns surrounded them to transport the remaining 6,000 to the gas chambers. The Roma resisted with knives made from scraps of sheet metal, iron pipes, clubs and stones. The Nazis did not confront them directly, but after removing work-capable adults, eventually murdered the remaining approximately 3,000 inmates in the gas chambers. The book of wider Roma resistance to the Porajmos (Romani Holocaust) is yet to be written (Tec, Nechama, 2013, pp28, 36). See also *United States Holocaust Memorial Museum*, 2023.

120 Shelley, Lore, 1996.

121 Witold Pilecki, a member of the underground Polish Home Army, voluntarily smuggled himself into Auschwitz in 1940 and set up an underground organisation whose main purpose was to send information out of the camp. He escaped in 1943 after realising that the Allies did not intend to liberate the camp (*Jewish Virtual Library*, nd(4); Pilecki, Witold, 2012, p168).

122 Those familiar with Slavic languages might think this is a nickname but it is in fact the real name of a woman who deserves recognition. She was hanged after the uprising shouting "Be strong and brave" (*Jewish Virtual Library*, nd(5)).

123 Tec, Nechama, 2013.

124 Tec, Nechama, 2013, p14.

125 Shelley, Lore, 1996, p8. Rosen, Klaus-Henning, 1985. Walsh, Mary Williams, 1997.

126 *United States Holocaust Memorial Museum*, nd(9).

127 *United States Holocaust Memorial Museum*, nd(10).

128 Tec, Nechama, 2013, p26.

129 Tec, Nechama, 2013, pp26-7.

130 One woman who was helped several times by non-Jews was Hanna Szper Cohen: "To this day I say—since Jews

Notes

have bad feelings about Poles…we who survived, a small percentage though it be, none of us would have survived if in some moment he did not get help, usually without ulterior motives, from some Pole" (Cohen, Julian, 2007). Many other personal accounts are given in Paul, Mark (ed), 2010.

131 Cited in Lukas, Richard, 1989, p13.

132 Lukas, Richard, 1989, p13.

133 Ascherson, Neal, 1987, pp96-100.

134 Unless otherwise indicated, information on Zegota is from Tomaszewski, Irene and Werbowski, Tecia, 1994.

135 Bingham, Marjorie, 2009.

136 Paulsson, Gunnar, 2002, pp123, 231.

137 Blatman, Daniel and Poznanski, Renee, 2001, pp182-3.

138 Zimmerman, Joshua, 2015.

139 Laqueur, Walter, 1982, p200.

140 Epstein, Barbara, 2008, p13.

141 Epstein, Barbara, 2008, p13.

142 Steven, Stewart, 1982.

143 Paulsson, Gunnar, 2002, p230.

144 Depending on which author is consulted, estimates of the number of Jews rescued by Poles vary from around 100,000 up to 450,000 with as many as 3 million Poles involved in the rescues (Lukas, Richard, 1989, p13; Davies, Norman, 2003, p200).

145 Gilbert, Martin, 2004, p103.

146 Paulsson, Gunnar, 1998 cited in Paul, Mark (ed), 2007, p287. Some authors think Paulsson is over optimistic and argue that modern research presents a less rosy picture. See for example Żbikowski, Andrzej, 2018, p408.

147 Connelly, John, 2002, p651. The main units were the Polish Police (known as the "Blue Police") and the Construction Service (*Baudienst*). The reasons for collaboration and participation in such activities are complex and cannot be discussed here, but it is worth pointing out that members of the *Baudienst* at least were conscripted and that there are many instances of people being shot for refusing to carry out instructions.

148 Żebrowski, Rafał, nd.

149 Żebrowski, Rafał, nd.

150 Gross, Jan, 2000.

151 Connelly, John, 2002, p644.

152 Connelly, John, 2002, pp644-5.

153 Stola, Dariusz, 2003, p141.

154 Connelly, John, 2002, p644.

155 Connelly, John, 2002, pp647-8.

156 Connelly, John, 2002, p656. The full sentence is: "We have the odd fact that a country pervaded by antisemitism could also produce one of the strongest resistance movements in Nazi-occupied Europe". Strangely blinkered, Connelly doesn't seem to realise that the latter fact actually contradicts the former statement.

157 Cited in Polonsky, Antony, 2001, p403.

158 Connelly, John, 2002, p57.

159 *Jewish Heritage Online Magazine*, nd.

160 Tec, Nechama, 2003, p13.

161 Henri Michel for instance, in his book on European Resistance during the Second World War, devotes four out of 360 pages to Jewish resistance (which he suggests involved only "a few thousand") and one sentence to the Warsaw Ghetto Uprising (Michel, Henri, 1972, pp177-180).

162 Paucker, Arnold, 2012, p8.

163 Pratt, Mike, 2020.

164 Paucker, Arnold, 2012, p67.

165 Patai, Raphael (ed), 1960, p6.

166 Klatzkin, Jacob, 1925, cited in Agus, Jacob, 1963, p425.

167 Weizmann, Chaim, 1983, p286.

168 Referring in this instance to the situation in Germany. Paucker, Arnold, 2012, p40.

169 Goldmann, Nahum, 1970, p149.

170 Epstein, Barbara, 2008, p268.

171 Epstein, Barbara, 2008, p284.

172 Epstein, Barbara, 2008, p285.

173 Epstein, Barbara, 2008, p291.

174 This is a comment by *Yad Vashem* historian Israel Gutman, cited in Shore, Marci, 2013.

175 See "Poland's Warsaw Rising" in Gluckstein, Donny, 2012, pp55-69 for more information about the underground state apparatus set up during the Nazi occupation.

176 Meed, Vladka, 1979, cited in Tec, Nechama, 2013, p10.

177 *Jewish Heritage Online Magazine*, nd.

Chapter 13
The impact of Palestine on the radical Jewish tradition
1   Urman, Menachem, 2015, p63.
2   Urman, Menachem, 2015, p72.
3   Urman, Menachem, 2015, p243.
4   Shur, Chaim, 1998, pp9-20 and pp331-350.
5   Rosenberg, Chanie, 2013, p12.
6   Rosenberg, Chanie, 2013, p12.
7   Rosenberg, Chanie, 2013, p28.
8   See Mendes-Flohr, Paul and Reiharz, Jehuda, 1995, p716.
9   At least half of the Third Aliyah were committed to one or other of these movements. See for example on the Second Aliyah Shafir, Gershon, 1996, pp1-5 and Shapiro, Yonathan, 1976, p17. This estimate was specifically related to the Third Aliyah.
10 Wolfe, Patrick, 2012, pp133-4.
11 Sternhell, Zeev, 1999, locs 565-566. Herzl was there for just a month in 1898 and met Kaiser Wilhelm II.
12 Dowty, Alan, Ha'am, 'Ahad and Ginzberg, Asher, 2000, p161.
13 See Lockman, Zachary, 1996, p31. The phrase itself is of uncertain origin.
14 Dowty, Alan, Ha'am, 'Ahad and Ginzberg, Asher, 2000, p162.
15 Dowty, Alan, Ha'am, 'Ahad and Ginzberg, Asher, 2000, p163.
16 Dowty, Alan, Ha'am, 'Ahad and Ginzberg, Asher, 2000, p173.
17 Dowty, Alan, Ha'am, 'Ahad and Ginzberg, Asher, 2000, p175.
18 Dowty, Alan, Ha'am, 'Ahad and Ginzberg, Asher, 2000, p176.
19 Dowty, Alan, Ha'am, 'Ahad and Ginzberg, Asher, 2000, p176.
20 Segev, Tom, 2019a, p101.
21 It was not until restrictions elsewhere forced migration to Palestine that numbers were substantial. By 1931, 58 percent of Jewish inhabitants were recent arrivals. British Census of Palestine, 1931.
22 Shapira, Anita, 2016, loc 799. Ben Gurion thought that 90 percent of the second Aliyah left. Segev, Tom, 2019(1), p61.
23 Ruppin, Arthur, 1934, p374.
24 This figure is for 1927. Hersh, Liebman, 1931, p514.
25 Ussishkin, Abraham, 1905, p11.
26 Katznelson, Berl, 1918, See also Pappé, Ilan, 2006, p82.
27 Shapiro, Yonathan, 1976, p11.
28 See McCarthy, Justin, 1990, and Cliff, Tony, 1945.
29 The rest was on land held by Jewish settlers three quarters of which had been sold by large Arab landowners (Shafir, Gershon, 1996, p41). Cliff gives the figure of 90 percent (Cliff, Tony, 1947).
30 This statistic comes from 1936 and the figure for 1914 would have been greater (Cliff, Tony, 1946, ch 1).
31 A figure of 76.8 percent for whom "wage labour is the only, or one of the main sources of income" is given for 1930 (Cliff, Tony, 1946, p104).
32 Ussishkin, Abraham, 1905, p26.
33 That came to just one fifteenth of the land purchased by Rothschild in the period up to 1914 (Shapiro, Yonathan, 1976, p11).
34 This was even less than the Jews' 10 percent share of the overall population. This is for the year 1907. Shafir, Gershon, 1996, p43. Ussishkin puts the figure at 2 percent in Ussishkin, Abraham, 1905.
35 In 1914 it was 86 percent. Calculated from Shapira, Anita, 2016, loc 1421.
36 Just 2 percent of Jewish immigrants knew farming (Shafir, Gershon, 1996, p67).
37 Shafir, Gershon, 1996, pp56-7.
38 Shafir, Gershon, 1996, p56, Ussishkin, Abraham, 1905, p26.
39 The figure is for 1905-9. Shafir, Gershon, 1996, p64.
40 Segev, Tom, 2019a, pp63-4.
41 See Borochov, Ber, 1916a.
42 Ussishkin, Abraham, 1905, pp27-8.
43 Lockman, Zachary, 1996, p51.
44 Quoted in Lockman, Zachary, 1996, p106. For Yitzhak Ben-Zvi, the leader after Borochov of Russian Poale Zion and future Israeli President, the new policy was a matter of life and death: "As long as employers from among our people contracted, explicitly or implicitly, with the fellaheen and the natives to reject and restrict the Jewish worker [we must] struggle for survival" (quoted in Shafir, Gershon, 1996, pp86-7).

Notes

45 Lockman, Zachary, 1996, p106.

46 Quoted in Mansour, George, 2012, p200. See Lockman, Zachary, 1996, pp50-57 and Pappé, Ilan, 2012.

47 Shapiro, Yonathan, 1976, p267.

48 Shafir, Gershon, 1996, p3.

49 Sternhell, Zeev, 1999, locs 179-181.

50 Pappé, Ilan, 2006, p42.

51 Shafir, Gershon, 1996, pp169-70.

52 Shapiro, Anita, 1977, p669.

53 Elkind, Menachem, 2007.

54 Margalit, Elkana, 1969, p41.

55 Leon, Dan, 1969, pp8-9.

56 Krausz, Ernest (ed), 1983, p405.

57 Krausz, Ernest (ed), 1983, pxii.

58 George Friedmann, quoted in Leon, Dan, 1969, p1.

59 Katznelson, Berl, 1918.

60 An analogous situation on a much larger scale was Russia under Stalin. Under the rubric of "socialism in one country", the economy was not based on private property and many assumed this was "actually existing socialism", despite labour camps, the show trials, and the complete lack of rights of working people. On this Tony Cliff wrote:

"If one examines the relations within the Russian economy, *abstracting them from their relations with the world economy*, one is bound to conclude that the source of the [capitalist] law of value, as the motor and regulator of production, is not to be found in it."

Russia was like "one big factory" in which "all the labourers received the goods they consumed directly, *in kind*" (Cliff, Tony, 1955). But, as Cliff pointed out, Russia *could not be* abstracted from the rest of the world because form was "in subordination to content". Military considerations due to threatening imperialist powers enforced a capitalist dynamic within the society even if its form was not market-based.

61 Shapiro, Yonathan, 1976, p72.

62 See Near, Henry, 1971.

63 Scholch, Alexander, 1985.

64 Levine, Mark, 2007,

65 *Jewish Virtual Library*, nd(6).

66 Metzer, Jacob, 1998, p7.

67 This calculation is for 1939.

68 See Avineri, Schlomo, 1981, p91, and Green, David, 2015.

69 Quoted in Avineri, Schlomo, 1981, p89.

70 Quoted in Chaver, Yael, 2004, p93.

71 Bachi, Roberto, 1974, p286.

72 See *YIVO Institute for Jewish Research*, 1946.

73 See Chaver, Yael, 2004, and Shohat, Ella, 2006.

74 Bachi, Roberto, 1974, p288.

75 Chaver, Yael, 2004, p45, pp61-2.

76 Metzer, Jacob, 1998, p7.

77 Metzer, Jacob, 1998, p106.

78 Metzer, Jacob, 1998, p85.

79 Metzer, Jacob, 1998, p106.

80 Two parties came together in 1930 to form Mapai. The larger one, which claimed to be Marxist (Ahdut Ha'avoda—Labour Unity), was the successor to Poale Zion. It had the support of around 4,500 of Palestine's 80,000 Jews (Lockman, Zachary, 1996, p65). The other party was Hapoel Hatzair (Young Worker). Established in 1905 it described itself as non-Marxist socialist.

81 Metzer, Jacob, 1998, p6.

82 Plunkett, Margaret, 1958, p162.

83 Shapira, Anita, 2016, loc 2710.

84 Shapiro, Yonathan, 1976, p18.

85 Metzer, Jacob, 1998, p134.

86 Shapira, Anita, 2017, p94.

87 Syrkin, Marie, 2018, p262.

88 Borochov, Ber, 2020, p91.

89 Ben Gurion, David, 1925. Katznelson contrasted Labour Zionism with bourgeois Zionism's aim of "a national home, in which the landlords will rule, which under 'national freedom' economic slavery will rule, in which gold will buy everything, in which the worker will pass under the rod of the oppressor" (Katznelson, Berl, 1918).

90 Berlin, George, 1970, p39.

91 Berlin, George, 1970, p54.

92 Berlin, George, 1970, p53.

93 Quoted in Metzer, Jacob, 1998, p197. This attitude towards the special requirements imposed by land colonisation had a long provenance dating back to Herzl. See Penslar, Derek, 2020, p166.

94 Shapira, Anita, 2017, pp89-90.

95 Lockman, Zachary, 1996, p86.

96 Shapira, Anita, 2016, loc 2143.

97 *Falastin*, 29 April 1914, quoted in Black, Ian, 2018, p36.

98 Haqqi Bey al-Azm quoted in Black, Ian, 2018, p32.

99 The year was 1937 (Mansour, George, 2012, p205).

100 See Black, Ian, 2018, p34.

101 Quoted in Shafir, Gershon, 1996, p87.

102 Our emphasis Allon, Yigal, 1970, p7.

103 Hertz, Deborah, 2017, p200.

104 Shafir, Gershon 1996, p167. Ben Gurion stayed there and it was a key formative experience for him: "Time and again in his speeches he harked back to Sejera" (Segev, Tom, 2019a, p307).

105 Hertz, Deborah, 2017.

106 See Allon, Yigal, 1970, pp113-6.

107 Pappe, Ilan, 2006, p46. "Established in 1920, its name literally means 'defence' in Hebrew, ostensibly to indicate that its main purpose was protecting the Jewish colonies."

108 Black, Ian, 2018, p109. S Shamir Hassan give figures of Haganah 40,000, Irgun 1,500, Stern Gang 300. Hassan, Shamir, 2001, p869. See also Pappé, Ilan, 2006, p87.

109 Shapira, Anita, 2016, loc 307.

110 Drory, Zeev, 2014, p167.

111 Leon, Dan, 1969, p139.

112 Elkind, Menachem, 2007, pp357-6.

113 Leon, Dan, 1969, ppxii-xiii.

114 Quoted in Lockman, Zachary, 1996, p75.

115 Cliff, Tony, 1947.

116 Shapiro, Anita, 1977, p670.

117 Lockman, Zachary, 1996, pp332-5.

118 Lockman, Zachary, 1996, pp315-7.

119 Lockman, Zachary, 1996, p276.

120 *Against the Stream, Collection of Articles and Speeches*, Tel Aviv 1943, Hebrew, quoted in Cliff, Tony, 1947.

121 Lockman, Zachary, 1996, p288.

122 Zafar, Saleem, 2010, p110.

123 Budeiri, Musa, 2010, p13.

124 Budeiri, Musa, 2010, pp98-115.

125 Pappé, Ilan, 2006, p224, and Budeiri, Musa, 2010, p115.

126 Ben Gurion, David, 1925.

Chapter 14
A balance sheet

1 See for example where 60 percent of British Jews identify as Zionists, and 90 percent support Israel's existence. *Full Fact*, 2018; Nortey, Justin, 2012; Morganti, Caroline, 2020.

2 Forty-six percent of Jews now reside in former Palestine compared to 3 percent in 1939 (*American Jewish Year Book*, 2020). It is interesting that current statistics need to be based on a very complex definition of what is Jewish. Six different versions are given in the table. The one that gives the 46 percent figure is on "all persons who, when asked, identify themselves as Jews, or, if the respondent is a different person in the same household, are identified by him/her as Jews; and do not have another religion. Also includes persons with a Jewish parent who claim no current religious or ethnic identity".

3 See for example Grabowski, Jan, 2022; Polonsky, Antony, 2001.

4 For example, a right-wing Polish member of parliament disrupted a lecture by Grabowski in Warsaw in January 2023 (Lepiarz, Jacek, 2023).

5 Kanye West has said "the Jewish community...milk us till we die" (*ADL*, 2022). Trump himself warned Jews to "get their act together and appreciate what they have in Israel—Before it is too late!" (Axelrod, Tal, 2022). There is a particular irony in Musk, the richest man of the world, invoking classic antisemitic tropes (Samuels, Ben, 2023).

6 *Hungary Today*, 2020.

7 Perry, Marvin and Schweitzer, Frederick, 2002, pxiii.

8 Apart from being a tool to stop campaigns for Palestinian rights, the antisemitism of the left theory is used to justify Israel's place in wider Western imperialist ambitions. The theory helped justify Islamophobia and the US invasion of Iraq. It still serves on-going hostility to the rival sub-imperialism of Iran.

9 Indirect evidence of this comes from the Spanish Civil War (1936-1939), for

example. Jews were up to a quarter of the International Brigades that fought Franco and his fascist allies. See Jackson, Michael, 1994, p84 and Sugarman, Martin, nd. Apart from the countries covered in this book, the Brigades had Jewish fighters from Argentina, Austria, Belgium, Bulgaria, Canada, Czechoslovakia, Hungary, Italy, Romania, Spain, Turkey, and Yugoslavia.

10 See for example the Israeli PM's recent reaction to a UN report on violations of international law, *Times of Israel*, 2022.

11 See for example Bernie Sanders: "No one is arguing that Israel, or any government, does not have the right to self-defense or to protect its people" (Sanders, Bernie, 2021). Likewise, Corbyn recognises "the terrible tragic history of Jewish people in Europe, the Nazis, the Holocaust, and the deaths of 6 million people" and believes "there was justice being sought for Jewish people hence the establishment of the state of Israel in 1948." He accepts the UN's two-state solution policy: "I want to see a recognised Palestine, recognising obviously 1967 borders within that. That is what the UN has said. That's what 242 said, and that's what many subsequent UN General Assembly and indeed some security council resolutions said" (Corbyn, Jeremy, 2020).

12 Schindler, Colin, 2018.

13 Rose, John, 2009a; Rose, John, 2009b. Other ghetto and Holocaust survivors have also opposed Israel's oppression of Palestinians. Chavka Fulman-Raban, a ghetto survivor, vehemently denounced the Israeli occupation of Gaza in 2013. Amira Hass, daughter of two Holocaust survivors, is world famous for her stand including calling Palestinian stone-throwing, "the birthright and duty of anyone subject to foreign rule", Silverstein, Richard, 2013; Hass, Amira, 2013.

14 Quoted in Wieczorek, Michał, 2021.

References

Abarbanel, Avigail, 2018, *Beyond Tribal Loyalties: Personal Stories of Jewish Peace Activists*, Kindle Edition.

Ackerman, Kenneth, 2017, "Trotsky in New York, 1917: reluctant Jew in a Jewish city", *Bnei Brith International*, www.bnaibrith.org/trotsky-in-new-york-1917-reluctant-jew-in-a-jewish-city-html/

ADL, 2017, "The International Jew", www.adl.org/resources/backgrounder/international-jew-1920s-antisemitism-revived-online

ADL, 2022, "Unpacking Kanye West's antisemitic remarks", 19 October, www.adl.org/resources/blog/unpacking-kanye-wests-antisemitic-remarks

Adler, Franklin, 2000, "South African Jews and Apartheid", in "After Apartheid: South Africa in the new century", *Macalester International*, vol 9.

Ages, Arnold, 1969, "Montesquieu and the Jews" in *Romanische Forschungen*, vol 81, h 1/2.

Agus, Jacob, 1963, *The Meaning of Jewish History*, vol 2, Abelard-Schuman.

Aktion Reinhard Camps, 2006a, "Bialystok Ghetto", www.deathcamps.org/occupation/bialystok%20ghetto.html

Aktion Reinhard Camps, 2006b, "Hirsh Glik", www.deathcamps.org/occupation/glik.html

Ali, Tariq, 2022, *Winston Churchill*, London, Verso.

Allen, Austin, 2017, "Emma Lazarus: 'The New Colossus'", *Poetry Foundation*, www.poetryfoundation.org/articles/144956/emma-lazarus-the-new-colossus/

Allen, Joe, 2021, "Confronting the fascist threat in the US in the late 1930s", *International Socialist Review*, 87, 1 September, isreview.org/issue/87/it-cant-happen-here/index.html

Allen, William Sheridan, 1989, *The Nazi Seizure of Power*, Penguin, London.

Allon, Yigal, 1970, *The Making of Israel's Army*, Valentine Mitchell, London.

Alpha History, nd, "Milyukov's note to the Allies (1917)", alphahistory.com/russianrevolution/milyukovs-note-to-allies-1917/

Alroey, Gur, 2003, "Journey to early-twentieth-century Palestine as a Jewish immigrant experience", *Jewish Social Studies*, New Series, vol 9, no 2, www.jstor.org/stable/4467647?seq=11

Aly, Götz, 2014, *Why the Germans? Why the Jews?*, Metropolitan Books, Henry Holt, New York.

American Jewish Year Book, 2020, "World Jewish Population, 2020", Table 7.14. link.springer.com/chapter/10.1007/978-3-030-78706-6_7/tables/14

ANU Museum, nd, "The Jewish community of Vilkaviškis", dbs.anumuseum.org.il/skn/en/c6/e121820/Place/Vilkaviskis

Arkush, Alan, 2009, *Voltaire on Judaism and Christianity*, ASJ Review, Cambridge University Press, Cambridge.

Ascher, Abraham, nd, "Russian Revolution of 1905", *YIVO Encyclopedia of Jews in Eastern Europe*, yivoencyclopedia.org/article.aspx/russian_revolution_of_1905

Ascherson, Neal, 1987, *The Struggles for Poland*, Channel 4 Books.

Aschheim, Steven, 1989, "Between East and West: reflections on migration and the making of German-Jewish identity 1800–1880s", *Studia Rosenthaliana*, vol 23, www.jstor.org/stable/41481729?seq=1

Auden, W H, 2022, "Refugee blues", www.facinghistory.org/resource-library/refugee-blues

Avineri, Schlomo, 1981, *The Making of Modern Zionism*, Basic Books, New York.

Axelrod, Tal, 2022, "White House blasts what it calls Trump's 'antisemitic' comments", *ABC News*, 17 October, abcnews.go.com/Politics/white-house-blasts-calls-trumps-antisemitic-comments/story?id=91634336

Bachi, Roberto, 1974, *The Population of Israel*, 1974, CICRED series, www.cicred.org/Eng/Publications/pdf/c-c26.pdf

Bacon, Gershon, nd, "Poland from 1795 to 1939", *YIVO Encyclopedia of Jews in Eastern Europe*, yivoencyclopedia.org/article.aspx/Poland/Poland_from_1795_to_1939

Bainton, Roland, 1995, *Here I Stand*, Read Books, Kindle Edition.

Baker, Zoe, 2021, "Bakunin was a racist', theanarchistlibrary.org/library/zoe-baker-bakunin-was-a-racist

Bakunin, Mikhail, 1872, "Aux Compagnons de la Fédération des Sections internationales de Jura", libcom.org/article/translation-antisemitic-section-bakunins-letter-comrades-jura-federation

Barnavi, Eli, 2017, "World War I and the Jews", *My Jewish Learning*, www.myjewishlearning.com/article/wwi-and-the-jews/

Baron, Salo, 1949, "The impact of the Revolution of 1848 on Jewish emancipation", in *Jewish Social Studies*, vol 11, no 3 (July 1949), Indiana University Press, www.jstor.org/stable/4464829?seq=1#metadata_info_tab_contents

Baron, Salo, 1987, *The Russian Jew under Tsars and Soviets*, Schocken Books, New York.

Batalion, Judy, 2020, *The Light of Days: Women Fighters of the Jewish Resistance: Their Untold Story*, Virago.

Bauer, Yehuda, 2001, *Rethinking the Holocaust*, Yale University Press.

Baxandall, Rosalyn, Gordon, Linda and Reverby, Susan (eds), 1976, *America's Working Women*, Vintage Books, New York.

Beider, Alexander, 2023, "Jewish Surnames Adopted in Various Regions of the Russian Empire", *Avotaynu Online*, avotaynuonline.com/1900/01/jewish-surnames-adopted-in-various-regions-of-the-russian-empire-by-alexander-beider/

Ben Gurion, David, 1925, *On the National Mission of the Working Class*, trans Ari Ne'man, www.sefaria.org/sheets/33911.3?lang=bi&with=all&lang2=en

Berenbaum, Michael, 2011, "Judenräte", *Encyclopedia Britannica*, www.britannica.com/topic/Judenrate

Berlin, George, 1970, "The Brandeis-Weizmann dispute", *American Jewish Historical Quarterly*, vol 60, no 1, www.jstor.org/stable/23877928

Bingham, Marjorie, 2009, "Women and the Warsaw Ghetto: a moment to decide", *World History Connected*, worldhistoryconnected.press.illinois.edu/6.2/bingham.html

Birchall, Ian, 2011, *Tony Cliff: A Marxist for his Time*, Bookmarks, London.

Bisno, Abraham, 1925, "When I went home I was aflame", in Michels, 2012, pp27-40.

Bittelman, Alexander, 2012, "The world of socialism and revolution", in Michels, 2012, pp49-58.

Black, Ian, 2018, *Enemies and Neighbours*, Penguin Books.

Blackbourn, David, 1997, *Fontana History of Germany: The Long 19th Century*, Fontana, London.

Blakeney, Michael, 1985, *Australia and the Jewish Refugees 1933–1948*, Croom Helm Australia, Sydney.

Blatman, Daniel and Poznanski, Renee, 2001, "Jews and their social environment: perspectives from the underground press in Poland and France", in Kosmala, Beate and Verbeeck, Georgi, *Facing the Catastrophe: Jews and non-Jews in Europe during World War II*, Berg.

Blatman, Daniel, 2003, *For Our Freedom and Yours: the Jewish Labour Bund in Poland 1939–1949*, Vallentine Mitchell.

Blatman, Daniel, 2010, "Bund", *YIVO Encyclopaedia of Jews in Eastern Europe*, yivoencyclopedia.org/article.aspx/bund

Blobaum, Robert, nd, *Rewolucja: Russian Poland 1904–1907*, Cornell University Press, Ithaca. Kindle Edition.

Bloom, Cecil, 1994, "The politics of immigration, 1881–1905", *Jewish Historical Studies*, vol 33 (1992–1994), www.jstor.org/stable/29779919?seq=3

Borochov Ber, 1905, *The National Question and the Class Struggle*, www.marxists.org/archive/borochov/1905/national-class.htm

Borochov, Ber, 1916a, *At the Cradle of Zionist Socialism*, en.wikisource.org/wiki/

Borochov, Ber, 1916b, "The jubilee of the Jewish labor movement", *Marxist Internet Archive*, www.marxists.org/subject/jewish/bb-jubilee.pdf

Borochov, Ber, 2020, *Class Struggle and the Jewish Nation*, Routledge, Abingdon-on-Thames.

Boyer, Richard and Morais, Herbert, 1980, *Labor's Untold Story*, United Electrical, Radio and Machine Workers of America, New York.

Brecher, Jeremy, 1977, *Strike!*, South End Press, Boston.

Brecht, Bertolt, 1964, "To posterity", in Schwebell, Gertrude (ed), *Contemporary German Poetry*, New Directions Books, Connecticut.

Breitman, Richard, Goda, Norman, Naftali, Timothy and Wolfe, Robert, 2005, *US Intelligence and the Nazis*, Cambridge University Press.

Brenner, Lenni, 1983, *Zionism in the Age of the Dictators*, www.marxists.org/history/etol/document/mideast/agedict/index.htm

Brent, Jonathan and Naumov, Vladimir, 2003, *Stalin's Last Crime: The Doctors' Plot*, John Murray, London.

Brinkmann, Tobias, 2003, *Review of Exclusionary Violence: Antisemitic Riots in Modern Germany*, in H-Antisemitism, networks.h-net.org/node/2645/reviews/4143/brinkmann-hoffmann-and-bergmann-and-smith-exclusionary-violence

Brooke, Mike, 2014, "Historian Bill Fishman, witness to 1936 Battle of Cable Street, dies at 93", *Hackney Gazette*, 30 December, www.eastlondonadvertiser.co.uk/news/20966972.historian-bill-fishman-witness-1936-battle-cable-street-dies-93/

Brossat, Alain and Klingberg, Sylvia, 2017, *Revolutionary Yiddishland: A History of Jewish Radicalism*, Verso, London.

Brumberg, Abraham, 1999, "Anniversaries in conflict: on the centenary of the Jewish Socialist Labor Bund", *Jewish Social Studies*, 5, www.jstor.org/stable/4467559?read-now=1&seq=1#page_scan_tab_contents

Brumberg, Abraham, 2003, "The Bund's last battles", *The Jewish Daily Forward*, 10 October, online at forward.com/articles/8322/the-bund-s-last-battles

Brune, Eva, 2020, "The Jewish roots of Labor Day", *Museum at Eldridge Street*, www.eldridgestreet.org/blog/the-jewish-roots-of-labor-day/

Budeiri, Musa, 2010, *The Palestine Communist Party 1919–1948*, Haymarket Books, Chicago.

Burrow, Gerard, 2008, *A History of Yale's School of Medicine: Passing Torches to Others*, Yale University Press.

Bush, Lawrence, 2017, "Herzl and Chamberlain", *Jewish Currents*, jewishcurrents.org/herzl-and-chamberlain

Butler, R A, 1938, (Under-Secretary of Foreign Affairs) "German and Austrian refugees", *Hansard*, vol 335, 4 May, hansard.parliament.uk/Commons/1938-05-04/debates/e9dc4e49-d691-444e-9547-624f9b0d2dbd/GermanAndAustrianRefugees

Caestecker, Frank and Moore, Bob (eds), 2010, *Refugees from Nazi Germany and the Liberal European States*, Berghahn Books, New York. Kindle Edition.

Callinicos, Alex, 2001, "Plumbing the depths: Marxism and the Holocaust", *The Yale Journal of Criticism*, vol 14, pp385-414, www.marxists.org/history/etol/writers/callinicos/2001/xx/plumbing.htm

References

Castle Jones, Rory, 2016, "Was Rosa Luxemburg a self-hating Jew? A response to Joseph Telushkin", in *Tablet Magazine* and Wesley Pruden in *The Washington Times*, rosaluxemburgblog, rosaluxemburgblog.wordpress.com/2016/08/26/was-rosa-luxemburg-a-self-hating-jew/

Cavitch, Max, 2006, "Emma Lazarus and the Golem of Liberty", *American Literary History*, 18, pp1-28, www.researchgate.net/publication/249274449_Emma_Lazarus_and_the_Golem_of_Liberty

Cesarini, David, 2004, *The Left and the Jews: The Jews and the Left*, No Pasaran Media, London.

Chamberlain, Neville, nd, www.goodreads.com/quotes/7905819-no-doubt-the-jews-aren-t-a-lovable-people-i-don-t

Charnock Smith, Jeremy, nd, *The Bolsheviks and the National Question 1917–1923*, SSEES, discovery.ucl.ac.uk/id/eprint/10108826/1/The_Bolsheviks_and_the_nationa.pdf

Chatzoudis, Georgios, 2015, "Arbeiterwiderstand hatte die größten Verluste zu beklagen" (Interview with Stefan Heinz), *Lisa Gerda-Henkel Stiftung*, 15 December, lisa.gerda-henkel-stiftung.de/gewerkschaften_widerstand

Chaver, Yael, 2004, *What must be Forgotten*, Syracuse University.

Childers, Thomas, 1976, "The social bases of the National Socialist vote", *Journal of Contemporary History*, vol 11, no 4, www.jstor.org/stable/260190?seq=15#metadata_info_tab_contents

Churchill, Winston, 1920, "Zionism versus Bolshevism", *Illustrated Sunday Herald*, London, 8 February, en.wikisource.org/wiki/Zionism_versus_Bolshevism

CJPME, 2022, "Demographics of historic Palestine prior to 1948", www.cjpme.org/fs_007

Cliff, Tony, 1945, *Middle East at the Crossroads*, www.marxists.org/archive/cliff/works/1945/12/mideast.htm

Cliff, Tony, 1946, *The Problem of the Middle East*, www.marxists.org/archive/cliff/works/1946/probme/index.html

Cliff, Tony, 1947, *On the Irresponsible Handling of the Palestine Question*, www.marxists.org/archive/cliff/works/1947/xx/palestine.htm

Cliff, Tony, 1955, *State Capitalism in Russia*, www.marxists.org/archive/cliff/works/1955/statecap/ch07-s1.htm

Cliff, Tony, 1963, *Deflected Permanent Revolution*, www.marxists.org/archive/cliff/works/1963/xx/permrev.htm

Cohen, Julian, 2007, "Escape from Belzec: saved by a pair of heels", *Holocaust Research Project*, www.holocaustresearchproject.org/ar/belzec/belzecescape.html

Cohen, Mitchell, 2017, "Does the Left have a Zionist problem?", in Jacobs, Jack (ed), 2017, *Jews and Leftist Politics*, Cambridge University Press. Kindle Edition.

Cohen, Rachel, 2014, "The erasure of the American-Jewish Left", *TheLi.st*, 18 November, medium.com/thelist/the-erasure-of-the-american-jewish-left-1dd41335a46b

Cole, Peter and van der Walt, Lucien, 2011, "Crossing the color lines, crossing the continents: comparing the racial politics of the IWW in South Africa and the United States 1905–1925", in *Safundi: The Journal of South African and American Studies*, vol 12, no 1.

Connelly, John, 2002, "Poles and Jews in the Second World War: the revisions of Jan T Gross", Contemporary European History, vol 11, no 4, pp641-658.

Corbyn, Jeremy, 2020, "Exclusive interview with Jeremy Corbyn on Palestine", in *Palestine Deep Dive*, YouTube, 17 May.

Cornell University, 2018a, Remembering the 1911 Triangle Factory Fire, trianglefire.ilr.cornell.edu/story/introduction.html

Cornell University, 2018b, "Let's Sing!" Educational Department, International Ladies' Garment Workers' Union, trianglefire.ilr.cornell.edu/primary/songsPlays/UprisingTwentyThousand.html

Corrsin, Stephen, 1998, "Literacy rates and questions of language, faith and ethnic identity in population censuses in the partitioned Polish lands and interwar Poland (1880s-1930s)", *The Polish Review*, vol 43, no 2.

Crabapple, Molly, 2018, "My great-grandfather the Bundist", *The New York Review of Books*, 6 October, www.nybooks.com/daily/2018/10/06/my-great-grandfather-the-bundist/

Crim, Brian, 2011, "'Our most serious enemy': the specter of Judeo-Bolshevism in the German military community 1914–1923", *Central European History*, vol 44, no 4.

Crouch, Dave, 2006, "Left history: rising from the East", *Socialist Review*, 307, socialistworker.co.uk/socialist-review-archive/left-history-rising-east/

Cunningham, John, 2023, "Roaring Twenties", *Britannia*, www.britannica.com/topic/Roaring-Twenties

Curley, Edwin (ed), 1994, *A Spinoza Reader*, Princeton University Press.

Dando, William, 1966, "A map of the election to the Russian Constituent Assembly of 1917", *Slavic Review*, vol 25, no 2, www.jstor.org/stable/2492782?seq=2

Datner, Szymon, 1945, "The fight and the destruction of Ghetto Białystok", *Landsmanschaft of Białystok and the Surround*, www.zchor.org/bialystok/testimony.htm

Davies, Norman, 2003, *Rising '44: the Battle for Warsaw*, Viking.

Davis, R W, 1996, "Disraeli, the Rothschilds and Anti-Semitism", *Jewish History*, vol 10, no 2, www.jstor.org/stable/20101265#

de Dijn, Annelien, 2012, "The politics of Enlightenment: from Peter Gay to Jonathan Israel", *The Historical Journal*, vol 55, no 3, www.jstor.org/stable/23263274?seq=7

Demoscope Weekly, 2023 "The First General Census of the Russian Empire of 1897", www.demoscope.ru/weekly/ssp/rus_lan_97_uezd_eng.php?reg=91

Deutscher, Isaac, 1968, *The Non-Jewish Jew and other Essays*, Merlin Press, London.

Diamond, Anna, 2020, "The 1924 law that slammed the door on immigrants and the politicians who pushed it back open", *Smithsonian Magazine*, www.smithsonianmag.com/history/1924-law-slammed-door-immigrants-and-politicians-who-pushed-it-back-open-180974910/

Dobroszycki, Lucjan, 1993, "Polish historiography on the annihilation of the Jews of Poland in World War II: a critical evaluation", *East European Jewish Affairs*, vol 23, no 2 cited in Tec, Nechama, 2001.

Doherty, Rosa, 2018, "Cable Street veteran dies at 103", *Jewish Chronicle*, 5 November, www.thejc.com/news/uk/max-levitas-who-fought-mosley-dies-103-1.471997

Dowty, Alan, Ha'am, 'Ahad and Ginzberg, Asher, 2000, "Much ado about little: Ahad Ha'am's 'Truth from Eretz Yisrael' Zionism and the Arabs", in *Israel Studies*, vol 5.

Dresser, Madge nd(1), "Blood libels, castration and Christian fears: opposition to Jewish citizenship", *Our Migration Story*, www.ourmigrationstory.org.uk/oms/blood-libels-and-castration-political-opposition-to-jewish-citizenship-

Dresser, Madge nd(2), "Jewish immigration and the Aliens Act", *Our Migration Story*, www.ourmigrationstory.org.uk/oms/jewish-immigration-and-the-aliens-act-1905

Drory, Zeev, 2014, "Societal values: impact on Israel security: the kibbutz movement as a mobilized elite", *Israel Studies*, vol 19, no 1, Indiana University Press Stable, www.jstor.org/stable/10.2979/israelstudies.19.1.166

Dubnow, Simon, 2012, *Jewish History: an Essay in the Philosophy of History*, HardPress Publishing. Kindle Edition.

Dubnow, Simon, 2020, *History of the Jews in Russia and Poland*, (vols 1-3), Musaicum Books. Kindle Edition.

Dwork, Deborah and van Pelt, Robert, 2002, *Holocaust: a History*, John Murray.

East End Women's Museum, 2016, "Women at the Battle of Cable Street", 4 October, eastendwomensmuseum.org/blog/tag/fascism

References

Eckhardt, Alice, 1989, "The Reformation and the Jews", *Shofar*, vol 7, no 4, www.jstor.org/stable/42941341?seq=4#metadata_info_tab_contents

Edelman, Marek, 1990, *The Ghetto Fights: Warsaw 1941–43*, Bookmarks, London.

Elkind, Menachem, 2007, "Die linkszionistische Organisation Gdud Avoda und die Komintern", *Jahrbuch für Historische Kommunismusforschung*, www.kommunismusgeschichte.de/jhk/jhk-2007/article/detail/menachem-elkind-die-linkszionistische-organisation-gdud-avoda-und-die-komintern-drei-dokumente-aus-den-jahren-192627

Ellenson, David, 1999, "Zionism in the United States", jwa.org/encyclopedia/article/zionism-in-united-states

Encyclopedia.com, nd, "Łódź Uprising", www.encyclopedia.com/history/encyclopedias-almanacs-transcripts-and-maps/lodz-uprising

Engel, Barbara, 2017, "Gesia Gelfman: a Jewish woman on the Left in imperial Russia", in Jacobs, Jack (ed), 2017, *Jews and Leftist Politics*, Cambridge University Press. Kindle Edition.

Engel, David, 2018, "World War I and its impact on the problem of security in Jewish history", in Rozenblit, Marsha and Karp, Jonathan, *World War I and the Jews*, Berghahn Books. Kindle Edition.

Engels, Friedrich, 1877, *Anti-Dühring*, www.marxists.org/archive/marx/works/1877/anti-duhring/ch09.htm

Englert, Sai, 2012, "The rise and fall of the Jewish Labour Bund", *International Socialism Journal*, 135, Marxist Internet Archive, www.marxists.org/history/etol/newspape/isj2/2012/isj2-135/englert.htm

Ephemeral New York, 2014, "A teenager leads the great rent strike of 1907", ephemeralnewyork.wordpress.com/2014/06/21/a-teenager-leads-the-great-rent-strike-of-1907/

Epstein, Barbara, 2008, *The Minsk Ghetto 1941–1943: Jewish Resistance and Soviet Internationalism*, University of California Press.

Facing History, 2020, "The Vilna Partisan manifesto", www.facinghistory.org/resource-library/vilna-ghetto-manifesto

Faigan, Suzanne, 2018, *An Annotated Bibliography of Maria Yakovlevna Frumkina*, openresearch-repository.anu.edu.au/bitstream/1885/155631/1/SuzanneFaigan_Thesis%202019.pdf

Farber, Samuel, 2017a, "Deutscher and the Jews: on the non-Jewish Jew: an analysis and personal reflection", in Jacobs, Jack (ed), 2017, *Jews and Leftist Politics*, Cambridge University Press. Kindle Edition.

Farber, Samuel, 2017b, "Lessons from the Bund", *Jacobin*, 3 January, jacobinmag.com/2017/01/jewish-bund-poland-workers-zionism-holocaust-stalin-israel

Feldberg, Michael, nd, "Jews in America: the kosher meat boycott (1902)", *Jewish Virtual Library*, www.jewishvirtuallibrary.org/the-kosher-meat-boycott-of-1902

Feldman, David and McGeever, Brendan, 2018, "Labour's antisemitism: what went wrong and what is to be done?", *The Independent*, 18 April.

Fine, Robert and Spencer, Philip, 2017, *Antisemitism and the Left: the Return of the Jewish Question*, Manchester University Press.

Fischer, Klaus, 1998, *The History of an Obsession*, p167, Constable, London.

Fischer, Lars, 2007, *The Socialist Response to Antisemitism in Imperial Germany*, Cambridge University Press, Cambridge.

Fischer, Lars, 2017, "Marxism's other Jewish questions", in Jacobs, Jack (ed), 2017, *Jews and Leftist Politics*, Cambridge University Press. Kindle Edition.

Fishman, William, 2004, *East End Jewish Radicals 1875–1914*, Five Leaves, Nottingham.

Flechtheim, Ossip, 1969, *Die KPD in der Weimarer Republik*, Europaische Verlagenanstalt, Frankfurt am Main.

Foner, Philip and Roediger, David R, 1997, *Our Own Time: a History of American Labor and the Working Day*, new ed, Verso, New York.

Foner, Philip, 1945, *Jews in American History 1654 to 1865*, International Publishers, New York.

Foner, Philip, 1973, *The Policies and Practices of the American Federation of Labor 1900–1909*, International Publishers, New York.

Foner, Philip, 1979, *Women and the American Labor Movement: from the First Trade Unions to the Present*, The Free Press, New York.

Forward, nd, forward.com/about-us/history/

Foster, William Z, 1945, "On the question of revisionism", 20 June, www.marxists.org/history/erol/1946-1956/foster.pdf

Frankel, Jonathan, 2009, *Crisis, Revolution and the Russian Jews*, Cambridge University Press, New York.

Freedland, Jonathan, 2005, "The end of the affair", *The Guardian*, 14 February, www.theguardian.com/world/2005/feb/14/religion.politicsphilosophyandsociety.

Full Fact, 2018, "Are the majority of British Jews Zionists?", 26 September, fullfact.org/news/are-majority-british-jews-zionists/

Furmanovsky, Michael, 2001, "Communism as Jewish radical subculture: the Los Angeles experience", *Organization of American Historians Annual Meeting*, Los Angeles, April 2001, www.world.ryukoku.ac.jp/~michael/docs/oah_paper.html

Geier, Joel, 2023, personal communications.

Gendzier, Stephen, 1973, "Diderot and the Jews", in *Diderot Studies*, vol 16.

Gilbert, Martin, 2004, *The Righteous: the Unsung Heroes of the Holocaust*, Holt Paperbacks.

Gilbert, Shirli, 2005, *Music in the Holocaust: Confronting Life in the Nazi Ghettos and Camps*, Oxford, Clarendon.

Gitelman, Zvi, 1988, *A Century of Ambivalence: The Jews of Russia and the Soviet Union, 1881 to the Present*, Indiana University Press, Bloomington, Indianapolis.

Gluckstein, Donny (ed), 2015, *Fighting on all Fronts*, Bookmarks, London.

Gluckstein, Donny, 1985, *The Western Soviets*, Bookmarks, London.

Gluckstein, Donny, 1994, *The Tragedy of Bukharin*, Pluto Press, London.

Gluckstein, Donny, 1999, *The Nazis, Capitalism and the Working Class*, Bookmarks, London.

Gluckstein, Donny, 2012, *A People's History of the Second World War*, Pluto Press, London.

Glynn, Sarah, 2005, "East End immigrants and the battle for housing: a comparative study of political mobilisation in the Jewish and Bengali communities", *Journal of Historical Geography*, 31, pp528-545.

Goebel, Malte, 1999, *Antisemitism during the Second Reich (1871–1918) and Antisemitism in Nazi Germany*, Grin Verlag.

Goitein, Schlomo, 1974, *Jews and Arabs: a Concise History of their Social and Cultural Relations*, Dover Publications. Kindle Edition.

Goldhagen, Daniel, 1997, *Hitler's Willing Executioners*, Abacus Books, London.

Goldman, Albert and Sprinchorn, Evert, 1964, *Wagner on Music and Drama*, Dutton, New York.

Goldmann, Nahum, 1970, *Memories: the Autobiography of Nahum Goldmann*, Weidenfeld and Nicholson.

Goldstein, Bernard, 2016, *Twenty Years with the Jewish Labor Bund: a Memoir of Interwar Poland*, Purdue University Press, West Lafayette.

Gordon, Oliver, 2018, "Israel in the Kimberley: how the top end nearly became a global Jewish hub", *ABC Kimberley*, 20 March, www.abc.net.au/news/2018-03-20/how-the-kimberley-almost-became-australias-israel/9566214

Grabowski, Jan, 2022, "The new wave of Holocaust revisionism", *South Central Review*, vol 39, pp60-65.

References

Grebing, Helga, 1985, *History of the German Labour Movement*, Berg Publisher, Leamington Spa.

Green, David, 2015, "This day in Jewish history first boy to be raised speaking Hebrew dies", *Haaretz*, 8 April 2015, www.haaretz.com/jewish/2015-04-08/ty-article/.premium/this-day-ben-yehudas-son-dies/0000017f-e0c7-d7b2-a77f-e3c72e050000

Greene, Doug, 2017, "The oath: the story of the Jewish Bund", *Left Voice*, 3 July, www.leftvoice.org/the-oath-the-story-of-the-jewish-bund/

Grinberg, Daniel, nd, "Jewish radicalism in Poland", *Kate Sharpely Library*, www.katesharpleylibrary.net/ghx4f3

Gross, Jan, 2001, *Neighbors: the Destruction of the Jewish Community in Jedwabne*, Poland, Princeton University Press.

Gross, Nachum (ed), 1976, *Economic History of the Jews*, Schocken Books, New York.

Haberman, Clyde, 2022, "Today in History: The Father Coughlin Story", *PBS*, 9 March, www.pbs.org/wnet/exploring-hate/2022/03/09/today-in-history-the-father-coughlin-story/

Haenisch, Horst, 2017, *Faschismus und der Holocaust*, M21, Berlin.

Haenisch, Horst, 2023, *Kann der Marxismus den Holocaust erklären?*, Aurora, Berlin.

Halamish, Aviva, 2014, "Palestine as a destination for Jewish immigrants and refugees from Nazi Germany", in Caestecker, Frank and Moore, Bob (eds), *Refugees from Nazi Germany and the Liberal European States*, Berghahn Books. Kindle Edition.

Halkin, Hillel, 2014, *Jabotinsky: a Life*, Yale University Press, Newhaven.

Halpern Amaru, Betsy, 1984, "Martin Luther and Jewish mirrors", in *Jewish Social Studies*, vol 46, no 2.

Harman, Chris, 1987, "Student power?", in *Socialist Worker Review*, no 94, January 1987, www.marxists.org/archive/harman/1987/01/students.htm

Harrington, John, 1935, "High meat prices stir wide protest", *NY Times*, 2 June, www.nytimes.com/1935/06/02/archives/high-meat-prices-stir-wide-protest-markets-chief.html

Hass, Amira, 2013, "The inner syntax of Palestinian stone-throwing", *Haaretz*, 3 April, www.haaretz.com/opinion/the-inner-syntax-of-palestinian-stone-throwing.premium-1.513131

Hassan, Shamir, 2001, "Zionism and terror: the creation of the State of Israel", *Proceedings of the Indian History Congress*, vol 62, www.jstor.org/stable/44155829?seq=1#metadata_info_tab_contents

Heller, Celia, 1980, *On the Edge of Destruction: Jews of Poland Between the Two World Wars*, Wayne State University Press.

Heller, Daniel, 2017, *Jabotinsky's Children*, Princeton University Press, assets.press.princeton.edu/chapters/i11134.pdf

Henry, Patrick, 2014, *Jewish Resistance Against the Nazis*, Catholic University of America Press.

Herberg, Will, nd, *The Jewish Labor Movement in the United States*, Berman Jewish Policy Archive, www.bjpa.org/content/upload/bjpa/1952/1952labormovt.pdf

Hernon, Ian, 2020, *Anti-Semitism and the Left*, Amberley Publishing, Stroud, Gloucestershire.

Hersh, Liebman, 1931, "International migration of the Jews", in Willcox, Walter (ed), 1931, *International Migrations*, vol 2: Interpretations, www.nber.org/books/will31-1, www.nber.org/chapters/c5117

Hertz, Deborah, 2017, "Manya Shochat and her traveling guns: Jewish radical women from pogrom self-defense to the first kibbutzim", in *Jews and Leftist Politics*, Cambridge University Press. Kindle Edition.

Herzig, Arno, 2010, *1815–1933: Emanzipation und Akkulturation*, www.bpb.de/shop/zeitschriften/izpb/7674/1815-1933-emanzipation-und-akkulturation/

Herzl, Theodor, 1920, *Der Judenstaat*, Jüdischer Verlag, Berlin, ldn-knigi.lib.ru/JUDAICA/Herzl-Judenstaat.pdf

Herzl, Theodor, 1986, *The Jewish State*, Kindle Edition.

Hickey, Michael, 1998, "Revolution on the Jewish Street: Smolensk 1917", in *Journal of Social History*, vol 31, no 4, www.jstor.org/stable/3789303?seq=4

Hirson, Baruch, 2005, *A History of the Left in South Africa*, Bloomsbury Academic, London.

Hitchen, Alice, 2010, in "Eyewitnesses to the Battle of Cable Street: 'Fascists did not pass'", *Socialist Worker*, 16 March, socialistworker.co.uk/art/20230/Eyewitnesses+to+the+Battle+of+Cable+Street%3A+Fascists+did+not+pass

Hochschild, Adam, 2019, "When America tried to deport its radicals", *The New Yorker*, 4 November, www.newyorker.com/magazine/2019/11/11/when-america-tried-to-deport-its-radicals

Hodgson, Keith, 2010, *Fighting Fascism: the British Left and the Rise of Fascism 1919–39*, Manchester University Press, Manchester.

Holocaust Education & Archive Research Team, nd, "Biala Podlaska", www.holocaustresearchproject.org/ghettos/bialapodlaska.html

Holocaust Research Project, nd, "Efraim Barasz: Chairman of the Bialystok Judenrat", www.holocaustresearchproject.org/ghettos/barasz.html

Holst, Ludolf, 1818, *Über das Verhältnis der Juden zu den Christen in den Handelsstädten*, Leipzig jewish-history-online.net/source/jgo:source-154, section 2-14-216

Horowitz, Brian, 2017, "Vladimir Jabotinsky: a Zionist activist on the rise 1905–1906", *Studia Judaica*, 20, no 1 (39), pp105-124.

Howe, Irving, 1976, *World of our Fathers*, Simon and Schuster, New York.

Hoyer, Katja, 2021, *Blood and Iron: the Rise and Fall of the German Empire 1871–1918*, The History Press, Cheltenham.

Hungary Today, 2020, "Orbán: Europe 'Must not succumb to Soros network'", 25 November, hungarytoday.hu/orban-soros-letter-post-eu/

Hyman, Paula E, 1980, "Immigrant Women and Consumer Protest: the New York City Kosher Meat Boycott of 1902", *American Jewish History*, vol 70, no 1, pp91-105, JSTOR 23881992.

Israel, Jonathan, 2021, *Revolutionary Jews from Spinoza to Marx*, University of Washington Press. Kindle Edition.

Jabotinsky, Vladimir, 1923, *The Iron Wall*, Razsviet, 4 November, en.jabotinsky.org/media/9747/the-iron-wall.pdf

Jackson, Michael, 1994, "Fallen sparrows: the International Brigades in the Spanish Civil War", in *Memoirs of the American Philosophical Society*, vol 212, archive.org/stream/bub_gb_GYjVTqWwLTkC/bub_gb_GYjVTqWwLTkC_djvu.txt

Jacobs, Jack (ed), 2001, *Jewish Politics in Eastern Europe: the Bund at 100*, Palgrave, Basingstoke.

Jacobs, Jack, 2011, "Bundist Anti-Zionism in interwar Poland", in Grabski, August, (ed), *Rebels Against Zion: Studies on the Jewish left anti-Zionism*, Jewish Historical Institute, Warsaw, pp67-88.

Jacobs, Jack, 2013, "Jewish Labor in interwar Poland", *AJS Perspectives*, perspectives.asjnet.org/the-labor-issue-fall-2013/jewish-labor-in-interwar-poland

Jacobs, Jack, 2017 (ed), *Jews and Leftist Politics Judaism, Israel, Antisemitism, and Gender*, Cambridge University Press. Kindle Edition.

Jacobs, Joe, 1978, *Out of the Ghetto*, self-published by Janet Simon, London.

Jacobs, Paul, 2012, "It wasn't difficult for me to reject Judaism", in Michels, Tony, 2012.

Jaher, Frederick, 2009, *The Jews and the Nation*, Princeton University Press.

James, C L R, 1938, *The Black Jacobins*, Penguin History Series, Penguin Books, Kindle Edition.

References

Jensen, Uffa, 2016, *Wirtschaft und Berufsstruktur*, juedische-geschichte-online.net/thema/wirtschaft-und-berufsstruktur

Jewish Chronicle, 2014, "The outbreak of the First World War—as told in the pages of the JC", 1 August, www.thejc.com/news/uk/the-outbreak-of-the-first-world-war-as-told-in-the-pages-of-the-jc-1.56010

Jewish Heritage Online Magazine, nd "Never say there's only death", poem by Hirsch Glik www.jhom.com/bookshelf/kovner_scrolls/glick_poem.htm

Jewish Heritage Online Magazine, 2001, "Di Shvue", www.jhom.com/personalities/personalities/ansky/the_oath.htm

Jewish Partisan Education Foundation, 2017b, "Abba Kovner", www.jewishpartisans.org/partisans/abba-kovner

Jewish Partisan Educational Foundation, 2016, "Bernard Druskin", www.jewishpartisans.org/t_switch.php?pageName=mini+bio+short+bio+1&parnum=34

Jewish Partisan Educational Foundation, 2017a, "Vitka Kempner", www.jewishpartisans.org/t_switch.php?pageName=mini+bio+short+bio+1&fromSomeone=&parnum=40

Jewish Partisan Educational Foundation, 2017c, "Gertrude Boyarski", www.jewishpartisans.org/t_switch.php?pageName=mini+bio+short+bio+1&fromSomeone=&parnum=8

Jewish Resistance: a Working Bibliography, 1999, Miles Lerman Center for the Study of Jewish Resistance, Center for Advanced Holocaust Studies, *United States Holocaust Memorial Museum*.

Jewish Telegraphic Agency, 1933, "Polish Zionists urged to support Pilsudski regime", 24 October, www.jta.org/archive/polish-zionists-urged-to-support-pilsudski-regime

Jewish Virtual Library, 2023, "The declaration of the establishment of the State of Israel", www.jewishvirtuallibrary.org/the-declaration-of-the-establishment-of-the-state-of-israel

Jewish Virtual Library, nd(1), "Modern Jewish history: the Pale of Settlement", www.jewishvirtuallibrary.org/the-pale-of-settlement

Jewish Virtual Library, nd(2), "Zionism: Po'alei Zion", www.jewishvirtuallibrary.org/po-alei-zion

Jewish Virtual Library, nd(3), "Zionism: American Zionism", www.jewishvirtuallibrary.org/american-zionism

Jewish Virtual Library, nd(4), "Witold Pilecki", www.jewishvirtuallibrary.org/jsource/biography/Witold_Pilecki.html

Jewish Virtual Library, nd(5) "The revolt at Auschwitz-Birkenau", www.jewishvirtuallibrary.org/the-revolt-at-auschwitz-birkenau

Jewish Virtual Library, nd(6), "Tel Aviv: from Spring Hill to independence", www.jewishvirtuallibrary.org/tel-aviv-from-spring-hill-to-independence

Jewish Weekly News, 1933, "Jewish debate in Polish parliament", (Melbourne), 29 December.

Johns, Sheridan, 1975, "The birth of the Communist Party of South Africa", *The International Journal of African Historical Studies*, vol 9, no 3.

Jones, Nigel, 2011, "Story of a secret state by Jan Karski: Review", *The Telegraph*, 4 May.

Joselit, Jenna, nd, "The landlord as czar: pre-World War I tenant activity", *TenantNet*, www.tenant.net/Community/history/histo1.html

Judd, Denis and Surridge, Keith, 2013, *The Boer War: a History*, I B Tauris.

Kaczerginski, Shmerke, nd, "Partizaner-marsh", *Rise up and Fight! Songs of Jewish Partisans*, collections.ushmm.org/search/catalog/bib66524

Kaplan, Chaim, 1973, *Scroll of Agony: the Warsaw Diary of Chaim A Kaplan*, Collier Books, cited in Dwork, Deborah and van Pelt, Robert, 2002.

Kaplan, Peisach, 1982, "Recalling our proud past", in Shmulewitz, I, 1982, p21, www.jewishgen.org/yizkor/Bialystok1/bia020.html

Kapp, Yvonne, 1976, *Eleanor Marx*, Pantheon Books, New York.

Kassow, Samuel, 2010, "Po'ale Tsiyon", *YIVO Encyclopedia of Jews in Eastern Europe*, yivoencyclopedia.org/article.aspx?poale_tsiyon

Katz, Daniel, 2011, *All Together Different: Yiddish Socialists, Garment Workers, and the Labor Roots of Multiculturalism*, New York University Press, New York.

Katz, Jacob, 1986, *The Darker Side of Genius: Richard Wagner's Anti-Semitism*, Brandeis University Press, Hanover and London.

Katznelson, Berl, 1918, *Facing the Days Ahead*, www.jewishvirtuallibrary.org/facing-the-days-ahead-by-berl-katznelson

Kaufmann, Thomas, 2019, "Luther and the Jews", in *Antisemitism Studies*, vol 3, no 1.

Kershaw, Ian, 1998, *Hitler, 1889–1936: Hubris*, Allen Lane, London.

Klatzkin, Jacob, 1925, *Tehumim*, Spheres, cited in Agus, Jacob, 1963.

Klehr, Harvey, 1984, *The Heyday of American Communism: the Depression Years*, Basic Books, New York.

Klein, Bernard, 1960, *Jewish Social Studies*, vol 22, no 1, pp27-42.

Koestler, Arthur, 1949, *Promise and Fulfilment: Palestine*, Macmillan, London.

Köhler, Ludwig, 1845, *Thomas Münzer und seine Genossen, Erster Band: Die neue Zeit*, Verlag von Joh Ambr Barth, Leipzig. Kindle Edition.

Korey, William, 1972, "The origins and development of Soviet anti-semitism: an analysis", *Slavic Review*, vol 31, no 1, www.jstor.org/stable/2494148?seq=3#metadata_info_tab_contents

Kornberg, Jacques, 1993, *Theodore Herzl: from Assimilation to Zionism*, Indiana University Press.

Krakowski, Shmuel, 1984, *War of the Doomed: Jewish Armed Resistance in Poland 1942–1944*, Holmes & Meier Publishers.

Krausz, Ernest (ed), 1983, *The Sociology of the Kibbutz*, Transaction Books, New Brunswick.

Krushchev, Nikita, 1956, *Secret Speech*, novaonline.nvcc.edu/eli/evans/HIS242/Documents/Speech.pdf

Kuhn, Rick, 2001, "The Jewish Social Democratic Party of Galicia and the Bund, in: Jack Jacobs (ed), *Jewish Politics in Eastern Europe: The Bund at 100* (Palgrave Macmillan), pp133-154.

Kuhn, Rick, 2002, "The tradition of Jewish anti-Zionism in the Galician socialist movement", *Jubilee conference of the Australasian Political Studies Association*, Canberra, www.researchgate.net/publication/251332888_The_tradition_of_Jewish_anti-Zionism_in_the_Galician_socialist_movement

Kuhn, Rick, 2011, "Jewish anti-Zionism in the Galician socialist movement", in Grabski, August (ed), 2011, *Rebels Against Zion: Studies on the Jewish left anti-Zionism*, Jewish Historical Institute, Warsaw, pp47-65.

Lambroza, Shlomo, 1981, "Jewish self-defence during the Russia pogroms of 1903–1906", *The Jewish Journal of Sociology*, 23, pp123-134.

Lanzmann, Claude, 2011, "Claude Lanzmann interview with Jan Karski", 4 May, US Holocaust Memorial Museum; Stephen Spielberg Film and Video Archive, www.ushmm.org/online/film/display/detail.php?file_num=4739

Laqueur, Walter, 1972, *A History of Zionism*, Holt, Rinehart and Winston, New York.

Laqueur, Walter, 1982, *The Terrible Secret: Suppression of the Truth about Hitler's "Final Solution"*, Penguin.

Laski, Neville, 1934, quoted in "The Deputies", *Jewish Chronicle*, 4 October, p18, archive. thejc.com/archive/1.344162?type=edition&editionDate=1935-10-04&wholeEdition=true

Lenin, Vladimir, 1901, "A talk with defenders of economism", *Iskra*, no 12, 6 December, in *Lenin Collected Works*, Foreign Languages Publishing House, 1961, Moscow, vol 5, pp313-320, www.marxists.org/archive/lenin/works/1901/dec/06.htm

Lenin, Vladimir, 1902, *What is to be Done?* www.marxists.org/archive/lenin/works/download/what-itd.pdf

Lenin, Vladimir, 1903, "Second Congress of the RSDLP: draft resolution on the place of the Bund in the Party", www.marxists.org/archive/lenin/works/1903/2ndcong/2.htm

References

Lenin, Vladimir, 1915, *The Collapse of the Second International*, www.marxists.org/archive/lenin/works/1915/csi/i.htm#v21pp74h-208

Leon, Abram, 1970, *The Jewish Question: a Marxist Interpretation*, Pathfinder Press, New York, www.marxists.org/subject/jewish/leon/ch1.htm

Leon, Dan, 1969, *The Kibbutz: a New Way of Life*, Pergamon, London.

Lepiarz, Jacek, 2023, "Polish radical right-wing MP disrupts lecture on Holocaust in Warsaw", *Deutsche Welle*, 6 January, www.dw.com/en/polish-radical-right-wing-mp-disrupts-lecture-on-holocaust/a-65795483

Lessing, Gotthold, 1894, *Nathan the Wise*, James Maclehose, Glasgow.

Lestchinsky, Jacob, 1936, "Night over Poland", *Jewish Frontier*, July, pp10-12.

Lestchinsky, Jacob, 1944, "Jewish Migration for the Past Hundred Years", *Yiddish Scientific Institute—YIVO*, New York, fau.digital.flvc.org

Leuschen-Seppel, Rosemarie, 1978, *Sozialdemokratie und Antisemitismus im Kaiserreich*, Neue Gesellschaft, Bonn.

Levine, Aaron, 2014, "Russian Jews and the 1917 Revolution", *Primary Source*, vol 4, issue 2, p13, psource.sitehost.iu.edu/PDF/Archive%20Articles/Spring2014/2014%20-%20Spring%20-%203%20-%20Levine%20Aaron.pdf

Levine, Louis, 1976, "Sweatshops", in Baxandall, Rosalyn, Gordon, Linda and Reverby, Susan (eds) 1976, *America's Working Women*, pp100-103, Vintage Books, New York.

Levine, Mark, 2007, "Globalization, architecture, and town planning in a colonial city: the case of Jaffa and Tel Aviv", in *Journal of World History*, vol 18, no 2.

Levy, Richard, 1991, *Antisemitism in the Modern World: an Anthology of Texts*, D C Heath, Lexington.

Levy-Hass, Hanna and Hass, Amira, 2009, *Diary of Bergen-Belsen: 1944–1945*, Haymarket Books., Chicago.

Library of Congress, nd(1), "Felix Mendelssohn and Jewish Identity", www.loc.gov/item/ihas.200156430/

Library of Congress, nd(2), "From haven to home: 350 years of Jewish life in America", www.loc.gov/exhibits/haventohome/haven-century.html

Lichtenstein, Izak, 1947, Excerpt from testimony, Relacje, ZIH, File 301/2441, 5 June, *Holocaust Encyclopedia*, encyclopedia.ushmm.org/content/en/article/izak-lichtenstein-testimony-excerpt

Liebman, Arthur, 1979, *Jews and the Left*, John Wiley, New York.

Lockman, Zachary, 1996, *Comrades and Enemies: Arab and Jewish Workers in Palestine 1906–1948*, University of California Press, Berkeley.

London, Louise, 2000, *Whitehall and the Jews, 1933–48: British Immigration Policy and the Holocaust*, Cambridge University Press, Cambridge.

Lukas, Richard, 1989, *Out of the Inferno: Poles Remember the Holocaust*, University Press of Kentucky.

Luther, Martin, 1543, *The Jews and Their Lies*, www.jewishvirtuallibrary.org/martin-luther-quot-the-jews-and-their-lies-quot

Luxemburg, Rosa, 1915, *The Junius Pamphlet*, www.marxists.org/archive/luxemburg/1915/junius/

Luxemburg, Rosa, 1918, *The Russian Revolution*, www.marxists.org/archive/luxemburg/1918/russian-revolution/ch01.htm

Luxemburg, Rosa, 1976, *The National Question: Selected Writings*, Monthly Review Press, New York.

Mahler, Raphael, 1971, *A History of Modern Jewry 1780–1815*, Schocken Books, New York.

Mangold-Will, Sabine, nd, *Die Reichsgründung zwischen Juden-Emanzipation und Antisemitismus*, www.demokratie-geschichte.de/index.php/3225/die-reichsgruendung-zwischen-juden-emanzipation-und-antisemitismus/

Mansour, George, 2012, "The Arab worker", in *Settler Colonial Studies*, vol 2, no 1, *Past is Present: Settler Colonialism in Palestine.*

Margalit, Elkana, 1969, "Social and intellectual origins of the Hashomer Hatzair Youth Movement, 1913–20", *Journal of Contemporary History*, April 1969, vol 4, no 2, www.jstor.org/stable/259660

Margolis, Peter, 1997, "Margolis on Urofsky, 'American Zionism from Herzl to the Holocaust'", *H-Judaic*, August 1997, networks.h-net.org/node/28655/reviews/30588/margolis-urofsky-american-zionism-herzl-holocaust

Marks, Jonathan, 2010, "Rousseau's use of the Jewish example", in *The Review of Politics*, vol 72, no 3, www.jstor.org/stable/20780332?seq=2

Marot, Helen, 1976, "The shirtwaist strike", in Baxandall, Rosalyn, Gordon, Linda and Reverby, Susan (eds), *America's Working Women*, pp187-194, Vintage Books, New York.

Marr, Wilhelm, 1879, *Der Sieg des Judenthums über das Germanenthum: Vom nicht confessionellen Standpunkt aus betrachtet*, www.gehove.de/antisem/texte/marr_sieg.pdf

Marx, Karl and Engels, Friedrich, 1846, "Idealism and materialism", in *The German Ideology*, www.marxists.org/archive/marx/works/download/Marx_The_German_Ideology.pdf

Marx, Karl and Engels, Friedrich, 1848, *The Communist Manifesto*, www.marxists.org/archive/marx/works/1848/communist-manifesto/ch01.htm

Marx, Karl, 1835, "Reflections of a young man on the choice of a profession", in *Writings from Karl Marx before Rhenische Zeitung*, www.marxists.org/archive/marx/works/download/Marx_Young_Marx.pdf

Marx, Karl, 1843a, *A Contribution to the Critique of Hegel's Philosophy of Right.*

Marx, Karl, 1843b, "Letter from Marx to Arnold Ruge, written September 1843", www.marxists.org/archive/marx/works/1843/letters/43_09-alt.htm

Marx, Karl, 1844, *On the Jewish Question*, www.marxists.org/archive/marx/works/1844/jewish-question/

Marx, Karl, 1870, "Marx to Sigfrid Meyer and August Vogt, 9 April 1870", in Marx, Karl and Friedrich Engels, Friedrich, 1975, *Selected Correspondence*, Progress Publishers, Moscow, www.marxists.org/archive/marx/works/1870/letters/70_04_09.htm

Marx, Karl, and Engels, Friedrich, 1844, *The Holy Family*, www.marxists.org/archive/marx/works/download/pdf/holy-family.pdf

McBrearty, Michael, 2020, "Fighting evictions: the 1930s and now", *Monthly Review Online*, 13 September, mronline.org/2020/09/02/fighting-evictions-the-1930s-and-now//

McCarthy, Justin, 1990, *The Population of Palestine*, Columbia University Press, New York, yplus.ps/wp-content/uploads/2021/01/McCarthy-Justin-The-Population-of-Palestine.pdf

McGeever, Brendan, 2019, *Antisemitism and the Russian Revolution*, Cambridge University Press.

McKeown, Adam, 2007, *Global Migration and Regionalization 1840–1940*, paper for conference on Mapping Global Inequalities, Santa Cruz, escholarship.org/content/qt4t49t5zq/qt4t49t5zq.pdf?t=lnqgsp

Medem, Vladimir, 2011, "The worldwide Jewish nation", in *Jews and Diaspora Nationalism*, Brandeis University Press. Kindle Edition.

Meed, Vladka, 1979, *On Both Sides of the Wall*, Holocaust Library, New York.

Mendelsohn, Ezra (ed), 1997, *Essential Papers on Jews and the Left*, New York University Press, New York.

Mendelsohn, Ezra, 1968, "Jewish and Christian workers in the Russian pale of settlement", *Jewish Social Studies*, vol 30, no 4, pp243-251.

Mendelsohn, Ezra, 1970, *Class Struggle in the Pale*, Cambridge University Press, Cambridge.

Mendelsohn, Ezra, 1987, *The Jews of East Central Europe between the World Wars*, Indiana University Press, Bloomington.

Mendelsohn, Ezra, 1993, *On Modern Jewish Politics*, Oxford University Press, Oxford.

Mendelssohn, Moses, 2011, *Jerusalem: Religious Power and Judaism*, www.earlymoderntexts.com/assets/pdfs/mendelssohn1782.pdf

References

Mendes, Philip, 2013, "The Rise and Fall of the Jewish Labor Bund", *Jewish Currents*, Autumn, jewishcurrents.org/rise-fall-jewish-labor-bund

Mendes, Philip, 2014, *The Jewish Left: the Rise and Fall of a Political Alliance*, Palgrave Macmillan, Houndmills.

Mendes-Flohr, Paul and Reiharz, Jehuda, 1995, *The Jew in the Modern World*, Oxford University Press.

Metzer, Jacob, 1998, "The divided economy of mandatory Palestine", in *Cambridge Middle East Studies*, 11, Cambridge University Press, yplus.ps/wp-content/uploads/2021/01/General-Metzer-Jacob-The-Divided-Economy-of-Mandatory-Palestine.pdf

Meyer, Michael, 2010, "The German-Jewish legacy in America", jsp.sitehost.iu.edu/docs/Legacy%20Indiana.pdf

Meyers, Joshua, 2020, "The Bund by the numbers", in *Geveb: A Journal of Yiddish Studies*, 6 May, ingeveb.org/blog/the-bund-by-the-numbers

Michel, Henri, 1972, *The Shadow War: European Resistance 1939–1945*, Harper and Row.

Michels, Tony (ed), 2012, *Jewish Radicals: a Documentary History*, New York University Press, New York.

Michels, Tony, 2012, "Introduction: the Jewish-Socialist nexus", in Michels, Tony (ed), 2012, *Jewish Radicals: a Documentary History*, New York University Press, New York.

Michels, Tony, nd, "Commitment and crisis: Jews and American Communism", University of Wisconsin, Madison, history.osu.edu/sites/history.osu.edu/files/commitment-crisis-jews-american-communism-tony-michels.pdf

Middleton-Kaplan, Richard, 2014, "The myth of Jewish passivity", in Henry, Patrick, 2014, www.academia.edu/43618470/Myth_of_Jewish_Passivity_PDF

Milken Archive of Jewish Music, nd, "Shtil di nakht (Still the Night)", nd, www.milkenarchive.org/works/lyrics/717

Minc, Matitiahu, 2003, "The Bund: Like All the Jews, With All the Jews", *Yad Vashem*, www.yadvashem.org/articles/academic/the-bund-like-all-the-jews-with-all-the-jews.html

Molyneux, John, 2020, *The Dialectics of Art*, Haymarket, Chicago.

Montefiore, Dora, 1902, "Wagner as a revolutionary", in Social Democrat, 7 July 1902, www.marxists.org/archive/montefiore/1902/07/wagner.htm

Morganti, Caroline, 2020, "Are 95% of Jews really Zionists?", *Jewish Currents*, 29 October, jewishcurrents.org/are-95-of-jews-really-zionists

Mullaney, Marie, 1984, "Gender and the Socialist Revolutionary role, 1871–1921: a general theory of the female revolutionary personality", in *Historical Reflections / Réflexions Historiques*, vol 11, no 2, www.jstor.org/stable/41298827?seq=18

Mullen, Richard, 2010, *Lenin and the Iskra Faction of the RSDLP, 1899–1903*, University of Sussex, PhD, sro.sussex.ac.uk/id/eprint/2356/1/Mullin,_Richard.pdf

Müller, Klaus-Jürgen, 1987, *The Army, Politics and Society in Germany, 1933–45*, St Martin's Press, New York.

Muraskin, Bennett, nd, "A short history of Jews in the American labor movement", www.jewishlaborcommittee.org/Jews%20in%20the%20American%20Labor%20Movement%20by%20Bennett%20Muraskin.pdf

Museum of London, 2023, "Establishing a Jewish East End in London, 1880–1914", www.museumoflondon.org.uk/discover/establishing-jewish-east-end-london-1880-1914

Nadel, Benjamin, 1986, "Bundism in England", *Jewish Socialist Group*, no 6/7, Marxist Internet Archive, www.marxists.org/subject/jewish/jsg-bundism-uk.pdf

Naison, Mark, 2005, *Communists in Harlem during the Depression*, University of Illinois Press

Naison, Mark, 2012, "Fighting evictions during the Great Depression", *International Socialist Review*, 81.

Near, Henry, 2011, *Where Community Happens: the Kibbutz and the Philosophy of Communalism*, Peter Lang AG, www.jstor.org/stable/j.ctv2t4foh

Necheles, Ruth, 1971, "The Abbé Grégoire and the Jews", *Jewish Social Studies*, vol 33, no 2/3, www.jstor.org/stable/4466643?seq=7#metadata_info_tab_contents

Nedava, Joseph, 1971, *Trotsky and the Jews*, Jewish Publication Society, Philadelphia.

Neserius, Philip, 1926, "Voltaire's political ideas", in *The American Political Science Review*, vol 20, February, www.jstor.org/stable/1945097?seq=5

Neufeld, Michael, 2000, "Introduction", in *Bombing Auschwitz: Should the Allies Have Attempted it?*, St Martin's Press.

New World Encyclopedia, nd, "International Women's Day", www.newworldencyclopedia. org/entry/International_Women%27s_Day

New York Times, 1902, "Brooklyn mob loots butcher shops", 23 May, www.nytimes. com/1902/05/23/archives/brooklyn-mob-loots-butcher-shops-rioters-led-by-women-wreck-a-dozen.html

New York Times, 1903, "Jewish Massacre Denounced", April 28. www.newspapers.com/ article/the-new-york-times-kishinev-pogrom-1903/78818573/

New York Times, 1910, "Peripatetic Philosophers", 29 May, in Michels, Tony (ed), 2012, pp174-178.

New York Times, 1976, "Butchers appeal to police for protection", 26 May, in R Baxandall, L Gordon, and S Reverby (eds), 1976, pp186-187.

New York Times, 1986, "Abel Meeropol", www.nytimes.com/1986/10/31/obituaries/abel-meeropol-83-a-songwriter-dies.html

Noakes, Jeremy and Pridham, Geoffrey (eds), 1991, *Nazism 1919–1946*, vol 1, *The Rise to Power 1919–1934*, University of Exeter Press, Exeter.

Nortey, Justin, 2012, "US Jews have widely differing views on Israel", *Pew Research Center*, 21 May, www.pewresearch.org/fact-tank/2021/05/21/u-s-jews-have-widely-differing-views-on-israel/

Novershtern, Avraham, nd, "Kaczerginski, Shmerke", *YIVO Encyclopedia of Jews in Europe*, yivoencyclopedia.org/article.aspx/Kaczerginski_Shmerke

Novick, Peter, 2000, *The Holocaust in American Life*, Haughton Mifflin.

Nykänen, Nooa, 2015, *Industrial Clusters in the Russian Empire 1860–1913*, jyx.jyu.fi/ bitstream/handle/123456789/46000/URN:NBN:fi:jyu-201505221958.pdf;sequence=1

O'Shea, Joe, 2016, "Battle of Cable Street: when the Irish helped beat back the fascists", *The Irish Times*, 24 September, www.irishtimes.com/culture/heritage/battle-of-cable-street-when-the-irish-helped-beat-back-the-fascists-1.2801873

Osterman, Nathan, 1941, "The controversy over the proposed readmission of the Jews to England (1655)", in *Jewish Social Studies*, vol 3, no 3.

Palestine Post, 1936, "The anti-Jewish excesses in Poland", 29 January.

Pallavicini, Stephen and Patt, Avinoam "Lachwa", nd, *Holocaust Encyclopedia*, www.ushmm. org/wlc/en/article.php?ModuleId=10007233

Papal Encyclicals Online, 2020, "Third Lateran Council, 1179 AD", www.papalencyclicals. net/councils/ecum11.htm

Pappé, Ilan, 2006, *The Ethnic Cleansing of Palestine*, Oneworld Publications. Kindle Edition.

Pappé, Ilan, 2012, "Shtetl colonialism: first and last impressions of indigeneity by colonised colonisers", in *Settler Colonial Studies*, vol 2, no 1, *Past is Present: Settler Colonialism in Palestine*.

Pappé, Ilan, 2017, *Ten Myths About Israel*, Verso, Kindle Edition.

Past Tense, 2016, "Jewish workers' demo protests pogroms in Russia 1903", pasttenseblog. wordpress.com/2016/06/21/big-london-jewish-anarchist-demo-protesting-pogroms-in-russia-1903/

Pasternak, Velvel, 1998, *The Mordechai Gebirtig Songbook*, Tara Publications, Owings Mills.

Patai, Raphael (ed), 1960, *The Complete Diaries of Theodor Herzl*, vol 1, Herzl Press and Thomas Yoseloff.

References

Paucker, Arnold, 2012, *German Jews in the Resistance 1933–1945: the Facts and the Problems*, Gedenkstaette Deutscher Widerstand.

Paul, Mark (ed), 2010, "Wartime Rescue of Jews by the Polish Catholic Clergy: the Testimony of Survivors", *Polish Educational Foundation in North America*, www.savingjews.org/docs/clergy_rescue.pdf

Paulsson, Gunnar, 1998, "The rescue of Jews by non-Jews in Nazi-occupied Poland", *The Journal of Holocaust Education*, vol 7, nos 1 & 2.

Paulsson, Gunnar, 2002, *Secret City: the Hidden Jews of Warsaw 1940–1945*, Yale University Press.

Peled, Yael Margolin, 1999, "Gusta Dawidson Draenger 1917–1943", *Jewish Women's Archive*, jwa.org/encyclopedia/article/draenger-gusta-dawidson

Peled, Yoav, 2020, "The Jewish minority in inter-war Poland", H-Nationalism, networks.h-net.org/node/3911/discussions/5740776/jewish-minority-inter-war-poland

Penslar, Derek, 2020, *Theodor Herzl: the Charismatic Leader*, Yale UP, New Haven.

Perlmann, Joel, 1993, "Russian-Jewish literacy in 1997: a re-analysis of census data", *Proceedings of the World Congress of Jewish Studies, Division B: The History of the Jewish People*, vol 3: *Modern Times*.

Perry, Marvin and Schweitzer, Frederick, 2002, *Antisemitism: Myth and Hate from Antiquity to the Present*, Palgrave, Houndmills.

Pilecki, Witold, 2012, *The Auschwitz Volunteer: Beyond Bravery*, Aquila Polonica.

Piratin, Phil, 1978, *Our Flag Stays Red*, Lawrence and Wishart, London.

Plunkett, Margaret, 1958, "The Histadrut: the General Federation of Jewish Labor in Israel", *ILR Review*, vol 11, no 2.

Pogorelski, Mordechaj, 1982, "The Jewish Labour Movement", in Shmulewitz, I (ed), 1982 p12, www.jewishgen.org/yizkor/Bialystok1/bia002.html#Page12

Polonsky, Antony (ed), 1988, *A Cup of Tears: a Diary of the Warsaw Ghetto by Abraham Lewin*, Blackwell, cited in Rose, John, 1990,

Polonsky, Antony, 2001, "What made the massacre at Jedwabne possible?", *The Polish Review*, vol 46, no 4, pp403-417.

Polonsky, Antony, 2017, "Jews and Communism in the Soviet Union and Poland", in Jacobs, Jack (ed), 2017, Jews and Leftist Politics, Cambridge University Press. Kindle Edition.

Polonsky, Antony, 2019, *The Jews in Poland and Russia*, vol III 1914 to 2008 (Littman, 2010), p537, cited in Tec, Nechama, 2001.

Portnoy, Samuel, (ed), 1979, *The Life and Soul of a Legendary Jewish Socialist: the Memoirs of Vladimir Medem*, KTAV Publishing House, New York, thecharnelhouse.org/wp-content/uploads/2018/03/Vladimir-Medem-Memoirs-1923.pdf

Postone, Moishe, 2017, "The dualisms of capitalist modernity: reflections on history, the Holocaust, and antisemitism", in Jacobs, Jack (ed), 2017, *Jews and Leftist Politics*, Cambridge University Press. Kindle Edition.

Prager, Dennis and Telushkin, Joseph, 1983, *Why the Jews?*, Touchstone, New York, Kindle Edition.

Pratt, Mike, 2020, "Soviet Russia's Reaction to the Nazi Holocaust and the Implications of the Suppression of Jewish Suffering", *The Saber and Scroll Journal*, vol 8, no 3, Spring 2020.

Presidential Library, nd, "The First All-Russian Congress of Soviets of Workers' and Soldiers' Deputies All-Russian Congress of Soviets (1 Petrograd, city, 1917) – 1931", www.prlib.ru/en/node/436742

Price, Richard and Sullivan, Martin, 1994, "The Battle of Cable Street: myths and realities", *Workers News*, March-April, retrieved from What Next Journal, www.whatnextjournal.org.uk/Pages/History/Cable.html

Pritsak, Omeljan, 1987, "The pogroms of 1881", *Harvard Ukrainian Studies*, vol 11, no 1/2, pp12-13, www.jstor.org/stable/41036239

Proudhon, Pierre, 1847, *On the Jews*, www.marxists.org/reference/subject/economics/proudhon/1847/jews.htm

Rabinovitch, Simon, 2012, "Diaspora, nation, and Messiah: an introductory essay", in Rabinovitch, Simon (ed), *Jews and Diaspora Nationalism*, Brandeis University Press, New Hampshire, Kindle Edition.

Redlich, Shimon, 1969, "The Jewish Antifascist Committee in the Soviet Union", in *Jewish Social Studies*, vol 31, no 1, www.jstor.org/stable/4466454?seq=3

Reinharz, Jehuda, 1980, "Ideology and structure in German Zionism, 1882–1933", in *Jewish Social Studies*, vol 42, no 2, pp119-146, www.jstor.org/stable/4467080

Rennap, Ike, 1942, *Anti-Semitism and the Jewish Question*, Lawrence and Wishart, London.

Report of the Royal Commission on Alien Immigration, vol 1, 1903, www.google. co.uk/books/edition/Report_of_the_Royal_Commission_on_Alien/ N4E3AQAAMAAJ?hl=en&gbpv=1

Resolutions of the 18th Zionist Congress, Prague, 21 August to 3 September, 1933, 1934, www. bjpa.org/content/upload/bjpa/reso/RESOLUTIONS%20OF%20THE%2018TH%20 ZIONIST%20CONGRESS%20PRAGUE%20AUGUST%2021ST%20TO%20 SEPT%203RD,%201933.pdf

Revolution's Newsstand, nd, "One day of Communist Party activities in New York City, Thursday February 16, 1928", revolutionsnewsstand.com/2022/10/10/one-day-of-communist-party-activites-in-new-york-city-thursday-february-16-1928/

Riddell, John, (ed), 1871, *The Communist International in Lenin's Time*, vol 1, *Founding the Communist International*, Pathfinder Press, New York, 1987.

Ringelblum, Emmanuel, 1975 "Comrade Mordechai: Mordechai Aniliewicz: Commander of the Warsaw Ghetto Uprising", in Suhl, Yuri (ed), 1975, *They Fought Back: the story of the Jewish resistance in Nazi Europe*, Shocken.

Ringelblum, Emmanuel, 1992, *Polish-Jewish Relations During the Second World War*, Northwestern University Press.

Robbins, Glyn, 2021, "New York's winter rent strike inspired generations", *Jacobin*, 26 December jacobin.com/2021/12/nyc-1907-rent-strike-paulina-newman-east-side-housing

Roberts, John Morris (ed), 1966, *French Revolution Documents*, vol 1, Oxford.

Rogger, Hans, 1983, *Russia in the Age of Modernisation and Revolution 1881–1917*, Longman, London.

Röhl, John, 1994, *The Kaiser and his Court*, Cambridge University Press.

Rose, John, 1990, "Introduction", in Edelman, Marek, 1990, *The Ghetto Fights: Warsaw 1941–43*, Bookmarks, London.

Rose, John, 2009a, "Marek Edelman: the ghetto fighter", *Socialist Worker*, 13 October, socialistworker.co.uk/features/marek-edelman-the-ghetto-fighter/

Rose, John, 2009b, "Marek Edelman—last surviving leader of the 1943 Warsaw Ghetto Uprising against the Nazis", *The Independent*, 17 October, www.independent.co.uk/news/ obituaries/marek-edelman-last-surviving-leader-of-the-1943-warsaw-ghetto-uprising-against-the-nazis-1798644.html

Rose, John, 2020, "The Bolsheviks and antisemitism", in *International Socialism*, no 168, 9 October, isj.org.uk/the-bolsheviks-and-antisemitism/

Rosen, Klaus-Henning, 1985, "Eine Stadt zeigt Betroffenheit", *Vorwaerts*, 1 June, no 23, cited in Shelley, Lore, 1996.

Rosenberg, Chanie, 1988, "The Labour Party and the fight against fascism", *International Socialism* (2), no 39, pp55-93, www.marxists.org/history/etol/writers/rosenberg/1988/xx/ antifascism.html#f19

Rosenberg, Chanie, 2013, *Fighting Fit*, Redwords, London,

Rosenberg, David, 1985, *Facing up to Antisemitism: how Jews in Britain Countered the Threats of the 1930s*, Jewish Cultural and Anti-Racist Project, London.

Rosenberg, David, 2011, *Battle for the East End: Jewish Responses to Fascism in the 1930s*, Five Leaves, Nottingham.

Rosenberg, David, 2015, "Ukip is nothing new: the British Brothers' League was

References

exploiting immigration fears in 1901", *The Guardian*, 5 March, www.theguardian.com/uk-news/2015/mar/04/ukip-nigel-farage-immigrants-british-brothers-league

Rosenberg, David, 2016, "The rebels who brought London to a standstill", *Jewish Chronicle*, 25 November, www.thejc.com/culture/books/the-rebels-who-brought-london-to-a-standstill-1.65742

Rosenberg, David, 2019, *Rebel Footprints*, Pluto Press, London.

Rosenberg, David, 2020, "Lessons for today from our history in London of combating racism", *Rebel Notes*, 26 November, rebellion602.wordpress.com/tag/british-brothers-league/

Rosenthal, Henry, 1987, "Eleanor Marx: 'I am a Jewess'", www.marxists.org/subject/jewish/marx-daughter.htm

Rosner, Hela, 1998, "Sister, sister", *Australian Memories of the Holocaust*, excerpts from Rosner Blay, Anna, *Sister, Sister*, Hale & Iremonger, pp106-138, www.holocaust.com.au/mm/j_sister.htm

Rowe, Leonard, 1974, "Jewish self-defense: a response to violence", in Joshua Fishman (ed), *Studies on Polish Jewry 1919–1939*, YIVO, New York.

Rowland, Richard, 1986, "Geographical patterns of the Jewish population in the Pale of Settlement of late nineteenth century Russia", in *Jewish Social Studies*, vol 48, no 3/4, www.jstor.org/stable/4467338?seq=6#metadata_info_tab_contents

Rozenblit, Marsha and Karp, Jonathan, 2017, *World War I and the Jews*, Berghahn Books, New York. Kindle Edition.

Rubenstein, Hilary, 1991, *The Jews in Australia 1788–1845*, vol 1, Heinemann.

Ruppin, Arthur, 1934, *The Jews in the Modern World*, Macmillan, London.

Sachar, Howard, 2005, *A History of the Jews of the Modern World*, Alfred A Knopf, New York.

Sampson, Elissa, 2016, "'Women resume riots against meat shops': the 1902 Great Meat Boycott", *Lower East Side History Month*, www.leshistorymonth.org/2016/05/22/women-resume-riots-against-meat-shops-the-1902-great-meat-boycott/

Samuels, Ben, 2023, "Elon Musk boosts antisemitic blood libel on Twitter", Haaretz, www.haaretz.com/us-news/2023-06-07/ty-article/.premium/elon-musk-boosts-antisemitic-blood-libel-on-twitter/0000188-9714-df21-a1b8-b79d7a5b0000

Sanders, Bernie, 2021, "The US must stop being an apologist for the Netanyahu Government", *New York Times*, 14 May, www.nytimes.com/2021/05/14/opinion/bernie-sanders-israel-palestine-gaza.html

Schappes, Morris, 1954, "Jews and the American labor movement 1850–1880", www.marxists.org/subject/jewish/schappes-50-80.pdf

Schappes, Morris, 1955a, "The heroic period of Jewish labor 1909–1914", www.marxists.org/subject/jewish/schappes-heroic.pdf

Schappes, Morris, 1955b, "The Jews and the post-war reaction after 1918", www.marxists.org/subject/jewish/schappes-reaction.pdf

Schappes, Morris, 1955c, "The thirties—and the Jewish masses", p18, www.marxists.org/subject/jewish/schappes-thirties.pdf

Schear, Stuart, 2017, "My grandmother, Yiddish and May Day", *American Jewish World Service*, ajws.org/blog/grandmother-yiddish-may-day/

Schilde, Kurt, 2007, *Jugendopposition 1933–1945*, Lukas Verlag, Berlin.

Schindler, Colin, 2018, "Orbán and Netanhau's meeting of minds", *The Jewish Chronicle*, 16 July 2018.

Schöffer, I, 1981, "The Jews in the Netherlands: the position of a minority through three centuries", in *Studia Rosenthaliana*, vol 15, no 1.

Scholch, Alexander, 1985, "The demographic development of Palestine 1850–1882", in *International Journal of Middle East Studies*, vol 17, no 4.

Schrag, Peter, 2010, *Not Fit for Our Society*, Berkeley: University of California Press, p145. Available at: urn:oclc:record:649914394

Segev, Tom, 2019a, *A State at Any Cost*, Apollo, New York. Kindle Edition.

Segev, Tom, 2019b, *The Seventh Million*, Farrar, Straus and Giroux. Kindle Edition.

Seidman, Hillel, 1997, *The Warsaw Ghetto Diaries*, Targum/Feldheim.

Serge, Victor, 1930, *Year 1 of the Russian Revolution*, www.marxists.org/archive/serge/1930/year-one/cho1.htm

Seventeen Moments in Soviet History, 2015, soviethistory.msu.edu/1917-2/kornilov-affair/kornilov-affair-texts/kornilov-responds-to-kerenskii/

Shafir, Gershon, 1996, *Land, Labor and the Origins of the Israeli-Palestinian Conflict 1882–1914*, University of California Press.

Shapira, Anita, 1989, "Labour Zionism and the October Revolution", in *Journal of Contemporary History*, vol 24, no 4, www.jstor.org/stable/260882?seq=12

Shapira, Anita, 2016, *Israel: a History*, Weidenfeld and Nicolson, London. Kindle Edition.

Shapira, Anita, 2017, "Socialist Zionism and nation building", in Jacobs, Jack, 2017 (ed), *Jews and Leftist Politics: Judaism, Israel, Antisemitism, and Gender*, Cambridge University Press. Kindle Edition.

Shapiro, Yonathan, 1976, *The Formative Years of the Israeli Labour Party*, Sage, London.

Sharot, Stephen, 1973, "The three-generations thesis and the American Jews", in *The British Journal of Sociology*, vol 24, no 2.

Shelley, Lore, 1996, *The Union Kommando in Auschwitz*, University Press of America.

Shimoni, Gideon, 1988, "South African Jews and the Apartheid Crisis", *The American Jewish Year Book*, vol 88, pp3-58 www.jstor.org/stable/23604147

Shindler, Colin, 2018a, "Mandela and the Jews", *Jewish Chronicle*, 12 July, www.thejc.com/news/features/mandela-and-the-jews-1.467000

Shindler, Colin, 2018b, "Orbán and Netanyahu's meeting of minds", *Jewish Chronicle*, 16 July.

Shmulewitz, I (ed), 1982, *The Bialystoker Memorial Book*, Bialystoker Center, New York, www.jewishgen.org/yizkor/Bialystok1/bialystok1.html

Shohat, Ella, 2006, *Le Sionisme du Point de Vue de ses Victimes Juives*, La Fabrique Editions.

Shore, Marci, 2013, "The Jewish hero history forgot", *New York Times*, 18 April, online version, nytimes.com/2013/04/19/opinion/the-jewish-hero-history-forgot.html?pagewanted=all&_r=0

Shur, Chaim, 1998, *Shomrim in the Land of Apartheid*, Members of Hashomer Hatzair South Africa and Havazelet in conjunction with Yad Yaari.

Siegelbaum, Lewis, 2014, "1917: Kornilov affair", *Seventeen Moments in Soviet History*, web.archive.org/web/20140330015438/www.soviethistory.org/index.php?page=subject&SubjectID=1917kornilov&Year=1917

Silber, Marcos, 2010, "Shomer ha-Tasa'ir, Ha-", *YIVO Encyclopedia of Jews in Eastern Europe*, yivoencyclopedia.org/article.aspx/Shomer_ha-Tsair_Ha-

Silberner, Edmund, 1946, "Charles Fourier on the Jewish Question", *Jewish Social Studies*, vol 8, no 4.

Silver, Steve, 2011, "They did not pass", 30 September, stevesilver.org.uk/blog/page/2/

Silverstein, Richard, 2013, "Last of Warsaw Ghetto survivors calls for rebellion against Israeli occupation", www.richardsilverstein.com/2013/04/09/last-of-warsaw-ghetto-survivors-calls-for-rebellion-against-israeli-occupation/

Simons, Mike, 2020, 25 October, personal communication.

Smith, Jack, 2017, "How square dancing became a weapon of white supremacy against an anti-Semitic jazz dance conspiracy", www.mic.com/articles/186892/how-square-dancing-became-a-weapon-of-white-supremacy-against-an-anti-semitic-jazz-dance-conspiracy

Smith, Stephen, 1983, *Red Petrograd: Revolution in the Factories 1917–18*, Cambridge University Press, Cambridge.

Smolenskin, Perets, 1872, *The Eternal People*, in Rabinovitch, Simon (ed) 2012, *Jews and Diaspora Nationalism*, Brandeis University Press. Kindle Edition.

References

Socialist Appeal, 1939a, "An end to Zionist illusions!", 7 March, www.marxists.org/history/etol/newspape/themilitant/socialist-appeal-1939/v3n13-mar-07-1939.pdf

Socialist Appeal, 1939b, "50,000 anti-Nazis answer SWP call", 22 February, reprinted at www.marxists.org/history/etol/document/swp-us/education/antifascism/silver.htm

Sohn, David, 1982, "The pogrom against the Jews", in Shmulewitz, I, *The Bialystoker Memorial Book* (English version), www.jewishgen.org/yizkor/Bialystok1/bia002.html

Soyer, Daniel, nd, "Jewish Socialism in the United States 1880–1920", *My Jewish Learning*, www.myjewishlearning.com/article/jewish-socialism-in-the-united-states-1880-1920/

Spencer, Joseph, nd, "New York City tenant organizations and the post-world war housing crisis", in *The Tenant Movement in New York City 1904–1984*, www.tenant.net/Community/history/histo2a.html

Srebrnik, Henry, 1995, "Class, ethnicity and gender intertwined: Jewish women and the East London rent strikes 1935–1940", *Women's History Review*, 4, 283-299.

Srebrnik, Henry, 2010, *Dreams of nationhood: American Jewish Communists and the Soviet Birobidzhan Project 1924–1951*, Academic Studies Press, www.jstor.org/stable/j.ctt1zxsj1m.6?refreqid=excelsior%3A5bbdb09fede7d598500a4203da385378&seq=4#metadata_info_tab_contents

Stalin, Joseph, 1954, *Works*, vol 10, Moscow.

Sternhell, Zeev, 1999, *The Founding Myths of Israel: Nationalism, Socialism, and the Making of the Jewish State*, Princeton University Press. Kindle Edition.

Steven, Stewart, 1982, *The Poles*, Collins/Harvill, cited in Slawinski Andrzej, "Those who helped Jews during WWII", www.polishresistance-ak.org/10%20Article.htm

Stevens, Richard, 1971, "Zionism, South Africa and Apartheid: the paradoxical triangle", *Phylon*, vol 32, no 2, p125, www.jstor.org/stable/273998?seq=3

Stola, Dariusz, 2003, "Jedwabne: revisiting the evidence and nature of the crime", *Holocaust and Genocide Studies*, vol 17, no 1.

Stone, Janey, 2015, "Jewish resistance in Eastern Europe", in Gluckstein, Donny (ed), 2015, *Fighting on all Fronts*, pp89-130, Bookmarks, London, www.jstor.org/stable/24660789?seq=2

Stone, Janey, 2022, "Revolutionaries, resistance fighters and firebrands: the radical Jewish tradition", *Marxist Left Review*, no 23, supplement.

Storrs, Ronald, 1943, "A little Jewish Ulster in a sea of potentially hostile Arabism", palcit.net/article-837-a-little-loyal-jewish-ulster-in-a-sea-of-potentially-hostile-arabism

Strobl, Ingrid, 2008, *Partisanas: Women in the Armed Resistance to Fascism and German Occupation (1936–1945)*, AK Press.

Stroop Report (Excerpts), 1946, excerpts from *Nazi Conspiracy & Aggression*, vol 1, ch 7, Office of the United States Chief Counsel for Prosecution of Axis Criminality, United States Government Printing Office, Washington, 1946, pp995-998, fcit.usf.edu/holocaust/resource/document/DocStroo.htm

Sugarman, Martin, nd, "Jews in the Spanish Civil War", www.jewishvirtuallibrary.org/jews-who-served-in-the-international-brigade-in-the-spanish-civil-war

Sydney Jewish Museum, 2018, "Oneg Shabbat", holocaust.com.au/resources/supplementary-material/oneg-shabbat/

Syrkin, Marie, 2018, Nachman Syrkin, *Socialist Zionist: a Biographical Memoir and Selected Essays*, Borodino Books. Kindle Edition.

Szaynok, Bozen, 2002, "The Anti-Jewish policy of the USSR in the last days of Stalin's rule and its impact on the East European countries with special reference to Poland", in *Russian History*, vol 29, no 2/4, 2002.

Tec, Nechama, 1993, *Defiance*, Oxford University Press.

Tec, Nechama, 2001, *Jewish Resistance: Facts, Omissions and Distortions*, Miles Lerman Center for the Study of Jewish Resistance, Holocaust Memorial Museum, www.ushmm.org/m/pdfs/Publication_OP_1997-02.pdf

Tec, Nechama, 2003, *Resilience and Courage. Women, Men and the Holocaust*, Yale University Press.

Tec, Nechama, 2013, *Resistance: Jews and Christians who Defied the Nazi Terror*, Oxford University Press.

Teller, Adam, 2010, "Economic life", *YIVO Encyclopedia of Jews in Eastern Europe*, yivoencyclopedia.org/article.aspx/Economic_Life

Tenorio, Rich, 2021, "20 years before the Holocaust, pogroms killed 100,000 Jews—then were forgotten", *Times of Israel*, 21 December 2021, www.timesofisrael.com/20-years-before-the-holocaust-pogroms-killed-100000-jews-then-were-forgotten/

The Guardian, 1936, "Fascist march stopped after disorderly scenes", 5 October, www.theguardian.com/theguardian/1936/oct/05/fromthearchive

The Telegraph, 2009, "Marek Edelman", 4 October, www.telegraph.co.uk/news/obituaries/politics-obituaries/6259900/Marek-Edelman.html

Times of Israel, 2013, "Putin: first Soviet government was mostly Jewish", 19 June, www.timesofisrael.com/putin-first-soviet-government-was-mostly-jewish/

Times of Israel, 2022, "Lapid slams 'antisemitic' UN report accusing Israel of violating international law", 21 October, www.timesofisrael.com/lapid-slams-antisemitic-un-report-accusing-israel-of-violating-international-law/

Tobias, Henry, 1972, *The Jewish Bund in Russia*, Stanford University Press, Stanford.

Tomaszewski, Irene and Werbowski, Tecia, 1994, *Zegota*, Price-Patterson, www.warsawuprising.com/zegota.htm

Tomaszewski, Jerzy, nd, "Zionism", *Virtual Shtetl*, sztetl.org.pl/en/glossary/zionism

Traverso, Enzo, 2016, *End of Jewish Modernity*, Pluto Press, London.

Traverso, Enzo, 2019, *The Jewish Question*, Haymarket, Chicago.

Treitschke, Heinrich, 1914, *His Life and Works*, Jarrold, London, archive.org/details/treitschkehislifootreiuoft/page/n15/mode/2up?q=contents

Trotsky, Leon, 1907, *1905*, www.marxists.org/archive/trotsky/1907/1905/index.htm

Trotsky, Leon, 1930, *History of the Russian Revolution*, www.marxists.org/archive/trotsky/1930/hrr/ch07.htm

Trotsky, Leon, 1931, *For a Workers' United Front against Fascism*, www.marxists.org/archive/trotsky/germany/1931/311208.htm

Trotsky, Leon, 1969, *Stalin*, vol 2, Panther History, London.

Tsvetkov, V Zh, nd, *Lavr Georgievich Kornilov*, pt 2, www.dk1868.ru/statii/kornilov2.htm

Tzur, Eli, 1998, "From moral rejection to armed resistance", in Rohrlich, Ruby (ed), *Resisting the Holocaust*, Berg Publishers, Oxford.

United States Holocaust Memorial Museum, 2023, "Genocide of European Roma (gypsies) 1939–1945", www.ushmm.org/wlc/en/article.php?ModuleId=10005219

United States Holocaust Memorial Museum, nd(1), "US immigration laws and the refugee crisis", encyclopedia.ushmm.org/content/en/article/wagner-rogers-bill

United States Holocaust Memorial Museum, nd(2), "Stephen Wise", exhibitions.ushmm.org/americans-and-the-holocaust/personal-story/stephen-wise

United States Holocaust Memorial Museum, nd(3), "Our town is burning", 1936, www.ushmm.org/wlc/en/media_so.php?MediaId=2621

United States Holocaust Memorial Museum, nd(4), "Jewish Councils (Judenraete)", encyclopedia.ushmm.org/content/en/article/jewish-councils-judenraete

United States Holocaust Memorial Museum, nd(5), "Jewish uprisings in ghettos and camps 1941–1944", nd, www.ushmm.org/wlc/en/article.php?ModuleId=10005407

United States Holocaust Memorial Museum, nd(6), "Killing center revolts", www.ushmm.org/outreach/en/article.php?ModuleId=10007747

United States Holocaust Memorial Museum, nd(7), "Kovno", encyclopedia.ushmm.org/content/en/article/kovno

United States Holocaust Memorial Museum, nd(8), "Group portrait of a Jewish partisan musical

References

troupe in the Narocz Forest in Belorussia", collections.ushmm.org/search/catalog/pa1134433

United States Holocaust Memorial Museum, nd(9), "Tomasz (Toivi) Blatt", www.ushmm.org/wlc/en/idcard.php?ModuleId=10006539

United States Holocaust Memorial Museum, nd(10), "Sobibor", www.ushmm.org/wlc/en/article.php?ModuleId=10005192

Urman, Menachem, 2015, Warrior, Entrepreneur, Lover of Life, Contento, Tel Aviv.

Ussishkin, Abraham, 1905, Our Program: an Essay, Federation of American Zionists, New York, archive.org/details/ourprogramessayooussiiala

Vallois, Nicolas and Imhoff, Sarah, 2020, The Luftmentsh as an Economic Metaphor for Jewish Poverty: a Rhetorical Analysis, www.researchgate.net/publication/343772681

Vaynshteyn, Bernard, 2012, "The birth of the Knee-Pants Makers' Union", in Michels, Tony, 2012, pp88-90.

Vedemosti, 2013, www.vedomosti.ru/opinion/articles/2013/06/17/ot-redakcii:-pyatyj-punktik

Vital, David, 1999, A People Apart: the Jews in Europe 1789–1939, Oxford University Press, Oxford.

Voigtländer, Nico and Voth, Hans-Joachim, 2012, Persecution Perpetuated: the Medieval Origins of Anti-Semitic Violence in Nazi Germany, crei.cat/wp-content/uploads/users/working-papers/voth_persecution_qje(1).pdf

Volkov, Shulamit, 2006, Germans, Jews, and Antisemites, Cambridge University Press. Kindle Edition.

Wachsmann, Nikolaus, 2015, KL: A History of the Nazi Concentration Camps, Little Brown Book Group, New York.

Wagner, Richard, 2002, Art and Revolution, www.public-library.uk/ebooks/11/97.pdf, www.marxists.org/archive/montefiore/1902/07/wagner.htm

Wald, Alan, 1987, The New York Intellectuals: the Rise and Decline of the Anti-Stalinist Left from the 1930s to the 1980s, University of North Carolina Press, Chapel Hill.

Waldinger, Roger, 1985, "Another look at the International Ladies' Garment Workers' Union: women, industry structure and collective action", Milkman, Ruth (ed), 1985, Women, Work and Protest: a Century of US Women's Labor History, Routledge, 131793af-e04d-55d4-55be-f2367680bd87.filesusr.com/ugd/90d188_351db7c5f137be258245f6dfe94f812a.pdf

Waldman, Louis, 2012, "Leon Trotsky on Second Avenue", in Michels, Tony, 2012, pp214-218.

Walsh, Mary Williams, 1997, "German Judge awards back pay to WWII slave laborer", Los Angeles Times, 6 November.

Walsh, Nick, 2006, "How Voltaire praised the 'enlightened despot' Catherine the Great", in The Guardian, 2 June, www.theguardian.com/world/2006/jun/02/russia.books

Walzer, Michael, 2017, "The strangeness of Jewish Leftism", in Jacobs, Jack, 2017 (ed), Jews and Leftist Politics: Judaism, Israel, Antisemitism, and Gender, Cambridge University Press. Kindle Edition.

Ward, Chris, 1993, Stalin's Russia, Edward Arnold, London.

Weibaum, Lawrence, 2008, "Jabotinsky and the Poles", in Polin: Studies in Polish Jewry, vol 5, pp156-172.

Weinberg, Robert, 1992, "The pogrom of 1905 in Odessa: a case study", in Klier, John, and Lambroza, Shlomo, 1992, Pogroms: Anti-Jewish Violence in Modern Russian History, pp248-89, Cambridge, faculty.history.umd.edu/BCooperman/NewCity/Pogrom1905.html

Weinberg, Robert, 1993, The Revolution of 1905 in Odessa, Indiana University Press, www.google.com.au/books/edition/The_Revolution_of_1905_in_Odessa/SIYt6hxoq18C?hl=en&gbpv=0

Weinryb, Bernard, 1980, "Stalin's Zionism", in Proceedings of the American Academy for Jewish Research, vol 46/47, Jubilee Volume (1928–29/1978–79) [Part 2] (1979–1980), www.jstor.org/stable/3622371?seq=7#metadata_info_tab_contents

Weinstein, Bernard, 2018, The Jewish Unions in America: Pages of History and Memories, Open Book Publishers, www.jstor.org/stable/j.ctv8j3sm.5

Weinstock, Nathan, 1979, *Zionism: False Messiah*, Ink Links, London.

Weiss, Aharon, 1977, "Jewish leadership in occupied Poland: postures and attitudes", in Yisrael Gutman, (ed), 1977, *Yad Vashem Studies*, vol 12, cited in Yehuda Bauer, 2001, *Rethinking the Holocaust*, Yale University Press.

Weitz, Eric, 1997, *Creating German Commmunism 1890–1990*, Princeton University Press, Princeton.

Weizmann, Chaim, 1983, *The Letters and Papers of Chaim Weizmann: series B Papers*, vol II, December 1931 to April 1952, Transaction Books, New Brunswick.

Weizmann, Chaim, 2013, *Trial and Error: the Autobiography of Chaim Weizmann*, book 1, Plunkett Lake Press, Lexington Mass.

Welch, Susan, 2014, "American opinion toward Jews during the Nazi era: results from quota sample polling during the 1930s and 1940s", *Social Science Quarterly*, vol 95, www.researchgate.net/publication/260604054_American_Opinion_Toward_Jews_During_the_Nazi_Era_Results_from_Quota_Sample_Polling_During_the_1930s_and_1940s

Wertheimer, Barbara, 1977, *We were There: the Story of Working Women in America*, New York: Pantheon Books.

Weston, Reg, 2005, "Fascists and police routed: the battle of Cable Street", 12 September, Libcom.org: libcom.org/library/fascists-and-police-routed-battle-cable-street

Wheeler-Bennett, John, 1953, *Nemesis of Power: the German Army in Politics*, Macmillan, London.

Wieczorek, Michał, 2021, "On their own terms: the Warsaw Ghetto and its heroic uprising", *Culture*, 16 April, culture.pl/en/article/on-their-own-terms-the-warsaw-ghetto-its-heroic-uprising

Wiese, Stefan, 2012, *Jewish Self-Defense and Black Hundreds in Zhitomir*, www.quest-cdecjournal.it/jewish-self-defense-and-black-hundreds-in-zhitomir-a-case-study-on-the-pogroms-of-1905-in-tsarist-russia/

Wiggins, Nick and Arnold, Ann, 2020, "A Yiddish poet's quest for a Jewish safe haven in the Australian outback", *ABC Radio National*, 12 March, www.abc.net.au/news/2020-03-12/yiddish-poets-quest-for-a-jewish-safe-haven-in-the-outback/12025644

Wisotsky, Isadore, 2012, "Our mecca", in Michels, Tony, 2012, pp99–103.

Wistrich, Robert, 1976, *Revolutionary Jews: from Marx to Trotsky*, Harrap, London.

Wolfe, Patrick, 2012, "Purchase by other means: the Palestine Nakba and Zionism's conquest of economics", pp133-4, researchbank.swinburne.edu.au/file/30c016d4-7dd5-454d-bba2-358a164cc3ec/1/PDF%20%28Settler%20Colonial%20Studies%202_1%20-%20Full%20issue%29.pdf

Wolpe, Rebecca, 2020, "'Poor Jews! You get blamed for everything!' Hope and despair in a Galician Yiddish newspaper during the Revolutions of 1848–49", *Quest*, no 17, www.quest-cdecjournal.it/poor-jews-you-get-blamed-for-everything-hope-and-despair-in-a-galician-yiddish-newspaper-during-the-revolutions-of-1848-49/

Woodhouse, Charlies and Tobias, Henry, 1966, "Primordial ties and political process in pre-revolutionary Russia: the case of the Jewish Bund", in *Comparative Studies in Society and History*, vol 8, no 3, www.jstor.org/stable/177570?seq=8-Tobias 344

Wrobel, Piotr, 2001, "From conflict to cooperation: the Bund and the Polish Socialist Party 1897–1939", in Jacobs, Jack (ed), 2001, *Jewish Politics in Eastern Europe: the Bund at 100*, Palgrave, Basingstoke, pp155-171.

Wynot, Edward, 1971, "'A necessary cruelty': the emergence of official anti-semitism in Poland 1936–39", *The American Historical Review*, vol 76, no 4, www.jstor.org/stable/1849240?seq=2

Yad Vashem, nd(1), "Call to armed self-defense, from an underground publication", www.yadvashem.org/about_holocaust/documents/part2/doc125.html

Yad Vashem, nd(2), "The discussion on fighting aims by the activists of the Bialystok Ghetto, February 27, 1943", www.yadvashem.org/odot_pdf/Microsoft%20Word%20-%20573.pdf

References

Yale Law School, nd, "Declaration of the Rights of Man, 1789", avalon.law.yale.edu/18th_century/rightsof.asp

Yelin, Chaim and Ghelpernus, Dimitri, nd, "The Gelpernus Diary: resistance in the Kovno Ghetto", *Holocaust Education & Archive Research Team*, www.holocaustresearchproject.org/revolt/gelpernusdiary.html

Yes! Solutions Journalism, 2013, "Where did International Women's Day come from?", 9 March, www.yesmagazine.org/democracy/2013/03/09/where-did-international-women-s-day-come-from

YIVO Institute for Jewish Research, 1999, "In Love and Struggle" (audio recording), savethemusic.com/album/in-love-and-in-struggle-the-musical-legacy-of-the-labor-bund/

YIVO Institute for Jewish Research, 1946, "Basic facts about Yiddish", www.yivo.org/cimages/basic_facts_about_yiddish_2014.pdf

Zable, Arnold, 1991, *Jewels and Ashes*, Scribe, Newham.

Zafar, Saleem, 2010, "War—a tool for political ends: the evolution of Israel's military psychology", in *Policy Perspectives*, vol 7, no 1, www.jstor.org/stable/42909257

Żbikowski, Andrzej, 2018, "The dispute over the status of a witness to the Holocaust: some observations on how research into the destruction of the Polish Jews and into Polish-Jewish relations during the years of Nazi occupation has changed since 1989", in Polonsky, Antony, Węgrzynek, Hanna and Żbikowski, Andrzej (eds), 2018, *New Directions in the History of the Jews in the Polish Lands*, Academic Studies Press.

Żebrowski, Rafał, nd, "Anniversary of the Jedwabne pogrom", *Jewish Historical Institute*, www.jhi.pl/en/articles/anniversary-of-the-jedwabne-pogrom,3752

Zhitlovsky, Chaim, 2012, "A Jew to Jews", in Rabinovitch, Simon (ed) 2012, *Jews and Diaspora Nationalism*, Brandeis University Press, New Hampshire, Kindle Edition.

Zimmerman, Joshua, 2003, "Was the Jewish Labor Bund in Czarist Russia a 'national movement'?", *Jewish Political Studies Review*, vol 15, no 1/2.

Zimmerman, Joshua, 2012, "The influence of the 'Polish question' on the Bund's national program, 1897–1905", in Jacobs, Jack (ed) 2001, *Jewish Politics in Eastern Europe: the Bund at 100*, Palgrave, Basingstoke, pp28-45.

Zimmerman, Joshua, 2015, "Rethinking the Polish Underground", interview about *The Polish Underground and the Jews, 1939–1945*, Cambridge University Press.

Zimmermann, Moshe, 1987, *The Patriarch of Antisemitism*, Oxford University Press, Oxford.

Zionist Congress, no 16, 1929, *Resolutions of the 16th Zionist Congress, Zurich, 28 July to 11 August, 1929*, www.bjpa.org/content/upload/bjpa/reso/RESOLUTIONS%20OF%20THE%2016TH%20ZIONIST%20CONGRESS%20ZURICH%20JULY%2028TH%20TO%20AUGUST%2011TH,%201929.pdf

Zionist Congress, no 2, 1898, Stenographisches Protokoll der Verhandlungen des II Zionisten-Congresses", *gehalten zu Basel* vom 28 bis 31 August 1898, Vienna 1898, www.worldcat.org/title/stenographisches-protokoll-der-verhandlungen-des-ii-zionisten-congresses-gehalten-zu-basel-vom-28-bis-31-august-1898/oclc/25349014

Zuckerman, Martin, 2020, *The Jewish Labor Bund: on the Occasion of its 100th Anniversary*, Capra Publishing, Los Angeles.

Zuckerman, Yitzhak, 1993, *A Surplus of Memory: Chronicle of the Warsaw Ghetto Uprising*, University of California Press.

Zukerman, William, 1936, "Blackshirts in London", *Jewish Frontier*, no 10, November.

Zukerman, William, 1937, "Jews in Poland: ghetto benches", *The Palestine Post*, 1 December, p4.

Index

Index

Index